EBURY PRESS
FROM DUBAI TO KARACHI

S. Hussain Zaidi is India's number one crime writer. He is the author of several bestselling books, including *Dongri to Dubai: Six Decades of the Mumbai Mafia*, *Mafia Queens of Mumbai*, *Black Friday: The True Story of the Bombay Bomb Blasts* and *My Name Is Abu Salem*. A veteran of investigative, crime and terror reporting in the media, he has worked for *Asian Age*, *Mumbai Mirror*, *Mid-Day* and *Indian Express*. He is also the associate producer for the HBO movie *Terror in Mumbai*, based on the 26/11 terror strikes. He lives in Mumbai with his family.

ADVANCE PRAISE FOR THE BOOK

'*From Dubai to Karachi* is as riveting a chronicle of the life of India's most wanted don, Dawood Ibrahim, as *Dongri to Dubai* was. This book is another unputdownable masterpiece by S. Hussain Zaidi, which will bring unmitigated delight to his legion of fans in India and overseas'—**Neeraj Kumar, former commissioner of police, Delhi**

'What David Simon and the Wire did to reveal life on a street corner of Baltimore, S. Hussain Zaidi has done for Mumbai and its criminal diaspora. A chronicler of pavement life and the police beat, he has become a go-to guide for anyone interested in the twilight hours in many of India's heaving cities'—**Adrian M. Levy, bestselling author of** *The Siege: The Attack on the Taj*

FROM DUBAI TO KARACHI

THE DAWOOD SAGA CONTINUES

S. HUSSAIN ZAIDI

EBURY PRESS

An imprint of Penguin Random House

EBURY PRESS

Ebury Press is an imprint of the Penguin Random House group of companies whose addresses can be found at global.penguinrandomhouse.com

Published by Penguin Random House India Pvt. Ltd
4th Floor, Capital Tower 1, MG Road,
Gurugram 122 002, Haryana, India

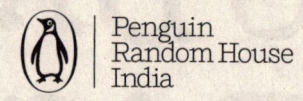

Penguin Random House India

First published in Ebury Press by Penguin Random House India 2024

Copyright © S. Hussain Zaidi 2024

All rights reserved

10 9 8 7 6 5 4 3 2 1

This book is a work of non-fiction and is based on the evidence collected from a variety of sources, interviews conducted and personal interactions of the author with various persons mentioned in the book. The views and opinions expressed in the chapters of this book are those of the author only and do not reflect or represent the views and opinions held by any other person.
This book is based on actual events and is based on evidence collected by the author with respect to the events enumerated. It reflects the author's representation of the events enumerated as truthfully as possible on the basis of the interviews conducted with various individuals and/or on the basis of materials that can be verified by research. All persons within the book are actual individuals.
The objective of this book is not to hurt any sentiments or be biased in favour of or against any particular person, society, gender, creed, nation or religion.

Please note that no part of this book may be used or reproduced in any manner for the purpose of training artificial intelligence technologies or systems.

ISBN 9780143424284

Typeset in Sabon LT Std by Manipal Technologies Limited, Manipal
Printed at Replika Press Pvt. Ltd, India

This book is sold subject to the condition that it shall not, by way of trade or otherwise, be lent, resold, hired out, or otherwise circulated without the publisher's prior consent in any form of binding or cover other than that in which it is published and without a similar condition including this condition being imposed on the subsequent purchaser.

www.penguin.co.in

MIX
Paper | Supporting
responsible forestry
FSC™ C016779

For Dr Shabeeb Rizvi,
The Twelfth Intellect,
My Teacher

Contents

Prologue: Kamaal to Kamal   xi

1. The Blue Fox   1
2. Pakistan's First Ten-Per Cent President   9
3. A Tale of Two Arrests   18
4. Grand Guest House   28
5. The Interrogation   35
6. Taufique Jaliawala   46
7. The Hanging   57
8. The Aftermath   66
9. Stockholm Syndrome   73
10. Mehwish Hayat   83
11. Uncanny Associations   90
12. Mexican Stand-Off in Bombay   96

13. Balance of Power	104
14. Do I Look like a Dog?	112
15. Race to Death	119
16. The Godman	126
17. Volcano of Weapons	133
18. Suburban Drug Lord	139
19. Trapped in Thailand	149
20. Shoot-Out at Bandra	159
21. A Long Trial	168
22. The Mad Man's Brother	176
23. *Yeda* on the Run	183
24. How Many Headleys?	190
25. With Friends Like These . . .	197
26. Kamran Faridi and The Beatles	204
27. Jostling for Jabir	211
28. Fallen Comrade	218
29. Prime Suspect	226
30. India's Escobar	235
31. Fugitive	244
32. Wily Wolf	251
33. Death of the Kingpin	258
34. Movies and the Mafia	266
35. Life Is a Game	276
36. Arrest at the Premiere	286
37. Five-Crore Bet	297
38. Snippets from Three Decades	308

39. A Tale of Two Brothers	318
40. If You Can't Beat Them . . .	326
41. Come to Dubai	333
42. Dubai to Jail	342
43. Legal Eagle	351
44. Law Minister	358
45. Calling D	365
46. Casualties of War	373
47. Dangerous Debts	381
48. Bankrupted	388
49. The Don's Garage	395
50. The Gold King	402
51. The Adopted Son	410
52. Return of the Badshah	416
53. New Lamps for Old	428
54. Where There's a Will	439
55. Ghosts of the Past	448
Epilogue: PAKmodia Street to PAKistan State	455
Acknowledgements	463
Notes	469

Prologue

Kamaal to Kamal

Competing with the razzmatazz in the great Etihad Arena that evening were the symbols of showtime: giant inflated egos, eager paparazzi, glitter and shimmering gowns, and outlandish costumes worn by both men and women. Howling fans waited for a glimpse of their favourite stars, and some wannabe item girl who came wearing a huge hat and a mermaid dress to flounce on a VIP seat not reserved in her name. Huge screens on either side of the podium brought the stars closer to the backbenchers. I was an invitee to the International Indian Film Academy (IIFA) Awards 2023, held in Abu Dhabi as the Sanjay Leela Bhansali-directed Alia Bhatt-starrer *Gangubai Kathiawadi* was nominated in the best adapted story category.

On the stage was India's most prolific actor and a titan of Indian cinema, Kamal Haasan. Kamal Haasan's presence commanded everybody's attention but strangely, he did not look in his element though he was being celebrated with much gusto. As a film aficionado, I was very happy to watch Kamal Haasan from such close quarters.

As I sat there in the special enclosure, cheek by jowl with so many stars and their overwhelming perfumes, I thought of the man whose name I initially assumed was a facsimile of the thespian on stage.

Days prior, an unexpected call shattered the monotony of my routine. However, it wasn't the familiar voice of the legendary Kamal Haasan that greeted me, but that of a Pakistani magnate, a green card holder and yet a fugitive from life's unyielding grasp. He introduced himself as Kamaal Hasan. The name did not ring a bell as it was distinctively different from Kamal Haasan. While our own Kamal Haasan has a name that echoes the duality of its origins—one blooming in the sanctity of Sanskrit, the other steeped in Arabic lore, the caller claimed his name was Kamaal Hasan.

Over the years after I wrote *Dongri to Dubai*, which traces the story of India's most famous don, Dawood Ibrahim, I have been deluged with callers of all hues who forget that I am a writer and presume I am Heimdall, the sentry from Norse mythology, who can help them magically cross over to Dawood Ibrahim's realm. They ask me all kinds of questions: How does he look? Can you tell me more about him? Will you recommend my name? How does he talk? *I want to be part of his team!*

These star-struck young men have pestered me for years and so when Kamaal Hasan called up, I was prepared for yet another barrage of 'requests'. But this particular caller was no ardent devotee of India's most wanted gangster and neither did he want to join the legion of followers of Dawood Ibrahim. Kamaal Hasan's very short conversation drew me into a vortex of intrigue and deception. I wanted to meet the man immediately. If the teaser he showed me held so much promise, the main story would definitely whet my appetite.

With a brusque edge to my voice, I insisted on meeting him, refusing to back down in the face of his dismissiveness. After a moment of contemplation, his response took me aback.

'I cannot come to India, but I am willing to meet you anywhere in the world. Even if that means I have to come to Saudi Arabia under the pretext of *Umrah*,' he offered.

His suggestion left me unsettled. While I was committed to pursuing the truth, I refused to exploit my religion for professional gains. The principles of integrity and honesty that guided my work as a journalist were non-negotiable, even in the pursuit of a story as compelling as this.

As I shared my plans to visit Abu Dhabi for the IIFA event next week, Kamaal Hasan's response sent a shiver down my spine. 'I will find you,' he declared, his words carrying an ominous weight that left me disturbed.

Before I could respond, the call abruptly disconnected, leaving me to ponder the implications of his cryptic message. In that moment, a chill of unease and self-doubt crept over me as I wondered whether I had bitten off more than I could chew. Was this a trap?

As Kamal Haasan stood, bathing in the spotlight, basking in the honour bestowed upon him by the illustrious

A.R. Rahman, another figure made his entrance into the Etihad Arena on Yas Island, the venue of the IIFA Awards. Amidst the sea of faces, a man clad in an elegant grey suit slipped into the seat beside me. Lost in the spectacle unfolding before me, I scarcely registered his presence.

Suddenly, he leaned in closer, his voice a whisper in the clamour of the hall. 'My name is Kamaal, Kamaal Hasan,' he uttered, punctuating his introduction with the traditional Muslim greeting, 'Assalamu-alaikum.'

The unexpected arrival of Kamaal Hasan caught me off guard. I had waited for him to contact me throughout the day, but his unanticipated appearance in the midst of such a significant event was not what I expected. From the moment I landed in Abu Dhabi, my senses were on high alert, scanning the crowds for any sign of the mysterious figure. Yet, despite my vigilant search, he remained elusive, like a spectre hovering just beyond reach.

Even within the confines of the hotel, where I had hoped to find respite, his presence continued to elude me. Each passing moment only served to heighten my sense of unease, as I awaited the inevitable encounter. I had waited for him to make his appearance through the day and as I left for the awards venue from my hotel, I was dejected and felt Kamaal Hasan had pulled a fast one on me.

And then, just as Kamal Haasan took the stage, delivering what promised to be a moment of cinematic brilliance, the apparition, whose real name I was sure was not Kamaal Hasan, was sitting next to me. The disruption was swift and unexpected, shattering the tranquillity of the moment and leaving me reeling in its wake. Now I took my gaze off the great Kamal Haasan on the stage and turned towards this man.

His smile was sincere, his eyes pools of depth and intelligence, and he exuded a charisma reminiscent of the legendary Sean Connery. In fact, his clipped British accent bore a striking resemblance to that of the late Hollywood icon.

'What took you so long?' I inquired, a tinge of impatience creeping into my voice.

His lips curved into a wry smile as he leaned in closer, his eyes darting around the room. 'I was making sure no one spotted me coming here,' he murmured, his voice barely audible above the din of the crowd. 'Once I was confident that the coast was clear and the VIP area was accessible without drawing undue attention, I made my move.'

While Kamaal Hasan confided his apprehensions, Kamal Haasan's speech resonated through the arena, its cadence threading into our conversation. 'The fact is, I'm a child of cinema,' he shared, his voice weaving through the bustle of the crowd. 'I grew up on cinema . . .'

As Kamal Haasan's words intermingled with our discussion, a sense of reverence filled the air, casting a moment of introspection amidst the grandeur of the event. Despite the captivating allure of the great actor's address, my attention remained anchored to Hasan's expression of fear and vulnerability, reminding me of the gravity of the meeting.

I caught a flicker of genuine fear in his eyes as he began the conversation. 'Dawood Ibrahim was the biggest power broker of your country . . . and now my country,' he said. 'The man can get the prime minister of my country appointed and removed in the wink of an eye. For him, getting me killed would be no big deal.' He paused. 'He pulled the strings, orchestrating Imran Khan's downfall with meticulous precision.'

Amidst the splendour and opulence of the glittering ceremony, Hasan's mention of Dawood Ibrahim strangely did not feel out of place. The Middle East had long since been Dawood Ibrahim's chosen turf that had sheltered him when he was an absconder from India. Both the journalist and writer in me were alert as Hasan began narrating his story, his voice barely audible in the cacophony of the loud music and celebrations on the podium. What Hasan told me did sound audacious, but he gave me ample evidence to support his claim.

Imran Khan, a cricketing legend-turned-politician, was more familiar to Indians as a handsome sportsman who led Pakistan to its first-ever Cricket World Cup victory. It was natural for Khan to gravitate towards politics after his mammoth cancer hospital initiative in Peshawar and Lahore. Imran was finally propelled to the highest office in the country in 2018 but in 2022, he alleged that the US was responsible for his removal from office.

Dawood Ibrahim orchestrating Pakistani Prime Minister Imran Khan's downfall surprisingly did not seem like a stretch, considering Dawood Ibrahim's insidious grip on the rich and the powerful of Pakistan.

'Aren't you aware that Dawood Ibrahim had earlier got Asif Ali Zardari appointed as the President of Pakistan?' Kamaal queried, his tone tinged with incredulity at my hesitation.

I grabbed his wrist.

'Why are you meeting me here? When can you tell me the whole story?' I demanded.

My determination to uncover the truth had overridden any desire to remain at the IIFA Awards. Reflecting on the events that led me to this moment, I couldn't help but acknowledge the role my wife had played in bringing me here. Her insistence, rooted in her admiration for Kamal Haasan, had compelled me to attend the event despite my initial reluctance. I did not know, once again, that I would be led to a treasure trove—a tale of treachery that reeked of tyranny and deception.

'Before you leave, do check the video link I have just shared with you. I know you will not take my word for it. But will you believe Javed Miandad making a candid confession on a national television channel?' Kamaal said, replacing his phone in his coat pocket and walking out of the hall.

I found myself grappling with the enormity of unravelling yet another story—the weight of the exposé bearing down upon me like a heavy yoke. And amidst the clamour and confusion and the fireworks at the podium, the enigmatic figure slipped away, leaving me to ponder the mysteries that had drawn us together.

We had agreed to meet at a secret location, where he would reveal the story in parts. But before I could press him for further details, he vanished into the thronging crowd, leaving me to contend with the tumultuous events unfolding around me. And as Salman Khan prepared to take the stage, I was left with a sense of anticipation as well as trepidation, knowing that the journey had only just begun.

Back in the hotel room, as I replayed the conversation in my mind, I couldn't help but wonder about Kamaal Hasan's intentions. I couldn't wait to Google and do my homework before my next meeting with Kamaal Hasan. As the laptop flickered to life, I clicked the link which he had shared with me. The voice of a news anchor filled the air, recounting the latest developments.

My gaze fixed on the screen as Javed Miandad's familiar face appeared, his words carrying the weight of its significance. A member of the historic World Cup-winning team alongside Imran Khan, Miandad's name commanded respect in the realm of cricket. Yet, what he revealed in that interview was significant in the light of his familial ties to Dawood Ibrahim through his son Junaid's marriage to Mahrukh, Dawood's daughter. The interview sent a shiver down my spine.[1]

The irony of public perception between two Pakistani cricketers couldn't be starker. In India, Imran Khan was a cricketing legend; he was a cultural icon. In his prime, he was hosted by the rich and famous of Mumbai and adorned the covers of magazines. On the other hand, Javed Miandad, a celebrated hero of Pakistan's cricketing triumphs, was vilified by Indian sports fans. His sixer to Chetan Sharma's last ball in 1986 changed the face of Pakistani cricket for half a decade, boosting it to a national obsession and catapulting the cricketers to the hall of fame and wealth. The Miandad sixer that made India lose the match destroyed the morale of Indian cricketers, an entire nation and the fans for a very long time. That one ball and one stroke became a defining moment in the strained relationship between the two countries.

So deep-seated was the antipathy towards Javed Miandad that Bollywood, ever quick to draw inspiration from real-life drama, began naming its villains after him, cementing his status as a cultural pariah.

In this particular news clip that I was watching in my hotel room, Javed was openly claiming that it was his recommendation that helped Imran Khan secure the premiership of the country. Miandad claimed that Khan was ungrateful and did not acknowledge his efforts.

'Imran had to lose his seat . . . because some powerful people who are believers in the power of Allah deposed him,' Miandad's words echoed. The news anchor who seemed to be totally flummoxed at this revelation from Javed Miandad thought it wise not to pursue this any more.

Dawood Ibrahim may have had a deep political nexus with Indian ministers or even chief ministers of some states in the country, but that he would now become a king-maker in Pakistan choosing presidents and premiers was such a preposterous idea. Nevertheless, as they say, the story had just begun . . . and I was determined to chase it from all corners, not just Kamaal Hasan.

1

The Blue Fox

In every man's life comes a moment which is defining in more ways than he can imagine. Dawood Ibrahim's life is a living testimony to the fact that he managed to scale new heights with every crime he perpetrated. Sometimes, in the process, he surprised himself as well.

Beginning from the biggest bank robbery since Indian independence, in 1974, registered by the Pydhonie police, Dawood moved on to bigger things with every phase of his life.

In a span of thirty years, a street-level hoodlum became the world's most-wanted gangster and then a global terrorist designated by the US Treasury Department. In this period, Dawood decimated the Pathan mafia of Mumbai, relocated to Dubai and then moved to Pakistan.

Dawood's life after the Mumbai bomb blasts of 1993 is plagued with as much complexity as it was prior to that event. The difference is that the scale of Dawood's operations increased massively while the violence took a back seat, at least on the surface. To analyse Dawood's move to Karachi and his eventual settling in Pakistan, we need to have a deeper insight into his initial foray, especially his debut in Karachi's civil wars in the 1990s. The decade was not just a watershed phase in the history of Karachi and the blood-toned history of Pakistan but also for Dawood, who decided to create strategic alliances for his future.

'He is human,' Kamaal Hasan told me. 'He makes mistakes. But his ability to correct his course makes him dangerous.'

'Why do you say that?'

'Because he once bet on the wrong horse,' Kamaal said, 'and then began riding the one that won the race.'

In June 1992, Karachi shimmered under the relentless sun, its oppressive heat mirroring the simmering political cauldron. The Mohajir Qaumi Movement (MQM), a party born from the anxieties of Urdu-speaking migrants who had fled India after Partition, clashed violently with the established power of the Pakistan People's Party (PPP), a party rooted in rural Sindh.

The MQM emerged in the late 1970s. Its fiery founder, Altaf Hussain, channelled the frustrations of a community which felt marginalized and discriminated against. Born in Karachi in 1953, Hussain belonged to the Urdu-speaking Mohajir community. Witnessing their marginalization, Hussain founded the MQM in 1978, initially as a student organization advocating for Muhajir rights. He later went on to become a powerful political force in Karachi owing to his mastery of oratory skills.

The PPP, founded by Zulfikar Ali Bhutto, had long held sway in Sindh, which was their stronghold. It was built on a populist message of social justice and rural development. Born in 1928, Zulfikar Ali Bhutto rose from a prominent Sindhi family and became a celebrated lawyer and politician. He championed socialism and populism, captivating the masses with his fiery speeches. As the President and later prime minister of Pakistan, Bhutto nationalized industries, implemented land reforms and pursued closer ties with the Muslim world. Yet, his tenure was marred by political turmoil, including accusations of authoritarianism and the controversial dismissal of the chief justice.

Zulfikar Bhutto had four children, of which two rose to prominence in the political sphere. Born in 1953, Benazir Bhutto inherited her father's charisma and political instincts. After her father's execution by military dictator Zia-ul-Haq, Benazir emerged as the torchbearer of the PPP, with Pakistan facing brutal suppression under military dictatorships. In 1988, she finally led the PPP to a historic victory and became the first elected female prime minister in a Muslim-majority nation.

While Benazir thrived in the political arena, her brother Murtaza Bhutto, born in 1954, carved a different path. Educated in Syria and Lebanon, he embraced a more radical socialist ideology and formed his own political party while aligning himself with the revolutionary movements. His fiery speeches and armed challenges to the government kept him in constant conflict with the authorities, including his own sister and her husband Asif Ali Zardari.

In the Pakistan of the early 1990s, the tension crackled like dry tinder. MQM rallies boomed with calls for ethnic recognition and political autonomy. Their supporters would be clad in vibrant green, the party's colour. PPP gatherings countered with promises of national unity and a more equitable distribution of resources. Beneath the surface, whispers of violence slithered: targeted killings, grenade attacks and drive-by shootings painted the city red with blood. Karachi, the economic engine of Pakistan, sat at the crossroads of these ideologies and became a fertile ground for clash and conflict.

Karachi had become the most violent and blood-soaked city in the world in the 1990s despite the unabated bloodshed that painted so many countries red. The killing spree in Iraq, Somalia, the freed states of the USSR and triad-ruled countries in Southeast Asia were no less shocking, but they paled in comparison when Karachi's civil wars were recorded in history.

In this tinderbox, the shadow of Dawood Ibrahim began to loom onto Pakistan. He was already on the run from Mumbai and looking for places where he could establish his stamp of authority. Dawood's stay in Dubai had started getting precarious as the growing political prominence of the United Arab Emirates and India's increasing clout internationally seemed like a tightening noose around his neck. He needed another safety net.

He saw in the MQM not just a political ally but a potential bridge back to his past life in Mumbai. He envisioned building Karachi as another stronghold, a base from where he could operate following his exile from Mumbai. Hence, he decided to supply arms to Altaf Hussain to aid them in his party's fight against the PPP. But for once, Dawood seemed to have placed his bets on the wrong horse.[1]

Four of Dawood's arms consignments to Hussain were intercepted from Nine-Zero's bustling bazaar, Haneefabad, Jinnah Terminal near Karachi Airport and Arambagh on M.A. Jinnah Road. The cache of weapons included AK-47s, explosives and advanced automatic pistols and guns.[2]

The MQM's dreams of supremacy fuelled by Dawood's guns and promises were shattered. The government responded with Operation Blue Fox; a large-scale, controversial military operation. While the planning for Operation Blue Fox likely began under Prime Minister Nawaz Sharif in early 1992, the official launch and implementation took place under Benazir Bhutto, who became prime minister in July 1993. It's important to note that the operation had strong backing from both Sharif's and Bhutto's administrations, reflecting the gravity of the situation in Karachi.[3]

The objectives of the operation were to disarm the MQM, curb their criminal activities, restore law and order and weaken their political influence. Raids were conducted on MQM offices and strongholds by Sindh Police and Pakistan Rangers with support from the Pakistan Army and intelligence agencies. MQM members and activists were arrested. Official figures report 1770 casualties in Karachi in 1995, while media sources suggest over 1990 killings (around 700 in 1994).[4]

The MQM was weakened, forced to renounce violence and accept government authority. Throughout all this, Dawood Ibrahim remained elusive.

Despite the Mumbai bomb blasts on 12 March 1993, and Dawood being named as the number one accused and main conspirator, the Indian government was not able to lay its hands on him. Dawood was ready to leave Dubai, and Karachi was still not ready to accept him. Dawood's alliances and support of Altaf Hussain had turned out to be a major fiasco.

One particular episode demonstrated Dawood's total desperation and vacillation. Dawood had reached out to the famous Indian lawyer Ram Jethmalani while the latter was in London and expressed his desire to surrender. He requested Jethmalani to negotiate on his behalf with the Indian government. However, his request to surrender, which also had a few peculiar conditions, was summarily dismissed by the Maharashtra government.

Experts say that the rejection of the surrender plea was more for the fear of some of the top politicians getting exposed by Dawood's return rather than being seen as buckling under a ganglord's *diktat*, if they would have accepted his terms. Nevertheless, Abu Salem's formal extradition in 2005 and the Indian government's submission to some grave conditions are clear evidence that the experts were not far off the mark.

Dawood seemed to be totally stuck after the dismissal of his surrender plea by the government. He was left with no option but to relocate. Dawood had quite a few options: London, Istanbul, but the best option was Karachi.

In the aftermath of Operation Blue Fox, Karachi witnessed a peculiar power shift. Asif Ali Zardari, the politician with a gaze as sharp as his suit, and husband of the then prime minister, Benazir Bhutto, emerged as the unlikely victor.

Born on 26 July 1955, in Karachi, Zardari had no idea that he would go on to become a prominent figure in Pakistani politics. He was a Sindhi and was engaged in several rackets in his early days.[5] He used to sell movie tickets in black for a living as his father Hakim Zardari owned a cinema house, Bambino, in Karachi. When he prospered economically, Asif Ali Zardari became a businessman. He faced various legal challenges and spent several years in prison on charges of corruption and other allegations, although he consistently denied any wrongdoing. His fortunes turned after marrying Benazir Bhutto, who was later, in 1988, elected as prime minister of Pakistan.

With the MQM crippled, Zardari and Bhutto's party, the PPP, seized control of the country. It was a double victory in the hushed corridors of power. For one, Zardari had dealt a decisive blow to the MQM. Yet, this wasn't just a political triumph; it was a message to another shadowy figure across the border—Dawood Ibrahim. The don, who dreamt of carving out a Karachi foothold, watched from afar as his pawns faltered. Zardari established himself as the undisputed power broker, the man who controlled the levers of Karachi's fate.

But in these twilight hours, a curious alliance began to bloom. Dawood, recognizing the new reality, offered Zardari an unexpected partnership. The politician, hungry for both wealth and power, found himself drawn to the don's vast criminal empire, its coffers a tempting source of sustenance for his political ambitions.

Zardari believed that Dawood was very resourceful as the don had delivered so many weapons to Altaf Hussain on Pakistani soil despite not being a native of the country. Zardari's and Dawood's friendship blossomed.[6] In the rubble of Blue Fox, a new Karachi was slowly taking shape. Dawood remained a silent but powerful partner, his tentacles ready to reach into the country's underbelly.

But amidst this power play, a stark counterpoint emerged—the human cost. Thousands of lives, caught in the crossfire of ambition and violence, were silenced. Mothers wept for sons lost in political wars and children were orphaned by stray bullets.

The Karachi Incident of 1992 stood as a stark reminder: the pursuit of power comes at a heavy price. Operation Blue Fox may have achieved its tactical objective, but the ethical questions lingered and were marked by the stamp of a single, elusive criminal.

For Dawood, he had opened the gateway to Pakistan. It did not matter to him whether the gatekeeper was Altaf Hussain or Asif Ali Zardari. From here, Dawood would go on to forge multiple partnerships with powerful and influential figures like Malik Riaz and Mehwish Hayat. But no one in Pakistan had any idea that the don was willing to go to such great lengths to see his friend, Asif Ali Zardari, capture the highest seat of power in the country rather than play second fiddle to his wife.

2
Pakistan's First Ten-Per Cent President

Mount Vernon Estate is the former plantation of the first President of the US, George Washington. It is a beautiful historic site in Washington, D.C. I am totally in love with the Potomac and various trails around the river. The lush greenery, the calmness and the spiritually exhilarating surroundings can make me walk around the massive riverside for hours or just stand there in deep meditation. Such places are a rare combination of peace and natural beauty.

However, I had never ventured inside this historical estate. So, when Kamaal Hasan suggested this as a site to meet, I was taken aback. I now understood that he had a penchant for choosing unusual venues for meetings—and I was willing to go to any length to hear a good story.

Kamaal had suggested that he would provide an analytical commentary on Pakistani politics and the rise of

Indian mafiosi in the badlands of Karachi during our tour of Mount Vernon. Listening to a deeply studied perspective of Pakistani politics inside a touristically important place in the US was the weirdest combination I could have imagined.

'Why this historical, touristy site?' I asked.

'Have you seen *Baadshah*? The comic thriller of Shah Rukh Khan?'

Of course I had. 'What about it?'

Kamaal said, 'I will narrate the story of one such *badshah*.'

We began the long walk and talk, not on the history of the US or Mount Vernon Estate but on the violent past of Pakistan. Not many Indians have tried to decipher why the violence and instability of Pakistani regimes were responsible for tumult in India and the country having to face so many terrorist attacks. Beginning with the mysterious death of Pakistan's founder Mohammad Ali Jinnah to the deaths of several of its rulers and leaders, rivers of blood kept flowing in Pakistan.

High-profile political killings such as those of Liaquat Ali Khan, Yahya Khan, Zulfikar Bhutto, Zia-ul-Haq and Benazir Bhutto continued ad infinitum. Ironically, all these murders are still unsolved.

'*Haakim ki saazish aamez maut, hukumati hawadees, mulk aur awaam ki taqdeer taiy karte hain,*' Kamaal said. (Conspiracies surrounding the death of rulers, and the shenanigans of governments determine the fate of the nation, and all its people.)

Standing among the crowd of Americans and English-speaking visitors, my suave friend took refuge in chaste Urdu.

He meant to use it as a code, which can be translated as 'the conspiratorial deaths of the rulers and the upheaval in the governments decide the fate of the country and its people'.

A seventy-seven-year-old country has only blood and bankruptcy writ large in its decree. Kamaal's reference to a twenty-five-year-old Indian movie to describe the status of Pakistani politics was strange if not downright baffling. *Baadshah* is one of the more films of Shah Rukh Khan that was released in 1999. The plot revolved around a Machiavellian husband of an all-powerful chief minister who decided to eliminate her and don the mantle of ruler himself. Kamaal was asking me to learn from it. Perhaps Kamaal or even Bollywood buffs do not know that *Baadshah* was inspired by the Hollywood political thriller *Nick of Time* (1995) starring Johnny Depp.

Shahnawaz Bhutto, the younger son of Zulfikar Bhutto, was poisoned in France in 1986. Ten years later, the elder son Murtaza Bhutto and his friends were killed in an incident of police firing in Karachi during the violent skirmishes in the civil war of the 1990s. The shocking part was that the high-profile killing was executed during the rule of Murtaza's own sister, Benazir Bhutto. The whole Bhutto clan had accused Benazir and her husband Asif Zardari to be the brains behind the killing. The tremors of this political killing spread so far and wide that within weeks, then President Farooq Leghari dismissed the PPP government of Benazir and she finally had to leave the country.

Pakistani politicians have a tacit understanding between themselves. They choose to go into exile to escape legal prosecution or prison and forge some kind of truce with the regime that succeeds them. There are scores of such examples in the political history of Pakistan. Despite being prime minister of Pakistan for two brief stints, Benazir led her life abroad for eight years and returned only after making a strategic plan to contest the 2008 elections.

This epoch-making return of the year 2007, which sealed the fate of Benazir, also changed the fortunes of many in Pakistan, including the then President, Pervez Musharraf, and above all, her own husband, Zardari. Political experts in India and Europe always suspected that it was Pervez Musharraf who cleverly invited Benazir to Pakistan and plotted her assassination.[1] However, Musharraf did not have to write the epitaph for Benazir; it was already crafted before she landed in Karachi in October 2007.

Soon after she left Jinnah International Airport, two explosions occurred.[2] They were believed to have been orchestrated through two suicide bombers and resulted in the deaths of over 190 people, with over 500 injured. Benazir remained unhurt but over seventy volunteers of her political party died in the attack. The Bhutto family was totally rattled by the attack, and its seismic waves were felt by intelligence agencies around the world, notably, the Central Intelligence Agency (CIA), Military Intelligence-6 (MI-6), Research and Analysis Wing (R&AW) and Mossad of Israel.

However, Musharraf and the Indian agencies were totally unfazed because the suicide bomber technique did not bear the signature of either of them. Even while the Bhuttos were seeking augmented security from various quarters, including the Americans and the Arabs, in less than two months, the terrorists succeeded in killing Benazir at a rally in Rawalpindi.

This time the assassination attempt was much more coordinated with foolproof methods. Subsequent investigations revealed that several snipers were stationed, who took shots at her, and in a concerted attempt, a suicide bomber also detonated a bomb. In fact, a video had gone viral, where one of her bodyguards was seen signalling to a sniper to target Benazir's neck.[3] This clearly indicated the involvement of an insider in the killing.

On 27 December 2007, she was rushed to the hospital with fatal wounds. The cause of death was never established. It was widely speculated that she suffered a bullet shot in her throat or the massive impact of the suicide bombing jerked her spine, while she was waving at the crowd, in such a manner that she suffered cranial injuries leading to her death. Benazir's husband, Asif Zardari, who returned to Pakistan the same evening after the incident, opposed the autopsy, which further deepened the mystery.

Wikipedia is rife with several theories of the assassination and multiple causes of death quoting several doctors and politicians of Pakistan, each making their own assertions and propounding different causes of death. Among the various theories, it was explained that several terror organizations, including Al-Qaeda, the Islamic State of Iraq and Syria (ISIS) and Lashkar-e-Jhangvi joined hands to plot the killing. The real reason and the perpetrators could never be traced.

After his return, Zardari stayed in Pakistan and appointed their son Bilawal as the head of the PPP. The party returned to victory with a majority in the September 2008 elections and Zardari was appointed as the President of Pakistan.

Zardari, whose career had begun with selling tickets in black, had come a long way in three decades. Until his marriage to Benazir in 1987, Zardari had nothing worth mentioning as accomplishments in his life. Soon after his marriage, Zardari shot into the limelight, but Benazir deliberately kept him out of politics. She had no clue of the extent of Zardari's ambitions.

In 1988, when Zia-ul-Haq's plane crashed and a political vacuum was created, Benazir's PPP romped to the Parliament with an absolute majority. Benazir was crowned as the first woman prime minister of Pakistan much to the chagrin of the clergy in Pakistan and the Arab world. Zardari basked in the borrowed glory as the de facto prime minister.

Between 1988 and 2008, Zardari was incarcerated several times and spent over eleven years in jail. He was also booked in a variety of corruption and criminal cases. Perhaps Benazir's aura totally eclipsed his unabated aspirations, though everyone in Pakistan knew what Mr Ten Per Cent was capable of. Zardari's ascent to presidency was a historical reality that the battle-scarred nation had resigned itself to accept.

In the span of nine months since the Bhutto killing and almost a year after the assassination attempt on her in Karachi, no progress was made in the investigation. Despite the PPP winning the elections and Zardari occupying the top post in Pakistan, no concerted efforts were made to find the mastermind behind the killing to unravel the whole conspiracy.

In fact, the British Broadcasting Company (BBC) conducted a full-fledged investigation only to find that there was a huge cover-up by government higher-ups with regard to nailing the culprits of the killing.[4] The obstacles in the probe were created not just by the Pakistan Army but even Zardari, who was considered to be the main suspect behind the sordid drama of Benazir's killing and his subsequent elevation. He appeared to be disinterested in finding out the truth or in punishing the perpetrators, claimed the BBC investigation.

Incidentally, Zardari was the only Pakistani President to have carried out his full tenure as the President of the country. Perhaps also the most controversial one too, for any head of a country anywhere in the world. The *Guardian UK* ran a headline that said: 'The Godfather as President'. *Chicago Tribune* and *France 24* wrote that Mr Ten Per Cent had become President. The 'ten per cent' reference was to a long-standing corruption accusation against Zardari for his involvement in various scandals where he was alleged to have received kickbacks of 10 per cent on any deal that he facilitated.[5]

However, the most shocking incident associated with Zardari was the hijacking of Singapore Airlines Flight 117 on 26 March 1991 by PPP workers. The flight was hijacked by four Pakistanis from an airport near Kuala Lumpur in Malaysia while it was en route to Singapore.[6] The hijackers demanded the release of Zardari from prison. However, commandos of the Singapore Armed Forces (SAF) managed to overpower the hijackers and release the passengers and crew members at Changi Airport in Singapore.

In 2008, Zardari ascended to the presidency and began whitewashing his blemished political career. The corruption and criminal cases against Zardari were dismissed summarily. Zardari, who was facing the biggest blot of his involvement in Murtaza Bhutto's killing, also got acquitted in the case after over twelve years of facing the allegation.

Political experts often claim that Zardari was a clever combination of Chanakya and Chandragupta. None had seen this side of him, except his own wife Benazir, who wanted to keep him on a leash, and his brother-in-law Murtaza Bhutto. Both had to be systematically ejected from the scheme of things for him to reach the top slot. The whole saga of Zardari's survival and success was intriguing and left me flummoxed. Comparing it with the Indian film *Baadshah* and its basic theme would be inaccurate, I felt.

The sun was about to set, a pleasant chill had begun to envelop the city. Kamaal and I had walked a long way from Mount Vernon Estate and had now reached the waterside of the Potomac River. Both of us were mentally tired and physically exhausted. We were ready to part when he sat on a bench nearby and said, 'Have you Indians ever thought that one of the biggest terrorist attacks on Indian soil orchestrated by Pakistan, was in 2008, which was within months of Asif Zardari's presidency?'

I looked at him with great interest despite my exhaustion.

'Terrorists who attacked India in 2008 came with the same ideology that had killed Benazir Bhutto,' Kamaal said with a distant look in his eyes. 'Zardari's involvement in either hasn't been established. But what is totally clear is that Dawood Ibrahim and his gang progressed and prospered since 2008 and rose to become the most powerful clan in Pakistan.'

I knew the story was far from over. I was never interested so much in Asif Zardari, but Kamaal was indicating that if I had to understand the power of Dawood Ibrahim, I had to understand the permutations and combinations of the power play in Pakistan. Dawood tramples over the authorities to demonstrate his domination, whether in India, Pakistan or Europe.

3

A Tale of Two Arrests

Neeraj Kumar has no dearth of accolades to his name since he began his career in the police force as an ACP. From doing a spectacular job in handling security operations in the 1982 Asian Games to cracking a puzzling serial murder case in which victims were mysteriously bludgeoned to death before being looted by their killer, Kumar's splendid career as a brave and intelligent police officer is replete with feats that are indescribably amazing and awe-inspiring at the same time.

But the case that stands out in terms of the diplomacy with which it was executed was his perseverance in persuading the Memon family to return to India and subsequently sneaking them out of Dubai from right under the Inter-Services Intelligence's (ISI) nose. Tiger Memon was among the chief accused in the Mumbai blasts case. His brother Yakub Memon was deemed to have played a pivotal role in executing the blasts as well.

Though responsible for the arrests of sixteen other absconders who were accused of the blasts, Kumar's success in getting the six family members of the Memon family to return to India to face the law made his name inseparable from the handling of the Memons' case. That was the reason I was compelled to fly back to Delhi to meet Neeraj Kumar and learn more about the only accused in the serial blasts who was sent to the gallows.

'The centrepiece of Yakub's arrest was his cousin whom we gave the cover name Suresh,' Kumar said. 'The CBI worked meticulously to exploit this source and lure Yakub to fly back to India. But, of course, there are a few versions floating around.'

Around late July or early August 1994, depending on which version one wants to believe, Yakub Memon flew from Dubai to Kathmandu with only a briefcase in his hands. He was the younger brother of Tiger Memon, the man who had executed the biggest terror attack on Indian soil in the form of the 1993 Mumbai bomb blasts.

Nondescript in its appearance, the briefcase was at the centre of the discussion Yakub was going to have with his cousin that day. It contained several incriminating documents that proved Pakistan's role in carrying out the blasts, along with the fake passports held by the Memon family. The Memons had been on the run since the blasts, living the lives of fugitives across the border in various countries before finding themselves holed up in Pakistan.

Apparently, Yakub was considering turning in the documents in the hope of receiving clemency from the Indian government and getting other members of his family (excluding Tiger) cleared of all charges. With this idea in mind, he travelled to Nepal to meet his cousin and discuss the potential of the idea of surrendering. There are theories that Indian agencies were in touch with this cousin of Yakub, codenamed Suresh, and were trying to convince him to return to the country and face the law.[1]

Yakub's plan, however, could not come to fruition as he was picked up by the CBI from Kathmandu while being detained in a routine security check. There were reports that a bunch of keys in his luggage showed up as a handgun in the X-ray machine and the security personnel stumbled upon the fake passports when the luggage was checked. He was then flown down to Delhi where he remained in CBI's custody.

He was presented to the court, and it was officially announced that a big arrest had been made by the CBI in the 1993 Mumbai blasts case.

The official account as per the CBI runs contrary to the one mentioned above. The CBI version, which was majorly picked up by the media, states that the cops captured Yakub from a railway station in Delhi where he was on one of his clandestine visits using his fake passport. The intelligence agencies got wind of his expedition and a group of undercover agents apprehended him at the station on 5 August 1994.

Then Union home minister, S.B. Chavan, broke the news of Yakub's arrest in the Parliament and the house erupted in cheers and thumping of desks. But as the years passed, different versions of Yakub Memon's arrest started floating around, some conforming with the official version and some granting credibility to the theory that he came into CBI's custody of his own volition.

B. Raman, a former R&AW officer, wrote an article in this context in 2007, stating:

> Yakub was right in claiming that he was not arrested in Delhi. In July 1994, some weeks before my retirement, he was informally picked up in Kathmandu, with the help of the Nepal police, driven across Nepal to a town in Indian territory, flown to Delhi by an aircraft of the Aviation Research Centre and formally arrested in Old Delhi by the investigating authorities and taken into custody for interrogation. The entire operation was coordinated by me.[2]

Raman, who used to head the Pakistan desk at India's spy agency, requested the article to be withheld from publishing until his retirement as he felt other accused might escape conviction if the higher court saw that the case had been vitiated as a result of the prosecution concealing a material fact from the sentencing court. The article was finally published in July 2015 by Rediff.com.

Some much wilder theories went largely underreported. One such theory, emanating from across the border, suggested that Yakub's voluntary arrival in India was a 'gift' from the Government of Pakistan ushered by then prime minister Benazir Bhutto. Her rivalry with Nawaz Sharif, who was the prime minister of Pakistan when the blasts took place, was made the basis of this theory to insinuate that the move was an act of political vendetta by the ruling prime minister to present Nawaz Sharif in bad light.

Bhutto, however, was quick to trash the theory and even went so far as to term Home Minister S.B. Chavan's observation of Pakistan's complicity in the bomb attacks as a 'pack of lies' and deny the ISI's involvement in the crime.

Interestingly, a building located on Dadabhai Naoroji Road in south Mumbai caught fire five days after Yakub had crossed the Indo-Nepal border at around 3 a.m. on 28 July. The Eruchshaw building was engulfed in flames and completely gutted in the fire. The building was taken up by R&AW offices on two of its floors and the fire, it was said, had destroyed all the data that the agency had stored in computerized form. The incident was followed by a theory doing the rounds that it was Yakub Memon's brother, Tiger's way of expressing his contempt for his brother's arrest.

The truth behind Yakub Memon's arrest is hidden by the smoke and mirrors; much like the man himself. Yakub was born on 30 July 1962 in Byculla, Mumbai to Mr and Mrs Abdul Razzak Memon. The third in a line of seven children—all boys—Yakub showed great interest in acquiring a decent education. He completed his SSC in 1978 following which he did several odd jobs until 1982, when he joined the Bombay Port Trust (BPT) as an audit clerk.

He, however, held on to his last gig as an accounts and sales supervisor for a showroom of VIP (a suitcase company) where he worked before joining BPT. Four years later, he left both the jobs and went on to do a chartered accountancy course. By this time, he was already writing accounts for eight or nine companies on a part-time basis. He completed his CA in 1990 and started a firm with his childhood friend Chetan Mehta under the name of Memon and Mehta Associates. Yakub had become a co-owner of a successful and flourishing CA firm even before he reached the age of thirty. He was showing all the signs of growing up to become an exemplary son of the Memons, unlike his brother born two years before him, Ibrahim Mushtaq Abdul Razzaq Memon aka Tiger Memon.

Tiger started as a bank clerk but ended up in police records when he was fired at, at a customs party in 1985. While the neighbourhood of Pydhonie had high hopes for Yakub, they made sure to maintain a safe distance from the reckless Tiger whose furious temper was like a ticking bomb.

Yakub's partnership with Mehta couldn't last long and the two eventually split. Mehta went on to remember Yakub as a gentle person and said that it was impossible for one to believe that Yakub got involved in any activity that was against the law.[3] The termination of his partnership in the Mehta firm did not stop Yakub from scaling new heights as he continued gaining clients.

Within a year of his separation from the Mehta firm, Yakub was handling the accounts of over a hundred bigwig firms. He also assisted his brothers in managing the accounts of their meat export firm, Tejarath International. He entered into a partnership with his brothers and founded the firm ARL and Sons in the year 1991. As they had shifted from Kurla to Al-Hussaini building in Mahim by this time, the operations of this firm used to be carried out from Mahim.

In the wake of the Babri Masjid demolition in 1992, the city was hit with violent Hindu–Muslim riots. The carnage gave Mumbai one of its most traumatic experiences in the history of independent India and was noted to have occurred in two phases. The first immediately followed the Babri Masjid demolition in December 1992 and the other was in the month of January 1993. Apart from the huge losses to private property and infrastructure, the riot left 575 Muslims and 275 Hindus dead, in addition to the deaths of fifty persons from other faiths.[4] The Babri Masjid demolition and perception that the local police were more than ready to throw them to the mobs through their acts of omission or commission had created an intense feeling of insecurity and mistrust among the Muslims. These feelings were exploited to the hilt by people like Tiger, who began propagating the idea of revenge.

Even prior to the blasts, when Tiger Memon was planning this mega operation of terror, he flew his family members to Dubai before counselling Yakub to join him. He exhorted Yakub to distance himself from the danger that he saw looming upon the Muslims of the country. Yakub, however, was busy renewing some important documents of a professional nature that got burnt in the riots. He chose to remain in the city where he had built a life and flourishing business for himself.

Yakub started establishing ties with new clients and entering into new business transactions. This went on till March 1993 when Tiger, on one of his visits to the country from Dubai, insisted that Yakub should leave for Dubai along with their parents and family as the situation in the city was getting worse by the day for the Muslim populace. Yakub finally submitted to his brother's incessant requests and left for Dubai a few days before the blasts.

Yakub owned a Hero Honda motorcycle, which was included in the many possessions he had to bid farewell to when he left Mumbai. The bike remained in the parking space of the Al-Hussaini building. It was later found out that the vehicle was used by two of the accused to throw hand grenades at an aircraft at Sahar Airport with the intention of causing the loss of civilian lives. Yakub claimed complete ignorance of his brother's activities in relation to the blast and the use of his motorcycle in carrying out the Sahar Airport explosion.

On 12 March 1993, Mohammad Iqbal Shaikh, one of the co-accused in the blasts, returned to Tiger's house after he had successfully parked an RDX-laden scooter outside Kailash Lassi Shop near Dadar (East) railway station. At Tiger's house, he met up with Javed Chikna and Bashir to take further instructions on the plan for causing mayhem. Naseem Barmare, another accused, was also present to receive his share of instructions from the duo.

'Javed and Bashir handed us the grenades,' Mohammad Iqbal recounted during his confession to participating in the blast. 'They asked us to go to Sahar Airport on the motorcycle parked outside the house.'

Iqbal did as he was told and rode the Honda to Sahar International Airport with Naseem riding pillion. As soon as they reached the airport, Naseem hurled the grenades at an aircraft and they both fled. The grenades, fortunately, didn't explode.

Back in Dubai in 1993, Yakub was growing restive with each passing day. He had heard of the blasts and began suspecting that their lengthy stay in Dubai translated to something more sinister than just an innocuous security measure taken against the growing atmosphere of hate against Muslims in the city. Ever since the blasts, Tiger was always on the phone, engaged in animated conversations that ranged from secretive to congratulatory. Yakub's version is that it was during this period that he deduced that Tiger had something to do with the gruesome bombings that had taken place on 12 March 1993.

Meanwhile, Indian authorities were piling on the pressure using diplomatic channels to get custody of the Memons after Tiger had emerged as the kingpin of the blasts. As a result, Tiger moved from Dubai and was ably assisted by the ISI to enter Pakistan on 14 March 1993. Yakub was still in Dubai.

Yakub arranged a call with Tiger in the hope that Tiger would allay his fears and inform him of his plans of arranging their return to India. But the call, on the contrary, fanned the flames of his suspicion as Tiger earnestly requested him to come to Pakistan along with the rest of the family.

'It's a matter of life and death for us,' Tiger told him on the phone.

Under pressure from his maliciously maverick brother, Yakub obliged and left Dubai on 17 March 1993 on a flight bound for Bombay via Karachi with his family. They were received by a bald man at Karachi Airport, who asked for their Indian passports. Keeping the passports with him, he escorted them straight outside the airport, waiving all immigration and customs formalities. The family would later learn that the man's name was Asif, and he was an official who worked for the Government of Pakistan.

As soon as Yakub stepped outside, his eyes fell on a Pajero car that was protected on all sides by three or four armed personnel dressed in civilian clothes. Seated inside the Pajero was none other than Tiger Memon. Yakub saw that his brother was being propped up by none other than one of the most dangerous intelligence agencies in the world, the ISI; and that life for him and others of the Memon family would never be the same again.

4

Grand Guest House

Situated in the vicinity of Indira Gandhi International Airport in Palam, the colossal Indian Air Force Museum is a marvellous site that compels commuters to stop and take notice. From the historic photographs, uniforms to personal weapons, the museum features an array of memorabilia associated with the Indian Air Force since its establishment in 1932.

Visiting the museum had been on my to-do list, and I was grateful to Neeraj Kumar for the once-in-a-lifetime experience and for the opportunity to be proud of the rich and valorous history of our air force.

'The formidable defence system of our nation has always been the key to keeping threats from our neighbouring countries at bay,' Kumar said. 'Much like our intelligence and diplomatic channels that played a major role in leading the Memons back to India from various countries.'

'What was Yakub's stay in Pakistan like?' I asked.[1]

'As per Yakub's confession,' Kumar said, 'a lot happened.'

After reaching Pakistan, Yakub and his family were escorted by the armed men to Taufique Jaliawala's bungalow, which was situated in Dhoraji Colony in Karachi. Jaliawala, who had emerged as a key aide of Tiger in Pakistan, was on an Umrah tour to Saudi Arabia with his family. Yakub was received by Taufique's eldest son Riaz and his would-be son-in-law, Farooq. Three or four armed men would guard the bungalow 24/7.

'Do not allow anyone to venture outside except for prayers to the nearby mosque,' Tiger had instructed these armed escorts, virtually placing his own family under house arrest.

On 24 March 1993, merely days after Yakub had landed in Pakistan, the family was moved to another of Jaliawala's bungalows in Karachi, which was located in an area called Gulshan-e-Iqbal. Tiger's mingling with obscure personalities in a foreign land and his avoidance of any kind of transparency was pushing Yakub to the edge. Their lives were getting more complex with each passing day and Yakub finally decided to confront Tiger. But, owing to Tiger's unyielding nature, the confrontation led nowhere and it only gave rise to frequent quarrelling between the two brothers. Yakub had begun feeling queasy and fell ill for the remaining days of their stay in Gulshan-e-Iqbal, which ended during the third week of April.

In the month of April, Taufique visited Tiger at the Gulshan-e-Iqbal bungalow bringing four men along with him. The four were addressed as Asif, Usman aka Captain Sarwar, Faisal Sa'ab and Umar Sa'ab by Taufique.

Smartly dressed, the four men conducted themselves in an officious manner. Yakub deduced that they were Pakistani government officials who were probably acting on the directions of the ISI.

One of them opened a bag and handed out a pocket-sized packet to Yakub. To his surprise, it was a new passport! The officials soon started handing out new passports to each of the family members that gave them Pakistani identities. The family's middle name was now 'Ahmed'. The assumed name of Tiger's father was Ahmed Mohammed while Yakub was to be identified as Yusuf Ahmed as per the new passports.

On 17 April 1993, Captain Sarwar visited the bungalow again.

'There is a lot of pressure on the Pakistani government from India to hand over the Memons,' he said. 'We have to move you to a different location.'

'Where?' Yakub asked.

'Pack your bags,' Sarwar responded curtly.

The family was flown to Bangkok under the assumed identities in two groups. Faisal Saab and Captain Sarwar accompanied each group separately. If Yakub held any second thoughts about Tiger's role in carrying out the blasts by colluding with Pakistani agencies, they had been dispelled.

Yakub started to keep his eyes and ears open to everything that was happening around him. In Yakub's words, his motive to return to India was to clear his family's name and this is why he began collecting evidence about those who were involved in the blasts, including the suspects in Pakistan. He started speaking to people around him so as to create a good rapport with crucial persons such as Taufiq and his son-in-law Farooq and squeeze as much info as possible out of them. On 29 April, the family was brought back to Karachi on the same passports while Tiger stayed behind. The bald man, Asif, was present to receive them in Karachi and he was accompanied by four or five guards. He took care of the customs and immigration formalities and escorted them out of the airport.

This time they were taken to the Defence Housing Authority in Karachi where Captain Sarwar had arranged a rented bungalow at Rs 7000 a month. Tiger joined them at the bungalow after fifteen to twenty days of their return from Bangkok.

Yakub had made good friends with Taufique and his immediate family by then and it proved successful in taking them into confidence. Taufique was impressed by Yakub's exceptional intellectual abilities and contemplated starting a real estate business in partnership with him. He took Yakub as his personal adviser in his existing businesses.

While the rest of the family remained confined to the bungalow, Yakub was able to roam freely due to his employment in Taufique's business. He also pulled in his two brothers to join him in looking after the business. Meanwhile, in an attempt to keep himself occupied, Yakub joined a computer course at the Institute of Computer Science in the city.

However, in the midst of everything, Yakub could not get rid of the feeling of being shadowed by the guards. In the first week of January 1994, the Memons were once again shifted to another location at Karachi Development Scheme, 1A. It was a palatial bungalow with all kinds of amenities and each family member had a separate room for themselves. It also had a couple of rooms for guests. On one of the days that followed, Taufique made an announcement of his daughter's wedding to Farooq.

Farooq was an Indian citizen, the son of Taufique's maternal uncle, Firoze Ammiwala. Taufique had given his eldest daughter, Rabia, to Farooq in marriage with the view of strengthening the relationship between the two families living across the border. Farooq had subsequently applied for Pakistani citizenship, notwithstanding the fact that he had a shop in Mumbai that dealt in computer spare parts.

When Taufique came to their bungalow to give them an invitation to the wedding, he advised them against attending the function as Farooq's guests from Mumbai would be present at the ceremony. 'There will be problems if someone among those guests recognizes you,' he said.

The Memon family did not attend the wedding and were later sent video cassettes of the function. The videotapes were a welcome cache for Yakub as they offered him a glimpse into Taufique's inner circle and the men he seemed to be in deference to.

A few days later, Tiger also had his trusted driver, Shafi Memon, come to Pakistan to avail his services. Shafi stayed with the family in the bungalow. Yakub stayed close to Shafi as he knew that long years of faithful service had turned the driver into Tiger's confidant. According to Yakub's confessions, he gained a lot of insights about the blasts from Shafi.[2]

Shafi often boasted about the role Tiger and his men had played in the blasts. He gave him the names of the boys whom Tiger had recruited to carry out the blasts and the locations where they were currently hiding.

Yakub wanted to know more about Taufique's role in the blast. He decided to broach the subject with Taufique. Yakub's counsel was often sought by Taufique in matters of business, but the subject was still a risky one. Establishing Taufique's role in the blast was of utmost importance as it would grant much needed credibility to his findings. So Yakub decided the risk was worthwhile.

Taufique would welcome Yakub's questions with an air of a VIP personality being asked to give an interview. He would ramble for hours on end about his role in the blasts and his contacts with the important people of his country. Yakub had also managed to record Taufique's voice surreptitiously where the latter boasted about his 'noteworthy' contribution in executing the crime.

Yakub, as per his admission, was in possession of enough proof and evidence by now, which he supposed would be sufficient to prove his case and bring an end to the troubles his family was facing. But to simply approach the law with the proof and materials gained in an amateurish investigation wouldn't have been a good idea. He needed something more substantial that would also act as a catalysing event and complement the findings of his investigation. He waited for such a moment.

In the month of June, he went to his brothers, Suleman and Essa, who were staying at Al Muraqabat in Dubai and were visiting the country for some business matters. During his stay in Dubai, Yakub learnt that Farooq had announced a trip to a foreign country with his wife on the fake passport that declared him a citizen of Pakistan.

Yakub then spoke to his cousin in Mumbai, whom Yakub would normally turn to whenever he was in need of sincere counsel. It is said that Yakub was planning a surrender and it was to formulate a strategy for this that a meeting between the cousins was arranged. Another theory doing the rounds is that the Indian agencies had learnt of Yakub's urge to return to India and were trying to get him back to the country to face the law. The agencies had also established contact with his cousin with the intention of bringing Yakub back to India, through cooperation or coercion.

On the morning of 21 July 1994, Yakub Memon took a flight from Dubai to meet his cousin who was waiting for him at the Grand Guest House in Kathmandu, Nepal. From that point, there are various theories about how he landed in India. Yakub may have been detained by authorities in Nepal on account of a bunch of keys that showed up as a gun during a security scan before his planned return to Dubai. Yakub may have been informally detained by Indian agents in Kathmandu as stated by B. Raman, who headed the Pakistan desk at the agency.[3] Or Yakub may have decided to show up at a railway station in New Delhi with many passports in his bag. Whatever the journey, the ultimate destination was that Yakub was back in India. He was taken to an undisclosed location where he was interrogated at length for several days.

5

The Interrogation[1]

In 1994, Neeraj Kumar, who was leading the probe into the serial blasts in the capacity of a CBI officer, managed to get in touch with Dawood Ibrahim over the phone. These calls were arranged by Manish Lala, who was known as Dawood's finance minister. After Yakub's arrest, Dawood had also given an interview where he claimed that he had never met Yakub Memon or conducted any business with him.[2] In fact, the don claimed that he was named in the case due to a political rivalry involving two former chief ministers of Maharashtra as one of them wanted to topple the other. As per Dawood Ibrahim, it was only on the basis of the testimony of landing agent Dawood Phanse aka Dawood Taklya that his name was dragged into the case. Dawood also admitted that he knew Taufique Jaliawala as a businessman based in Dubai and not as someone who worked for the ISI.

'A lot was learnt when Yakub was grilled for the first time after his arrest, wasn't it? I asked Neeraj Kumar.

In his peculiar style, Neeraj Kumar adjusted his spectacles on the ridge of his nose. Then, he nodded. Yakub had apparently revealed *a lot*.

In stark contrast to the self-congratulatory atmosphere in the Parliament spurred by the arrest of a Memon, the air in the interrogation room had been tense. Over a period of several days, Yakub Memon was questioned by an interrogator who was trained in effectively building an equation with a suspect and eliciting all possible information. Yakub sat across from his interrogator, as calm and calculated as ever. The first salvo was fired.

'How do you know Amjad Ali Meherbaksh?' the interrogator asked.

'He was a classmate of Ayub, my younger brother,' Yakub said.

Amjad also used to live in Mahim. He was a part of the regular crowd of spectators at the Khandwani Shield Tournament where Yakub used to sponsor a match or two. Amjad Ali Meherbaksh ran a communication centre near the Memon residence at Mahim and Yakub would go there often when his telephone was out of order.

These were times when smartphones and the Internet were still years away from the country. Public call offices (PCOs) were common until the late 1990s. People would often visit a public booth to make phone calls. International call rates were very expensive. With the passage of time, many citizens found the business lucrative and bought a set-up of their own and started running private booths with lower call rates. These units functioned as private telephone exchanges and were called *Khancha* exchange. A khancha means a bracket, in common parlance. The telephone lineman used to connect an international subscriber dialling (ISD) line to a telephone line. The ISD line was never accounted for by Mahanagar Telephone Nigam Limited (MTNL), so the racketeers made illicit profits of thousands of rupees daily, causing massive losses to the government.

Yakub's acquaintance, Amjad Ali Meherbaksh, ran such a communication centre, which was found to have been a crucial thread in the planning and execution of the blasts.

The interrogation then moved on to questions about Abdul Gani Ismail Turk and Anwar Haji Jamal Theba. Yakub paused to catch his breath before he could answer the question presented to him. He remembered the days when the duo used to come to their Al-Hussaini building in Mahim to pay their respects to his brother, Tiger.

A trusted lieutenant of Tiger Memon, Abdul Gani Ismail Turk had played a crucial role in the blasts. He had driven a Mahindra Commander SUV to Prabhadevi and parked it outside Century Bazaar, a place bustling with people at all hours of the day. At 2.45 p.m., after the three bombs had gone off, the explosives-laden SUV turned a buzzing market filled with animated buyers into a site of mourning and despair. This explosion claimed the highest number of casualties in comparison to the other blasts that took place on that ill-fated day.

Anwar Haji Jamal Theba, another accused in the blasts, managed to evade arrest and was said to have escaped to Pakistan. Notorious for dabbling in various illegal activities in addition to specializing in extortion, Theba was said to have participated in the explosions by personally setting off some of the bombs. Yakub claimed that he knew both of them merely as Tiger's associates and they knew him as Tiger's younger brother.

For a while, the interrogator kept throwing one name after another at Yaqub, while the latter categorically kept denying having anything to do with them.

These were names of those involved in the blast.

'I assert, on the basis of confessional statements of the accused,' said the interrogator, 'that the jeep containing ammunition was parked in the compound of Amjad Ali Meherbaksh on your instructions and was likewise removed from the compound on your orders. Do you admit to this act?'

'Incorrect,' Yakub said. 'Such statements are misleading and false.'

'Do Amjad Ali Meherbaksh, Altaf Ali Mushtaq Ali, Abdul Gani Ismail Turk and Rafique Madi harbour ill will against you?'

'Not that I know of.'

'Then why do these people want to implicate you in the blasts by giving false statements against you?'

'Maybe because they expect leniency from the court for divulging some names,' Yakub said. 'Or maybe they are afraid that naming Tiger will invite his wrath. So, they are using my name as a proxy.'

The interrogator then brought up the subject of East West Tours and Travels, a travel agency through which Yakub used to book tickets for his domestic as well as international travels. The agency was situated in Juhu. Investigations revealed that tickets on which several accused had flown to the UAE and other locations during the planning and execution of the blasts were arranged via the same agency. As per the CBI, the employees of the agency had named Yakub as the person who had arranged the tickets for the conspirators.

Yakub once again denied the allegation and insisted that he had only asked his staff to arrange the tickets during that period for his family members who were travelling to Dubai on Tiger's requests. 'My father and mother left for Dubai on 11 March,' he said. 'The rest of the family boarded the Dubai-bound flight the next day.'

The interrogator questioned whether Yakub had arranged a Protector of Emigrants (POE) for another group of co-accused, which included Mohammad Rafique Usman, Niaz Mohd Iqbal and Firoz Amani Malik. Their travels were arranged through East West at Yakub's behest.

Again, Yakub denied any such charges. Protector of Emigrants or POE refers to the obligation of nation states to accord basic universal human rights to the migrants fleeing persecution, violence or conflicts, as enshrined in the Universal Declaration of Human Rights, 1948, as well as various other treaties that were ratified in the course of the following years.

The interrogator flipped through the pages of the file in front of him that enumerated the allegations and charges pressed against Yakub. They were over an hour into the interrogation now and Yakub hadn't let go of the stoic expression he had brought along while entering the interrogation room. He listened to each question and allegation intently and never so much as flickered his eyelids in his terse responses or denials. The interrogator stopped turning the pages abruptly as he seemed to have found something interesting.

'How do you know Asgar Yusuf Mukadam?'

'He worked for Tiger as an accountant and used to come to see him very often,' said Yakub. 'I had also taken his help once or twice in my banking work.'

Asgar Yusuf Mukadam was the first person to be arrested in the case, merely two days after the blasts. He, along with another accused, Shahnawaz Abdul Kader Qureshi, had driven an RDX-laden car to Dadar West and parked it outside Plaza Cinema. The 880-seater cinema hall was running to full capacity as it was screening the 3 p.m. show of the Nana Patekar-starrer *Tirangaa*. The bomb exploded at around 3.13 p.m., resulting in the death of ten of the audience members and injuring thirty-seven others. Among other felonies that the duo were found guilty of was distributing funds for the conspiracy.

Mukadam and Qureshi were among the twelve who were later sentenced to death for their role in the blasts. Shoeb Ghansare was also in the same list as he was found to have parked a scooter rigged with RDX near Zaveri Bazaar that claimed the lives of seventeen people. Most of the twelve verdicts (excluding one) were commuted to life sentences by the Supreme Court of India in 2013.

The interrogator pressed on. 'Then why did you ask Mukadam to arrange for one crore rupees from Moolchand Choksi?'

Of all the persons arrested in connection with the March 1993 blasts, Moolchand Choksi was perhaps the most curious one. The owner of a small jewellery shop near Zaveri Bazar, Choksi was a Marwari businessman who would handle the money of other businessmen in exchange for a sum charged against each lakh of rupees deposited with them. In financial lingo, Choksi was a *hawala* (informal funds transfer system) operator.

Tiger had opened an account with Choksi, which was operated under the codename 'Hathi'. The money trail led the CBI to Choksi's jewellery shop as it held the account used to deposit and disseminate the money used in the blasts. He was slapped with charges of rendering financial assistance to terrorists and was sentenced to five years' rigorous imprisonment along with a fine of Rs 5 lakh, though the courts ruled that Choksi was not aware of the motives for which the money was being moved.

'I had never asked Mukadam to make such transactions on my behalf,' Yakub said. 'The only time I asked Tiger for such an amount was when I was running short of a crore for acquiring a property in Goa.'

The property in question was being purchased by Yakub in partnership with one of his friends. Tiger had given him Rs 1 crore at 2 per cent interest. The money was delivered to him by Mukadam at Tiger's instance.

The interrogator flipped through a couple of more pages till he came across the section that enlisted the businesses Yakub was personally involved with. He slowed down, perused the page and asked Yakub about Tejarath International. Founded by Yakub's brother Ayub Memon, Tejarath International turned up as yet another portal used to launder the money to carry out the blasts.

Yakub informed the interrogator that the firm was set up by Ayub Memon as a proprietorship concern that operated from an office in Mahim. The firm, he said, was dealing in exporting meat to Dubai and the main buyers were Evergreen Export and Parco Trading. He added that the firm had bank accounts in Mahim's DCB Bank, Union Bank of India and Syndicate Bank. 'In the capacity of one of the two chief accountants of Memon and Mehta associates,' Yakub said, 'I handled and oversaw the accounts of Tejarath International.'

The interrogator then went on to lay out before Yakub the accusation that it was on his instructions that Asgar Mukadam arranged passports for Parvez Farooq and Salim, who were then sent to Pakistan to receive training in firearms.

Yakub responded that he had only heard about the two boys when Tiger had once called and asked him to tell Mukadam to pick them up from a hotel in Mahim and drop them at the airport so that they could take a flight to Karachi.

The interrogator then questioned Yakub about financial transactions related to a certain Mr Devrukhkar who was one of Yakub's clients.

'Did you advise Devrukhkar to open an account with DCB Bank in September 1992?' asked the interrogator. 'And subsequently, did you take a loan of forty-two lakh rupees from him?'

Yakub explained that Devrukhkar had approached him for expert advice regarding the best method to receive money from a customer who was a foreign resident and had purchased Devrukhkar's hotel.

'I suggested that he receive the money via cheque,' said Yakub.

But the interrogator dug in his heels. 'How did he end up opening an account in DCB Bank, which is adjacent to your Mahim office?'

Yakub explained that the buyer had refused to pay the entire sum by cheque to Devrukhkar. So Yakub asked Devrukhkar to open an account in DCB Bank and receive the money through foreign remittance, which comes with the benefit of the immunity scheme floated by the government in 1991.

In the Union Budget of 1991–92, the then finance minister, Manmohan Singh, had announced the introduction of two new schemes with the aim of attracting a larger flow of foreign exchange. It was given the President's assent and passed in September 1991. The two schemes, the Remittances in Foreign Exchange (Immunity) Scheme, 1991 and the India Development Bonds Scheme, granted several immunities and exemptions to the person or entity receiving a remittance from foreign exchange, which included the exemption from any kind of inquiries against the money received via such a channel. Yakub had in-depth knowledge of India's laws and financial systems and had made use of them to serve his purpose legally in this case.

The interrogator proceeded to ask Yakub if he had received a sum of Rs 42 lakh as a loan from the same DCB account with a view to benefiting from the immunity scheme. Yakub responded that the remaining price of the hotel, i.e. Rs 37 lakh, was transferred to Devrukhkhar's DCB account without any such deal taking place.

'Then do you also deny receiving Rs 20 lakh from Mr Devrukhkhar as a loan on 10 March 1993, which was disbursed through an account payee cheque in favour of Tejarath International?' asked the interrogator.

This time, Yakub confessed that he did ask him for such a loan and received it on 10 March 1993 in the name of Tejarath International. He had taken the loan to pay the initial amount of Rs 60 lakh to a party from whom he was buying a plot at Peter Dias Road in Bandra. 'But since I had to leave India the day after receiving the loan,' Yakub said, 'I returned the loan to Mr Devrukhkhar by debiting the twenty lakh from the accounts of Tejarath International.'

After further grilling on the subject of Yakub's various financial and business activities, the interrogator brought up the connection of people who were involved in the film industry.

'How do you know Samir Hingora and Hanif Kadawala of Magnum Video?' the interrogator asked.

The owner of a thriving restaurant in the upscale Mumbai suburb of Bandra, Hanif Kadawala also dabbled in the film industry.

Kadawala was also alleged to have convened meetings where one of the invitees was his close associate and friend, Samir Hingora, another accused in the blasts. The duo had produced a few Bollywood movies featuring some of the leading superstars of the day. Kadawala was shot dead by Chhota Rajan's men at his Bandra office when he was out on bail.

Yakub responded that Kadawala and Hingora were Tiger's acquaintances. Tiger had mentioned Samir's name under the 'care of' section in the address he had provided to East West Tours and Travels.

Yakub stated that he had once accompanied Samir to the trial show of the movie *Saajan* on the latter's request, apart from which he had had no contact with the two whatsoever. The romantic musical starring Sanjay Dutt, Salman Khan and Madhuri Dixit was one of the biggest blockbusters of 1991. In stark contrast, the tale of the bomb blasts was nothing like this. It was a dark, grisly and spine-chilling conspiracy of terror in which Yakub was being accused of riding pillion with his brother, Tiger.

Tiger, on the other hand, seemed to have received a lot of support from Taufique Jaliawala. And Yakub was about to spill the beans on that too.

6

Taufique Jaliawala

In Dawood's own words, he knew Taufique Jaliawala from the time they had spent in Dubai. Tiger had also been Taufique's business partner. Some of the explosives recovered after the blasts were packed in material that mentioned an ordnance factory in Pakistan as its origin. Later investigations revealed that Taufique Jaliawala, a Pakistani national, was among those who had played a crucial role in sending the explosives from across the border. However, Indian agencies did not have sufficient evidence for this.

I was aware that Yakub had revealed many things about Taufique during his interrogation. And a lot of other facts were revealed during my discussions with Neeraj Kumar.

To the rest of the world, Yakub Memon's arrest might have come across as a surprise. But a core team of the CBI and other personnel, including Neeraj Kumar, were part of the backdoor negotiations being conducted to get Yakub back to the country.

One of Yakub's cousins was in constant touch with him. The CBI group would hold frequent meetings with this cousin and make sure to keep him in the loop. The government's stance was that if Yakub had done nothing wrong, he should come back and face trial. But even after employing all the techniques and resources at their disposal, the CBI couldn't see Yakub returning any time soon.

When Yakub announced an impromptu trip to Kathmandu to meet his cousin, the CBI was in for a surprise. Yakub's visit to Nepal along with the incriminating evidence he had collected from Pakistan became a source of delight for the CBI.

At this point, things become a little unclear. Was Yakub still undecided on returning to India? Or had he arrived in Kathmandu with the intention of returning to India? Apparently, Yakub had been arrested when the security personnel suspected there was some contraband in his baggage and found numerous passports during the check. But if he didn't want to surrender, why was he carrying evidence of his conversations with Taufique Jaliawala with him? Jaliawala was the man who had given them support in Pakistan at the behest of the ISI.

Since the Memons had been given Pakistani citizenship by then, Yakub's arrest seemed to foreshadow the manner in which the ISI protected those who could cause trouble in the diplomatic arena.

Many years after the blasts, the Thai police arrested one of Dawood's most feared sharpshooters, known as

Munna Jhingada. He was nicknamed 'Jhingada' for his scrawny physique, which resembled that of a prawn. But what he lacked in muscle, he more than made up for by his ability to shoot and kill without remorse.

Munna Jhingada had already committed a murder before he came into the D-Company, under the mentorship of Chhota Shakeel. His most audacious claim to fame was the deadly attack on Chhota Rajan in Bangkok in 2000, which nearly killed the latter.

Jhingada then fled to Dubai. He was later caught by the Thai police, who had found a Pakistani passport on him, and was sentenced to eleven years' imprisonment. Towards the end of his sentence, Indian authorities sought to extradite him for his involvement in various crimes in India.

This is where the ISI barged in and appealed to the Thai court to hand over Jhingada to them. When the lower court adjudged the case in India's favour, the ISI moved to the higher court, which ruled that Jhingada was a Pakistani citizen by virtue of the passport he was carrying. Jhingada refused to give his blood samples to undergo a DNA test requested by the Indian authorities to establish his Indian identity. Since doing so without the person's consent was illegal under Thai law, Indian authorities had no option but to step down and let Jhingada get away. He flew to Pakistan to reunite with the D-Company.

Similarly, ISI's strong influence in Nepal wasn't hidden from anyone. But for some reason, the ISI was caught napping in the case of Yakub. It was quite an embarrassment for them that the Indian agencies had managed to get a man into their custody and they didn't even react until the man landed on Indian soil. Perhaps this loss taught them a lesson they would never forget and so, they were better prepared in the case of Jhingada.

Whatever their apprehensions about the CBI might have been, the Memon family, including Yakub, weren't harbouring high hopes in Pakistan and the ISI. They strongly felt that Pakistan was keen on protecting just Tiger. When the time came, they would disown the rest of the family by making them scapegoats. A close examination of the ISI's indifference to Yakub's arrest and its lack of involvement with the matters that transpired thereafter was sufficient proof that the Memons were right in their assessment of the shady agency that the ISI was and still remains.

The Memon family kept receiving feelers from India to return to the country and face the law. The family sought legal opinion regarding their decision to turn themselves in. They were informed that none of them except Tiger had strong cases against them. The terms that each one would be punished with were going to be minor. In a few years, they would be out, walking free and cleared of all charges. The Memons trusted this legal advice. Most of the family was longing to return to the city. While in Pakistan, Suleman, Tiger's elder brother, had even said in a very emotional tone, 'I often go to Bombay in my dreams. I will go there again.'[1]

But the consequences of Tiger's transgressions were going to be disastrous not just for him but for the entire family. Out of all the evidence that Yakub had gathered, the voice recording that he had stealthily taken of Taufique Jaliawala was probably the most incriminating one. Yakub had probably lost count of the times he had found Taufique speaking highly of Tiger during their conversation about the blasts.

'If I had a valiant lieutenant such as Tiger,' Taufique had said, 'we would win all wars against our enemies.'

Yakub had recognized Taufique for the narcissist that he was and therefore used to articulate his questions in a manner that sufficiently massaged the man's inflated ego.

'Do people in Dubai know that you are involved in the bomb blasts?' Yakub had asked him.

'Oh yes,' Taufique replied. 'They came to know of it within four to five days (of the blast). They also know very well that I am Tiger's business partner and that I am always at the forefront of such tasks.'

'How did the idea of causing the bomb blasts occur to you?'

'I was well informed of the atrocities that were being committed in India. I offered my help to Dawood as I had enough contacts to mobilize and train people in handling weapons. The arrangement of arms and explosives would be handled by the ISI at my behest. But Dawood declined, saying that the matter pertains to India, and he would deal with it. I told Tiger that Dawood and his team will never go beyond holding meetings. If they want some real action, they will need my help.'

Yakub let Taufique ride his high horse a little more while probing the matter further.

'Who chose the spots for the bombings?' Yakub asked.

Taufique responded that the ISI chose the sites. And he claimed that he pulled the right strings so that the Memons as well as Dawood could be given a safe haven in Pakistan.

'There is a lot of pressure on Dubai to hand over Dawood and Tiger,' Taufique said. 'Their phones are being tapped and their movements are being watched. So those two can't even think of going to Dubai. I advise you and your family to avoid going to Dubai at all costs.'

Sporting a short boxed beard, fancy spectacles and with a dainty sense of dressing, Taufique Jaliawala was a megalomaniac whose contact list consisted of people who wielded considerable power and influence within the country and outside, be it a politician or a high-profile mafioso. The 'curry-favour' attitude had paid off well for Taufique as apart from owning many bungalows in Pakistan, he also had a flat in Dubai which he would frequently fly to, for leisure. The Indian media identified him as a high-profile smuggler who played a major role in the planning and execution of the 1993 bombings.

Yakub had revealed that Taufique was also the owner of several firms in Karachi and was involved in construction businesses, but all of that was just a facade to cover up his illegal activities.

Among many things, he boasted to Yakub that he had sheltered and procured fake passports for the perpetrators of the blasts. Besides Tiger and Dawood, he claimed to have offered a safe haven to other accused such as Yeda Yakub, Javed Chikna, Basheer Khan, Shafi Memon and a few others, in one of his bungalows in Karachi.

In the revelatory tapes released by the CBI, Taufique can be heard speaking with flair about how he had arranged for the explosions, and single-handedly managed to keep things under control by summoning his political influence in the aftermath.

Over the period of his investigation, Yakub had precisely figured out the persons who needed only a little provocation before they started prattling on sensitive information about the blasts. One such person was Shafi Zariwala.

Shafi Zariwala was none other than Tiger's driver and prized confidant, Shafi Memon. On account of his job, Zariwala was glued to his boss like a shadow. He was not only a witness to the preparation that came before the blasts but was also an active partner in transporting and caching the arms and explosives smuggled from across the border. During his many conversations with Yakub, Zariwala admitted to being a part of the group that offloaded the smuggled arms and ammunition from the shore.

'I knew that the goods we offloaded were anything but gold and silver,' Zariwala told Yakub. 'I told Anwar, who offloaded the goods with me, that the packages contained something far more significant and consequential.'

'How did you know?' Yakub asked.

'I've accompanied Tiger bhai in the exercise of offloading smuggled gold and silver, countless times. I knew what was in those boxes was different than our usual goods. My suspicions turned out to be true as the packages contained arms and explosives.'

'Who stashed those weapons and explosives? And where?'

'Tiger bhai gave me the packages which I carried to Mumbra and hid them there. Some packages were also given to Anwar and Javed Chikna for concealing.'

Yakub then asked Zariwala if he knew the purpose for which the weapons and explosives were smuggled into the country. Zariwala answered that Tiger claimed to have imported arms and explosives with the intention of seeking revenge for the atrocities being committed in the city in the aftermath of the Babri Masjid demolition.

'Who was given the responsibility of carrying out the blasts?' Yakub had asked.

'Tiger bhai assigned that task to Ejaz Pathan, Anwar Theba, Javed Chikna, Bashir and Yeda Yakub.'

'And who sent the Muslim youths to Pakistan for training to handle arms and ammunition?'

'Tiger bhai.'

Zariwala also disclosed that he along with Tiger and Javed Chikna had arranged the vehicles used in the blasts. Anwar Theba had booked the hotels with Javed Chikna's assistance. Yakub drove the conversation to non-essential elements of the attacks deliberately so as to avoid raising Zariwala's suspicions before asking him one of the key questions related to the absconding accused.

'Did Tiger bhai arrange for your escape out of the country?' he asked.

'Tiger bhai gave us money and instructed us to escape to Calcutta. From Calcutta, I, along with Javed Chikna and Anwar Theba, reached Bangladesh. The other boys remained in Calcutta.'

Zariwala added that Tiger reached out to some of his friends in Bangladesh and arranged Bangladeshi passports for them to fly to Pakistan. He also expressed his gratitude to Taufique Jaliawala, who made their sojourn in Pakistan comfortable by accommodating them in his bungalow in Karachi.

'Who all are presently living in Karachi?' Yakub asked.

'Anwar Theba and Javed Chikna are staying there with their families,' Zariwala said. 'Bashir Khan, Nasir Dakhla, Ejaz Pathan and Yeda Yakub are also staying in one of Taufique's bungalows.'

One of the conversations with Taufique even had Yakub wondering about the extent to which the man was obsessed with himself. The conversation took place in a car. Taufique clearly sounded petrified that his photo had been published in a *Times of India* news article that spoke about Dawood still being at large. But he soon started bragging about the central role he had played in keeping Dawood out of the CBI's vice.

Taufique said, 'Everybody in Dubai and Karachi knows that I sheltered Dawood and Tiger. I am the main person. This photo was taken without my knowledge, otherwise I would have never allowed it.'

'Perhaps the article just wants to show that Dawood is still with his men,' Yakub said.

'No . . . no. I am in a lot of trouble for protecting Dawood. They know that I am taking care of Dawood, otherwise he would have been in a dire situation.'

As the conversation progressed, Taufique sensed that Yakub was not getting impressed by his high talk portraying himself as more important and bigger than Dawood.

'Dawood is an intelligent person,' Yakub said to probe the matter further. 'He hasn't left a clue behind and nobody knows how he got here. He had even been to *Umrah* with you and back, leaving no trails.'

The statement stung Taufique as he responded pertly, 'That was before . . . when his name wasn't published. But once his name got out, he came running to me for help and I told the ISI right away that if they wanted to abandon Dawood, they would have to do it over my dead body.'

'That's so brave of you. You took great risks to save Dawood from being handed over to the CBI.'

'I certainly did.'

Then it was Taufique's turn. He asked Yakub if he had come in contact with any of the persons accused in the blasts. Yakub replied that he had only met Mohammed Dossa, who had once asked for his help for income tax-related work.

'I keep my distance from these people,' Yakub said. 'Tiger had even castigated Dossa for giving me the work.'

'But Taufique bhai,' Yakub broached the subject slyly when they were in the car, 'I find it difficult to wrap my head around the fact that the embassy has taken it upon itself to answer for Dawood if he travels to Dubai on his fake Pakistani passport.'

'What is so difficult to understand? I have spoken personally to *them* to ask the embassy to handle that matter.'

'To whom?'

'Big men.'

'ISI?'

'Yes. Nobody except me could have done that favour to Dawood. You can tell that even to Tiger. There is a complete file on Dawood. Anybody can check it.'

Taufique was trying to reiterate that Dawood had never been in such big trouble before and it was because of him that Dawood was able to evade the law.

'But isn't Dawood topping the most wanted list from 1985?'

'Topping the most wanted list of India,' Taufique snapped. 'Interpol wasn't after him then. Even his passport was revoked in 1993.'

Taufique then went on to denounce Dawood, saying that he had ended up becoming a criminal who was too invested in gang wars. He further said that he envisaged Dawood being forced to come out in the open and surrender one day, and Tiger rising up to take on the mantle.

'I swear on god,' Taufique said, 'even Dawood knows very well that Tiger will go on to become more powerful.'

Taufique rambled on for a while and tried to prove how thick he was with Tiger, something which even Dawood was well aware of. Yakub had enough experience by now to tell when the conversation had drifted to something inconsequential. He rested his head against the seat of the car, glanced at the window and patiently waited for the destination while letting his companion chatter away. Perhaps he had already made up his mind to return to India. The only question that remained was that of the quantum of punishment he would face for his crimes, and those of his brother.

7

The Hanging

India's judicial history has seen many firsts. It is also notable that the judiciary has been an active player in the world's largest democracy. In fact, the legislature, executive and judiciary are regarded as the three pillars of democracy. A strong and independent media, which I have wanted to be a part of since my days in journalism, was supposed to be the fourth pillar. But in my opinion, that pillar today is on the verge of collapse, if it has not collapsed already.

The judiciary has also promoted activism by allowing citizens to file petitions and public interest litigations (PILs). It allows citizens to attract the court's attention to matters where they may not have a personal interest but affect the general public nonetheless. In 2015, a petition filed in the Supreme Court led to a three-judge bench being called in the middle of the night to decide what was going to become of the man who had been found guilty on several counts in the serial blasts case.

Traditionally, India has not been a big proponent of capital punishment. Even the Supreme Court mandates that capital punishment must be provided only in the 'rarest of the rare' cases. The doctrine of 'rarest of rare' was established in the case of *Bachan vs State of Punjab*. In the Machhi Singh case, the court provided guidelines to determine whether a case fell under the 'rarest of rare' category by taking into account the manner of commission of the murder, the motive, the socially abhorrent nature of the crime, the magnitude of the crime and the personality of the victim of murder.

Of the twelve people whom the Terrorist and Disruptive Activities (Prevention) Act (TADA) court had awarded capital punishment, the Supreme Court lowered the sentence for all others except Yakub Memon. 'Given the circumstances of Yakub's return,' I told Neeraj Kumar, 'his hanging is a rare conclusion to a rare case.'

30 July 2015

At 4 a.m., the iron gate of the *faasi-khana* (gallows) at Nagpur Central Jail rattled as the prison guard pushed it open and entered the cell where inmates were held before they were sent to the gallows. The guard walked towards the inmate who was fast asleep. He tapped the prisoner on his shoulder to wake him up.

Yakub Memon, the inmate, did not respond. The guard had known Yakub for the time he had been lodged at the jail and the latter never needed prodding to be woken up on normal days. This morning was anything but normal for Yakub. It was his 53rd birthday. Ironically, this was also the day he would be hanged to death for his role in the 1993 Mumbai bomb blasts.

All his efforts to overturn the death penalty awarded to him by the court were futile. Yakub hadn't slept since his pleas at different forums had been dismissed one after another. Last night was particularly difficult. He woke up after the third tap on his shoulder.

'The hour has arrived,' the guard said.

Yakub pushed against the hard floor of the cell and sat up straight. He stared at the ground and mumbled some prayers. His white beard had grown to his chest. Yakub had pinned his last hopes of relief on the mercy plea that noted lawyer Prashant Bhushan and other civil society activists had carried to the Supreme Court during the early hours of 30 July 2015.

The plea was a last-ditch attempt by the defendant to delay the hanging by at least two weeks. Yakub's last mercy plea had already been rejected by the President of India. The newer plea argued that there should be at least fourteen days' gap between the disposing of the mercy plea of the defendant and his execution.

The Supreme Court decided to take an unprecedented action. It convened a three-judge bench to hear the petition at 3 a.m. Such a move was only taken keeping in mind the serious nature of the petition. The petition was requesting for the postponement of the hanging of Yakub Memon, which was supposed to be executed that morning at 6.45 a.m.

Inside the jail, Yakub rose to take a bath. He did his ablutions, offered *namaz* (prayer) and sat down to recite some verses from the Quran. He kept on reciting without even looking at the breakfast that had arrived and remained unattended. He had shunned food over the past few days. The prison guard returned and urged him to have his breakfast. Yakub appreciated the guard's courteous words and ate the biscuits and drank the tea.

Yakub's battle to avert the judgment that awarded him the death sentence went at least a couple years back. After he was declared guilty of several offences in the blasts by the TADA court in 2007, the State of Maharashtra filed a reference before the Supreme Court to confirm Yakub's death sentence. The Supreme Court sustained the charges pressed by the TADA court and upheld the State of Maharashtra's application to award Yakub the death sentence.

On 21 March 2013, the apex court ordered capital punishment to Yakub on the grounds of conspiracy and financing the attacks. The court held that Yakub's role was not just limited to lending support to the attackers and arranging correspondence between them. As per the confessional statements of several accused, he was also responsible for the handling of the explosive bags and their safekeeping. He was also found by the court to have been actively involved in hawala transactions that assured the execution of the blasts.

Yakub denied all charges and claimed innocence. He filed a review petition seeking a review of the Supreme Court judgment confirming his death sentence. On 30 July 2013, a Supreme Court bench headed by Chief Justice P. Sathasivam and Justice B.S. Chauhan dismissed the review petition. At the same time, Yakub also filed a petition seeking an oral hearing.

Yakub's brother, Suleman Memon, who was acquitted by the court in 2006 due to lack of evidence, moved heaven and earth to send his brother's bail pleas to the appropriate office and get them heard. Unlike Suleman, his wife, Rubina Memon, was sentenced to life imprisonment after being found guilty of conspiring in the blasts. A vehicle that was used to ferry explosives around the city was registered in her name. Even as the matter of oral hearing was being heard by the Supreme Court, Yakub filed another writ petition seeking a revaluation of the death sentence.

Yakub's mental condition during this time had deteriorated significantly. According to eyewitnesses, he was seen having emotional outbursts on a few occasions during his hearings. He would scream at the top of his voice and declare that he was innocent. On occasions of such extreme emotional episodes, he would also ask the judge what the law had done to bring the culprits identified by the Srikrishna Commission to book. The Srikrishna Commission was established by the Government of Maharashtra to investigate the Mumbai riots of 1992–93 in which the minority community had suffered substantially. However, the commission's findings and recommendations were not binding on the government since it was not a court of law. The recommendations were neither accepted nor acted upon by successive state governments.

'This is no justice,' Yakub would say. 'I am being made a scapegoat.'

On 11 April 2014, the then President of India Pranab Mukherjee rejected Yakub's mercy petition. But that did not deter Yakub from pursuing the commutation of his death penalty as he filed yet another petition that resulted in an order directing his execution to be put on hold. Yakub had argued in the petition that the review of death penalties should be heard in an open court rather than in closed chambers. Justices J. Khehar and C. Nagappan ordered a constitution bench of the Supreme Court to hear the plea, while passing a stay order on the execution in June 2014.

'We are running out of legal avenues to stop the execution,' Suleman would say to Yakub in the *mulaqat* (meeting) room. His voice would be sombre and his eyes glazed with tears.

'Stay strong,' Yakub would reply. 'You have to take care of my family after me.'

While lawyer Prashant Bhushan was jostling up and down the streets of Delhi in the hope of overturning Yakub's hanging, an official was already on his way to see Suleman.

Suleman met the official at 2.30 a.m. and was handed the *hamdast* (hand-delivered execution order) that mentioned the exact hour of Yakub's hanging. Meeran Bowankar, the additional director general of police, and Yogesh Desai, superintendent of police for Nagpur Central Jail, said that they were sure of the apex court's decision and so delivered the letter to Yakub's brother even before the late night Supreme Court bench had given its final verdict in the case. It was time for Suleman to deliver the terrible news to his family.

A dejected Yakub spotted Suleman standing in the corridor as he was being escorted to the cell. The officials refused permission for the brothers to meet.

'Take care of my wife and my daughters,' Yakub yelled as he was ushered by the cops towards the hanging ground.

The last writ petition Yakub had filed before the Supreme Court had challenged the order that was passed rejecting the curative petition he had filed in May 2015. Yakub had contended that at the time of passing an order that rejected the curative petition, the required quorum was not present, which ran contrary to the interpretation of the Supreme Court's rules. Two judges appointed to decide the validity of the challenge held opposing views, which prompted the Chief Justice of India to constitute a larger bench on an urgent basis. The bench, on 29 July 2015, dismissed the challenge as invalid and upheld the order of execution.

At 5.30 a.m., when Yakub was still busy in his prayers ahead of his final walk to the gallows, the lights of the jail went off and the entire premises was plunged into darkness. It was a signal to the jail authorities to get ready for the exercise scheduled to take place an hour and fifteen minutes later.

'They knew that I was clean,' Yakub had reportedly told the prison guard. 'I don't like the way all of this has been taken into a different direction.'

After Yakub filed a plea for an open court hearing, the proceedings had begun on 24 March 2015. The argument presented by Jaspal Singh, senior counsel who represented Yakub in the open court hearing, was that the prosecution had failed to produce any independent evidence to refute Yakub's assertion that he knew nothing about the blasts. Singh argued that Yakub was convicted on flimsy grounds such as the statement by one approver and the retracted confessions of the co-accused. The open court hearing ended within a month and Yakub's review petition was dismissed.

Following this, on 30 April 2015, the Maharashtra government issued a death warrant that set the date of 30 July 2015 for Yakub's execution. Yakub filed a curative petition the following month that got rejected on 21 July 2015. He then went on to file a mercy petition with the Governor of Maharashtra, which allowed him to subsequently file a writ petition in the Supreme Court asking for a stay on the execution till the mercy petition was decided upon.

On the fateful morning, Yakub was headed for the gallows. An eerie silence prevailed over the entire jail. His inmates, who were fast asleep, had bid goodbye to Yakub two days ago as he was taken into an isolated cell, well aware that they were seeing him for the last time.

'*Ab toh Allah hi malik hai*,' Yakub had said to one of them as the date of execution came near. '*Uske darbar mein sahi insaf hoga. Aur Allah Tiger ko bhi maaf nahi karega. Kaash wo mera bhai nahi hota.*'

Yakub had wished for justice in the court of the divine, and implied that it was his misfortune that Tiger was his brother. It was learnt from a few of the inmates that he had spent the last few days reminiscing about the days when he lived in Mahim with his family. Yakub was led to a room where the final medical tests were to be conducted. After the test, he was led into the execution chamber where he was asked if he had any last wish.

'I want to talk to my daughter Zubeida,' Yakub said.

Zubeida was only five years old when Yakub was arrested. She had visited him one week prior to the date of hanging with her mother Rahin in Nagpur Central Jail. One of the officials called Zubeida's phone number and handed the phone to Yakub. No other phones were allowed so that no one could record the hanging secretly.

Yakub fought back his tears during the first few seconds of the call where they exchanged salutations. Then he broke down and said, 'I wish I could see you getting married.'

Zubeida reportedly broke down too.

'Take good care of your mother,' Yakub said before he ended the call.

Outside, not even a bird could flap its wings over the entire stretch that led to the Nagpur Central Jail. A huge contingent of police personnel carrying automatic weapons was deployed around the jail. Yakub resumed his recitation of prayers as he stepped on to the execution platform. The authorities waited till the clock struck seven to avoid further complications and abide by the timing mentioned by the TADA court.

The clock struck the deathly hour. An official pulled the lever. The trapdoor opened. Yakub called upon his Lord one last time before he plunged through the trapdoor and hung from the noose till the last breath of air escaped his chest.

And thus, a saga that had begun with Yakub Memon's return to India nearly two decades ago came to a conclusion; a rather unpredictable end.

8

The Aftermath

At approximately 1 p.m., the IndiGo flight made its descent, touching down on the tarmac of what now stands as the Chhatrapati Shivaji Maharaj International Airport. Amidst the bustling airport activities, a group of men and women gathered, unified by a shared purpose. The cargo, a poignant label adorning a long rectangular box, read, 'Human Remains'. The gravity of the moment unfolded as Yakub Memon's lifeless form, encased in the solemn box, was claimed from the area by his family.

The procession, consisting of Yakub's family and his earthly remains, set course for Bismillah Manzil, the Memon family's residence in Mahim. The drive, already fraught with emotional turbulence, grew more arduous as they approached their destination. The streets, once familiar, now pulsated with an unusual energy. People filled every available space, their numbers rivalling the presence of the vigilant police force.

Closer to Mahim, the familiar visage of Rakesh Maria flickered among the cops who were posted there to ensure that no untoward incident took place at Yakub Memon's funeral. The wheel of time had completed a full circle. Maria, the seasoned investigator who had spearheaded the inquiry into the 1993 blasts, was now at the helm of the force as the commissioner of police, Mumbai.

The deployment, a force of over 40,000 inspectors, sub-inspectors and constables, was not just a logistical necessity; it was a poignant return to a painful origin. The reason behind this massive show of force was the hanging of Yakub Memon, brother of Mushtaq alias Tiger Memon, at Nagpur Central Jail at 7 a.m. that morning. The body was now making its journey back home.

The intricacies of Maria's role during the 1993 blasts investigation painted a fascinating tableau. At that time, he held the position of DCP Traffic, with an additional charge of the Worli area due to the absence of its DCP, who was on leave. In a twist of fate, Maria found himself leading the team that discovered a crucial breakthrough—the unexploded bomb-laden scooter. In the glove compartment, a treasure trove awaited: registration papers that served as the vital link connecting the police to the Memons and, subsequently, to India's most wanted fugitive, Dawood Ibrahim Kaskar.

Maria's reputation for a razor-sharp memory had become legendary among both law enforcement officers and reporters. Addressing press conferences with an air of confidence, Maria never glanced at a piece of paper—a testament to the vast reservoir of information he carried in his mind. Equally renowned was Maria's wit, a quality that had endeared him to both the media and his colleagues.

The sun blazed overhead, casting shadows across the bustling streets and crowded alleys. Things were vastly different from the dark days of 1993. The authorities had learnt from the past, and strengthened their intelligence gathering and equipped the police force with state-of-the-art weaponry following the painful lessons of the 2008 Mumbai attacks.

Hours ticked away relentlessly. The city seemed to hush in anticipation of the grim event. The weather offered no respite from the oppressive heat; the air hung thick and stifling.

As the hearse passed through the lanes leading to the Memon house, a silent transformation occurred. Those who had gathered to pay respect began to walk behind the vehicle, forming an unspoken procession. In their collective grief, the Memons were keenly aware of the myriad eyes that observed them—judgemental, sympathetic or indifferent. The family sought refuge within the walls of Bismillah Manzil, a sanctuary where memories intertwined with the stark reality of the present.

Meanwhile, the police, cognizant of the potential for emotional fervour, mobilized its Rapid Action Force. Barricades strategically lined the lanes, ensuring that the growing crowd remained contained. Rakesh Maria assumed a prominent role at the forefront of the security arrangements. Hours were spent communicating sternly to the gathered multitude, emphasizing a zero-tolerance stance towards any attempts at fomenting unrest. '*Koi naarebaazi nahi,*' he announced, reiterating a zero-tolerance policy towards any sloganeering.

Maria's demeanour, usually accommodating towards the media, underwent a marked shift on this solemn day. He was curt, almost brusque, questioning the presence of reporters with an uncharacteristic bluntness. 'Why are you even here?' he asked the reporters. 'Why aren't you in Rameshwar?'

On the same day, former Indian President A.P.J. Abdul Kalam had been laid to rest in Rameshwar, but his farewell had garnered far less attention—an unfortunate truth that would linger in the nation's conscience.

On the second floor of the building, Yakub's body had been bathed as per tradition. Outside, a loudspeaker announced that the *namaz-e-janaza* would be held at the Bada Qabrastan in Marine Lines. Barely half an hour later, the decision was changed and it was decided to hold the funeral prayer at the Mahim Dargah nearby. There was no other option; the crowd had swollen to nearly ten thousand by now.

Around 3.45 p.m., Memon's body was brought out and carried to the Dargah. A confidential report later filed for the Maharashtra government by the police would state that more than 10,000 people prayed at the Mahim Dargah that day, and over 15,000 at the Bada Qabrastan, where the body was later taken and buried. According to this same report, the majority of the people who turned up had nothing to do with the Memons. Details about his body's expected time of arrival and the funeral had been forwarded far and wide through WhatsApp. The attendees included not only Muslims from all over Mumbai, but also from areas like Mumbra, Padgha and Bhiwandi, who came by road and train.[1]

The Bada Qabrastan, a vast expanse of resting souls in Marine Lines, awaited Yakub Memon's arrival. The crowd, now a unified force of mourners, watched as the burial rites began. The imam, a figure of reassurance in uncertain times, led the funeral prayers. The air was thick with sorrow, the echoes of prayers mingling with the city's ceaseless sounds.

In an opinion piece, journalist and columnist Aakar Patel later observed in *India Today* that the massive gathering of the crowds, if taken out of context, would naturally elicit anger in anyone.[2] But hardly anybody had taken into account the fact that the death penalty itself had been a matter of intense debate. Especially because it was due to Yakub's cooperation that the Indian law enforcement had been able to get crucial information about the planning and execution of the blasts. It is said that the Indian government reneged on its deal, that the original plan was to grant leniency to Yakub in exchange for his cooperation. Indeed, that was why he had come back to India in the first place and spared the CBI the whole headache of extradition. His own direct involvement in the blasts had been oblique at best, and yet, he was the only one of the over 100 convicts—which included the men who assembled and planted the bombs—who had been sentenced to death.

I had also written an article for the *Telegraph*, where I made the point that Yakub had returned to India with evidence of Pakistan's involvement in the blasts and he had expected clemency in return. But the powers-that-be were under tremendous pressure to show that tough actions had been taken. They decided to hang the Memon who was as close as they could have got to Tiger—the main perpetrator of the blasts. The article was aptly titled: 'Any Memon Would Do.'[3]

I had also written another article for *Mumbai Mirror* stating Yakub had provided Indian officials with details of the identities and passport numbers that were assigned to his family members in Pakistan. Abdul Razzak Memon, his father, was given the name of Ahmed Mohammad Jamal. His mother was now Zainab Ahmed. Tiger Memon was Ahmed Jamaal, Suleman Memon was Aftaab Ahmed, while Yakub himself had been renamed as Yusuf Ahmed.[4]

While the Memons were in Pakistan, India had stepped up diplomatic pressure against the country for sheltering criminals who were wanted in India. In return, Pakistan had announced that international agencies like the United Nations were free to come to the country and verify that none of the Memons were in Pakistan. But nervous that its bluff would be called if someone took up that offer, Pakistan had moved the entire Memon clan to Thailand in April 1993. The documentary evidence provided by Yakub helped the Indian authorities establish concrete links to Pakistan's involvement in the blasts.

Within a month of Yakub's landing in India, his other family members also returned. He was said to have engineered their return as well. In the entire conspiracy, it is only Yakub who was sent to the gallows.

For the next two weeks after his hanging, Bismillah Manzil and the neighbouring Al-Hussaini remained the subject of intense vigil, with the police keeping watch round the clock, aided by State Reserve Police Force companies. Social media was continuously monitored and on-ground intelligence was sifted through. Nobody said it out loud, but the entire city was on edge.

However, further controversy erupted when Chhota Shakeel gave a telephonic interview to an Indian news channel and claimed that Yakub had been unjustly punished for the deeds of his brother, Tiger.[5] He also said that Dawood Ibrahim would have also suffered a similar fate if he had returned to India had the negotiations around his surrender not faltered. Shakeel warned that even the D-Company would deal with this event in their own way. It was an outright threat on national television. However, no retaliatory act was witnessed in the days that followed. Perhaps, the story of a man who was once a promising chartered accountant has been finally laid to rest.

9

Stockholm Syndrome

Stockholm Syndrome, a psychological disorder linked with a beautiful city's name. When I heard about it for the first time, in the early years of my crime writing, I was totally flummoxed and fascinated. The genesis of the whole condition was discovered or diagnosed in 1973 during a failed bank robbery in Stockholm, Sweden. The victims developed a bond with the captors and despite government investigations, refused to identify or testify against the captors. Instead, they began to gather money for the defence of the bank robbers. This bond was referred to as the Stockholm Syndrome.

I was called again by my mysterious friend Kamaal Hasan to the same city to explain the syndrome. 'The strange bond between the captors and the captive can be understood only if you are in this city and walking and breathing the air,' he said.

Much as I hate travelling, this man was really enjoying his sadistic hold on me because he knew that I would span several continents to get one good story. By now, I have understood that my erudite friend will always flaunt his deep knowledge about the world.

'Sweden has suddenly reported over 140 explosions in 2023. And sixty gun shootings. It is one of the most violence-affected countries in Europe,' he said. 'Most of the crimes are perpetrated by the immigrants.'

I gave him a look and simply nodded. Swedish people still love immigrants. They have Amir Rostami, a Persian-origin crime expert, to help them make sense of the crime happening in their country.

'Does this happen only in Stockholm?' I asked.

I had been to Stockholm earlier in October 2010 on the invitation of my author, teacher and savant friend Amitava Kumar, who teaches in a university in New York. Amitava had organized a panel discussion with Sabrina Dhawan, a gifted writer and me on the movie *Black Friday*, which was based on my first book.

The discussion was organized by charming Annette Taranto of Earsounds. I was totally bowled over by Annette's intelligence, Sabrina's charm and Amitava's profound wisdom. I felt so much like a pygmy among those intellectual giants. They dissected *Black Friday* as no one had earlier. *Fear turning into love.* I can never forget that conclusion even after thirteen years of that panel discussion.

Kamaal laughed. 'Stockholm syndrome *hai yeh*.' Pakistan is suffering from the same problem. They never liked Dawood Ibrahim in the first place and now they are protecting him and prospering with him. 'Pakistan gained prosperity through an Indian ganglord.'

I looked at him with absolute disbelief. He was now warmed up and ready to go into the story that he wanted to narrate today.

Malik Riaz Husain was a small-time civil contractor in the 1990s. Around the time when the Karachi civil wars were at their peak, he happened to come in contact with Dawood Ibrahim.

Dawood had learnt the art of grabbing prime real estate in Mumbai and giving it to builders to develop and construct premium residential and commercially owned premises. The construction business is an enterprise that has massive returns on investment at nominal seed capital. Strangely, Riaz, a builder with humble beginnings, found a partner in the Pakistan Navy and a promoter in a controversial politician, Asif Zardari.

Zardari was known for keeping a 10 per cent cut in every deal that he facilitated and never bothered that he was stealing from Peter to enrich Paul. Within a few years, Malik Riaz rose to become a name synonymous with opulent houses and the brand of Bahria townships with sprawling premises in Karachi, Lahore and other cities. Malik Riaz's meteoric rise brought him immense wealth and influence. It also drew scrutiny, suspicions, allegations of political favouritism, controversial acquisitions, corruption, forcible land grabbing and a nexus with the omnipresent Dawood Ibrahim.

Malik Riaz Hussain was born on 8 February 1954, in Sialkot, Punjab, Pakistan. He had experienced financial struggle in his youth because his father did not have sufficient contacts in the business. Malik Riaz realized that talent alone is not enough in life; one has to have connections if one wants to fulfil one's ambitions. Miserably failing to continue his education, Malik had to abandon school at the matriculation level. Malik's struggle began as a clerk with the Military Engineering Service (MES) in Rawalpindi.

Malik soon aspired to go to the next level and he decided to become a civil contractor in the government department. It helps to have connections in the Pakistan defence circuit and Malik's first big break was with the Pakistan Navy. In 1995, Malik launched Hussain Global and in collaboration with the Pakistan Navy, started the Bahria Foundation.

'Have you read Mario Puzo?' Kamaal suddenly asked me.

I looked at him. 'He inspired me to write about the mafia.'

'Then you must remember,' he said, 'behind every successful fortune there is a crime.'

Of course, that was the cornerstone of his book: *The Godfather*.

Malik Riaz had two godfathers—Dawood and Asif Zardari. It is widely alleged that during his tenure with the Pakistan Navy, Malik was approached by Dawood Ibrahim through Asif Ali Zardari for a collaboration. Dawood had mastered the tricks of land grabbing, illegal encroachments and evicting land plots. He proposed the same kind of support to Malik with serious muscle, financial backing and political blessings for the establishment of Bahria Town in Rawalpindi.

Dawood had the habit of replicating his successful businesses of Mumbai in Karachi. He introduced Fire brand gutkha in Pakistan after forcibly acquiring know-how and machinery from Mumbai gutkha czars like Manikchand Dhariwal and Jagdish Joshi, after getting them to Karachi for arbitration. Then he built the controversial Karachi Exchange on the lines of his earlier Mumbai Exchange, which dealt with unofficial foreign exchange. It was not strange for him to prop up another builder and get continued support from politically powerful politicians.

When legal disputes arose, the Pakistan Navy locked horns with Malik Riaz for using the Bahria Foundation name. But Malik Riaz was trained well. He reportedly gifted bungalows to army personnel, political leaders and judges to gain approval for the use of the word 'Bahria' in his projects. He won the case against the Navy. The Supreme Court intervened in favour of Malik. In early 2000, the Pakistan Navy transferred its shareholding to Malik Riaz. This did not become clear until the Al-Qadir Trust case controversy came out in the open.

In 2008, Dawood's strategic initiatives and project launches propelled Bahria Town into a new era, solidifying its status as a real-estate powerhouse and sparking both admiration and controversy. This was the year when Asif Zardari became the President of Pakistan. After that, everything was for sale in Pakistan, including the judiciary.

'What we see is only the tip of the iceberg,' Kamaal said.

He was right. Even in European countries, it appeared that the judiciary could be managed, as was evident in the cases of Iqbal Mirchi and Nadeem Saifee, who was accused of being involved in the murder of music magnate Gulshan Kumar.

'In such cases,' I said, 'the judiciary is committed to the cause of the government, rather than justice.'

'There is no better place on the global map to expose a committed judiciary than Pakistan.'

'Which case are you talking about?' I asked.

The Al-Qadir Trust case came to light in 2019 as a monumental testament to the interplay between corruption and political manoeuvring within the Pakistani landscape. The case gained prominence against the backdrop of Malik Riaz's colossal financial settlements with the UK's National Crime Agency, totalling a staggering PKR 460 billion. The agency first froze £20 million of Riaz's funds in December 2018. In August 2019, the agency secured a court order that covered £120 million across eight bank accounts. It was the largest amount frozen in an NCA investigation since the Criminal Finances Act 2017 came into force.

The seeds of this scandal were sown in the Al-Qadir Trust. Named after the revered Pakistani cricketer Al-Qadir, it was ostensibly established for charitable purposes. Presented as a charitable endeavour, the trust served as a conduit for financial transactions associated with Riaz's settlements in the UK. Imran Khan's trusteeship, coupled with the trust's exclusive nature, invited scepticism about the objectives of the trust.

The Supreme Court, under the leadership of Chief Justice Saqib Nisar, found itself thrust into the spotlight. The judiciary's intervention was prompted by the need to address the alleged financial irregularities surrounding Malik Riaz's ventures, particularly the Bahria Town projects. Chief Justice Saqib Nisar intervened on concerns that Bahria Town had not fully compensated land sellers. This potential injustice required redressal.

Simultaneously, the political landscape faced its own upheavals. Imran Khan, the prime minister at the time, found himself at the centre of the storm. The dynamics of the Al-Qadir Trust case forced him to navigate a delicate balance between addressing corruption allegations and managing the political fallout. Imran Khan's government had played a key role in the creation of this trust, purportedly to receive large financial settlements from Malik Riaz.

The 'sealed envelope incident' during a cabinet meeting to approve transfer of funds to the trust added an air of secrecy and intrigue to the events. The method employed to secure signatures of public representatives without revealing the contents fuelled public curiosity. Ministers were presented with sealed envelopes, concealing the contents which could be viewed only in the designated signing area.

The deliberate effort to keep the details concealed led to dissent among the cabinet members. Attempts to inquire about the contents were met with stern resistance, reportedly enforced by intelligence agencies present in the meeting. This sealed envelope approach stood as a testament to the clandestine nature of the transactions associated with the Al-Qadir Trust.

On 3 December 2019, Prime Minister Imran Khan received approval from his cabinet for the settlement with the UK crime agency without revealing the specifics of the private accord. According to the arrangement, the money would be presented to the Supreme Court on Malik Riaz's behalf.

Dawood Ibrahim's looming presence played a pivotal role in shaping the financial landscape and intricate dealings surrounding Malik Riaz Hussain's ventures. The Moin Palace land where Dawood had once lived in Karachi was reportedly in the name of Asif Ali Zardari. Indian news agencies, including *Indian Express*, had previously identified Zardari's ownership of the land.[1]

In a bold move, the Supreme Court swiftly imposed a ban on the construction of the Bahria Icon Tower and directed Bahria Town to halt development works in Bahria Town Karachi. The financial penalty imposed was unprecedented, amounting to a staggering PKR 460 billion—a sum equal to the settlements caught by the UK crime agency.

In the weeks that followed the decision, Islamabad saw the founding of the Al-Qadir Trust. Malik Riaz allegedly gave up the land for the construction of an educational institution in exchange for legal protection for the monies he had.

On 21 March 2019, the Supreme Court accepted Bahria Town Karachi's PKR 460-billion offer for the land it occupied in the Malir district of Karachi and restrained the National Accountability Bureau (NAB) from filing references against it. Surprisingly, the court was not allowing an investigating agency to intervene in a case where it should have!

Bahria Town Karachi was to pay the entire amount over seven years. A sum of PKR 25 billion was to be paid by August that year. From September onwards, it was to pay monthly installments of PKR 2.25 billion for the next three years. If the company failed to deposit two instalments, Bahria Town would be considered a defaulter.

In an unusual turn of events, Malik Riaz and the Supreme Court entered into an agreement to recover the outstanding amount. Chief Justice Saqib Nisar worked in tandem with the government and Imran Khan to facilitate the recovery process. The intricate negotiations raised questions about the independence of the judiciary and its alignment with political forces.

This period coincided with Malik Riaz's settlements with the UK crime agency, raising suspicions about the synchronized nature of these financial manoeuvres. The Supreme Court's decision to adjust the UK crime agency settlements against the fine instalments sparked controversy. The seemingly illogical move left observers questioning the court's motives and raised speculation about external influences, particularly the alleged connections between Dawood Ibrahim, Malik Riaz and the broader political landscape.

Following the adjustment of the settlements, Malik Riaz appealed to the Supreme Court to revisit the case. In a surprising turn of events, the court declared that the case against Malik Riaz was not justified, leading to a favourable judgment that overturned the earlier financial penalties. Mysterious circumstances surrounding this reversal prompted further scrutiny of the justice system's integrity.

In conclusion, Malik Riaz emerged not only as a real estate mogul but as a puppet master in a complex dance involving the Supreme Court, Dawood Ibrahim and the political stage led by Imran Khan. The financial penalties, initially imposed by the court, were ultimately reversed. Funds caught by the UK crime agency found their way back into Dawood Ibrahim's hand via Malik Riaz's.

On 9 May 2023, Islamabad Police released a statement quoting Inspector General (IG) Akbar Nasir Khan as saying that Imran had been arrested in relation to the Al-Qadir Trust case, which alleges that the PTI chief and his wife obtained billions of rupees and land from a real-estate firm for legalizing PKR 50 billion that was identified and returned to the country by the UK during the previous PTI government.[2]

The Al-Qadir Trust case leaves a lingering question mark over the integrity of the justice system, the influence of organized crime and the symbiotic relationship between business and politics in Pakistan. This left Prime Minister Imran Khan totally discredited and his reputation in ruins.

I knew Kamaal would now dispense his pearls of wisdom at the end of the story.

'Everything in the end was left with an appalling stigma; the judiciary, the executive, which included an incumbent like Imran Khan, a nouveau riche philanthropist like Malik Riaz, but people did not want to throw out Dawood Ibrahim. The man is still rock solid in Pakistan,' Kamaal said. 'The army does not act against him. No new dispensation wants to jettison him and the judiciary is happy turning a blind eye. This is what I call the Stockholm Syndrome.'

It has been over three decades. Pakistan is reeling under the Stockholm Syndrome. It can very well be called the Dawoodholm Syndrome.

10

Mehwish Hayat

Kamaal's knowledge about cinema continued to amuse me. He would often cite anecdotes from movies to make his point. His latest analysis was based on Robert Redford's obsession which led him to make an irresistible offer to Demi Moore in the iconic Hollywood movie *Indecent Proposal*. The film effectively conveyed a message that rich men know that money cannot buy love, but it can hire the company of beautiful people at will.

Mehwish Hayat, the reigning top actress of the Pakistani film industry, had been struggling for several years while working in television serials or even doing item songs. Mehwish's name, derived from the Farsi language, means 'moon face' and she indeed had magnetic, charming looks. But her beauty alone failed to carve a niche in the top echelons of Lollywood, the Pakistani film industry.

Punjab Nahi Jaungi in 2017 made her an overnight success and she then gave five consecutive hits, never having to worry about failures of her movies any more. She stunned the Pakistani film industry when the Imran Khan government conferred the highest civilian award—Tamgha-e-Imtiaz (medal of excellence)—on her in 2019. The award is a recognition of extraordinary contribution to the field of arts and culture. This award had eluded several stalwarts of the industry but Mehwish managed to get it with relative ease.

Apocryphal stories of her instant stardom and continuous success were connected to a rich businessman of non-Pakistani origin. She was introduced to him at a private party and Mehwish found that the man dressed in expensive suits and spoke in a soft tone, lacing his words with delectable Urdu. She was told that he was a very influential man and was on a first-name basis with many Pakistani politicians. He was the Robert Redford of Mehwish's life who had given a golden touch to her career.

This rich businessman with a Midas touch in Mehwish Hayat's life is actually Dawood Ibrahim. Their rumoured relationship began much earlier, around 2015–16, but it was the coveted award that convinced everyone that Dawood was behind it. Apparent signs of affluence like a bungalow in the posh locality of Clifton, which is about eight miles away from Dawood's own Moin Villa, raised many eyebrows.

The exact nature of the relationship between the two remains in the shadows. There is an age gap of over twenty-seven years between the two of them. However, such an age difference never meant much in real life. When newspapers were writing about them, it was claimed that they could be the Indian subcontinent's Michael Douglas and Catherine Zeta-Jones.

For Mehwish it meant wading through troubled waters. But association with Dawood was never a source of downfall for anyone in Pakistan. Rather, his associate's fortunes soared north. Some may call it a collaboration of convenience and not necessarily a scandalous affair.

Mehwish soon realized that Dawood Ibrahim was a very rich, powerful and influential man. Dawood already had the experience of barging into the film industry since his days in Mumbai. He knew how the industry worked. During one of their meetings, Dawood suggested to her that the best way to succeed is to have a production house in your name.

'All the stars and actors have production houses,' he told her.

Mehwish did not exactly understand the business part of it though she liked the suggestion very much. But the think tank around Dawood suggested that the production house should not be registered in her name but under any of her family members who could be a proxy owner. And then they launched a production house which had one office in Karachi and one office in London. Mehwish had no idea what she was getting into but this production house boosted her clout in the Pakistani movie industry.

Nobody seemed to realize that amidst all these developments, Dawood Ibrahim was seeing a future opportunity. In 2015, he made friends with Mehwish Hayat with the thought that ten years later, he was going to move his money to London through her. The best route for this purpose was to establish a production house because the movie industry remains a big business and moving crores of rupees for that was not difficult, nor would it attract much attention. That was the reason why Dawood made friends with Mehwish and gave her a bungalow and helped her establish the production house. The surprising thing was, after this, whichever movie Mehwish worked on went on to become successful.

Mehwish Hayat has now established a production house in London, named Pink Llama Films (https://pinkllamafilms.com/) and another, Fine Cut PR, in her brother Danish Hayat's name in Pakistan. These production houses collaborate for cross-border money movement, currently framed as investments with plans to transition to project payments. Dawood had gifted her a luxurious house in DHA Phase 7, Karachi, a significant upgrade from her previous residence in North Karachi. The generosity extended to a 500-square-yard bungalow at a prime location in Karachi, a gift symbolic of the beginning of their partnership. Despite Mehwish's inability to afford such a residence, Dawood's offering marked the start of a unique relationship.

Indian agencies keeping a tab on Dawood's associates in Pakistan claim that they frequently meet on Mondays and Fridays in Karachi, often in a secure 500-square-yard house, close to her gifted home. Security measures in this block include CCTV cameras, guards in black uniforms and a controlled entry system. Dawood initially allowed Mehwish to travel freely, including trips to the UK and Dubai, offering her exposure to international settings.

London is an important geographical location for Dawood Ibrahim's business interests. While local film stars look for offices in Los Angeles to connect with Hollywood and have their offices in the US, Dawood's friends are content with connections in the UK. Malik

Riaz, Dawood's front man, was previously involved in transferring Dawood's money from Pakistan to London.

Mehwish was vocally agitated when a retired army officer made a claim against a few Pakistani actresses who were used as honey traps by the Pakistani intelligence and reacted in a much softer manner on her nexus with Dawood Ibrahim. She tweeted on the subject: 'I know the agenda of the Indian media. I would not comment on such kinds of news reports.'

Dawood also chased actresses from the Indian and Pakistani film industry. Apart from other actresses, earlier Dawood was close to Anita Ayub in the early 1990s. Anita, who debuted in the Dev Anand-directed film *Pyar Ka Taraana* (1993), soon hit the cover page of Indian glossies and was front-page news for her connections with Dawood Ibrahim. In fact, when film producer Javed Siddiqui refused to cast Anita in his movies, he was shot dead in broad daylight in 1994.[1]

After that, none could refuse the underworld diktat or their darling damsels. The writ was considered sacrosanct on both sides of the border and in both the film industries.

Istanbul Airport is a specimen of thriving chaos. I couldn't figure out whether Heathrow was more of a jungle than Istanbul Airport. Two of the most beautiful things are the swimming pool at Singapore Airport and the beautiful masjid at Istanbul Airport.

Spending three days with Kamaal Hasan was interesting, intriguing and full of stories. We both decided to return to our destinations through Istanbul. It was quite a stay with him. At the airport, he wanted to have a beer and I was avoiding letting him have a drink in my presence.

The best tactic I could use was to drag him to the beautiful prayer room at the airport. I was totally surprised when someone told me there are more than forty prayer rooms in the entire airport, twenty for men and twenty for women.

Kamaal chuckled. 'Religion kills more people in Pakistan than toxic liquor.'

He was taking a swipe at my naivete, apparently, enjoying it. Before we could part ways, he asked another question.

'Do you know there is something called Reverse Stockholm Syndrome?'

'I guess it is called Lima Syndrome,' I said.

Lima Syndrome is a psychological disorder where abductors develop sympathy or compassion towards their hostages. This is a more recently developed theory after a 1996 hostage crisis where the Japanese ambassador was held at his house in Lima, Peru.

'I believe Dawood Ibrahim has Lima Syndrome towards Mehwish Hayat. Her success and her unstoppable rise to stardom is evidence,' Kamaal concluded.

I will never be able to fathom the depth of these conundrums that he keeps bouncing off me. She claimed to have given seven back-to-back hits, which is a record of sorts in the Pakistani or Indian film industry. The girl who was not well known before that not only became a top actress but also holds Tamgha-e-Imtiaz. There is more in store for Pakistan.

Mehwish, who was a struggling actress until a few years ago, has now become too ambitious for her young age. In an interview with Geo TV, she recently claimed that she would like to follow in Imran Khan's footsteps and become the prime minister of Pakistan.

This was the Redford moment indeed, when an item girl can harbour dreams to lead the country just because she happens to hobnob with the really powerful people in her country.

As Mario Puzo observed: Finance is a gun. Politics is knowledge when to pull the trigger.

11

Uncanny Associations

If an Indian and a Pakistani meet in any part of the world, it is unlikely that they won't discuss cricket. Hence, it wasn't surprising that one of the conversations between me and Kamaal turned towards cricket. While India has held a better record against Pakistan in recent times, the 1980s and 1990s was an era where Pakistan dominated India in the game. This fact has been acknowledged by many Indian cricketers of those days.

'If one Pakistani player was a thorn in India's scheme of things,' Kamaal said, 'it was none other than Javed Miandad.'

Born on 12 June 1957, in Karachi, Pakistan, Miandad is hailed as one of the greatest cricketers to have ever played for Pakistan. He played a pivotal role in many of Pakistan's most memorable victories, including their triumphant 1992 World Cup campaign.

One of the most iconic moments of Miandad's career occurred on 18 April 1986, at the Sharjah Cricket

Association Stadium against India. The match was the final of the Australia–Asia Cup, and Pakistan needed four runs to win from the last ball. Facing Indian bowler Chetan Sharma, Miandad executed a flawless swing, sending the ball soaring over the boundary for a six. This not only secured Pakistan's victory but also had a huge psychological impact on future India–Pakistan cricket matches. But that was not the end of Javed's rocky relationship with India.

Miandad has openly acknowledged and expressed pride in his family ties with Dawood Ibrahim. In an interview, Miandad declared it an 'honour' to have such connections, highlighting the marriage between Dawood's daughter, Mahrukh, and his own son, Junaid, which took place in Dubai in 2005.

Miandad's family has been associated with a company called Pak Armoring Pvt. Ltd. Javed's brother, Bashir Miandad, emerges as a mere pawn on the chessboard of power. He served as the perfect front for Dawood's empire, shielding the true mastermind from prying eyes and probing questions.

While Bashir Miandad may have occupied the position of CEO of Pak Armoring Pvt. Ltd, it is Dawood who pulls the strings from the shadows. From the outside, Pak Armoring appears to be a legitimate business, catering to the security needs of government institutions, private corporations and high-net-worth individuals. However, behind closed doors, a different story unfolds—one of corruption, money-laundering and clandestine operations.

The Pakistan Navy, Pakistan Air Force and ISI stand as silent partners in Dawood's empire, their need for security solutions providing the perfect cover for his nefarious dealings. The Pakistan Rangers, Coast Guards and various police departments across the country fall under Dawood's sway, their armoured vehicles supplied by Pak Armoring Pvt. Ltd serving as instruments of both protection and coercion. Even the judiciary, represented by the High Court of Sindh, finds itself ensnared in Dawood's web.

A key trait of Dawood is that no matter which country he goes to, he knows how to make money. When he was in the Gulf, he had virtually forced the Hindi film industry to assign overseas territories of films to his frontmen. In Pakistan, he founded Pak Armoring Pvt. Ltd and penetrated deep into the heart of Pakistan's establishment. It is also said that he owns a famous five-star hotel in Karbala through his Pakistani associates.

Similarly, he also founded another company called Advance Business Systems (ABS) through Saleem Zaveri. This company became a computer company with a sister company named Shaffaq Computers. They started to import used computers, laptops and parts from Europe, the US and other markets. Half of these computers were brought empty from inside without spare parts, i.e the CPU box was empty. In these CPU boxes, they smuggled gold, drugs and foreign currency.

Their troubles at various ports were sorted out by Bashir Miandad who had deep ties with the Coast Guard, Navy and port authorities on account of his Pak Armoring Pvt. Ltd business. The port authorities began looking the other way for their share of money and let these CPU boxes pass without any scrutiny.

The smuggled gold was also given to ARY Jewellers for selling and earning money via this channel. The drugs found their way to various cartels operating in Pakistan. But in 2014, Nawaz Sharif's government was forced by various Chinioti groups to crack down on these businesses.

The Federal Board of Revenue (FBR) arrested officials from ABS, including Attiq Ur Rehman, Saleem Zaveri and Sheikh Mohammad Yaqoob, for their involvement in a significant tax evasion scheme amounting to approximately Rs 1.04 billion. This action followed the rejection of their bail plea by the Supreme Court. Investigations revealed that civil proceedings were initiated against the ABS under the Section 11 of the Sales Tax Act to recover evaded sales tax. A complaint forwarded by the NAB highlighted the tax evasion involvement of various computer product importers, including ABS. Upon scrutinizing ABS's declarations and import records, it was confirmed that the company engaged in tax evasion and fraud.

ABS imported computers and related equipment from international markets from major brands with declared imports significantly lower than actual purchases, which resulted in evaded sales tax amounting to over Rs 1 billion. Investigations uncovered the company's involvement in under-invoicing products in Dubai, followed by their smuggling into Pakistan to evade sales tax. Furthermore, ABS operated *benami* bank accounts in Islamabad to understate its tax liability, depositing evaded tax money to conceal its transactions. ABS's partners also maintained a dummy company in Dubai, IT Station FZE, to ship consignments purchased from international manufacturers and divert tax liabilities, which caused substantial losses to the national exchequer.

Despite making payments to manufacturers through Dubai's banking channels, ABS routed most payments from Pakistan to Dubai through non-banking channels, contravening State Bank of Pakistan directives and enabling lower-rate imports. Their negligible input tax payments allowed them to make sales without charging sales tax, with evidence revealing substantial sales made without GST. To conceal sales proceeds, ABS maintained benami bank accounts under their employees' names and directed customers to deposit payments into these accounts.

ABS claimed that they purchased in bulk quantities, importing 20 per cent of goods to Pakistan and selling the remaining 80 per cent in Singapore. However, investigations contradicted their claims, revealing discrepancies between their declarations and sell-through reports submitted to their principal international IT companies. Moreover, the company's business in Singapore was not declared in the income tax return of Saleem Zaveri. This contradicted the sell-through reports, suggesting that products were massively under-invoiced in Dubai and then shipped to Pakistan, where the sales tax liability was understated. These findings also indicated that all products were not imported through legal channels and were smuggled into Pakistan to evade sales tax.

The investigation concluded that ABS had violated several provisions of the Sales Tax Act, engaging in tax fraud punishable under the relevant sections. The agency initiated criminal proceedings against ABS's partners and their managers, with FIR No. 1 of 2014 registered against them. Despite their claims regarding foreign sales, investigations exposed ABS's massive tax evasion, prompting the agency to finalize a contravention report for assessment and adjudication as per the Sales Tax Act's provisions. But just like Al Capone, the famous American gangster who was convicted only for tax evasion despite his public criminal record, a similar situation emerged in the Saleem Zaveri fiasco.

This completed another saga where Dawood and his associates had subjugated the system. The extent of Dawood's influence can also be gathered from another admission by Javed Miandad who claimed, on video, that Imran Khan became the prime minister of Pakistan because he had the blessings of a powerful person. It wouldn't be too difficult to guess who this powerful person is. His name is Dawood Ibrahim Kaskar.

12

Mexican Stand-Off in Bombay

Considering his impeccable record, former IPS officer Neeraj Kumar has investigated several high-profile criminal cases in a career spanning more than three and a half decades. He joined the coveted Indian Police Service (IPS) in 1976. By 1993, he was deputed to the CBI and promoted to the rank of deputy inspector general of police.

During his tenure with the CBI, he was instrumental in unearthing the cricket match-fixing scandal that rocked our cricket-crazy nation and put several prominent sportsmen across countries and bookies in the dock. His work in this domain also earned him a position as the chief adviser to the BCCI for their Anti-Corruption Unit in the later stages of his career.

'But no case presented me with the kind of challenges I faced when investigating the Mumbai bomb blasts in 1993,' Neeraj Kumar says. 'Layers upon layers of conspiracies had to be unearthed to get to the bottom of this act of terror.'

As an investigative journalist, I had tracked the blasts closely from 1993 to 2003. The mention of the subject piqued my interest. Much water had flowed under the bridge since I had covered the blasts and the subsequent investigation in my book *Black Friday: The True Story of the Bombay Bomb Blasts*.

But a subject as massive as this warranted a conclusion. To trace the conclusion, it was essential to go back in time. What stories remained to be told? Where were the perpetrators now?

Ironically, when the mastermind of the blasts, Dawood Ibrahim Kaskar, was scaling the heights of crime as a petty smuggler in 1970s' Mumbai, Neeraj Kumar was rising through the corridors of law and order having joined the police force after passing the civil services examinations conducted by the Union Public Service Commission (UPSC). He was first posted as the ACP for the Chanakyapuri subdivision of New Delhi in 1979. Dawood went from a small-time smuggler to becoming the most wanted man in the country and gained international notoriety. Neeraj Kumar ended his career as the commissioner of police in New Delhi. As fate would have it, they were destined to cross each other's paths.

The 1993 blasts put tremendous pressure on the security apparatus to act swiftly and bring the culprits to book. Mumbai Police stepped up to the task but very often found themselves staring at allegations of excesses. Mounting pressure from the higher-ups and the common public often compelled the cops to detain, arrest and torture men from the minority communities who had nothing to do with the blasts. A prominent hotelier of the city, Raj Kumar Khurana, whose name cropped up during the investigation, was summoned to the police station and subjected to such mental torture that he ended up shooting his wife and children and then killed himself.[1]

The CBI was called in and asked to take over the investigation. Neeraj Kumar was asked to lead the Special Task Force (STF) by his CBI bosses. By virtue of his investigation, he remains an authority on the topic of the Mumbai bomb blasts. It was essential for me to collude with him on the events of three decades ago.

The coffee shop of a golf club in Delhi was chosen for the first of many rendezvous that would stretch out for months to unearth more facts about the case. He was there before me, smiling with a cup in his hands. Kumar's soft-spoken demeanour remains unscathed even after thirty-seven years of working with law enforcement. The man can quote poetry from Ghalib as easily as he can detail provisions of the Indian Penal Code.

The first topic of our discussion was none other than Ibrahim Mushtaq Abdul Razzaq Memon aka Tiger Memon, the man who had played a key role in the planning and execution of the blasts.

My mind veered towards the time when Tiger's mercurial temper had caused him to draw a weapon on one of his former bosses and known associates. 'Wars have been fought over women,' I said. 'This was no different.'

The cocking of the revolver silenced every sound in a room that was bustling with laughter only a few moments ago. Tiger Memon was holding the weapon inside a small office in Nakhuda Mohalla. The area was popular among street shoppers in Mumbai (known as Bombay back then) and was located hardly six minutes away from Dongri, which had emerged as the epicentre of the mafia in the mid-1980s. Many shops selling ethnic wear for women were located in the area. Often, Tiger had purchased dresses from these shops—not for his wife Shabana but for another lady who was the root cause of this particular incident.

Now, Tiger was inches away from pulling the trigger on Mustafa Dossa aka Mustafa Majnu, who had been a former boss, an acquaintance or associate until this moment but never an enemy. Their entire equation was about to change in a few moments.

Tiger snarled, as he usually did when his temper took over. He was one of the top men in the D-Company. He had earned the nickname of Tiger due to his ferocious nature. Even customs officials who had been at the receiving end of his anger when they tried to confiscate his goods feared him a lot.

Dossa, however, was not going to be cowed down easily. If Tiger had drawn his weapon, he was not going to hold back either. He drew his weapon and aimed it at Tiger. This created a Mexican stand-off, where any act of aggression could lead to annihilation of both parties.

The tiny office was co-operated by Tiger and Dossa. Dossa's boys were sitting in the office but they knew better than to step into the path of an angry Tiger. Not many in the room had an idea why the two men were baying for each other's blood. But as history had witnessed several times, it was the lure of a woman that had caused bad blood between two powerful and dangerous men.

Mustafa Dossa had earned the sobriquet of Majnu on account of his promiscuous ways, and it was this precise habit that had created trouble between him and Tiger. At the centre of the controversy was Roma Singh, a woman who had arrived in Mumbai from Delhi in 1975 with aspirations of becoming an actress. Inspired by the success of Rekha and Reena Roy, who were walking the red carpet of Bollywood during that period, Roma had also moved to the city of dreams with stars in her eyes.

But Roma's Bollywood ambitions came crashing down swiftly. Work was hard to find and exploitation was not uncommon, if not the norm. Bollywood was not governed by corporate standards. In an industry dominated by glamour, the casting couch was very much a reality.

Even in those days, living in Mumbai was an expensive affair. Maintaining an image, wearing expensive clothes and applying high-quality make-up accounted for a lot of money. Roma had to figure out ways through which she could sustain a lavish lifestyle. Fate lured Roma into the dubious space of prostitution. Her prime years flew by in a jiffy and then she shifted to supplying escort services for the rich and powerful of Mumbai from her apartment near Carter Road.

Roma Singh was introduced to Tiger Memon by Anees Ibrahim—Dawood's younger brother. Tiger and Anees were thick friends. A fiery, passionate affair began between Tiger and Roma despite him being married at that time. Tiger's father was not too happy about his promiscuous ways and once even asked Tiger to leave their familial abode in Mahim. Despite her glamorous ambitions, it is said that Roma was, at best, average in looks and had an uncouth manner of speaking. But all of this did not deter Tiger, who continued the affair with Roma much to the surprise of his family and associates.

Things came to a point where Tiger issued strict directions to everyone in the D-Company that Roma was off-limits to all. And all the men of the underworld knew that Tiger's threat was to be taken seriously. All, except Mustafa Majnu, who had a long list of girlfriends that he was always looking to grow.

Roma would often call Tiger at his Tejarath International office in Mahim. On the day the Mexican stand-off occurred, she had called the Mahim office and learnt that Tiger was out for some work. That was the era of landline telephones. If Tiger was not in Mahim, Roma knew that he would most likely be found at the Nakhuda Mohalla office with the Dossa brothers as they were business partners.

So she called up at the Nakhuda Mohalla office. As luck would have it, Tiger was not present there either. The phone was answered by Mustafa Majnu who was *in the mood*, even at the afternoon hour, as he always was. When Roma asked if she could speak with Tiger, Majnu retorted with the cheesiest pick-up line of the year.

'Try me for a change,' he said cockily. 'After that, you will know who the *real* Tiger is.'

'Who is this?' Roma asked.

In response, Roma only heard the laughter and snide remarks of Dossa and his men. Roma immediately hung up but was seething with rage. She may have bedded many men, but she had bedded them on *her* terms. Besides, her involvement with Tiger was too strong at that time. She tried reaching him frantically and could only get in touch with him in the evening when he returned to Tejarath International.

Tiger was furious. A pass at Roma was an insult to his manhood. He asked Roma if she was aware of the identity of the man who had answered the phone. Roma told him that she had no clue.

'Don't worry,' Tiger said. 'I will find out.'

Tiger picked up his revolver and the keys to his car and drove like a madman towards Nakhuda Mohalla. His temper was rising with each passing second. His driving was known to be super fast. On more than one occasion, he had saved the Dossa brothers from the cops by driving recklessly through the streets when the cops or customs were chasing them. Those days, he used to work for the Dossa brothers. But times were different now. Tiger was his own man, and his rise in the underworld had irked many already.

Finally, the car screeched to a halt outside the office and Tiger stormed inside. Mustafa Dossa was still sitting there with his errand boys. Tiger's entry changed everything in a moment. The room went silent.

'*Kaun bhenchod phone uthaya*?!' Tiger growled, wanting to know who had answered the call.

His words were as much of a challenge as they were a question. Mustafa Dossa knew that if he didn't man up, he would lose the respect of his boys. He stood up and went toe to toe with Tiger.

'*Main uthaya*,' Dossa said defiantly. '*Kya ukhad lega*? (It was me. What are you going to do about it?)'

The next moment, Tiger pulled out his revolver and placed it on Dossa's forehead. Not to be outdone, Dossa responded in the same fashion. Things were about to go out of hand when Mohammad Dossa (Mustafa's elder brother) intervened and cooled down the tempers of the two men.

Mustafa pulled his weapon down and Tiger did likewise, but not before warning Mustafa, the perennial Romeo, that he would blow his head off if he even dared to think about Roma in his wet dreams. And then Tiger stormed out of the office, leaving everyone in the room stunned with his fury. The business relationship between Mustafa and Tiger was irreparably broken.

However, both were also aware that the news of this event would soon reach Dawood Ibrahim's kingdom in Dubai. If the underworld was a game of chess, Tiger and Mustafa were the knights who worked for the king. To keep their position in the company stronger than ever, both of them began preparing for their next move. All roads would now lead to Dubai.

13

Balance of Power

'Dossa knew that Tiger was no less than a ticking time bomb,' I said. 'He wanted to seek refuge in Dawood's camp.'

Kumar sipped on his coffee and waved his hand for another cup. 'Why wouldn't he?' He paused. 'Dawood Ibrahim had de-throned powerful old-timers of the mafia, like Karim Lala and Haji Mastan to gain absolute control of the underworld.'

Kumar was right. Dawood was born into a family that struggled to live. His father, an influential man within the community, was a constable in the Mumbai Police at a time when cops were paid such measly wages that they would never risk life or limb in the line of duty. At that time, brick by brick, Dawood built an empire and a fortune way beyond anyone's imagination. He operated in more than forty countries across six continents. To obtain this power and money, he had ruthlessly decimated his opponents.

'But something always troubled Dawood,' I said. 'He always dreaded that someone would repeat with him what he had done to others.'

'To retain absolute power after it is gained, it is essential for the apex predator to maintain the balance of power in his favour,' Kumar said. 'Otherwise, his position is threatened.'

'Therefore,' I said, 'it was essential for Dawood to maintain this balance of power between Tiger and Dossa.'

Neeraj Kumar leaned forward. 'There was no other way.'

As much as Tiger would have wanted to maim them, the Dossa brothers were not small fry who could be intimidated easily. Their wealthy family had played a huge role in establishing Manish Market, a wholesale and retail shopping complex located between Masjid Bunder and Chhatrapati Shivaji Maharaj Terminus. Ahmed Umar, the patriarch of the Dossa clan, had three sons of which Mohammad Dossa was the first, Mustafa—the Majnu—was the second and Haroon was the third. None of the three brothers showed any interest in academics and dropped out of school. They were Kutchi Memons from the Kutch region of Gujarat. The community is known for its keen sense of business.

The Dossa family controlled the trade of electronic goods in Manish Market. During that time, electric goods had a huge black market because of the high import duties levied on them by the government. Smugglers had field days by illegally shipping these goods from Dubai to Bombay. The electronic market was built in the place of a theatre which the Dossa family had bought after its fortunes had soared by smuggling gold and electronic items from Dubai.

Mohammed Dossa was introduced to smuggling by one Haji Mohammed in the 1970s. Haji was also said to have taught Dawood many tricks of this trade. Mustafa Dossa followed his elder brother into the business, and they became a force to reckon with. The Dossa brothers founded one of the biggest gold jewellery showrooms at Gold Souk, which they named Mignas. Gold Souk became one of Dubai's traditional and opulent markets that houses over 350 retail gold shops that sell tax-free gold in different carats and designs.

Tiger, on the other hand, also belonged to the Memon community and had worked for the Dossas in his early days. It was Mohammad, Dossa's elder brother, who had introduced Tiger into the crime world by initially hiring him as a driver. While Mustafa was romancing his girlfriends, Tiger's focus was laser-sharp. He wanted to mark his territories and control them. Thus, he soon outgrew his loyalties to the Dossa family and set out on a path of becoming his own boss.

But not even in his wildest dreams had Mustafa Majnu imagined that Tiger would pull a gun on him over a woman like Roma who had such a dubious past. To be challenged by someone like Tiger was a huge blow to the pride of not just Mustafa Dossa but also his elder brother Mohammed Dossa. They had to protect the family's power which they had worked hard to build.

But what Tiger lacked in dynastic credentials, he made up for with his bravado. He had climbed up the ranks of the underworld rather quickly. His ferocious temper was well known in the entire D-Company. His expulsion from his first job as a menial in a bank is a testimony to that effect. After passing his matriculation, Tiger could not pursue higher education due to his family's strained financial conditions. He went about looking for a job to sustain his house and got a petty one in the Memon Co-operative Bank. While working in the bank, Tiger got into a feud with the manager of the bank over serving tea. The manager had barely mouthed two abusive words before Tiger pounced on him and beat the daylights out of him. He met Mohammad Dossa after losing his job at the bank.

Tiger would always stand his ground, not just against the Dossa brothers but even against Dawood Ibrahim. In the mid-1980s, Dawood had sent a huge consignment of smuggled goods from Dubai to India. He had assigned the management of the landing to Tiger. Everything was going as planned until the authorities got wind of the illegal operation. Close to the landing site, the consignment was apprehended by the customs in the Konkan region. Dawood was shocked to hear this news. The financial loss was huge, but Dawood was more worried about the loss of face. He could not digest the fact that Tiger had screwed up a landing and sensed something amiss. The don picked up a telephone from his office in Dubai and called Tiger.

Tiger, on the other hand, was also expecting a call from the boss after the fiasco. He steeled himself and answered the phone. Dawood wasted no time in getting to the point.

'*Seedhe kaam mein itna lafda*? (How was a simple landing botched up?)'

Tiger paused before answering. 'Bhai, you've screwed up so many times too. We never question you, do we?'

Dawood was taken aback. Not many had the *gooda* (strength of the bone marrow) to talk to him like that.

More than a few men had paid with their limbs and lives for even looking at him with disrespect. The most famous example was that of strongman Mehmood Kalia. He was a thick-set man, as strong as a bull and his name evoked raw fear from the locals. He ran a couple of dormitories and guest houses in Mumbai near Novelty Cinema, Grant Road. He also had a *zari* (embroidery lace) business. Much like Tiger, Kalia was his own man and refused to accept Dawood's hegemony in the underworld. He refused to be tamed.

In 1987, Dawood called Kalia to Dubai on the pretext of a partnership. All arrangements like flight tickets and a lavish stay were put in place. Kalia thought he was being treated like a king. However, Kalia did not know that Dawood was treating him like a sacrificial lamb that was about to be sent to the butcher.

Kalia boarded the return flight and had only stepped out of Sahar Airport (as Chhatrapati Shivaji Maharaj International Airport was known then) when he was accosted by sub-inspector Emmanuel Amolik and shot dead. It is said that Mehmood's whereabouts were leaked to the cops on Dawood's orders. In 1986, Amolik had also tried to shoot dead Charles Sobhraj after the serial killer's arrest in Goa and only a severe reprimand from his senior stopped him from carrying out the act. Still, Amolik went on to have a controversial career before being arrested for involvement in the murder of builder Sunil Kumar Loharia in 2013.

However, Tiger Memon was not Mehmood Kalia who could be disposed of so easily. Dawood knew that Tiger's rage was not only his weakness but also his strength, which could be put to use in the future. So when Tiger bared his teeth, Dawood swallowed a bitter pill and immediately disconnected the call. The don began thinking of ways through which Tiger's rise could be curtailed and controlled. Immediately, he ordered Anees to build a bond with Tiger and keep him under check.

Tiger and Anees became good friends. They shared a common dislike for Mustafa Dossa's flamboyance. Anees showed scant respect for Dossa's riches and would treat him like an errand boy. So after the Mexican stand-off between Tiger and Dossa, the first thing Tiger did was to call Anees and narrate the entire incident to him. Anees assured Tiger that he would protect his interests in the D-Company and that Tiger had nothing to fear from Dossa.

On the other side, Dossa also made his move. In 1981, Dawood's elder brother Sabir was killed in a shoot-out near a petrol pump at Prabhadevi. Dawood was closest to Sabir among his siblings. The two had forayed into crime together. After Sabir's death, Dawood became closer to Anees.

Anees was the number two in the company. Mohammed Shakeel Babu Miyan Shaikh aka Chhota Shakeel was emerging as a challenger to the throne of Dawood's deputy. Another strong contender at that time was Rajendra Sadashiv Nikalje aka Chhota Rajan.

The power dynamics of the D-Company would undergo a substantial change after the blasts. But at that time, Anees was the undisputed number two.

Mohammad Dossa learnt that Tiger had sided with Anees. He was also aware that Anees hated the sight of him and his brother. Dossa understood that only the number one could save him from the wrath of the number two. So he booked a flight to Dubai, landed at the don's *durbar* and narrated his ordeal to none other than Dawood himself. Dawood was waiting for this opportunity. The don also pretended to give him a sympathetic ear.

Dawood promised refuge to Dossa and told Anees to ensure that Dossa did not face the brunt of Tiger's fury after that point. Dossa returned to Mumbai fully satisfied that he had the big don on his side of the ring. But what none of the players in the game could understand was that they were being played by the shrewdest criminal mind in the history of the underworld.

Ever since Tiger had shown the gall to speak up after the botched landing, Dawood was looking for ways to stall his rise in the D-Company. One may ask why Tiger did not meet the same fate as Mehmood Kalia for his temerity. The answer lies in the fact that Dawood realized that Tiger's resourcefulness was worth way more than his nuisance value. That is why Tiger only needed to be put on a leash and not eliminated. So Dawood had advised Anees to develop a bond with Tiger and keep him caged, only to be unleashed when the need arose. Dawood's methods of dealing with Tiger were proven correct when Tiger played a major role in executing the Black Friday bombings of March 1993.

To curtail Tiger, Dawood also used Dossa as a counterweight. Dossa's rise was assured after he grew close to the big don himself. He purchased a fleet of double-engine boats that could transport goods between Dubai and Mumbai in half the time than the established benchmarks. His wealth continued to soar to even greater heights.

Now, Tiger was under Anees's control and Dossa was aligned with Dawood himself. Using this strategy, Dawood was able to maintain the balance of power in the D-Company. Dossa would go on to make a name for himself in the underworld. But what is more surprising is that Dossa's bonhomie with Dawood and his involvement in the 1993 bombings would have never surfaced if a top don of the D-Company had not been arrested in a secret operation of the CBI in not-so-distant Kathmandu. And it was none other than Neeraj Kumar who arrested this dangerous man in a cross-border operation.

14

Do I Look like a Dog?

Salim Mira Moideen Shaikh was one of the strongest men in the D-Company. He was also always ready for a fight. Due to his rabid nature and dark complexion, he was nicknamed Salim Kutta. He was a native of Kotta Nellore in Tamil Nadu. In Mumbai, he was involved in rioting cases.

'But how did Salim get involved in the blasts?' I asked.

His name also evoked a reaction from Neeraj Kumar, who had conducted a cross-border operation to arrest him; a surgical arrest in the mid-1990s, for sure, if not a strike.

Salim Kutta used to be a bodyguard for the Dossa family. Mohammad Dossa used to help Salim with medical expenses and gained the latter's undying loyalty. Salim's violent nature was of good use for Dossa. In the late 1980s, Salim was also part of a gang known as the 'Arjun' gang which was modelled after the gang led by Sunny Deol in his superhit film of the same name. This gang also had the blessings of Mustafa Dossa aka Mustafa Majnu. By 1992, Salim was firmly entrenched in Mohammad Dossa's good books. Members of the Arjun gang were also sent to Pakistan for training in the usage of arms and ammunition.

While Neeraj Kumar was investigating the bombings, he was hell-bent on chasing down those who played a key role in the bombings.

Salim had participated in landing the arms and ammunition at the Gosabara Coast in Gujarat. These were used for the Black Friday bombings in 1993. Hence, he was on the radar of the Gujarat Police. The Gujarat landings were orchestrated by Mustafa Dossa, whereas two other landings were organized by Tiger Memon at Dighi and Shekhadi coasts in Raigad district of Maharashtra. Thus, Salim Kutta became a natural target for Neeraj Kumar.

After weeks of waiting, things heated up with the arrival of an intelligence report at the CBI headquarters in New Delhi.[1] Holding the INTREP in his hands, and reading it over and over again, Neeraj Kumar (then joint director of the CBI) made a concrete effort to keep his zeal in control.

The CBI Headquarters had pint-sized cabins for members of their Special Task Force who were investigating the blasts. The walls of those cabins were so thin that officers seated in adjacent cabins could hear each other's conversations even if they were top secret! For this precise reason, Kumar resisted the urge to call his juniors to his cabin and brief them about the report which had come from India's top agency—the famed Research and Analysis Wing (R&AW).

According to the report, dreaded terrorist Salim Kutta, an accused in the Bombay bomb blasts, was said to be working at a grocery shop named 'Abhinandan' in

Kathmandu. There were also reports of two other accused, Shabir and Firoz, who were said to be spotted around the same area in Kathmandu. Neeraj Kumar stifled a chuckle. Who could have imagined that a most wanted man from the D-Company would be hiding in a grocery shop in Nepal's capital?

In all honesty, Kumar expected this intel to turn out to be another dud, the likes of which would get thrown at them with abandon in this game of cops and criminals. Now he had two options. To put in a half-hearted attempt or go all in. He gave it some serious thought and allowed his policeman's instincts to take over. Finally, he decided to take a leap of faith.

But there was one problem in going after Salim Kutta. Though he oversaw the STF, Kumar lacked the manpower he would need to arrest Kutta if the intel was legit. The CBI is a tremendously understaffed organization suffering from a perennial crunch in resources.

Kumar was aware that his batchmate from the IPS academy, Kuldeep Sharma, who was currently working with Gujarat Police, was also on the lookout for Salim Kutta as the criminal had taken part in landing explosives and ammunition on the coast of Gujarat.

Since they had trained together at the police academy, Kumar decided to team up with Kuldeep Sharma and launch an operation to arrest Salim. Another officer from the Jammu and Kashmir cadre was chosen by Kumar as a part of the CBI team for this mission.

The joint team reached Kathmandu and camped at the Annapoorna Hotel while awaiting formal approval from the Nepal government to commence their operation.

Contrary to popular belief, the CBI is barred from carrying out any secret operations that are not sanctioned by the government. This is the direct result of the diplomacy involved between the two countries and the fact that the CBI reports directly to the Central government. Misadventures or even the slightest of mistakes of the CBI can cause direct embarrassment to the prime minister's office. Kumar was bound to the established protocol and procedures.

The red tape of bureaucracy began taking its toll. As with any kind of government work, there was an inordinate amount of delay in procuring the requisite approvals. Kumar was getting edgier by the minute. *What if Salim got wind of their plans? If he escaped now, tracking him again would prove to be a monumental task.*

Kumar decided to act. He took along his CBI subordinates and a sub-inspector from Nepal Police down the streets of Kathmandu in a private vehicle. He wanted to inspect the location of the Abhinandan grocery shop where the three suspects (Salim, Shabir and Firoz) were supposedly working.

The team finally reached a spot from where they could keep an eye on the shop but they were still unsure of the presence of their quarry. Kumar spotted a telephone booth located right in front of the shop. On the pretext of making a call, Kumar entered the booth to get a closer look at the people inside the store. Much to Kumar's surprise, a tall, muscled man was seated at the counter of the shop. From the photographs sent by the R&AW, Kumar recognized the man as none other than Salim Kutta!

Kumar headed back to their vehicle and convinced the local Nepali sub-inspector to approach the accused and nab them even before securing approval from the Nepal government. The sub-inspector agreed after a discussion that went back and forth for several minutes.

Kumar checked his weapon and entered the shop. He looked squarely at the man on the counter.

'Are you Salim?' Kumar asked.

The unanticipated question left Salim open-mouthed, leaving his mind to do the maths on his chances of an escape. A desperate Salim looked around for an exit but found that the cops had blocked all routes. Salim also did not live up to his reputation of shooting first and talking later. He surrendered without offering any resistance. Kumar was relieved at this but also overjoyed with the success.

Salim was hustled into the waiting car. It was decided that Kumar would drive back to their location. The other two cops, who could match Salim's physique, would guard him in the rear seat. Kumar, being a stranger to the land, had some difficulty initially in making the right turns and following the correct path. But he picked it up eventually and managed to drive back to the destination without any difficulty.

Salim was produced at the local police station. The local Indian embassy was briefed about the development and was asked to speed up the process of securing formal approval from the Nepal government so that the arrest could be made official. One of the Intelligence Bureau officers deployed in Kathmandu termed the arrest of Salim a 'gold mine' and helped Kumar in completing the paperwork.

Salim's arrest also alerted Firoz and Shabir, who managed to flee the scene. The Nepal Police later played a sizeable role in arresting Shabir. There was a small problem, though. Since Kumar had acted impromptu, the Gujarat

Police contingent had been completely left out of the action. Kuldeep Sharma was highly disappointed that his team's chances of getting some laurels from this operation had been washed away. Sensing Sharma's predicament, Neeraj Kumar made a generous offer.

'You take Salim Kutta,' Kumar said. 'We will take Shabir.'

From his past experience, Kumar realized that the CBI never receives appropriate recognition for their work in arresting any dreaded criminal. The CBI's achievements are not highlighted enough in the media. Besides, the job was done and Kumar did not mind sharing the credit for it. So he decided to hand over his trophy catch to the Gujarat Police led by Sharma in the hope that it would garner the requisite attention and recognition.

Following the completion of formalities, the two teams boarded an Air India flight from Kathmandu to Delhi with Salim Kutta and Shabir in their custody. The teams demanded the flight operator allot them the two rows of seats at the rear of the aircraft to keep the handcuffed Salim and Shabir out of the public eye throughout the journey. To not cause any panic among the general public, Salim's and Shabir's handcuffed arms were covered with newspapers.

Upon arrival in Delhi, Salim was taken to Ahmedabad by the Gujarat Police and Shabir was taken by the CBI team to Delhi. Kuldeep Sharma, who had kept the prized catch, made sure to credit the CBI team for their efforts. During a press conference, Sharma told the media that Salim's arrest was possible only because the CBI team was keeping an eye on the suspect's location through satellite surveillance!

Neeraj Kumar, who was also invited to this press conference, could barely contain his laughter at Sharma's notion, which was lapped up by the media like a hot cake. The CBI did not have such technical surveillance capabilities during those years. And until this day, this fact was a well-guarded secret between the two teams.

Since his arrest, Salim has spent a lot of time in jail and used to get into violent fights with other prisoners. Even in prison, Salim spared no effort to justify the epithet of a ferocious dog that was bestowed upon him. One of the co-accused, Naseem Barmare, had told the court that Salim Kutta had threatened to kill him and sought protection from the burly gangster.

But in 2013, Salim entered a plea in the TADA court that he should not be addressed as Salim Kutta. 'Do I look like a dog?' he had asked the judge. On hearing his plea, the judge passed an order to drop the offensive word from all official records.

Salim's arrest indeed proved to be a gold mine as it was he who revealed Dossa's involvement in the 1993 bombings in Mumbai. Salim Mira Moideen Shaikh aka Salim Kutta was sentenced to life imprisonment and a fine of Rs 2,00,000 was imposed upon him. His arrest also boosted the confidence of Neeraj Kumar and his boys who were then ready to take on the next challenge in that massive investigation.

References

'1993 Mumbai Blasts Convict Had Urged Tada Court to Drop 'Kutta' Tag', Firstpost, 21 March 2013, available at https://www.firstpost.com/mumbai/1993-mumbai-blasts-convict-had-urged-tada-court-to-drop-kutta-tag-670093.html.

15

Race to Death

Dawood Ibrahim's rise to the top was funded by bags full of money obtained from various criminal activities and businesses. Starting from smuggling, the gang had diversified into other crimes like extortion rackets, contract killings, construction, funding movies, cricket betting and stock markets. They had a share in every profitable business in the city.

'Naturally,' I said, 'all these illegal businesses were generating a lot of cash.'

'And the money had to be whitewashed,' Neeraj Kumar said. 'For this, Dawood had engaged men who had the ability to move cash around the world. He owned one of the biggest laundries in the world that could turn black money into white.'

Kumar was right. Dawood had understood the importance of a solid hawala network and how it could help him outrun the competition by miles. The same hawala network was later used for moving money that was deployed to execute the Mumbai bomb blasts in 1993. The illegal routes that Dawood had mastered to move gold and other contraband in his earlier years were also used to smuggle arms and ammunition. In an ideal state, the cops should have taken due action and destroyed these networks before they turned into the proverbial Frankenstein's monster. The existence of these systems provided an easy passage for the perpetrators to execute their plans.

The interest of Haji Mastan and Karim Lala in conducting business overseas was marginal. The same could also be said of Arun Gawli, who was a contemporary and rival of Dawood.

But Dawood's international ambitions propelled him to the top when compared to his opponents. A well-established hawala network allowed him to achieve the desired results. Dawood also employed the services of several financial wizards who could move huge sums of money over ten-second phone calls.

'But it wasn't long before Dawood's enemies realized that they could target these men to weaken the D-Company,' I said. 'One of Dawood's associates paid a huge price for this very reason.'

'Who was this man?' Kumar asked.

Thus, I told him what I had learnt from one of my sources during a sojourn into the dark alleys of the city, where such tales are told in whispers.

The year was 1989. The Mahalaxmi Racecourse was packed to its capacity. The oval-shaped track where the fortunes of many have been made and destroyed was built in 1883 and designed like the Randwick Racecourse in

Sydney, Australia. At a time when most of the country was suffering from rising inflation and unemployment, the Mahalaxmi Racecourse was a place for the gentry of the city to assemble in their fedoras and gowns.

Seated in a special box, Mahendra Chordia peered into his binoculars. The last race of the day was in progress. Huge money was at stake. The oval-shaped track was spread across the heart of the city. The punters cheered wildly for their wagers. The rich and powerful of the city hobnobbed with each other in the higher stands.

Chordia was impeccably dressed for the races, as would be expected for a man of his wealth. He lived in a huge sea-facing mansion near Worli. He also owned a couple of horses and had a lot of wealth for a man in his mid-forties. As soon as the race ended, Chordia made an exit from the VIP gate.

Chordia was born with the proverbial silver spoon in his mouth. He was also related to Kamal Chadha, who used to live in Colaba. It is said that Kamal Chadha had a huge influence with the D-Company on account of his business relationship with Dawood Ibrahim. Reportedly, Chordia was also a huge hawala operator and was laundering money for Dawood. He was a financial shark who had the knack of making money appear, disappear and reappear on his command. He knew a lot about the D-Company's financial interests.

Dawood's power was peaking in the late 1980s. A particularly famous photograph of the don sitting next to a budding actress caught the fancy of the general masses, giving rise to obvious speculations. The actress appeared one last time in a movie that was released in 1996 following the incident before disappearing from the public sphere and choosing to remain low-key for a long period of time. Dawood was also photographed watching cricket matches in Sharjah along with his coterie. During this time, even celebrities were *not* afraid to be seen or photographed with him as he was yet to play a role in the Mumbai bomb blasts, after which, no one wanted to be associated with him, at least publicly. So in 1989, Chordia was also known to be close to the D-Company.

Chordia did not have any personal bodyguards or any kind of security as he dealt with matters of money rather than matters of violence. But he had no inkling that he had appeared on the radar of Arun Gawli's gang who were looking to make a statement after the untimely deaths of Babu Reshim and Rama Naik.

Arun Gulab Gawli and his brother Kishor Gawli aka Papa Gawli were among the initial founders of the Byculla Gang, which functioned in the same area. Babu Reshim and Rama Naik were the other main players in this gang. The birth of the Byculla Gang is rooted in the social upheaval that followed the widespread closure of mills where most of the labour class had found work and livelihood. Gawli once used to work for Khatau Mills. The loss of jobs and the poverty that followed pushed young men towards a life of crime.

Dawood and Gawli soon had a fallout and a bloody rivalry followed. In 1987, Babu Reshim was killed by his rivals in an audacious raid while he was lodged inside Agripada Police Station. Rama Naik was killed by the cops in an encounter in Chembur in 1988. The troika of Reshim, Naik and Gawli had started their gang together, but now

Gawli was the sole survivor who was left to contest the might of the D-Company.

Gawli wanted to cut off Dawood's financial lines. With this intent, he had chosen his target, Mahendra Chordia. As soon as Chordia stepped out of the racecourse, he was accosted by Gawli's men. One of them pointed a pistol at his head and another put a blade to his throat. Chordia was bundled into a car, which began speeding towards Dagdi Chawl. They took him to an under-construction building that was being redeveloped by the Maharashtra Housing and Area Development Authority (MHADA).

At the same time, another team of Gawli also picked up Hamid Dafedar alias Hamid Chuha, who was known to be close to Dawood. Dawood's men went into a tizzy, trying to trace both Chordia and Chuha.

Chordia was put through brutal torture at the under-construction building. The news soon reached Dawood Ibrahim in Dubai. The don flew into a rage. But storming Dagdi Chawl would have meant more dead bodies for the D-Company to count. For the locals of Dagdi Chawl, Arun Gawli was a revered figure and was referred to by its residents as 'Daddy'. Such high reverence came from the fact that Gawli would open his *darbar* (court) in the chawl for all kinds of disputing parties and pass judgments that would bring about swift settlements. Those seeking remedies in financial, real estate or even domestic matters would happily pay the consultation fees seeking judgment from Gawli.

Even if the police came looking for him, the men of Dagdi Chawl would block their paths, whereas the women would shower the cops with scalding hot water and chilly powder from the balconies. A famous encounter specialist from Mumbai had also reported to have stumbled upon a hidden passage that was carved out meticulously through the chawl, enabling Gawli to escape from under the police's nose whenever there would be a raid on the chawl to nab him.

Gawli then decided to rub salt into Dawood's wounds by calling him up. As Chordia was put through torture, his screams were broadcast to Dubai through the telephone. The D-Company offered money to secure the release of Chordia. But Gawli was having none of this. He wanted to make an example out of Chordia. They tortured Chordia relentlessly before dumping his lifeless body outside a building.

The loss of a financier hurt Dawood a lot. He then ordered that all his financial information should be kept secret and not revealed to anyone. He even told his finance handlers that they were free to badmouth and even abuse him if that would help them avoid the suspicion of their enemies. Dawood's financiers began keeping a low profile after this incident.

Dawood also began to smell a rat when it emerged that even though Chordia had been cut into pieces, Hamid Chuha was let go by the Gawli gang and he returned safe and sound. Dawood could not digest the fact that one of his men had returned alive from Dagdi Chawl. Surely, he felt, something was amiss. Hamid was his associate, but he had been nicknamed Chuha (rat) for a reason. He was suspected of ratting on his colleagues to the cops to protect his own interests. Dawood suspected that Hamid had ratted on Chordia. Otherwise, there was no reason why the man was still walking on the face of the earth.

Dawood's men began pressuring Hamid to file a police complaint against Gawli. But whether it was the fear of meeting the same fate as Chordia or whether Dawood's suspicions were true, Hamid refused to go to the cops against Gawli. He told the D-Company that Gawli had not harmed him and he did not want to give 'Daddy' a reason to come after his life. This strengthened Dawood's suspicions about Hamid.

The war between Dawood Ibrahim and Arun Gawli also took a communal turn as they were deemed to be the 'bhais' of their respective communities.

Gawli's attack had to be countered. Dawood responded by eliminating Arun Gawli's brother Papa Gawli in 1990. At the peak of the rivalry, four of Gawli's men entered Dawood's turf and killed Ibrahim Parkar, who was married to the don's sister, Haseena. Shailesh Haldankar was the main shooter and he was accompanied by Dayanand Pujari, Bipin Shere and another accomplice. After the murder, Haldankar was caught by a mob and had to be admitted to the JJ Hospital for treatment.

To avenge the death of his brother-in-law, on 12 September 1992, Dawood Ibrahim launched an audacious attack on the JJ Hospital by sending an entire contingent of twenty-four shooters armed with machine guns and revolvers to kill Haldankar. Though he was killed, two policemen also died in the melee. The heat on Dawood Ibrahim only increased after this incident.

As for Hamid Chuha, Dawood was waiting for an opportunity to fix him. That opportunity presented itself to the don only a few months after the JJ Hospital attack. But to trace that story, I would have to meet a source in another part of New Delhi.

16

The Godman

My return to the northern part of the capital brought me to the Swarna Jayanti Park. I was about to meet a man who knew a lot about the D-Company by virtue of being a confidant of Chhota Rajan. Most of Chhota Rajan's men were dead, behind bars or had given up their lives of crime and were trying to lead quiet, legit lives. For days, I had been trying to get a meeting with a former aide of Chhota Rajan who was addressed only as Shetty. He was an old-timer who had been through good and bad times with Rajan and was now running an Indian restaurant in Malaysia.

After days of dilly-dallying, Shetty told me that he was planning to visit Delhi. The timing seemed perfect as my plans to meet Neeraj Kumar in the capital city were already in place.

Shetty was close to Rajan. The latter had chosen him to oversee his affairs in Chembur, Rajan's home base. Rajan had started his underworld career by selling cinema tickets in black in Tilak Nagar, a sprawling middle and lower-middle-class suburb adjoining Chembur. After joining hands with Bada Rajan, Chhota Rajan climbed to the top in a very short time and became the indisputable don who controlled the Chembur–Tilak Nagar suburb unopposed. From dabbling in securing redevelopment projects for his favoured builders in exchange for a sum to erecting ridiculously huge-sized pandals in a show of his enormous wealth and dominance, Rajan's ever-increasing sway in the region would compel even the police force to stay clear of him.

But when Rajan left the country and fled to Dubai, he appointed a few of his minions to act on his behalf in looking after his affairs in the area and maintaining the power he held over its people and businesses. One such person was the man I was going to meet, who was assigned the task of maintaining and organizing the Ganpati pandals along with drawing the extortion money from the people or businesses Rajan would direct him to collect from.

Being an old-timer, he knew about a side of Dawood's personality that had not been covered much in the media. Apparently, Dawood and his family had high regard for certain godmen.

'Religion and crime don't mix well,' I said.

'Who would know this better than Dawood Ibrahim?' my source replied.

Dawood Ibrahim was known to take revenge upon his rivals when they least expected it. Hamid Chuha may have thought that he had pulled a quick one over Dawood's gang by ratting upon Chordia and living to tell the tale.

Chuha was an associate of Dawood, even if not a very close one. That is also one of the reasons Dawood did not spill his blood. Otherwise, the word in the market would be that the D-Company killed one of their own.

'But there are ways to kill a man without spilling his blood,' my source said. 'And the path to finish Hamid Chuha was opened up by an unlikely wish made by another man.'

In the early 1990s, a cavalcade of cars stopped outside the dargah of Amanatullah Peer. A man dressed in a white coat, wearing dark sunglasses and an imported Seiko watch on his wrist stepped out of one of the vehicles and walked into the prickly summer heat. The man's name was Mohammed Hussain Merchant (alias Mohammed Hussain Macchi). His henchmen immediately brought out an umbrella to protect him from the harsh sunlight. Macchi was visiting the dargah to follow up on his *mannat* (wish) that was pending in the darbar of Amanatullah Peer.

Chunabhatti, an industrial area in the central region of Mumbai was the *asthana* of the seer. *Chuna* (Hindi) means lime and *bhatti* means kiln. As such kilns were in abundance in this area, it came to be called Chunabhatti. The first cotton mill in Mumbai, Swadeshi Mills, was located in this area. There were also many small but influential dargahs and shrines in the locality.

Amanatullah Peer, one of the more famous seers, was highly popular among his followers. His sermon was in full swing on that fateful day. Those who believe in the notion of visiting dargahs hold the seers in extremely high regard. Mohammed Hussain Macchi walked into the dargah and Amanatullah Peer recognized him from a distance. An all-knowing smile descended on the sage's face. People would throng the dargah to get their wishes fulfilled. His *mureeds* (followers) came from all areas of the social spectrum. Many top police officials of the day, rich businessmen and even daily wage workers would visit the dargah. Some came to him seeking his influence to get a promotion or preferred position. Some wanted export licences to be cleared. Childless couples would come to the dargah in the hope of gaining an heir to their family. And there was hardly anyone among his visitors who wouldn't be ready to go to any lengths to follow his advice.

But Mohammed Hussain Macchi was seeking Amanatullah Peer's assistance with a rather strange request. He (Macchi) wanted to forge a business partnership with none other than Dawood Ibrahim.

The path was cleared so that Macchi could speak with Amanatullah Peer in the seer's private chamber. Macchi's men placed the electronics and gifts they had brought along at the seer's feet. Macchi himself sat on the floor, whereas Amanatullah Peer sat on the couch while a rosary dangled from his hands. Two of the sage's disciples stood behind him. Macchi kissed Peer's hand as a mark of respect and reverence. Above, a huge ceiling fan rotated slowly.

'Peer sahib,' Macchi said. 'When will my wish get fulfilled?'

Amanatullah Peer took a long pause. 'Good things come to those who wait.'

Then the seer stood up and left. Even Macchi was left confused by the cryptic response, but he did not dare to raise any counter questions. Amanatullah Peer had great influence and power, even in the political circles of the day, across party lines.

During those days, many people wanted to become business partners with Dawood Ibrahim. Having the don on their side assured them of making more money in one day than they would possibly make in their entire lives. Their buildings got easy clearances. Their containers did not attract the eye of the customs department. Extortion in the city was on the rise but those bestowed with 'Bhai's' support were protected from such calls. Macchi knew well that the benefits of allying with Dawood were way too many.

Amanatullah Peer, on the other hand, had access to powerful men. For some reason, even Dawood Ibrahim's family had a lot of reverence for godmen. Whenever a godman visited the Kaskar household, it was not uncommon for the brothers and associates to place him on a high pedestal and afford him the kindest hospitality. So, as a matter of course, Dawood Ibrahim Kaskar and his brothers were also regulars at the Baba's durbar. Macchi knew that only Amanatullah Peer could grant what he was seeking so desperately—a business relationship with Dawood.

It had been a while since Amanatullah had kept Macchi's requests on hold. Naturally, the latter was getting impatient due to the unexplained and seemingly unending delay. However, it was not that the seer was not interested in making Macchi's dream come true. He was only waiting for the right moment. And when it arrived, he caught a flight to Dubai and landed at the don's office.

Dawood was operating from his bungalow in a prime location in the city. The bungalow had swimming pools and a private elevator. Many film stars would also come to meet Dawood at this bungalow. The security was also super tight but adequate arrangements had been made to ensure that Amanatullah Peer did not face any inconvenience during his visit. He was accorded the highest protocol by the D-Company.

Dawood also extended a hearty welcome to the sage in his private cabin and inquired about the pressing problem that had brought him to the UAE.

'Last night, I dreamt of something special,' Amanatullah Peer said.

'What was it, Peer sahib?' Dawood said.

'I dreamt about your new business partner. The two of you had started new businesses which were soaring to great heights. Money was flowing through your coffers, so much that all the banks of the world would not have enough vaults to store your wealth.'

'Really, Hazrat sahib?' Dawood asked. 'You saw me in your dream?'

Amanatullah Peer smiled and nodded.

'Where will I find such a partner?' Dawood said.

'I've already discovered him in Mumbai,' Amanatullah Peer said. 'And his name is Mohammed Hussain Macchi.'

Dawood leaned back in his chair. He promised the seer that he would consider the request and then he bid goodbye to Amanatullah Peer. As soon as the sage left, Chhota Shakeel entered the don's cabin and was surprised to find Dawood smiling in a bemused manner.

'All okay, bhai?' Shakeel asked.

Dawood chuckled. '*Aaj kal main hazrat sahib ke khwab mein aa raha hoon.* (Nowadays, I appear in the dreams of godmen).'

Both men began laughing at this. Notwithstanding his family's reverence towards the sage, Dawood was a very shrewd man. Sometimes, he allowed people to live in the illusion that they were being successful in manipulating and deceiving him if it helped serve his own purpose. In reality, he would allow them to continue believing that, so he could pull the wool over their eyes and end up using them to further his own cause.

He could now sense an opportunity after listening to Mohammad Macchi's case. With a keen desire to expand his swelling empire in other countries, the don was eagerly looking for men who would handle his businesses back in Mumbai and Mohammad Macchi sounded a perfect candidate. Macchi was a well-to-do businessman. He had men and money at his disposal and Dawood was going to need both of these resources to conduct his illegal activities.

As soon as he landed in Mumbai, Amanatullah Peer learnt that Dawood's men had already established contact with Mohammed Hussain Macchi and inducted him into the D-Company. Macchi was on cloud nine now. His wish had finally come true. Little did he know that this partnership was going to land him in big trouble and eventually pave the way for Hamid Chuha's downfall.

17

Volcano of Weapons

I was about to return to Mumbai after a brief stay in Delhi. Neeraj Kumar wanted to drop me to the airport, being the generous host that he has been through these years. As we navigated through the Delhi traffic, Neeraj Kumar brought forth some interesting facets of his life.

'I had no plans of becoming a police officer,' said the man who went on to become the commissioner of police, New Delhi, which is one of the most sought-after postings in the country.

After his MSc from Delhi University, Kumar was egged on by one of his friends to prepare for the UPSC exams. Kumar's preparations for these exams were hampered when his hometown, Patna, was flooded days before the exam. 'My preparation was subpar,' he said.

But on his mother's insistence, Kumar appeared for the exams without even being thoroughly prepared for them. Days later, his uncle purchased a newspaper that had published the names of candidates who had cleared the UPSC exams. Kumar's name was on the list of selected personnel!

'Quite a twist of fate,' Kumar said as the car stopped at a traffic junction.

I noticed that there was a lot of digging and drilling going on around in the city. It reminded me of my home city, Mumbai, which was also perennially dug up. But one never knows what skeletons can be hidden under the ground. Kumar seemed to have noticed my brooding.

'There came a time when a volcano of weapons erupted in Mumbai,' he said. 'Nobody had seen anything like that before.'

In April 1993, police inspectors Kamble and Navghare landed up in the compound of Picnic Guest House, which was located behind a restaurant near Lido Cinema in Santacruz, Mumbai. The guest house had four blocks consisting of about twelve rooms each. The rooms were rented out to couples looking for a few good hours of privacy in the otherwise crowded city.

A five-foot wall was constructed to cover three sides. The two policemen headed straight to the southeast corner and asked their men to start digging. After digging for about three and a half feet, a gunny bag was found. Inside the bag, Kamble and Navghare found six AK-56 rifles and twelve magazines. It appeared as if the weapons had burst out from the ground like the lava of a volcano.

The cops were shocked. After all, it was hardly a month ago, in March 1993, that twelve bomb blasts had been triggered by Dawood's men at well-known landmarks, including the Bombay Stock Exchange, the Juhu Centaur Hotel and the Air India building.

Three men were arrested for their connection to Picnic Guest House. Two of them were Mohammed Hussain Merchant aka Macchi and Hamid Chuha. The third was Mohammed Farooq Yusuf Batki who was the erstwhile tenant of the plot. Macchi had gone to great lengths to forge a partnership with Dawood, whereas Hamid Chuha was also known to the don. But how had these two come to be associated with this plot?

The answer to this question could be traced to the preceding events—the demolition of Babri Masjid in December 1992, after which most of Mumbai was engulfed in communal riots. The streets were filled with rioters shedding blood and burning down houses and offices, one of which happened to be Tiger's Tejarath International.

Tiger's unruly temper was no hidden affair for those who knew him. He had a knack for taking revenge for the pettiest of slights. After his office suffered damage, Tiger was ready to do anything that would bring peace to his vengeful mind and perturbed heart.

Soon after, Anees called Tiger and it was decided that they would avenge the demolition of the masjid, the subsequent riots as well as the burning down of Tiger's office. So, when the planning of the bomb blasts started, Dawood Ibrahim saw an opening and devised a plan to get even with Hamid Chuha, against whom he had held a grudge after the murder of Mahendra Chordia. Dawood suspected that Hamid had played a role in leaking information that had eventually led to Chordia's death.

The story goes that the Picnic Guest House plot was purchased as a benami property by Anees Ibrahim. After Macchi's partnership with Dawood, the don asked Macchi to transfer the plot to his name. Macchi had gone to great lengths to build a business relationship with Dawood. If their partnership was a boon to Macchi in some ways, it was also a bane in many other ways. It was impossible for Macchi to refuse whatever the don would ask him to do. He agreed to take ownership of the plot, not knowing the game that was being played.

Additionally, Yusuf Batki was brought in as a tenant of the property after the plot was vacated. During this period, Mustafa Dossa would also frequently land up in Dubai at the don's darbar. Dawood had a habit of planning and executing his devious schemes along with his associates during their late-night conclaves. He would sleep late, wake up in the late afternoon, and make his way down to the central area of his bungalow where his associates would already be waiting for him.

Dossa would be present each day and he would try to bring the attention of his bosses to his suspicions of Hamid Chuha being a veritable rat, a police informer. Treason in the D-Company was an offence punishable by death. 'A police informer is *wajib-ul-qatl* (mandated to be killed),' Dossa said.

But since Hamid was known to be his associate, Dawood hesitated from getting him executed as it would harm his reputation among his other associates. The bomb blasts, however, were going to give him an opportunity to settle the score with Hamid Chuha too.

So prior to the blasts, Dawood moved the twelve AK-56 rifles and magazines to the compound of the Picnic Guest House and had them buried under the ground. Then he began pressuring Hamid Chuha to take over as the developer of the plot. Hamid was reluctant at first as he did not have much experience as a realtor. But he failed to squeeze himself out of this situation and finally agreed to do the don's bidding.

Macchi then signed an MoU with Hamid and gave him the development rights. He even let go of his site watchman, and Batki and Hamid got a new man for the job. Hamid then submitted a proposal to the BMC (then Bombay Municipal Corporation) for approval of his redevelopment plan. Thus, his name came to be closely associated with this plot. So when the weapons were recovered by the cops, his arrest was inevitable.

The cops' version states that P.I. Kamble and P.I. Navghare arrested Hamid Chuha as they had received credible intelligence that he was suspected to be a part of the conspiracy to illegally smuggle firearms and explosives that were used for the bomb blasts into the country and their distribution and storage. The police had received specific information that Hamid was responsible for smuggling two hundred AK-56 rifles through one vessel near Gujarat. The cops first apprehended him in this matter and when they interrogated him, Hamid revealed the location of the hidden weapons.

But another version is that when Hamid took over the plot, he was unaware that the weapons had already been planted underground by the D-Company. That information was leaked to the cops at Dawood's behest and then they arrested Hamid Chuha after recovery of the weapons.

When Macchi was picked up by the cops in the case, he presented his agreement papers and clarified that he had given development rights to Hamid and that he had no involvement in the plot when the weapons were found. Machchi, however, was in jail for two to three months before coming out. He was given bail in the case, but his passport was seized. Batki was also able to wash his hands off the case and get bail. Hamid emerged as the main accused in the entire case.

Hamid kept insisting that the police should trace the watchman who was working at the site to uncover the truth behind the weapons. But the man was nowhere to be found. Hamid, however, had good connections in the police department. It is said that he would often come out of jail with police escorts who would mention in the logs that they were taking him to trace the watchman. They would go to Panchgani and other places and he would then come back to the prison. Cases were filed against him under the provisions of the TADA Act, 1987. In the past, he had also been prosecuted for smuggling.[1]

In this manner, Dawood was able to fix Hamid Chuha. It was a lesson that the latter wouldn't be able to forget for the rest of his life.

Lido cinema has since gone defunct and other establishments have come up in its place. The city, for better or worse, tends to move on very quickly. I remembered this as I entered the airport to catch a flight back to Mumbai after bidding a temporary goodbye to Neeraj Kumar. The first of our parleys had ended, but more was yet to come.

18

Suburban Drug Lord

After the last meeting in Delhi, Shetty had promised to call me the next time he was in Mumbai. I thought he had made a perfunctory promise before bidding me goodbye, and thus I was surprised when the man kept his word and his number flashed on my phone screen.

We met in Bandra, where the seeds of Rajan's split with Dawood had been laid. The key players involved in the 1993 blasts were living in areas around Bandra and Mahim and were known to Tiger and his associates. Rajan had sworn revenge upon these men, but I was curious to know what had happened behind the scenes.

Shetty basked in the old memories of the days when 'Nana' (the nickname Rajan used to be called by his near ones) would be regarded as the Robin Hood of the area.

'Nana held a good command in the D-Company,' he said. 'But it was pure mayhem since he parted ways with Dawood after the blasts.'

However, a third player who had an interest in the scene happened to move quickly to turn this friends-turned-foes situation to their advantage. Shetty wanted to tell me about that, and I was all ears.

During the mid-1990s, Chhota Rajan was sitting in one of the high rises in Malaysia when he got a call from a handler of an *Agency*. The handler had sent feelers to Rajan through a layer of emissaries and a phone call between the two had been arranged. When the phone was passed to Rajan, he was surprised to find a woman speaking on the other end of the line.

'Yes Madam,' he said. 'My men said you had something important to discuss.'

'What can be more important than revenge?' the woman replied.

Rajan understood. Having broken away from the D-Company after the blasts, Rajan was looking to establish himself as a rival to Dawood Ibrahim who had gained international notoriety by that time. On the other hand, many of Dawood's aides who were involved in the blasts were getting bail from the court because the evidence against them was rather weak or there were enough loopholes in Indian laws that could be exploited to their advantage.

The Agency knew that these men had aided Dawood in the blasts directly or otherwise. They just did not have evidence that would stand in a court of law. Seeing these men walk free was creating an international embarrassment for the Mumbai Police and the CBI. The handler's offer was simple. The Agency would provide money and materials to Rajan to eliminate these men. Rajan would have to run the operations on the ground and put the fear of death in the D-Company.

'Killing Dawood's men is not child's play,' Rajan said. 'Who are you after?'

'Somewhere on the top of our list is Bakhthyar Ahmed Khan,' the handler said. 'Also known as Philoo Khan.'

'But according to my sources,' Rajan said, 'he doesn't have a direct hand in the blasts. At most, he is guilty of being an associate of Tiger and Yeda Yakub.'

'And with Dawood,' the handler said. 'Do I have to remind you that the rocketing sales of Philoo's drugs are filling up Dawood's coffers?'

The mere mention of Dawood's success was enough to set Rajan's blood boiling. After all, Dawood and Shakeel had heaped much humiliation upon him during the last phase of his association with the D-Company.

The Agency's offer suited Rajan. Though he claimed to have separated from his erstwhile boss because of the 1993 bombings, this claim is disputed by many from the D-Company. Chhota Shakeel went on record to say that Rajan was dancing on a yacht on the occasion of Dawood's birthday party on 26 December 1993, a good nine months after the blasts.[1]

I knew that Shakeel had claimed that Rajan ran away from the D-Company on the pretext of a visit to another country for some business and never returned. In fact, some of Shakeel's claims fall in line with the words spoken by the renowned encounter specialist Pradeep Sharma in his interview with a magazine, wherein he was invited to expound upon the famous rift in the gang world.[2] Sharma was the last of the country's encounter specialists, who had 112 encounters registered in his name. He was at the forefront of encounter operations that were initiated in 1994 and went on for a decade during which the Mumbai officials were given free rein to wipe out the scourge of rising organized mafia syndicates.

'The split happened because Chhota Shakeel started to grow powerful in the gang,' Sharma said. 'Shakeel's rise unnerved Rajan. His eventual breaking away from the Dawood group was in keeping with the internal developments. The split of the Dawood gang along religious lines is a myth.'

Sharma was responsible for killing several of Rajan's men in the encounter and was declared as the main accused in the fake encounter case of Chhota Rajan's close aide Lakhan bhaiya. Out of the fourteen cops arrested in the case, Sharma was the only one who was acquitted by the Mumbai Court in 2013.

But according to Shetty, the proposal from the Agency was a divine offering for Rajan to turn public opinion in his favour and warm up to the authorities at the same time. If he killed Dawood's men, he could claim to be a *patriotic* don and dissociate and insulate himself from being implicated in the 1993 bomb blasts. In fact, Rajan had already started to create a public perception of himself as a don rising for the national cause. The remarks such as 'traitors of the nation' and 'betrayers' featured prominently in the statements that he issued in the public domain while describing the perpetrators of the serial bombings. The proposal from the Agency couldn't have come at a better time and Rajan agreed to go after Philoo Khan.

As of date, not many who have known Philoo want to speak about him. Shetty had stayed close to Rajan during the days when Rajan was virtually the second-in-command in the D-Company. This provided him plenty of opportunities to rub shoulders with the lanky Pathan, Bakhtiyar Ahmed Khan aka Philoo Khan. Not many who knew Khan identified him with his real name and would simply address him as 'Philoo'—the nickname that got stuck with him for no specific reason. The occasional but numerous liaisons of Shetty with Philoo left him with enough memories to create a clear portrait of Philoo's life.

Philoo was only nine when his family had fallen upon bad times and were looking to rent out a room. His mother used to work at Topaz, a razor blade company and his father was an athletic Pathan. His brother was a good cricket player who played in the Kanga League.

Shetty was well versed in Philoo's enterprising ways even in his early years. He had heard Philoo on many occasions recalling how, as a young lad, he would be asked by some adult to get a cigarette from the paan shop. Philoo would give the cigarette to the person and slip the change into his pocket. He would spend that change buying eclairs not only for himself but also for his friend Mangesh.

The two boys used to study in the same school in Bandra. Philoo's foray into the world of crime happened because of his association with Mangesh, even before he could realize it. At school, none of them had any inclination towards academics. The kids were mischievous. They would often sneak out of the school during recess and head to Mangesh's home at the police headquarters. Philoo thought that Mangesh's father, a police constable in the Bombay Police, would rebuke them for bunking classes. But the boy was taken aback when Mangesh's father did not reprimand them. Instead, the constable took out a wrapped packet from a drawer in his cupboard and put it in Mangesh's schoolbag. 'Deliver this to Ali Chacha,' he told Mangesh.

Mangesh asked no questions. He had been through this drill several times, but it was a first for Philoo. Though he was a cop, Mangesh's father had dealings with several drug peddlers. He was cutting deals with drug dealers and even helping them distribute small amounts of *charas* (cannabis concentrate) to various retailers. In the late 1970s and early 1980s, the salary of someone low in the police hierarchy did not account for much. Living conditions in the police quarters were also sub-optimum. The smuggling mafia was turning out to be more powerful—they were the ones with imported cars, sea-facing bungalows and tailored suits. In fact, it won't be an overstatement to say that the affluent mafia system was kept sufficiently oiled by the money it acquired through the illegal drug trading business.

Mangesh's father, to supplement his income, would transport drugs through his own child who would take Philoo along on their sojourn to the ghettos of Bandra (East) which were a far cry away from the plush areas of Bandra (West).

Ali Chacha was one of the peddlers on the other side of the suburb. He owned a part of the slums in Khar. Mangesh and Philoo would carry the consignment in their schoolbags and deliver it each time. No cop would ever stop the two children because the plot that two young boys in their school uniforms were delivering small *golis* (balls) of charas instead of going to their tuition classes was indeed unimaginable.

In their early days, Mangesh and Philoo had no idea what they were delivering. But they soon smartened up to the business and realized that there was serious money to be made. Once, Philoo noticed a handsome young man with flowing hair, in a white Fiat, drive to Ali Chacha's *adda* to get his fix. A few days later, he saw the same man's photo on the poster of his debut film. Philoo was mighty impressed. To witness a leading actor of Bollywood frequenting Ali Chacha's place and indulging in drugs was as good as a final verdict for Philoo.

Inheriting a tall frame and handsome features, Philoo was fascinated with the entertainment industry and considered himself no less than any famous and good-looking Bollywood star. There are reports that describe him as possessing excellent acting skills.[3] These skills were the subject of much fascination among his inner circle of friends and acquaintances who wouldn't spare a chance to heap praises upon him whenever he performed in front of them and Mangesh would invariably be found at the head of such admirers.

So, in a way, Philoo and Mangesh grew up in the business of drugs. Philoo was what they called a *tartari bhavra* (wild spinning top) in the lanes of Bandra. He was always restless, wanting to earn money and fame through any means possible. He began peddling around theatres in Bandra and made good money. Reportedly, Philoo was also a huge fan of the reigning superstar of those years and tried to imitate the same angry persona, with long sidelocks and bellbottoms.

Soon, Mangesh and Philoo came into contact with a man whose last name was Biyani. The duo called him Biyani Seth and the man had links with Kashmiri drug dealers who were eager to sell in the city. The Kashmiri *maal* (drugs) was of a far higher grade than what was generally available on the streets. Distributing such high-grade stuff put Philoo and Mangesh leagues ahead of others in this business. They started supplying near areas where they hadn't ventured before. The disco culture was catching up in the city and the duo was often seen outside the dark alleys of the Blue Nile near Sassoon Dock and Studio 29 near Marine Drive.

Philoo would also look for innocuous ways of delivering the stash. Early on, not many of his friends and relatives were aware of his doings. One of his brother's acquaintances owned a Vespa scooter and Philoo would often borrow this scooter on the pretext of 'some work'. Years later, when his brother's acquaintance realized that Philoo's 'work' was actually putting pouches of drugs into the storage compartment of the scooter and delivering them around the city, he swore to never let Philoo come within an inch of his vehicle.

Philoo and Mangesh also began supplying at Caesar's Palace, which was located at Linking Road and owned by two brothers who would later make a foolhardy attempt to cross swords with Dawood Ibrahim and the D-Company. The owners were none other than Mahesh and Arvind Dholakia, and Caesar's Palace was nothing short of a sinner's paradise. The hotel had a disco named Cleo, and apparently, every vice was available there for a price. It was said to be one of the joints where strip dancers would perform for rich men in private settings. The discotheque, however, was closed when the police, after a series of attempts at finding concrete evidence against the club, were able to raid the premises and round up twenty-eight prostitutes.

The elder of the two brothers, Arvind Dholakia, and two managers were also arrested. Things went downhill for the Dholakias from there on. In 1987, the younger brother, Mahesh Dholakia, was shot dead by a posse of at least six men who shot him ten times in his chest from point-blank range at a place barely 200 metres away from their apartment at Peddar Road. The police theorized that the murder, which bore all the evidence of a gangland slaying, came as a retaliation to Babu Reshim's killing, which took place in a police lock-up earlier in March. The Dholakia family, however, rubbished all such claims that connected them to the underworld and denied having ever been involved in the smuggling business.

As their business began booming, Philoo and Mangesh met Iqbal Mirchi, who would go on to become one of the biggest drug lords in the subcontinent. They had hit the jackpot and cash was raining down from the skies for them. During those days, Philoo had proudly proclaimed to one of his elderly neighbours, whom he called Chacha, that he was a man worth Rs 2 crore. 'Dekho Uncle,' he had said with a smug smile, *'main do khoke ka aadmi ban gaya!'*

This chacha, who had learnt of Philoo's misdeeds and always exhorted him to renounce the path of evil, plainly warned him to stop right there and mend his ways while there was still time.

'A life of crime is only good while it lasts,' Chacha told him.

But Philoo was a reckless and temperamental man who was in no mood to slow down. Little did Philoo Khan know that his flight was about to crash in a manner that he could never have imagined.

19

Trapped in Thailand

A couple of men arrived to meet Shetty at the restaurant where we were having our discussions. One of them sported a bushy moustache while the other had a lean frame.

Shetty moved to a corner where they had an animated discussion that lasted only a few minutes. Then, they left. There was no exchange of material. That may have been reserved for another day, another time. Shetty came back and there was a certain spring in his step. He was charged up. I didn't ask him why. But he was eager to tell me how Rajan had trapped one of the smartest underworld operators in Thailand. It turned out to be an interesting story of friendship and betrayal.

Philoo's introduction to the D-Company happened due to a rather interesting incident. His exploits were garnering attention in criminal circles. Soon, even the cops began hearing about the young man. Once, Philoo was returning after delivering a consignment to one of his retailers near Linking Road when he was stopped by a couple of policemen led by Inspector Shaikh near a traffic signal. Philoo was caught completely off guard.

'Move your vehicle to the side of the road,' Shaikh said.

'Please sir,' Philoo said, 'I have to go to the hospital to meet an ailing relative.'

'Really?' Shaikh said. 'Is he suffering from addiction to the drugs you peddle?'

The constables flanked Philoo as he moved his scooter (which he had borrowed from another of his unsuspecting acquaintances) to the side of the road. They searched the entire vehicle, including the storage in the front and under the seat. They were unaware that he had already made the delivery and the vehicle was not loaded with narcotics at that time. However, Shaikh's instincts did not let Philoo off the hook so easily.

'Pat him down,' Shaikh told his men.

The constables conducted a physical search on Philoo during which they found a small quantity of powder in the pocket of his trousers, which was for his personal consumption. Shaikh took Philoo into custody and put him in the lock-up.

Philoo's arrest sent his colleagues into a frenzy. They started mobilizing their resources to ensure that their ringleader would get out of trouble soon. One of the newer acquaintances that Philoo had made had a direct line to Dubai, and managed to establish contact with none other than Dawood Ibrahim to request the don's intervention in getting their boy out of jail. Dawood, who had heard of Philoo's rise from other sources, was also interested in him.

Dawood used his sources and managed to get a *rafa-dafa* (no action taken) on the case. Since the quantity of narcotics recovered from Philoo was small, the cops let him go, thinking that he was nothing more than a hyped-up newbie. But Philoo had grown way bigger than the cops could have imagined. After his release, Philoo was indebted to Dawood for his intervention and an association began brewing between the two. He began working for the big don.

Though Philoo's association with the D-Company began growing by leaps and bounds, he was not averse to hobnobbing with Dawood's enemies too. He was a frequent visitor to an apartment of Malad Khan in D.N. Nagar. Malad was a close associate of Samad Khan, who was Karim Lala's nephew and involved in a heavy rivalry with Dawood Ibrahim and his brother Sabir. During his visits to D.N. Nagar in Versova, Philoo became romantically involved with Malad's stepdaughter and they soon got married.

Philoo was making big money and rented an apartment in Bandra where a famous Bollywood hero once lived. However, Philoo's temperamental nature often put him in conflict with others. He would bash up people for merely looking at him (or his wife) in a manner he didn't approve of. He had also begun carrying a weapon, a gun, which he often used to scare people.

He purchased a second house in Yari Road. Drug barons of those times often settled into peripheral areas to keep away from the cops. Though it may be one of the most happening places in the city these days, there was not much police presence in Yari Road during those years as the area was considered far-flung.

To purchase some material that was required for civil repair in the house, Philoo went to a shop along with the contractor whom he had hired for the work. The contractor gave a list of materials that were needed, and the supplier prepared a bill. Philoo asked for a discount from the supplier.

'Sir,' the shopkeeper said. 'There is no scope for a discount. I have already provided you with the *best* rate.'

'Okay,' Philoo said. 'No problem.'

Smiling like a gentleman, he put his hand in his pocket and pulled out his wallet and gun at the same time. He placed the gun on the supplier's counter and started counting the currency notes to make the payment. 'How much did you say I have to pay?' he asked, innocuously.

By now, the shopkeeper had seen the weapon and understood Philoo's subtle message. He was shivering from head to toe. He agreed to give a hefty discount to Philoo, who had a good laugh when he was out of the shop. He enjoyed putting fear into people.

Despite being a rich man, Philoo was always ready to fight even over a matter of Rs 500. This would often lead to many petty quarrels that he always managed to dominate with his aggressive personality.

Another time, Philoo and his wife were out for a walk when a few boys from the area happened to pass them. Philoo felt that one of the boys had cast a second glance at his wife. Soon, an argument broke out. Though the group of boys had the advantage of numbers, Philoo was not the kind who would back down easily. He pulled out his gun and fired a round in the air that sent his opponents running helter-skelter. This caused quite a scandal and again Philoo was arrested. But thanks to an influential lawyer hired by the D-Company, he was able to get out of jail quickly.

Things blew out of control when his name began cropping up in the investigations of the 1993 bombings in Mumbai. Tiger Memon, the chief conspirator and executioner of the blasts, lived in Mahim. Many of his associates who participated in the blasts also lived in the same area or around Bandra. Philoo, having grown up and operated in Bandra, was also known to Tiger and his associates.

When the blasts were being planned, Tiger was supported by Yeda Yakub, who helped him store the RDX in the godowns owned by his brother and Majid Khan. The latter used to run a construction company by the name of M.K. Builders. He was on good terms with several cops as he was in charge of clearing slum dwellers and other small house owners from the land, which would then come into the possession of builders who would construct tall towers for the rich in those parcels.

Yakub was also a highly temperamental man whose anger bordered on insane levels. For this reason, he was nicknamed *Yeda*, i.e. mad man. Yakub and Philoo were on decent terms during their early days but fell out over some trivial manner and their oversized egos. Things came to a point where Yakub wanted to beat Philoo to death.

When the blasts were being planned, Tiger called Philoo and Yakub to a popular restaurant in the suburbs and brokered peace between them. Yakub went on to play a key role in the blasts, which put the cops on his trail. When he had gone absconding, his brother and sister-in-law (Majid Khan's wife) were also picked up by the police and questioned at length. To lose some heat, Yakub brought up the subject of Philoo's association with Tiger to DCP Arup Patnaik. He was trying to negotiate a way out for himself and his family. Yakub's resentment also stemmed from the fact that he believed that Philoo had instigated the cops against him.

As DCP Zone VII, Patnaik was also involved in the investigations of the blasts during which he made the largest-ever seizure of RDX, to the tune of 1500 kg at Mumbra in 1993.

After Yakub put the cops on Philoo's trail, the latter was in deep trouble. The Mumbai Police started hunting for him as well as Mangesh. The cops would show up at his home and several of his properties came under the scanner. Philoo went underground and managed to evade arrest. Still, he continued operating his business through the men he had recruited. His family also started feeling the heat, and his siblings began moving their residences to Europe and North America.

Moving away from Mumbai put the relationship between Mangesh and Philoo under strain. The strong bond that had once existed between the two friends was now tied with sinewy threads. When their business was small, they always looked out for each other and protected each other's interests. But as the business grew beyond borders, to countries like Thailand, both of them started feeling that they were being short-changed by the other. As a result, they began double-crossing and cutting into each other's shares. Mangesh would eat up Philoo's pie in some deals and vice versa.

Once, Philoo was supposed to distribute a big consignment to their dealers. Mangesh called up Philoo and asked him for an update.

'Bad news, brother,' Philoo said. 'The bloody cops confiscated the entire consignment.'

'What are you saying?!' Mangesh said.

'Nothing but the truth.'

Mangesh sensed that Philoo was speaking anything but the truth, though he didn't let Philoo catch on to his feelings. And his fears came true a few months later when Mangesh ran into the dealer and apologized for not being able to make the delivery of the maal.

'Didn't your partner Philoo inform you?' the dealer told Mangesh. 'He delivered the consignment a few weeks later. I also paid him in full. Hard cash.'

Mangesh was shocked. He understood that Philoo had delayed the deliveries for a few weeks while informing Mangesh that the deliveries were not done because the consignment had been confiscated by the cops. Mangesh was livid that his friend, whom he had introduced to the business, was trying to outsmart him. He swore to teach Philoo a lesson he would never forget.

News of the brewing rift between Philoo and Mangesh reached Chhota Rajan. As per the mission that had been assigned to him by the Agency, Rajan was looking to eliminate Philoo. Mangesh seemed like the perfect chink in Philoo's armour. In 1994, Rajan decided to approach Mangesh and was able to strike a rapport with him. Rajan even brought up the subject of the bomb blasts that had divided the Mumbai mafia on communal lines and came up with a daring plan to eliminate Philoo.

As per Rajan's plan, Mangesh flew down to Bangkok where Rajan had already assembled a team that included sharpshooter Vilas Mane. From Bangkok, Mangesh contacted Philoo and asked him to come over on the pretext that he had found a new party that was interested in doing business with them. Philoo was anyway on the run from the Mumbai Police and thought it would be a good idea to spend some time in Bangkok until matters cooled down.

Still, Philoo kept his cards close to his chest and arranged for his own stay rather than letting Mangesh book a hotel for him. On the decided day, Philoo met Mangesh where the latter was staying. The two friends shared a few drinks and reminisced about the old times. Mangesh drank in moderation while egging Philoo to consume more. The alcohol lowered Philoo's defences.

'But where is the person who wanted to strike a deal with us?' Philoo asked.

'He'll be here any minute,' Mangesh said.

Just then, the doorbell rang. As a last gesture, Mangesh patted Philoo's cheek before he stood up to open the door. The messengers of Philoo's death had arrived. Philoo was shocked on seeing Vilas Mane and his boys. But he could hardly stand up. He was quickly overpowered, and his weapons confiscated. 'Get out of the room,' Vilas told Mangesh. 'Your eyes won't be able to bear the sight of the blood of your childhood friend.'

Philoo looked at Mangesh, and the latter could not match his gaze. Mangesh lowered his head and exited the room, closing the door behind him. Vilas and his men tortured Philoo for eight long hours. By the time Vilas was done, Philoo's body was not even in a recognizable state.

The boy from Bandra who went on to become a feared drug lord met his end in a tiny room in Bangkok.

Dawood was livid when he heard the news of Philoo's killing. He often used to refer to Philoo as 'darling', a term of endearment he was known to use only for those whose guts he admired the most. Dreaded sharpshooter Feroz Konkani was another, for whom Dawood used the same moniker. The don was keen to avenge the death of one of his favourites. Years later, the D-Company tracked down Mangesh in South Africa and killed him. In December 2000, Vilas Mane was killed in an encounter with the Mumbai Police by DCP Dashrath Awhad. He was thirty-five years old.

In the same year, Dawood had also received inputs of Rajan staying in Bangkok. He zeroed in on the location and hatched a plan to get rid of the mini menace once and for all. Chhota Shakeel volunteered to lead the mission. Posing as pizza delivery boys, Dawood's men gained entry into the room Rajan was staying in along with one of his close aides, Rohit Varma. But luck seemed to be on Rajan's side as he managed to dodge the attacks and make an escape at the expense of Varma's death.

In March 2016, in their continued efforts to crack down on Dawood's men, the Mumbai Crime Branch arrested Nadeem Ghulam Mistry. Absconding for nearly two decades, Mistry was one of the key members of the D-Company who is said to have worked closely with Philoo. The cops tracked him down to Gujarat and arrested him in Vadodara. Mistry was arrested for jumping bail in a case where he, along with Philoo and Mangesh, had fired on a man known as Haji in 1990. It was one of the cases that Philoo was wanted in. The Crime Branch had received inputs that Mistry was staying with his family in Vadodara, where he worked as a real estate agent.

The police, in its statement following the arrest, said that Mistry was a close associate of Philoo Khan, a trusted aide of Dawood who had put the latter in charge of the illegal drug business he controlled from Dubai.[1] The police added that Philoo was also wanted in various cases of assaulting the police.

Decades after his death, Bakhtiyar Ahmed Khan alias Philoo is still remembered as one of the top members of Dawood's huge narcotics empire. His murder was among the early ones in a series of killings and counter-killings between Chhota Rajan and Dawood Ibrahim. The war between the two dons had just begun.

20

Shoot-Out at Bandra

Shetty went to great lengths to explain how Chhota Rajan escaped from the Samitivej Hospital in Bangkok where he was admitted following the attack by the D-Company. One of Rajan's top shooters, Rohit Verma, died while protecting him. Such was the brutality of the attack that the age-old principle of keeping family members away from bloodshed was thrown to the dogs and Rohit Verma's wife also died in the attack.

The Thai Police were guarding Rajan at the hospital around the clock.

'One of my community brothers played a key role in the escape,' Shetty said. He was referring to Santosh Shetty, former aide turned foe of Chhota Rajan.

Apparently, Santosh Shetty, Bharat Nepali and Farid Tanasha had flown to Thailand to help Chhota Rajan escape from the hospital. It seemed like there were greater forces at work. How else could one explain how a man who was guarded round the clock, for whose extradition a team had been sent by the Government of India, managed to escape by climbing down a rope from the hospital room window?

Even Chhagan Bhujbal, then deputy chief minister of Maharashtra, was questioned by the press on Rajan's escape. He had politely asked them to direct the question to the then Central home minister, L.K. Advani. 'The Central government was dealing with Thai authorities,' Bhujbal had said.

'Nevertheless,' Shetty said, 'Rajan managed to move out of Singapore and was eager to resume the war with Dawood.'

For the next target, the handler from the Agency called Rajan, who was then holed up in Iran.

'Who is it this time?' Rajan asked.

'Hanif Kadawala,' the handler said.

'Oh yes,' Rajan replied. 'I don't like his movies anyway.'

On 7 February 2001, Hanif Kadawala was going about his business despite his particularly pensive mood. Of late, he had been receiving extortion calls from Rajan's men. Reportedly, he had also paid them for getting off his case, but the waters of the underworld had turned so murky that no one could be trusted. Kadawala had good reason to be worried.

He was accused of providing assistance to Tiger Memon in storing and transporting explosives that were used in the 1993 blasts. He was arrested on 16 April 1993, and spent five years in jail before getting bail in 1998. However, freedom proved to be a double-edged sword for him. Inside the walls of the jail, he was safe and surrounded by policemen. Outside those walls, he was fair game for Rajan, who had already displayed his prowess by taking out Philoo Khan in 1994 and Thakiyuddin Wahid in 1995.

Still, Kadawala was trying to get back into the movie business where he had made his mark. His office was situated at Orbit Corporation, on the third floor of the Vaz bungalow at Bandra. The popular Gaiety-Galaxy cinema was also located nearby, where several of Hanif's movies had run to houseful shows earlier.

As he parked in his assigned parking space, Hanif called the actor whom he wanted to cast in his new movie. His call went unanswered. 'Bloody bastards,' he muttered. 'There was a time they would give an arm and leg for a cameo in my films.'

Besides being in the movie business, Hanif and his family also owned a restaurant in the suburbs which was popular among the students of plush colleges located in the vicinity. But the blasts had rendered Kadawala a persona non grata. No actor wanted to be seen around him. He produced two movies along with his partner Sameer Hingora: *Dil Hi Toh Hai* in 1992 and *Sanam* in 1997 starring Jackie Shroff and Sanjay Dutt, respectively.

During the riots that followed the demolition of the Babri Masjid, mobs were running rampant through the city. Sanjay Dutt, whose family had received several threats for organizing aid for riot victims, wanted to procure a few weapons for his own protection.

When arms and ammunition were being transported through the city before the blasts, two cars were diverted to Dutt's house at different times at the behest of Hanif and Samir. Each time, Dutt retained a few weapons and the cars then continued towards their next destination. It was Hanif and Samir who had named Dutt in the case after their own names had surfaced in the investigation of the blasts. Dutt's conviction and imprisonment followed after the duo's arrest in April 1993. Hanif was released on bail in 1998.

Five years after he last produced a movie, Hanif wanted to revive his film production business but his thoughts were overshadowed by one man—Rajendra Sadashiv Nikalje aka Chhota Rajan, the man who was fast gaining public sympathy by eliminating the accused of the blasts. And Hanif was one of *them*.

When Hanif walked into his office, his workers noticed a strange apprehension on his face. It was not normal, and Hanif was not speaking about it to anybody. Furrows on his forehead surfaced again. He was anxious and scared that something bad or unpleasant would happen.

Whispers were already doing the rounds that Indian agencies were handpicking the targets of the blasts and assigning the kills to Rajan for plausible deniability in the court. By the time Hanif settled in his chair and was greeted by his assistant, Jafar, the thought of producing a new movie was eclipsed by the fear of death. Amidst all the chaos in his mind, three men came to Hanif's office around 12.30 p.m. Jafar could not sniff anything suspicious from the way they entered the office. They stopped at the reception. Their leader introduced himself as Yusuf.

'We want to meet Hanif bhai,' Yusuf told Jafar. 'We have a car deal to discuss.'

Jafar used the newly installed intercom to connect to Hanif's cabin. 'Yusuf has come to meet you with two others in connection with a car deal.'

'Bugger's been calling me for days,' Hanif replied. 'Send them in after five minutes.'

Two of the three men entered Hanif's cabin while one man stood at the door like a guard. Jafar was confused as to why the man was guarding the door of Hanif's cabin if they had really come to discuss a deal. Before he could make any sense of it, Jafar heard three *thak-thak* sounds.

His blood froze. Shakil Ahmad, the other attendant, and Jafar looked at each other. They realized what had occurred. The man who had stood guard at the door pulled out a gun and aimed it at them. 'If you twitch even one muscle, I'll blow your brains out,' he said.

Jafar and Shakil Ahmed knew the drill. They raised their hands to signify surrender. Then the three assailants made their way out of the office. Yusuf warned them that they would meet the same fate as their boss if they tried to follow them. Jafar and Shakil ran towards Hanif's cabin. Their boss's cabin, for the first time, looked like a haunted room of an ancestral *haveli*. Cold, with no movement from Hanif's body. The smell of gunpowder was still fresh.

Both of them could not see Hanif from the entrance of the cabin. Jafar made the brave step of moving further into the room and sneaked towards the other end of the table. The shirt Hanif had worn was soaked in red. Hanif bhai was lying in a pool of blood near the table from where he used to run an empire worth crores of rupees.

Jafar gathered his bearings and called Hanif's elder brother, Farooq Kadawala. Jafar could not explain what had happened at Hanif's office, he was only blabbering and all his efforts to sound coherent were coming to naught. It took a few curses for Farooq to make Jafar reveal what had happened.

'They killed Hanif bhai!' he blurted.

Farooq was shocked. He asked his son Asif to call for an ambulance at Hanif's office. Asif did not know his uncle was killed but the fear on his father's face prompted no questions. He immediately called for an ambulance.

Both Farooq and Asif left for Hanif's office. Farooq told Asif what had happened while they were running through the city traffic in their car. They reached the Vaz bungalow before the ambulance could. Farooq did not wait for the elevator, he made his way into Hanif's office on the third floor running up the stairs.

Farooq joined the sobbing Jafar and Shakil and lifted Hanif from the ground. His body was riddled with the entry and exit wounds of multiple bullets. They rushed Hanif to Bhabha Hospital where the medical officer declared him dead. All of Farooq's hopes vanished after the official confirmation from the doctor. The news of Hanif Kadawala's murder soon spread like wildfire.[1] News channels started flashing the 'breaking news'.

Senior Police Inspector Subhash Dattaram Jadhav, Inspectors Rauf Shaikh and Pandurang Bhargude along with other police officers of Bandra Police Station reached the hospital and met Hanif's family and colleagues. They also sent Hanif's body for a post-mortem. A police team visited the crime scene at Vaz bungalow to collect evidence. Two pairs of spectacles, diaries of the deceased and blood samples were collected from the spot. These were sent for chemical analysis at the Forensic Science Lab (FSL) located in Kalina, Mumbai.

The police began tracking the men behind the murder. From his two-storeyed villa in one of the posh residential areas of Bangkok, Rajan had assigned the task of eliminating Kadawala to one of his top henchmen, a shooter who went by the name of Yusuf Bachkana. Though *bachkana* meant 'child-like' in Mumbai's streetsmart lingo, there was no child-like innocence in Yusuf's behaviour. He was nothing but pure evil.

As Chhota Rajan's primary hitman, who would later go on to switch sides and start working for the gangster Ravi Pujari, Yusuf Bachkana is believed to have eliminated several members of Dawood Ibrahim's gang in Mumbai, including Kaliya (murdered in 1998), Devi Prasad Hegde (in 1999), Dawood Ibrahim's financiers Sohail Rizvi (in 1999) and Mutalik Patel (at Bandra Railway Station in 1999). But Hanif Kadawala was a bigger fish than all of them.

'*Ho jayega bhai*,' Yusuf had assured Rajan on the phone when the latter had given him Hanif's *supari* (contract killing), confirming that the job would be done. Yusuf recruited Jagannath Balkarn Jaiswal aka Deshmukh, Ashok Kotiyan aka Shetty and Nitin Ramchandra Sawant for the job. Then Yusuf went about establishing contact with Hanif Kadawala. Coming from a wealthy family, Kadawala was fond of cars and Yusuf contacted him on the pretext of arranging a top-end car for him. Hanif let his guard down and ended up dead in a government hospital.

After Hanif's post-mortem, the Bandra Police booked a case based on a complaint filed by Shakil, one of the employees, who was also an eyewitness of the crime. ACP Subhash Jadhav of the Bombay Police led the investigation into the matter.

During the investigation, ACP Jadhav unravelled the involvement of the organized crime syndicate in the offence and proposed invoking the Maharashtra Control of Organized Crime Act. Introduced in 1999, the MCOCA provides the state government special powers to tackle organized crime and terrorism. The widespread powers provided to the cops under this act include surveillance, relaxed evidentiary standards and procedural safeguards, and prescribing additional criminal penalties, including the death penalty.

Jadhav named Jaiswal, Sawant and Shetty in his chargesheet. Following Yusuf's arrest, he was also charged in the case. Shakil, who had filed the police complaint, was then called to Kalyan Jail for the identification parade of the arrested accused. Shakil had received the notice from the police a couple of times. He had skipped the earlier notices as he was nervous about being in the midst of notorious criminals and those who killed his boss. He was also scared for his life as he believed identifying the accused might sabotage his family's security.

After much insistence from Hanif's family, Shakil agreed and finally reached Kalyan Jail. He was nervous, anxious and edgy. He walked into the jail escorted by a group of policemen, but he did not want to get identified by these criminals at the jail. He used his handkerchief to sneakily cover his face whenever he came across an inmate or a constable who could have been bribed by Rajan's men to leak his details.

Shakil thought he would have to come face-to-face with the accused and identify them. But, much to his relief, he was made to stand behind a blind spot from where nobody could see him but he could see the accused lined up in a room inside the jail premises.

When he saw Jagannath Jaiswal at the jail, lined up for the identification, he felt more nervous. He went into deep thought. He had to take the call to identify him or let it go. He took a deep breath and thought of all the good things Hanif bhai had done for him and his family.

'*Yeh aadmi tha sahab! Yahi andar gaya tha sahab ke office mein* (He is the one, sir! He had gone inside Hanif Kadawala's cabin).' Shakil's loyalty to Hanif bhai prevailed over his fears and insecurities. But would his testimony stand the scrutiny of the defence lawyers? And what new twists would this case throw up? Those were crucial questions that would be answered soon.

21

A Long Trial

I told Shetty about the time I had got involved in Hanif's case, despite my reluctance to be a part of it. 'Chhota Rajan Picks off Blasts Accused like Flies' was the headline of an article I had written for Rediff.com under the pseudonym of Jake Khan in April 2001, merely months after Hanif Kadawala's murder.[1]

These were the years of the dot-com boom. The Internet bubble had ushered in a new era and Rediff was one of India's earliest Internet portals modelled after the US's very own Yahoo!. I had written the article under a pseudonym as I was employed with another national newspaper at that time.

As a part of my journalistic duties, I interviewed Chhota Rajan a few years before he was attacked in Bangkok by Chhota Shakeel's men. This may sound sacrilegious to the public, but interviewing criminals is a professional necessity in the realm of crime reporting. Though the Mumbai mafia has produced quite a few dons, Dawood Ibrahim and Chhota Rajan are considered to be the two who fought for the top spot. Chhota Shakeel has given interviews to many TV journalists. Rajan had also done the same. I had already interviewed Dawood in the late 1980s and then it was time for an interview with his ex-aide turned arch-enemy.

I sent messages to Rajan through his emissaries and waited for a response. For days, there was nothing. Radio silence. And then, one day I got a call from one of Rajan's men that he would speak with me around midnight. I waited in my office and then called at the scheduled time. The phone passed hands a few times before Rajan came on the line. He was vocal about his objective, or at least the perception he wanted to create.

'I have vowed to kill those traitors who were involved in the blasts even if the courts have granted them bail.''

'Why are you targeting them?' I asked.

'To convey the message that such a thing should never be repeated. Nobody should ever dare to orchestrate another round of explosions in the country. Getting bail does not mean that they have been sufficiently punished. Justice means an eye for an eye, a tooth for a tooth and a life for a life. Nothing less than death could be the retribution for the blasts accused.'

'How many people are you going to kill?'

'My hit list has about forty key persons involved in the blasts,' he said. 'I will get them, come what may.'

He kept his promises until he was attacked in Bangkok in 2000. Fifteen years later, Chhota Rajan was arrested from Bali in October 2015 after the Australian Police tipped off the authorities that he had boarded a flight from Sydney. The CBI had issued a Red Corner Notice (RCN) against Rajan in 1995 and has been on the lookout for him ever since.

An RCN is a request to law enforcement agencies worldwide to locate and provisionally arrest a person pending extradition, surrender or similar legal action. Rajan had always been on the run after the attack on him by the D-Company in 2000. The death of his top lieutenants Rohit Varma (in 2000) and Farid Tanasha (in 2010) had also virtually finished off his gang.

The CBI began coordinating with international agencies for Rajan's return to India. As such, all cases against Rajan were transferred to the CBI, including the Hanif Kadawala murder case.

Rajan was named as accused number five in this case. He was represented by senior advocate Sudeep Pasbola, who is known to be one of the sharpest criminal lawyers in the country. He has represented many high-profile cases involving murder, organized crime and even political activities.

In Rajan's defence, Pasbola stated to the court that the don was not involved in the murder of Hanif Kadawala in any manner whatsoever. During the attack in Bangkok in 2000, Rajan suffered injuries on his stomach and thighs and was subsequently admitted to Samitivej Hospital located on Sukhumvit Road in Vadhana, Bangkok. He was operated on twice during that period. On 28 November 2011, Rajan escaped from the hospital. It is alleged that professional mountain climbers were hired by his gang to help Rajan slide down from the window of the fourth floor of the hospital, nearly 40 metres. How Rajan managed to pull off this act despite his grave injuries and considerable police presence in the hospital is beyond anyone's imagination (or maybe it is anyone's guess).

After the escape, Rajan was shuttling between Cambodia and Singapore and finally landed in Iran. Pasbola argued that due to the ongoing conflict in Iran, it was not possible for Rajan to contact anyone and plan the conspiracy for Kadawala's murder. He claimed that Rajan had been framed in the murder by his enemies.

Another twist in the tale came through a completely different angle that ultimately benefited Rajan. Prosecution witness number 18, CBI officer Natram Meena, had recorded the confession of Yusuf Bachkana, who was the main shooter in the attack on Kadawala. There was also a voice recording of Bachkana claiming that the murder of Hanif Kadawala was committed at the insistence of his elder brother, Farooq Kadawala!

Farooq was the same brother whom Shakil and Jaffar had first called after the murder, and who had taken Hanif to Bhabha Hospital. Many years later, Fahad, the son of Hanif Kadawala, filed an application in court seeking direction to the cops to charge his uncle, Farooq, as an accused in the murder case. However, nothing much came out of this application.

Much of the prosecution's case was based on the statement of one person, i.e. Shakil Ahmed Shaikh, who was designated as prosecution witness number 10. Besides Shakil, all other witnesses in the case were police witnesses whose testimony could not decisively turn the case in the prosecution's favour as the testimony of an independent witness holds greater value.

In December 2020, I also received a request from the CBI to depose as a prosecution witness in the Hanif Kadawala murder case on account of having written several articles around the subject of Rajan's killing streak of the bomb blasts accused. My protests that my statement would have no direct impact on the case fell on deaf ears. Yet, I visited the court, answered the questions I was asked and returned home, knowing where the case was eventually headed.

The defence lawyers for the accused then focused on dismantling Shakil's statement so that the prosecution's case would come crashing down.

Shakil had been working for the Kadawala family since 1998, starting at the restaurant. The defence lawyers pointed out that there were contradictions in Shakil's statement. At times, he had stated that Hanif had called all three men, who visited the Orbit office, into his cabin. At times, he stated that only two people went inside. Also, in his first statement, Shakil claimed that after Hanif's family arrived at the site, all of them had taken the body to Bhabha Hospital. But during the cross-examination, Shakil claimed that he did not know which hospital Hanif was taken to and he came to know the name of the hospital much later. This meant that he was not involved in taking the deceased to the hospital.

Out of the two people who had gone inside Hanif's cabin, Shakil was unable to say which of them had finally gone inside Hanif Kadawala's cabin and who was standing outside.

Shakil was also the one who had identified the accused Jagannath Jaiswal at Kalyan Jail. There were discrepancies about the location where the identification parade was conducted. In one statement, it was claimed that the parade was conducted in Kalyan Jail. But in another statement, he stated that he was called for the parade on 2 November 2001 at Adharwadi Jail, Thane.

Prosecution witness number 2, Aslam Karim Mansoori, a special executive officer, who held the test identification parade, was cross-examined by Advocate D.S. Manerkar. The lawyer was representing the accused, Jagannath Jaiswal. By that time, the trial had already stretched for many years.

'Do you remember which accused was identified by Shakil during the parade?' the lawyer asked.

'Eighteen years have passed,' Mansoori said. 'I do not remember it now.'

'Can you describe the dummies who were part of the parade?'[2]

Mansoori shook his head. Dummies were essentially other men who were put in the parade so that the court could be sure that a witness had clearly identified an accused from a crowd, leaving no doubt about their identity. However, given the nature of Mansoori's responses, there was reason to believe that the guidelines for conducting an identification parade issued by the high court had not been duly followed.

Dy SP Sudam Sadhu Rakhpasare had recorded the memorandum statement of accused Jagannath Jaiswal in another case filed at Dombivali Police Station. At that time, Jaiswal had voluntarily disclosed that the firearms used in that offence were kept at his house at Juchandra Pada. Accordingly, the cops visited the house at Juchandra Pada and recovered three .9 mm pistols, one .455 mm revolver, two magazines and eight live cartridges. The public prosecutor had argued that the same weapons were used for the murder of Hanif Kadawala.

However, the defence argued that Jagannath Jaiswal was acquitted by the Special Court at Thane in the trial held in respect of Crime no. 203 of 2001 registered with the Dombivali Police Station. That raised the question of which weapons were sent to the FSL for analysis and which weapons were seized from Jaiswal. Thus, the weapons used in the murder could not be decisively linked to Jaiswal.

Through their manoeuvres, the defence lawyers were able to create sufficient space for doubt. And in any legal case, the benefit of the doubt always favours the accused. Jaiswal and Chhota Rajan were acquitted from the case on 22 April 2021, whereas Yusuf Bachkana had already been acquitted in 2004.

Rajan's string of acquittals in criminal cases continued. The Mumbai Police had listed seventy-one cases against Rajan, which were transferred to the CBI on 21 November 2015. By April 2021, the CBI had already filed closure reports in forty-six of such cases before the respective special MCOCA and magistrate courts set up to try the gangster.

Pradeep Gharat, the prosecutor who had also represented the CBI in the Kadawala case, stated that several cases against Rajan had been closed because it was not possible to trace witnesses and collect further evidence. The complainants had either died or were not traceable.

Collecting primary evidence like the call data records of the accused involved was also impossible. Thus, the agency had filed for closure of these cases.

Rajan's lawyer claimed this as a victory for the don. He claimed that Rajan was not at all involved in these cases, and could not clear his name as he was out of the country. 'After his return to India,' the lawyer said, '*facts* became evident, and it was found that he was not involved.' But as it is said, sometimes, facts are stranger than fiction.

22

The Mad Man's Brother

My conversation with Shetty shifted to another character from Bandra, one who was temperamental to the point of insanity. This man was none other than Haji Yakub, also known as Yeda Yakub. In Mumbai slang, *yeda* means a crazy man. A seemingly calm man, Yakub had the tendency to fly into a rage at the slightest provocation. It was as if there were two personalities living inside him.

'Tiger used Yeda Yakub effectively,' Shetty said.

Tiger knew that the huge dump of explosives sent from Pakistan to Mumbai would need to be stored in the city. Yakub proved his utility when he made the requisite arrangements to hide the RDX in the godowns of his brother, Majid Khan, who owned M.K. Builders. Yakub's involvement in the blasts was largely proven. As for Majid, he had managed to secure bail after being charged in the case. Yakub, on the other hand, fled to Pakistan along with his associates.

'But little did Yakub know that his kin would have to pay the price for his crimes,' I said.

In the early 1990s, the streets of Mumbai had turned into a battleground. Gangsters were fighting gangsters. Cops were fighting the gangs. Communities were fighting with each other. It seemed like everyone was fighting everyone. The air was thick with tension as rival gangs fought for control of the lucrative markets that could fill their coffers. Sometimes, the reasons *appeared* to be beyond the financial ones, though that perception could have very well been an altered version of reality. Each day brought news of one brutal killing after another. By the turn of the century, things had blown up into an all-out war.

On 1 March 1999, a vehicle made its way through the busy streets of Bandra. Inside the car were five people. Most prominent among them was Majid Khan, proprietor of a construction company called M.K. Builders. The others were his trusted associates.

Suddenly, the sound of screeching tires and rapid gunfire filled the air. The car jolted violently as bullets pierced through the windows and doors, shattering glass and metal. Majid Khan and his associates were under attack by a group of heavily armed gunmen sent by Chhota Rajan aka Nana.

The driver of the car, a seasoned veteran of the streets, swerved left and right, trying to avoid the bullets. But the gunmen were relentless, firing at least thirty rounds at the vehicle. The car spun out of control and crashed into a parked car, its engine sputtering and smoking. In the midst of this, Majid and two of his associates lay motionless on the floor of the car, their bodies riddled with bullet holes.

The surviving driver, his face covered in blood, crawled out of the car to find cover. But it was too late. The gunmen had already caught up with him, grabbing him by the collar and pointing a gun at his head.

The driver closed his eyes, resigned to his fate. He knew he was going to die. But then, something unexpected happened. A crowd began gathering on the street. The gunmen, caught off guard, made a run for it. Of the five people in the car, Majid Khan and two of his associates were dead. Two others died the next day. A small girl was also caught in the crossfire. It was a great miracle that she survived. For those who lived in the city, the threat of violence was always present. But what had caused Rajan to come after Majid Khan? The answer lay in his familial ties. Majid's bond of blood with his brother Yakub aka Yeda Yakub led to his death.

Earlier that year, Chhota Rajan was sitting in his plush office in Bangkok, staring at his handler with steely eyes. The handler from the Agency had reached out to him for another job. Rajan studied her tone, his expression impassive.

'Majid Khan,' she said, handing over a file to his agent. 'He *has to* go.'

The gears in Rajan's mind began moving. 'Hmm,' he said.

'His godowns were used for storing the explosives,' the agent said, her voice low and filled with cold venom. 'Fifteen hundred kilos? They could've blasted a hole to the centre of the earth with that.'

Yeda Yakub had used his brother's godowns to store the explosives that were later used in the 1993 Mumbai bombings. Yakub was a key conspirator in the bombings. His logistical planning to store the RDX had linked Majid Khan and his family to the attacks. Rajan's penchant for killing those involved in the bombings was well-known, and he was willing to go to any lengths to get even with them.

'He's usually surrounded by people. Won't be easy.'

The agent leaned forward, a glint in her eye. 'Easy doesn't pay the big bucks.'

Rajan nodded, while one of his men picked up the file and tucked it into a bag. He leaned back in his chair, his mind already racing with the possibilities. Khan's death would be a blow to the masterminds behind the bombings, a message to those who thought they could get away easily.

Rajan picked up his phone and dialled a number. It was time to set his plan in motion, to spill blood in Mumbai where he had started—selling movie tickets in black outside the theatres of central Mumbai. In 1979, the police launched a crackdown and had lathi-charged the black ticket sellers outside Sahakar Cinema. Chhota Rajan, a young man then, snatched a constable's lathi and injured five cops. That was a sign of bigger things to come.

Now Chhota Rajan was enjoying support from different agencies. The government had failed to prove the involvement of some of the accused in the bomb blasts case. This allowed him to operate with relative impunity, striking fear into the hearts of his enemies and furthering his quest for justice. Rajan was aware that simply killing those whom he wanted to take revenge against would land him in a legal soup. But to have the Agency on his side would grant him the opportunity to accomplish the task while allowing him to manoeuvre his way out of the legal implications. Rajan wanted to relish the fruits of his labour borne through his liaison with the Agency.

The blast accused, like Majid, who were out on bail, had tried to secure protection from the court as Rajan's men were coming at them with all guns blazing. The courts had turned down their requests since they were involved in a serious crime and could not be protected by the state, against whom they had waged war. The accused were asked to make arrangements for their own protection.

On the other hand, Yeda Yakub's personality was as explosive as the RDX he had stored in the city. Whenever he lost his grip over his emotions, which was often, Yakub was uncontrollable. He was known for his short fuse. Those who crossed him did so at their own peril and regretted it later.

Majid and Yakub had set up their stronghold in Bandra. In their early days, Majid was trying to break into the construction business, whereas Yakub was known to bash up people with abandon.

In the 1980s, a low-income colony in which they owned a house was being taken up for redevelopment by a builder who later went on to become one of the biggest names in the construction business in the city. But there was a *small* problem. The settlement had houses of varying sizes that were occupied by different families. Yakub's house was among the bigger ones. The builder was insisting that all house owners should get units of equal sizes in the redeveloped property. This news sent Yakub into a fit of rage. Majid reasoned with him to accept what the builder was offering. The builder was too powerful to be messed around with. But Yakub, being Yeda Yakub, decided to make an offer to the builder; an offer the builder could not have refused.

On one of those days, the same builder was visiting a construction site at Bandra. The news reached Yakub. Without warning, he stormed into the site, grabbed the builder's collar and dragged him to the edge of the under-construction floor, five storeys above the ground.

'Give me the big house,' Yakub said. 'Or fall to your death.'

'Take what you want,' the builder said, as the wind bellowed. 'Take it!'

Yakub pulled the builder back to safety. And the builder, who needed muscle to expand his growing empire, was also impressed by Yakub's boldness. The same builder hired Yakub to clear prime land of squatters and even legal dwellers, land which could be used to construct high rises in the city.

Yakub's experience in land clearing and his connections in the industry made him a valuable asset to anyone looking to make a name for themselves in the business. Majid made strides in his own real estate ventures and started M.K. Builders. Yakub became the force behind his brother's rise by securing prime pieces of land for Majid's business.

People feared Yakub's anger, but there were those who often sought his help. One of his acquaintances, Afzal, had invested in a property in Mumbra, where many Muslims had started moving to. The developer who had sold the property to Afzal reneged on his promise of delivering the project and was holding up Afzal's money and delaying to return it. Afzal approached Yakub for help.

'Who is the builder, Afzal bhai?' Yakub said.

'Orange Constructions in Mumbra,' Afzal said.

'That's Shafi bhai's company. I know him well,' Yakub replied. 'He is not returning your money?'

'Yes.'

'Don't worry,' Yakub said. 'If your money is with him, consider that it is with me.'

The next day, Yakub sent one of his men named Riyaz with Afzal to meet Shafi of Orange Constructions and work out a settlement. The duo reached Shafi's home just as he was about to eat dinner. Shafi's face went pale on spotting Riyaz as he knew that Riyaz used to work for Yakub. 'What brings you here at this hour, Riyaz bhai?' Shafi asked. 'You could have called me to Bandra.'

'We heard that there is an *amaanat* (possession kept for safekeeping) of Afzal bhai which you are not returning,' Riyaz said.

'Oh, that?' Shafi said. 'I will pay it next week as soon as one of my payments is cleared.'

'Very well,' Riyaz said. 'But if you fail to keep *this* promise, remember that next time it will not be me but Yakub bhai who will knock on your door.'

The last few words of that sentence had such a chilling effect on Shafi that he quietly went inside his room, opened the cupboard and gathered the entire amount he owed Afzal. The bundles of currency were wrapped in a newspaper and handed over to Afzal. Such was the fear of Yakub among those who knew what he was capable of. Perhaps, it was this quality of Yeda Yakub that made Tiger Memon summon him for executing one of the biggest terror attacks in the history of India. But the price of this collaboration would be a mighty one to pay.

23

Yeda on the Run

Even before he shot to infamy for his role in the blasts, the name of Yeda Yakub would strike fear among the general populace in his stronghold of Bandra. He was good friends with Sabir, Dawood Ibrahim's elder brother, and was known to be a frequent visitor to Pakmodia Street near Nagpada, where the D-Company had its headquarters. Ultimately, it was the death of Sabir at the hands of the Pathan gang that sent the entire Mumbai mafia into a bloody frenzy and triggered the gang war which catapulted Dawood to such heights that he was able to execute a terror attack as huge as the Black Friday bombings in March 1993.

'Through his association with Dawood's gang, Yakub also got acquainted with Tiger, who had grown into an influential figure in the underworld,' I told Shetty.

Tiger used to work for the Dossa family earlier but eventually upstaged them at least in terms of bravado. Given Yakub's sheer disregard for authority, Tiger decided to enlist him for the March 1993 bombings. Several meetings were held between Tiger and Yakub at different locations in the city, including a few at Stomach Restaurant in Bandra, which was owned by Rakesh Khurana. Philoo was also known to visit this restaurant as it used to serve delectable Chinese cuisine.

Due to this association, Khurana also came under the scanner of the cops and was put through severe mental torture. Reportedly, the cops called him to the police station and made him witness the humiliation that the other blast suspects were being put through. The experience scarred Khurana to such an extent that he first shot his wife and daughters and then killed himself. Perhaps, Khurana was a case of a man being at the wrong place at the wrong time.

On the other side, Tiger was purposeful in setting his plans in motion after the ISI had colluded with Dawood to make the RDX and other arms and ammunition available for the attack. In the preceding months, he had also sent several men from Mumbai to Dubai from where they were whisked to Pakistan to get the requisite training in handling arms and explosives.

The ISI controlled the shipping routes that extended from the Gulf to the west coast of India. It promised to deliver the explosives in the first week of February. Tiger was looking for more men to help him with the logistics. The godowns owned by Majid, brother of Yeda Yakub, would serve as the storehouses until D-Day arrived. Yeda Yakub backed Tiger's plan to the hilt and was even present when the maal was delivered by the ISI on 7 February 1993 at Shekhadi, a coastal village near Shrivardhan in Maharashtra's Konkan region.

The arms and ammunition were transported via two trawlers, both of which were owned by Mohammad Dossa. While the first trawler headed for the Gosabar coast in Gujarat, the second trawler made its way to the Raigad district, making Shekhadi its final destination. The consignments on both the trawlers contained AK-47 and AK-56 rifles, pistols as well as grenades.

The village in question had become a haven for landing smuggled goods over the years and even the customs department was on the payroll of many smugglers like Tiger and Dawood, who would land their smuggled gold and silver over there. The villagers were also accustomed to this, as they made good money by unloading the goods without asking any questions. This mechanism, which had evolved over the years, made landing the arms easier than expected. The customs department and the villagers were paid off and they were all under the impression that it was only silver that was being smuggled through the route (like always).

On the other hand, Tiger's team was ready. Among his top lieutenants was Javed Chikna, who had been hit by a bullet fired by the police to control a riot in the Bandra area. Many of those involved in the blasts had been recruited by Javed and brought to Tiger, who completely brainwashed these men through emotive issues. They were ready to give their limbs and lives for him and reached Shekhadi on 7 February 1993 to unload the consignment sent by the ISI. By 9 p.m., the maal arrived.

Tiger's boys offloaded the smuggled goods at the seashore. Two tempos were already parked there. Yeda Yakub and Javed Chikna were standing near the white tempo. The arms were packed in wooden crates and gunny bags and were loaded in both the tempos. Tiger Memon, Javed Chikna and Yeda Yakub opened the sacks to check the *gifts* from the ISI. Javed was blown away by the sight of rifles, hand grenades and bags containing black powder in them.

'*Kala saboon* (black soap),' said Tiger with a glint in his eyes.

The codeword for RDX was kala saboon, which meant black soap. It was derived from the black colour and soapy texture of the explosive. Javed picked up some of the bullets. Bullets were often referred to as *daana* (bird feed), whereas the guns in which they were supposed to be used were called *kabootar* (pigeons). After the tempos were filled, they were unloaded at a building named Wangni Tower. The goods were then reloaded in the Commander jeeps that left for Bombay. One tempo which was now empty followed the jeeps.

One particularly interesting man was seated in the tempo. He was actively involved in the blasts but was later deserted by Tiger and his associates and left to fend for himself. This man was eventually arrested by the cops and later, he turned an approver in the case. The cops codenamed him Badshah Khan to protect his identity from the other accused until the trial began.

Police action after the blasts was rather swift. Once the cops caught hold of Asgar Mukaddam, Tiger Memon's manager, the names of those who were involved started popping up left, right and centre. Yeda Yakub's name also cropped up and the cops began hunting for him. He quickly went underground but his family had to face the impact of his actions. The cops picked up Majid Khan and his wife Nafeesa and put them through severe torture.

Meanwhile, Yakub was on the run—moving from Delhi to Rajasthan and other cities. The condition of Majid and Nafeesa broke Yakub completely. To get some heat off his family, Yakub started tipping the cops about the explosives that were still stored in different warehouses in the city. He was in constant touch with DCP Arup Patnaik of the Mumbai Police to negotiate a release for his brother. He provided Patnaik with the address of a godown in Mumbra from where the cop recovered 1500 kg of RDX. It was the largest seizure made during the course of the investigation of the bomb blasts.

Majid took legal recourse and was able to secure bail. He continued with his business until Rajan's men bumped him off.

Tiger, who had already moved to Dubai, had dumped many of those who had helped him execute the blasts. It was this use-and-throw policy adopted by Tiger that led to Badshah Khan turning an approver in the case and then testifying against the same men with whom he had planted bombs in the city.

However, Yeda Yakub was too important for Tiger Memon. The latter ensured that Yakub crossed the border and was then provided a new identity and a passport by the ISI.

Apparently, Yeda Yakub settled in the city of Karachi, living there with his second wife and children. Indian agencies were working overtime to bring back those who were involved in the blasts either through extradition or even negotiation. Those who had escaped from Mumbai wanted to come back to the city as their businesses and families were rooted here. Even Dawood Ibrahim had contacted noted lawyer Ram Jethmalani and tried to negotiate an arrangement with the Indian authorities.[1]

However, the don wanted to make a conditional surrender. Some of these conditions, besides the expectation of a fair trial, were that he would not be put in jail but placed under house arrest. He also wanted all cases against him except the bomb blast cases to be quashed, and that the police should not subject him to torture or third-degree interrogation. These conditions were not acceptable to the Indian authorities. The then chief minister, Sharad Pawar, baulked at the don's offer and the government at the Centre refused to entertain the plea.

'It is true that Ram Jethmalani had given a proposal about Dawood's willingness to return,' former chief minister Sharad Pawar said in one of his interviews. 'But there was a condition that Dawood should not be kept in jail. Rather he should be allowed to remain in a house. This was not acceptable. We said he had to face the law.'

The subject of Dawood's surrender was never mentioned from that point on.

Like Dawood, even Yakub wanted to return to Mumbai. In 2011, it is said that he came to Dubai to surrender to Indian authorities but changed his mind at the last minute. His family wanted him to clear his name from the blasts and were pressuring him to come back. In 2015, he died of a heart attack in Karachi—forever a fugitive. Rakesh Maria, who had investigated the blasts in 1993, had been promoted to the post of commissioner of police, in Mumbai by then. Maria had confirmed to the press that the news had been received by the cops.[2]

'Yeda Yakub will forever remain among those fugitives who could not be brought to book for his role in the blasts,' Shetty said. 'The same cannot be said about his brother Majid, who received an unofficial death sentence.'

With that, Shetty glanced at his watch. Our parleys had continued late into the night. He had to leave. I have to meet an old friend, he confessed. He was also scheduled to fly to another country in three days. 'We'll catch up for a round of drinks and talk about the old times,' Shetty said.

'Perhaps I will have more stories for you the next time we meet.'

On my part, I thanked Shetty and shook hands with him, bidding him goodbye with a smile on my face.

24

How Many Headleys?

The next time, Kamaal and I met in the UAE again before he was about to embark on a trip to London. Great Britain had once ruled over most of the Indian Subcontinent. Now, they were dealing with the influx of Indians and Pakistanis along with various other nationalities in the cities. This immigration had brought along its own problems like overcrowding and petty crime.

'But organized crime is a far greater problem,' Kamaal said.

I couldn't help but agree. A horde of financial fugitives from India had flown to the country.

'There's one fugitive from Southeast Asia we haven't heard about a lot,' Kamaal said.

'Who?' I asked.

In 2018, Jabir Motiwala, a wealthy businessman from Pakistan, arrived in the UK. He had flown in from Cyprus, an island country located to the south of the Anatolian

Peninsula in the eastern Mediterranean Sea. It is considered to be a tax haven for individuals who can move mountains of money around the globe, which can be used for nefarious purposes like trafficking and terrorism.

Jabir was accompanied by his family. He had planned this trip for months, and after being invited by a *friend* for an important business meeting. Jabir and his family checked into the Hilton. The hotel was grand and the staff was friendly, which added to the experience. However, he was completely unaware of the ordeal that was looming upon him.

A mole of Scotland Yard was holed up in the hotel, and he tipped the cops about Jabir's presence. Scotland Yard, famous for their investigative skills, rushed to the location with the sirens of their cars blaring, cutting through the streets. The police cars screeched to a halt outside the Hilton's entrance. A team of officers rushed out, their guns drawn and pointed low. Guests and staff of the hotel stopped in their tracks and looked on in surprise.

The officers swiftly made their way towards Jabir's room, their footsteps silenced by the soft and plush carpets in the corridor. Near the door of the suspect's room, the cops readied their guns. Finally, the lead officer signalled to his team and they burst into the room.

Jabir was in shock as he was grabbed by the officers and pushed to the floor. They quickly subdued him and took him away, leaving behind a trail of confusion and fear among his family, who were left in a state of shock and uncertainty. They were afraid for Jabir and worried about what would happen next. How could they help him? They had no clue where the cops had taken him. And why had he been arrested in the first place? The answer to the last question was one of Pakistan's best kept open secrets. Jabir Motiwala was, apparently, a key associate of the world's most wanted gangster—Dawood Ibrahim Kaskar.

Taken to an undisclosed location, Jabir was sitting in a small, well-lit room, his hands cuffed to a metal table. He felt anxious and helpless, but he was smart enough to know why the cops had brought him here. They had uncovered his dangerous associations. By now, he had also figured out that the *friend* who had called him to the UK had ratted him out to the cops. He would make this *friend* pay, one way or another. But first, he had to ensure his own safety.

When an interrogator entered the room, Jabir immediately asked to be allowed to make one phone call which was his legal right. The interrogator had no choice but to concede to the request. Unsurprisingly, Jabir called his lawyer in the UK. Surprisingly, the lawyer's name was Deepak Vij and he hailed from India—a country that was fighting a long-drawn-out battle with Pakistan, from where Jabir hailed, and Dawood Ibrahim, a man wanted by India who had taken shelter in Pakistan. Within an hour, Deepak Vij arrived at the location. Jabir was relieved to see him.

Deepak had a serious look on his face. He wore a tailored suit, and his hair was neatly combed. He was the head of the Fraud and Complex Crime department at ABV Solicitors, and had over twenty-five years of experience in defending high-profile, complex white-collar and grey-collar serious fraud cases. His track record was impressive, built entirely on recommendations from satisfied clients.

He had already figured out the charges that were going to be pressed against Jabir.

Deepak explained to Jabir that he was indeed arrested for his links to Dawood Ibrahim, international money laundering, drug dealing and extortion on the request of the investigating agencies of the USA. An RCN from Interpol against Jabir had been issued to Scotland Yard at the request of the FBI. He warned Jabir that the US was planning to extradite him for their larger plans of getting their hands on Dawood Ibrahim.

Jabir's eyes darted nervously around the room. 'What do we do now?'

Deepak reassured him that he would use every legal manoeuvre he had perfected over the years to delay the extradition. 'But the FBI seems to have strong evidence against you,' he said. 'Otherwise, Scotland Yard wouldn't risk the public embarrassment of arresting a foreign national.'

Apparently, the FBI, through their *agent*, had caught Jabir on camera discussing the drug trade and financial crimes he had conducted for Dawood.

But Jabir had hired the best legal assistance he could have sought. Somehow, if Deepak could delay the extradition, Jabir would personally make sure that Scotland Yard and the FBI, two of the world's most powerful agencies who were behind his arrest, would have egg on their faces by the time this trial was over. 'I'll teach them a lesson they'll never forget,' Jabir said.

Jabir's confidence stemmed from the fact that he was aware of the man who had betrayed him. A while ago, he had been befriended by a man named Kamran Faridi, who lived in the US but was also of Pakistani descent, much like Jabir. Kamran was the one who had called him to the UK. And clearly, Kamran had played a role in Jabir's arrest. There was no way the cops could have acted so swiftly.

Jabir's mind raced with questions about Kamran Faridi. How had he been so easily fooled by someone he thought was a friend? What was Kamran's motive in setting him up? And most importantly, where was Kamran now? The answer was unclear but Jabir had friends in high places who could help him out if he could withstand this storm.

During the 9/11 attacks, the Al-Qaeda network of Osama bin Laden brought down the World Trade Center in New York by blowing up the twin towers with hijacked planes. The event was seen as a huge failure of the famous US agencies such as the FBI and the CIA, whose operating budgets were close to or even exceeded the budgets of a few third-world countries.

In the aftermath of the attack, the FBI and CIA were scrambling to gather intelligence on terrorist groups. But they were short of agents with the necessary skills to infiltrate these organizations. They needed people who could blend in seamlessly, who could go unnoticed and gather information without drawing attention to themselves. They needed the much-coveted human intelligence (HUMINT) to bring down these terror networks.

Hence, they started looking for people with criminal backgrounds like drug addicts and petty criminals as potential recruits who would take up these risky jobs while giving the agencies a cover of plausible deniability. The African-American community, which had been targeted by the FBI and CIA for years, was understandably hesitant to work with them. So the agencies began to turn to other groups, including Pakistani migrants.

David Headley was one such recruit of the US agencies. Headley had a troubled past and had been involved in drug-related crimes. He was living a difficult life with his girlfriend when the FBI picked him up. They saw potential in him and soon put him to work.

Headley was used by the FBI, the CIA and the DEA. He was sent to Pakistan, where he was trained by the ISI. Somewhere during this period, the ISI recruited him and sent him to Mumbai to be part of the reconnaissance team that provided the intelligence needed to carry out the 26/11 Mumbai attacks in 2008.

Headley used his US passport to travel to Mumbai, and he checked into several hotels and took videos and photographs of potential targets for the attack. He also helped to plan the attack and provided the terrorists with detailed maps of Mumbai, including locations of police stations and other key buildings. Headley was in touch with the Lashkar-e-Taiba (LeT) handlers who were directing the attackers during the attack. He was later arrested in Atlanta, Georgia, in 2009 and sent to serve a thirty-five-year sentence in the US for his role in the terror attack.

However, the FBI had also recruited another agent who matched Headley's profile very closely. This agent was none other than Kamran Faridi, the man who later trapped Jabir Motiwala.

Kamran had moved to the US in the 1990s and had a criminal background. He had been in trouble with the law in both Pakistan and the US. Like Headley, Faridi's criminal record was cleaned after he started working with the agencies. Faridi later infiltrated various terrorist organizations, including ISIS and IS, to gather intelligence for the FBI. Faridi had a long and sordid history with the FBI, having been recruited by them years ago to work as a pawn in their HUMINT operations.

Over time, Kamran was sent on various missions by the FBI to gather intelligence on terrorist organizations and their activities. He was trained extensively in spycraft and covert operations and became an expert in infiltration and surveillance. Kamran's skills and experience made him an asset for the FBI, and they used him to establish connections with various intelligence agencies around the world.

Kamran's job was to carry out the FBI's operations and report back to them upon completion of tasks. Despite the danger and risk involved in his work, Kamran stayed committed to his mission, mostly to remain in the good books of Uncle Sam rather than believing that he was 'saving the world'.

When the US agencies intensified their quest for Dawood Ibrahim, they were surprised to see the name of Jabir Motiwala pop up on their radar. He was believed to be laundering money for Ibrahim. In fact, it was the amount of money he was moving for Dawood that attracted the FBI's attention, as intelligence agencies always keep an eye out for suspicious transactions of high value. Soon, the FBI deputed Kamran Faridi to trap Jabir Motiwala. The agent was now ready to begin his mission and lock horns with Jabir Motiwala. The only mistake Faridi made was that he underestimated the consequences of messing with Dawood Ibrahim.

25

With Friends Like These . . .

After being recruited by the FBI, Kamran Faridi underwent an intensive training programme that was designed to prepare him for his role as an undercover operative. The training was gruelling and mentally exhausting, but Kamran knew that it was necessary if he wanted to succeed in his new career and wipe off his past.

The training programme was divided into several phases, each of which focused on a different aspect of espionage and undercover work. The first phase focused on skills such as surveillance, counter-surveillance and communication techniques. Kamran learnt how to blend in with his surroundings and how to avoid drawing attention to himself.

The second phase of the programme focused on more advanced skills such as interrogation, intercepting communication, breaking codes and infiltration techniques. Kamran learnt how to gather information from different sources and how to develop and maintain a cover identity.

The third and final phase of the training programme was the most challenging of all. It involved a series of real-world simulations that were designed to test Kamran's ability to operate in high-pressure situations. Kamran was put through a series of scenarios that ranged from simple surveillance tasks to complex undercover operations that required him to infiltrate any criminal organization and gather sensitive information.

Throughout the training programme, Kamran was pushed to his limits both mentally and physically. The instructors were tough and demanding, but Kamran knew that he needed to stay focused and work hard if he wanted to succeed. Kamran Faridi then worked as an undercover agent for the FBI for years, infiltrating terrorist organizations and collecting intelligence for the agency. He had become one of their most valued assets, and they trusted him to carry out their operations with great success. One day, Kamran received a call from his handler at the FBI. The directive was laid bare and simple.[1]

'We want you to trap Jabir Motiwala. According to our intel, he's the money launderer for Dawood Ibrahim.'

Kamran listened carefully, taking in the information. 'Why Jabir?'

'Because he's managing the spine of Dawood's financial network. And we want to crush each bone in that spine,' his handler replied.

Kamran nodded, understanding the importance of the mission. 'I'll do it.'

The next few weeks were spent preparing for the operation. Kamran underwent intense training from the FBI, learning the ins and outs of money laundering and how to approach someone like Jabir Motiwala. He had to be careful not to arouse any suspicion and not to give away his true intentions. Through a series of middlemen, he slowly inched his way towards Jabir Motiwala. Their common origins, from Pakistan, made the task for Kamran easier than he had expected.

Finally, the day came for Kamran to meet Jabir. They bonded over their shared experiences and soon became friends. They started meeting at various locations in different countries, including Pakistan, Armenia and the UAE, among others, for their business dealings.

Over time, Kamran gained Jabir's trust, and Jabir began confiding in him about his business dealings. Kamran listened carefully, taking mental notes and passing on the information to the FBI. One day, Kamran learnt of Jabir's plan to fly to the UK from Cyprus, where he was visiting to manage a deal for the D-Company. The FBI was quick to get an RCN issued against Jabir, and subsequently, Scotland Yard swooped upon Jabir at the Hilton in London.

Back then, Kamran was the toast of the FBI. The operation to catch Jabir Motiwala had turned out to be a stupendous success. Extradition proceedings had already been initiated and it seemed only a matter of time before Motiwala would be rotting behind bars in a highly secure facility in the US. But both Kamran and Uncle Sam had forgotten that messing with a D-Company man was akin to messing with the entire D-Company. Kamran's Pakistani origins had made it easier for him to get access to Motiwala. That same reason would eventually cause this entire case to collapse.

While Kamran was basking in the glory of his achievements, he received a call from an unidentified number. Kamran froze when he heard the unmistakable voice of Chhota Shakeel, the dreaded deputy of Dawood Ibrahim. The stakes had just been raised to a whole new level. Shakeel's warning to Kamran was clear. 'How are you, my friend? And how are your relatives in Pakistan?' Chhota Shakeel said. 'I pray for their health and their long lives.'

Kamran understood the threat. The D-Company had the full blessings of the ISI and bumping off a few people in Pakistan was no big deal for a criminal syndicate powered by one of the most dangerous and rogue intelligence agencies in the world. As Kamran hung up the phone, he felt a sense of dread wash over him. From that moment, life would never be the same again for him.

Dawood Ibrahim and Chhota Shakeel had moved quickly to prevent further damage after Jabir's arrest. If the Americans were successful in getting Jabir to the US, then it would open a can of worms that would put not just Dawood on a sticky wicket, but also the Government of Pakistan, who had harboured the dreaded gangster for years. The US was providing a huge amount of funds to Pakistan for their collaboration on the 'war against terror', which the US had launched in the region. This funding continued even after Osama bin Laden was killed on Pakistani soil in May 2011 under Operation Neptune Spear. Dawood Ibrahim was another high-value target for the US and the confirmation of his presence in Pakistan would again lead to much heartburn between the two countries.

Jabir Motiwala was too important for the D-Company. A quiet man with a sharp mind and an ability to navigate the murky world of money laundering, he rose up the ranks of the D-Company rather quickly. Dawood had established great connections with the Turkish and Cyprus mafia and needed a man to manage his financial operations in the region. Anees Ibrahim was not a financial wizard, and Chhota Shakeel was already managing Russia. Thus, Jabir was *the* man for the job.

Jabir's promotion was due to his sharp mind and ability. His task was to handle the financial operations in Turkey and Cyprus. Jabir deliberately kept a low profile due to which the authorities didn't notice him for quite a long time. He went about his business with diligence, making sure that Dawood's illegal money was laundered and moved around with ease. He was the man behind the scenes, the invisible hand that made sure everything ran smoothly. But even as Jabir rose through the ranks of the Dawood Ibrahim gang, he knew that he was playing a dangerous game. One wrong move could mean the end of his life, or worse, even put his loved ones in a lot of trouble.

Yet, he continued to do his job, knowing that the stakes were high, and the consequences were dire. As the FBI intensified its quest to capture Dawood Ibrahim, they began to closely monitor his financial transactions. They soon discovered a pattern of money laundering, with large sums of money being transferred to various countries through a network of middlemen. Through their investigations, the FBI was able to trace one of these middlemen to Jabir Motiwala.

Further surveillance and intelligence gathering led the FBI to build a strong case against Jabir, and they began to consider him a valuable target in their mission to bring down Dawood Ibrahim's criminal empire. The FBI had been listening in on phone calls between Jabir Motiwala and Dawood Ibrahim for months but they hadn't been able to catch them discussing anything incriminating. That is, until one day, they heard something that piqued their interest.

'Get me a Versace suit from Cyprus,' Dawood told Jabir during one of their calls.[2] At first glance, it seemed like an innocuous request, but the FBI suspected it was a coded message. Why would Dawood need Jabir to bring him a suit? He had billions at his disposal and could purchase a hundred suits if he wanted to. They decided to bring Kamran Faridi in and play him the recording.

As they did so, Kamran looked thoughtful. 'This is how they operate. This is a message for Jabir. "Versace suit" is a code for money. Jabir is being tasked with moving the money from Cyprus to somewhere else.'

The FBI had to tread carefully. They had intelligence that Jabir was the money launderer for Dawood, but without solid evidence, they couldn't take him down. After his arrest, the FBI planned to use Kamran's testimony as the evidence they needed to get Jabir extradited. The bureau had full faith in Kamran's abilities. But they had discounted the lengths to which Dawood would go to protect his man.

Kamran Faridi had been working undercover for the FBI and pretended to befriend Jabir Motiwala in order to gather evidence against him. He thought he had everything under control and that he could outsmart anyone who tried to stop him. But after Jabir's arrest, Kamran started receiving threatening calls and messages from unknown numbers. He realized he had exposed himself and his family to great danger and things were only about to get worse for him from this point.

26

Kamran Faridi and The Beatles

Kamran Faridi was sweating profusely as he stepped off the plane at Heathrow Airport. His stomach was churning with a mix of fear and anxiety. He had flown in from the US and was about to depose before the court in the UK in the Jabir Motiwala case. Faridi made his way through customs. He couldn't help but feel that he was being watched. While he was waiting for his luggage at the conveyor belt, he was surrounded by a bunch of men wearing suits with their identity cards around their necks.

'Mr Faridi,' a gruff voice said. 'Come with us.'

'What's going on?' Faridi asked.

'We'll explain everything in due time,' one of them said.

Kamran's mind was racing. He had worked enough with the FBI to know they were behind this. As the British agencies bundled him away, Kamran knew his game was over. His hands were shaking as they led him into a small interrogation room. FBI agents were already waiting for him. He tried to put on a brave face, but he knew he was in trouble with his former employers. Once he was their blue-eyed boy, but a certain sequence of events had turned him into a persona non grata.

After being recruited by the FBI, Faridi began establishing contacts in the Middle East so that he could eventually break into terror organizations and gather information that could be passed to the agency. With the money he was making from secret service funds, Faridi's lifestyle became affluent. He was fond of luxury watches and purchased a Rolex. He also moved about in a red Mercedes. He used the cover of a businessman and would tell people that he was in the business of antiques and artefacts. To build his image, he would display Buddha statues to cement his business credentials among those he would meet.

Faridi came under the scanner of Turkish authorities in November 2015 when the counterterrorism task force of the country raided a villa in Silivri, near Istanbul, after receiving a tip-off about the property being used for terror activities. Faridi himself was not arrested in the raid as he quietly left for New York only days before the raid. It is believed that Faridi had infiltrated the group planning an Islamic State type of attack on the country, and then passed the information to the FBI who alerted their Turkish counterparts. But Al-Walid Khalid Alagha was arrested in this raid.

To break into the circles of terror, Faridi had befriended Al-Walid Khalid Alagha, a man of Palestinian origins who had grown up in Pakistan after his father travelled to the country in the 1980s to fight against the Soviet forces. The Russians were fighting the Taliban for control of Afghanistan and Alagha's father joined the growing ranks of the mujahideen. Since Alagha's father had quite a reputation in the folklore of Afghani fighters, Faridi used Alagha as a means to break into these networks.

Among others who were arrested by the Turks in Silivri included a British national named Aine Davis who had crossed into Turkey from Syria. He was allegedly one of the four British nationals—nicknamed 'The Beatles'—who had risen to commanding positions in ISIS. The most infamous of the Beatles of ISIS was Mohammed Emwazi, who had been christened 'Jihadi John'.

A terrifying character, Jihadi John would wear a black mask and appear live on the Internet channels of ISIS. In these videos, he beheaded several foreigners from the US, the UK and even Japan. Emwazi was killed in Raqqa, Syria, in a targeted drone strike by US forces on 12 November 2015—around the same time the Turkish forces had raided the villa in Silivri where Aine Davis had been arrested.

Davis's phone records showed that he was in touch with both Alagha and Faridi while crossing over to Turkey from Syria. However, in the court, Davis denied any association with Emwazi or ISIS. Questions were raised on Faridi's conduct in the case as officials struggled to produce evidence that could undeniably link Alagha and Davis to acts of terror. But they remained in jail for a year before being convicted on lesser charges of being members of a terror group. It is largely believed that Faridi set them up by assembling them at the villa and then getting them arrested, which increased his stock with the FBI.

Faridi grew up in the middle-class area of Gulshan-e-Iqbal in Karachi. Even as a student, he was interested in politics and became a member of the student wing of the Pakistan People's Party (PPP).

Keeping in line with the violent traditions of Pakistan's politics, Faridi's days of student activism were also plagued by fights, following which he became involved with smuggling weapons and kidnapping and even learnt to handle weapons.

The area where Faridi lived was the stronghold of the rival Muttahida Qaumi Movement (MQM) party, previously known as Mohajir Qaumi Movement. Such was the rivalry between the PPP and MQM that it became difficult for Faridi, a flagbearer of the PPP, to stay in the area, so he moved to another locality where the presence of the PPP cadre was higher. During this period, he also got support from a popular student leader of the PPP.

Faridi's exploits had made him quite a few enemies. The cops and the MQM cadre were looking to get even with him. He became a man on the run, hiding from his enemies to prevent himself from becoming another statistic in the long list of Pakistan's political killings. This experience made Kamran master the mode of survival and he smuggled his way into Sweden. Even in foreign lands, he could not give up on his violent instincts. He picked up fights with the Albanian and Bangladeshi gangs. Tired of his delinquent ways, the Swedish authorities refused to renew his visa, which turned him into an illegal immigrant.

From Sweden, he made his way into the US and purchased a gas station in Atlanta, Georgia. The local cops there began harassing him for bribes and Faridi approached the FBI against them. This was how he first came into contact with the FBI. Since they were looking for resources who could infiltrate Southeast Asian gangs and terror networks, the FBI found great value in Faridi and recruited him.

Faridi did not disappoint the G-men. The term G-man is used informally to refer to any representative of US agencies, the FBI in particular. The slang originated during the September 1933 arrest of gangster George 'Machine Gun' Kelly. The Bureau of Investigation (BOI), a forerunner to the FBI, had surrounded the gangster in Memphis when Kelly repeatedly shouted, 'Don't shoot, G-men! Don't shoot!' However, this anecdote is believed to be an exaggeration and the amount of truth in it has often been disputed.[1]

As a part of the FBI's network, Faridi worked with several intelligence agencies, including MI6 and the CIA. Each time, he found ways to deliver even if some of the results had a certain spin around them, like in the case of Alagha and Aine Davis, one of the supposed members of the Beatles of ISIS. The FBI was so impressed with Faridi's work that they sponsored visas for Faridi's parents and moved them from Karachi to the US.

In May 2011, Faridi was tasked with infiltrating the D-Company. With the intention of working his way up to Dawood, Faridi chose Jabir Motiwala as his target out of a list that the agency gave him. He met Motiwala several times in different parts of the world. Sometimes, they would meet up in Karachi, Dubai or the US. Even after seven years, Faridi was playing the waiting game. Motiwala had controlled him well and prevented him from getting access to Dawood Ibrahim, who was well protected by the ISI.

In 2018, Faridi prevailed on Motiwala to come to London, where the latter was arrested. Interestingly, in 2017, the British agencies had arrested Asif Hafeez on similar instructions from the FBI. Hafeez, also a Pakistani, was detained from the same area of London where Motiwala was picked up. A gold trader and alleged drug smuggler with links to Dawood, the agencies asked Hafeez about the Taliban and Dawood. He denied knowledge about the Taliban but admitted to knowing Dawood, with whom he had watched cricket matches in Sharjah before the don moved from Dubai. Faridi had played a key role in Hafeez's arrest also.

Faridi's testimony was to play an important role in Motiwala's case. The D-Company and the ISI swung into action to prevent their man from being extradited to the US. After receiving subtle threats to his own life as well as those he loved, Faridi realized that he was on the radar of Chhota Shakeel and the D-Company. He told his FBI bosses that he did not want to testify in the case. The G-men were aghast. They tried convincing Faridi that he and his family would be protected. But Shakeel's threats had turned Faridi into a paranoid man. He began seeing Dawood's men all around, even in his dreams and nightmares.

'I can't testify,' Faridi said finally. 'How can I sell out Pakistan and my countrymen?'

His FBI handlers were puzzled. Faridi had not only developed cold feet but also a *conscience*. Unable to convince their blue-eyed boy, the FBI terminated Faridi's contract and cut back on the privileges they had extended to him. During that period, Faridi's wife was diagnosed with cancer. His foray into the network of the D-Company had strangled him like a curse that destroys anyone who dares to disturb the mummy of an Egyptian pharaoh.

A distraught and disoriented Faridi sent multiple death threats to his FBI bosses. To add a layer of recklessness to his actions, he chose email and SMS as his preferred mode of communication, leaving behind undisputed evidence of his actions. The G-men finally ran out of patience when Faridi made his way to the UK, not to testify against Jabir Motiwala but against the FBI!

Having established contact with Motiwala's legal team, Faridi had landed in the UK to depose in court that the FBI had pressured him to provide false testimony against Dawood Ibrahim, Chhota Shakeel and Anees bhai. The FBI acted quickly to control the damage, even though the embarrassment had turned them into a laughing stock in this case. Faridi was taken into custody from Heathrow Airport. Hours later, he was deported to the US from where he was taken to a prison.

Faridi was charged with the crime of issuing death threats to federal agents. He would now have to face trial in that case while Motiwala's case was headed in a completely different direction than expected. The tables had turned, and how!

27

Jostling for Jabir

The trial for Jabir Motiwala had turned into a multipronged contest. On one side, the D-Company was trying to save their man. On the other, the FBI was determined to make him face the music on US soil. The Americans had used this strategy many times, including in their war against the narcotics cartels in South America, especially in Columbia. In the mid-1980s, the kingpin of the Medellin Cartel, Pablo Escobar Gaviria, even formed an alliance—Los Extraditables—of drug lords to fight against the extradition treaty between the US and Colombian governments.

The Los Extraditables organization launched a campaign of fear to make the judiciary surrender to their demands. Far-left guerrilla organizations were recruited to attack the Colombian Judiciary building. Half of the justices of the Supreme Court were killed in the attack. In late 1986, Colombia's Supreme Court declared the treaty illegal as it had been signed by a presidential delegation, not the President. Escobar's victory over the judiciary was short-lived as the new President, Virgilio Barco Vargas, quickly renewed his agreement with the US.

However, in the twenty-first century, the rules of engagement had changed and attacks on emblems of the State were not, exactly, the best strategy to fight someone's case. The D-Company, aided by the ISI and a section of the Pakistani press, launched a multi-pronged campaign to keep the FBI from taking away Jabir.

Pakistani media channels began running a campaign to build a positive perception of Jabir Motiwala in the public domain. The effort was backed by none other than the Government of Pakistan, which vouched in the court that Jabir Motiwala was an honest businessman and a good citizen. His grandfather had played a key role in establishing the Karachi Stock Exchange and he came from a family with impeccable business credentials.

Jabir's legal team also had a solid game plan in place to defend their client. Deepak Vij and Amirah Ajaz of ABV Solicitors were instrumental in devising the overall strategy. Amirah, a dynamic lawyer, was fluent in many languages, including English, Urdu, Hindi and Punjabi. She was adept in dealing with cases of serious business crime and heavyweight fraud, and an expert in matters dealing with extradition.

On the second day of the trial, the defence called upon Barrister Rehan Kayani, a legal expert from Pakistan to depose before District Judge John Zani, who was hearing the case. Over the years, through Kamran and other agents, the FBI had collected a lot of evidence against Jabir.

Three US agents—who were only referred to as CS1, CS2 and CS3 during the course of the trial to protect their identity—had conducted a series of meetings with Jabir in Karachi and Atlantic City in the US to smuggle drugs across the US's borders. Kayani's testimony stated that it was illegal for the FBI to conduct a sting operation on Pakistani soil as it amounted to entrapment.[1] In court, an accused person may allege that he wouldn't have committed a crime if a law enforcement officer had not induced him into the crime. This act of the law officer can be categorized as entrapment and is considered illegal in many countries.

Barrister Edward Fitzgerald, who was part of Motiwala's legal team, raised the issue of 'passage of time'. The FBI had their agents tail Motiwala between 2014 and 2018, and Fitzgerald asked why the US had not acted upon the case earlier and asked for the arrest years after the alleged offences had been committed.

Eric Lewis appeared on the first day in person before the extradition judge to testify that prisoners in US jails—whether convicted or awaiting trial—suffered as a result of being put in inhumane jail conditions. Previously, he had played a key role as counsel to the liquidators of Bank of Credit and Commerce International, Laker Airways, Carlyle Capital, Madoff International, China Medical and Akai Electronics. He had also represented a number of sovereign governments and served as an expert on extradition and enforcement of judgments. Naturally, his words held much weight in a court of law. Lewis opined that Jabir's extradition to the US to face trial would adversely affect his mental health and that Jabir should not be extradited for the same reason.

On the third day of the trial, the defence called upon Maureen Baird, a US national who had served with the

Federal Bureau of Prisons for nearly twenty-eight years. Maureen deposed via a video link and opined that conditions in federal prisons of the US were pitiful. Motiwala would lose all communication with the outside world. Any form of human interaction would occur only if he was being served food or during inspections of the facilities by the authorities. 'Motiwala will be at risk of suicide as he will be sent to a prison where there is no twenty-four-hour monitoring,' she said.

The third witness, Zachary Philip Katznelson, also agreed with the two previous experts. Katznelson was a lawyer and formerly legal director for the human rights group Reprieve. Along with his colleagues, he had formerly represented over fifty people imprisoned in Guantanamo Bay.

Guantanamo Bay was a US detention camp located on the coast of Cuba where suspects of terror were detained and interrogated after the 9/11 attacks. The presence of the camp created a huge controversy when numerous incidents of illegal detention, torture and human rights abuse that led to several deaths were reported in the media.[2]

Katznelson had also represented Shaker Aamer, a national of Saudi Arabia who had been captured in Afghanistan by American bounty hunters and handed over to US forces in December 2001. For thirteen years, Aamer was held at Guantanamo Bay without charge or trial where interrogators who represented themselves as MI5 officers offered him a choice. 'Work for us and spy on the jihadis living in the UK,' one of the interrogators told Aamer. 'Or rot in here forever.'[3]

At one point in time, the interrogators offered this choice to Aamer and then left him alone in a room with a gun on the table—implying that there were only three ways out of the situation. He could either comply with their directive, live in detention forever or kill himself. Aamer was later freed in October 2015 after a sustained campaign by civil society for his release.

In Motiwala's case, Katznelson told the court that US prisons were full of gang culture and violence, and Motiwala would be subjected to harsh conditions given the kind of allegations levelled against him. He also categorized Motiwala at a high risk of suicide as he suffered from extreme levels of depression, tension and anxiety, and had attempted suicide on at least three occasions.

But the most bizarre twist of the case came on 19 March 2021. Kamran Faridi landed in the UK with the intent to depose in favour of Motiwala and was stopped by UK immigration authorities at the request of their US counterparts. Faridi wanted to admit under oath before the court that the process to trap Jabir Motiwala was filled with the abuse of legal rights. Faridi also wanted to implicate his former FBI bosses on charges of manipulating evidence to trap Jabir. Faridi was sent back to the US at the FBI's request. He was immediately arrested when he set foot on US soil and sent straight to a US prison from the airport.

Faridi's U-turn, said to be engineered by the ISI and the D-Company, proved to be the final nail in the coffin of the FBI's case. The UK court wanted the US government to confirm if Motiwala would face 'enhanced terror' charges in the US if the extradition request was granted. In the current case, only drugs and extortion charges had been levelled against Motiwala but the prosecution had harped a lot on his association with Dawood Ibrahim. However, no irrefutable proof of this had been provided either by the US or the Crown Prosecution Service (CPS) of the UK. Further, despite multiple correspondence by the court to come clear on the question of 'enhanced terror' charges, the US authorities had chosen not to provide a proper response.

The defence also made a reference to the deplorable jail conditions that had played a part in the death of Jeffrey Epstein on 10 August 2019. A high-flying US financier before he was arrested on various charges of sexual offences, Epstein was in custody at the Special Housing Unit where he was kept in solitary confinement prior to his suicide in the Metropolitan Correction Center in New York.

Deepak Vij and the rest of Motiwala's lawyers knew that they had put up a strong defence and the FBI's game plan had collapsed like a pack of cards. They were waiting for the court judgment to come through when a huge surprise came their way. On 6 April 2021, the CPS reached out to the lawyers and conveyed that the US Department of Justice had decided to dismiss all charges against Jabir Siddiq aka Jabir Motiwala and was formally withdrawing the extradition request. Vij had defended Jabir for nearly three years and their efforts had finally borne fruit.

On 15 April 2021, Jabir flew to Pakistan—a free man. But he was still not done with the UK government. He filed a case against them at the high court of the UK for cancelling his ten-year visit visa. When he was arrested in the UK and under detention from 2018 to 2021, then Home Secretary Preeti Patel had cancelled his visa on charges of overstaying. How could he have left the country when his Pakistani passport had been confiscated and he was in the custody of the UK authorities? The government conceded that the home secretary had acted unlawfully when cancelling the visa and had not applied due discretion before making the decision.

After the case was filed, the Home Office not only restored Motiwala's visa but also awarded him damages for being held unlawfully at Wandsworth Prison for seven days. They also agreed to return the legal fees in five figures that Motiwala had paid for this case. Motiwala's revenge was now complete. Not only had he outsmarted the agencies of two of the most powerful nations on the planet, but he had also set straight his personal record with Kamran Faridi.

For issuing death threats to FBI handlers, Kamran Faridi was sentenced to seven years in jail in December 2020. Judge Cathy Seibel of New York's Southern District Court described it as 'perhaps the most difficult sentencing I have ever done'.[4] She had taken note of Kamran's work with the FBI, which had led to the prevention of several terror attacks, and even though his mistakes had caused a critical case to collapse, his contributions to the home nation could not be overlooked.

'Kamran is still serving the sentence as of May 2023,' Kamaal Hasan said. 'He hopes that he will be offered some leniency on account of his service to the US; and plans to return to Pakistan as soon as he is out of jail.' He paused. 'On the other hand, Jabir Siddiq aka Jabir Motiwala, an alleged top henchman of Dawood Ibrahim, is a free man.'

'Such are the shadow games played between the underworld and powerful sovereign governments,' I said and wished my friend good luck for his trip to London.

28

Fallen Comrade

Crime reporting and investigative journalism are among the most exciting subjects of the larger field of journalism. As a crime reporter, one can unearth dark secrets and break the big news. The ability to go undercover and conduct sting operations is also essential for a crime journalist. As exhilarating as it may sound, the profession is quite a dangerous one. It involves spending a lot of time on the ground, visiting shady places and working in tough conditions.

In the midst of this, there is a thin line, almost imaginary, which one must learn to recognize. The line is: to not wine and dine with your source. Crossing this boundary can have fatal consequences. Some brave reporters have paid a heavy price for even slight miscalculations. When we talk about the killings for which Chhota Rajan was put on trial, there exists a victim whose profile does not match with the don's other targets like Philoo Khan, Majid Khan or Hanif Kadwala.

I shared a close professional and personal relationship with this victim with whom I first interacted during my stint with *Indian Express*. In the late 1990s, I was managing the hectic crime and investigation desk at the paper when a tall, well-built man walked into my cubicle.

'Hussain bhai, I want to *do* crime,' he said.

I tried to act a little funny. 'You have entered the wrong place then,' I said. 'We do not do crimes. We only report them.'

The man looked at me quizzically. I laughed and asked him to take a seat.

His name was Jyotirmoy Dey. He had predominantly been an environmental journalist. He earned his first break writing for the *Afternoon* on the environment beat. But more than birds and trees, it was guns and gangsters that interested him. Hence, he chose to move to the crime beat. I got involved instantly and facilitated his entry into the crime department by speaking to Sai Suresh. Sai was our editor at *Indian Express* who sported a ponytail and was an Aamir Khan look alike. I had recently moved from *Asian Age* to *Indian Express* and it suited me to have more hands to cover a large beat.

We made a deal. J Dey promised to help me with fitness tips and I would help him learn the ropes of crime reporting. He was quite a fitness fanatic and had also worked out in the gym with Pravin Kumar, who had played the role of Bheem in the epic *Mahabharat* serial. Years passed quickly, and J Dey went on to become quite a famous crime reporter, eventually heading the investigations desk at *Mid-Day*.

But J Dey was the kind of man whose aspirations would only get bigger each time he crossed a milestone. He soon became the author of two books, which recounted the stories of some of the dons who came from ghettos and made it to the top of the underworld. One such story was that of Chhota Rajan.

While heaping praises upon J Dey, his colleagues often describe him as a journalist par excellence. His quest to get the news directly from his source increased and so did his trysts with the big players in the underworld. One of the striking features of J Dey was that he spoke very little to people and safeguarded his interests as well as sources passionately. Such reticence eliminated the chances for someone concerned about his welfare to warn him when he might have at some point crossed that thin line and put his life on the line in exchange for a crucial piece of information.

On 11 June 2011, 56-year-old J Dey was getting ready to leave his home. It was an unusual morning at Dey's house in Powai where he lived with his wife Shubha Sharma. For the past few weeks, J Dey was not his usual self. He was shaken, seemingly worried over something he was not ready to discuss with his wife despite her best efforts to elicit that information out of him.

J Dey had started isolating himself and was bothered by something he would not talk about since his return from London. Shubha was unaware of what had transpired on her husband's trip to the UK and was equally confused and concerned by her husband's body language.

The month of June was the typical time when the rains began in Mumbai. Before stepping out of the house, J Dey casually checked the scale of the rain. It was still a drizzle, and not the downpour that the city was sometimes infamous for. J Dey put on his helmet and drove away nervously. But he was unaware of the bike-borne assailants who were tailing him amidst the rain as he was trudging through the waterlogged roads in Powai. Prominent among the criminals was Satish Kaliya, a feared sharpshooter of the Chhota Rajan gang.

Other than the bikers, a Toyota Qualis car was also following Dey as part of a meticulously planned shoot-out. The men in the Qualis were backup shooters to avoid any lapses in the plan and to pick the shooters up and escape in case their bikes broke down or slipped due to the rain.

J Dey took a turn near CRISIL House and moved towards the Spectra building in Powai. Kaliya, who was riding pillion, asked the rider to speed up towards Dey's bike. As soon as they got close enough, Kaliya opened fire. Dey's bike skidded. Five rounds were fired at the reporter, resulting in his death. The incident sent shockwaves through the area, but the people present at the crime scene were too stunned to react.

J Dey was taken to Powai Hospital, but they did not have the proper facilities to attend to him. He was later rushed to Hiranandani Hospital where he was reported dead on arrival. Though the cell phone that Dey had the habit of keeping inside his shirt pocket was completely damaged by the four bullets he sustained in his chest, the police were able to recover the SIM card, which they sent for an analysis of the call and text records. But death had followed J Dey long before the faces of his assailants showed up in the rear-view mirror of his bike.

The Mumbai Police speculated the murder was a professional job and may have been related to his reporting on the oil mafia. This mafia, which pilfers oil being transported and also dilutes it before sale, had been under pressure since the killing of Yashwant Sonawane in January 2011. Sonawane was the additional district collector of Malegaon, who was allegedly burnt alive by the oil mafia near Nashik. Later, the CBI decreed that Sonawane himself was under investigation for graft and was killed by those who were paying him when his demands started skyrocketing.

However, since J Dey was also investigating the oil mafia, the cops had started thinking about this angle. Dey had also recently reported that Chhota Rajan was the mastermind behind a recent shooting involving Dawood Ibrahim's brother Iqbal Kaskar in Mumbai.

Himanshu Roy, who was then joint commissioner of police (crime), started probing the case. Roy was pretty much a supercop in the police sphere, thanks to his Herculean personality. He was an IPS officer from the 1988 batch. His mere appearance was enough to send a chill down the spine of many criminals. Like Dey, Roy was also quite a bodybuilder and would conduct regular press conferences with his biceps bulging under the half-sleeve shirts he usually wore. He was praised among his colleagues as a unique mix of fitness, exceptional policing skills and personality.

The police investigation eventually revealed a meticulous plan to gun down J Dey on the orders of Chhota Rajan. Theories suggested that Rajan had been irked by J Dey's articles, which he thought were demeaning his stature.

One of the articles in question concerned the piece that Dey wrote titled 'Did Rajan Plan Hit on Kaskar?'

The article was published on 30 May 2011, and in one of its passages, Dey had suggested that the attack in the discussion was probably a desperate attempt by the 'ageing gangster' Chhota Rajan to oust Dawood and 'seize a lion's share of the underworld pie'. On 2 June of the same year, Dey penned another article in which he claimed that Rajan's men had gone missing from their hideouts as per police reports, which proved that the don's clout was on the decline.[1]

Asrani started as a small-time telephone booth operator and later turned into a cricket bookie with the help of Chhota Rajan. He then went on to become a well-known builder in the Chembur area, hence earning the moniker 'Vinod Chembur'.

Asrani was arrested earlier in 2005 under the stringent MCOCA, along with Chhota Rajan's wife Sujata Nikhaje and other accomplices. They were arrested for aiding Rajan in legitimizing the money he raised through an extortion racket.

Asrani facilitated the extortion of funds from builders in Tilak Nagar, Chembur and other areas at the behest of Pradip Madgaonkar alias Bandya Mama and made sure that the money found its way into the accounts of Rajan's family members. He also got several tenders with Rajan's help.

As per Asrani's statement, on 7 June 2011, he got a call from Rajan. The underworld don was furious and wanted to know the whereabouts of J Dey. During Dey's recent foreign trips, Rajan suspected that the reporter had met Iqbal Mirchi in London and was also planning to meet Chhota Shakeel. J Dey was also trying to speak with Rajan for professional reasons, which made the don suspect that he wanted to pass his location on to Dawood's gang. Rajan had made up his mind and wanted to eliminate J Dey.

Asrani, who knew J Dey, then called the latter to Uma Bar in Mulund for a drink. He pointed the journalist out to one of the shooters, Satish Kaliya, who had been called there by Asrani and was sitting at a table adjacent to theirs. Kaliya imprinted J Dey's face in his memory and was ready for the hit. All he needed was the right time.

Rohit Thangappan Joseph aka Satish Kaliya, seated on the bike behind co-accused Arun Doke, had shot five rounds at Dey that fateful day. Kaliya, the son of a mill worker from Khar, dropped out of school in Grade IX after being influenced by friends and allegedly got pulled into the world of crime. While in jail for an attempted murder case in 1996, he came in touch with Sunil Madgaonkar alias Matya. Matya was allegedly Rajan's spokesperson and was said to have risen to prominence after ordering high-profile murders such as that of Mahesh Dholakia (owner of Caesar's Palace in Khar) and Thakiyuddin Wahid (promoter of East-West Airlines). Once he joined Matya, Kaliya could allegedly get away with everything. In J Dey's case, he was later nabbed from Rameswaram in Tamil Nadu.

Kaliya later told the police that he received a call from Rajan about twenty days before the murder, offering him a contract killing worth Rs 5 lakh. Kaliya accepted the job without asking any questions or seeking to know anything more about the person he was likely to kill. He later claimed that he was shocked after learning through news channels that he had shot a senior journalist. But the most shocking twist was yet to be revealed, when a female crime journalist, as famous as J Dey, was arrested for playing a key role in his murder.

29

Prime Suspect

J Dey's murder had sent shockwaves through the media fraternity. I was the resident editor of *Asian Age* in Mumbai at that time and the incident had caused the fraternity, despite all their differences, to close their ranks. Prominent journalists took a delegation to the top police hierarchy and to the office of R.R. Patil, then home minister of Maharashtra, to demand swift action in the case.

For obvious reasons, the murder was also heavily reported in the media. Journalists from print and TV were taking the cops to the cleaners for not being able to solve the case. At that time, no one had a clue that another prominent crime journalist in the city was getting sucked into the vortex of this case.

Jigna Vora, who was the deputy bureau chief of *Asian Age* at the time, was also among the top crime journalists in the city. Much like J Dey, I had also mentored Jigna and we had worked together at *Asian Age* since 2008. She was one of my direct hires. At that time, she was famous, or infamous, for her outspokenness. Together, we worked on many stories that were deemed far too risky by others. To witness the feisty Jigna bothered over *something* had rattled me but nothing had prepared me for the reason behind her nervousness.

'The cops might arrest me for J Dey's murder,' she said.

'Ridiculous!' I said. 'Where did you hear that from?'

Apparently, reporting circles were abuzz with rumours that the cops were soon going to arrest a 'female journalist' for her involvement in the crime. Jigna had an inkling that the cops were coming for her. She had come under the scanner for being in touch with Rajan during the days leading up to the murder of J Dey.

'The cops think I instigated Rajan to commit the crime,' Jigna said.

It was true that Jigna had spoken to Chhota Rajan in May 2011. As I have explained earlier, such things are a part of a crime reporter's job. Earlier in that same month, armed assailants had attacked Iqbal Kaskar at Pakmodia Street. Iqbal was one of Dawood's brothers, and the attack in the heart of the D-Company's turf seemed like the fallout of the war between Dawood and Chhota Rajan. While Iqbal escaped unhurt, his driver-cum-bodyguard—Arif Syed—was killed in the attack. Jigna was following up on that story and needed a quote from Rajan.

So she worked through her contacts in Ghatkopar and Chembur, areas known to be dominated by the Rajan gang. Her efforts finally bore fruit when she received news that Rajan had agreed to the interview and would call her late in the night. I remember sitting with Jigna in the office and receiving a call from Rajan from the number he used those days.

Rajan spoke but the call didn't last for long. The story was published. Jigna had no idea that this interview would prove so costly for her. As the cops began investigating the J Dey murder, they constructed a theory that Jigna Vora and J Dey were involved in a professional rivalry. It was also implied that Jigna had incited Rajan against Dey by claiming that the latter had aligned with Dawood Ibrahim's gang and had specifically met Iqbal Mirchi in the UK for that purpose. In reality, J Dey was far too senior than Jigna for any kind of professional rivalry to exist. But there were other factors at play, due to which Jigna's troubles refused to end.

Himanshu Roy had taken over as joint commissioner of police (crime) in May 2010. This position is the second most powerful in the hierarchy of the Mumbai Police, next only to the commissioner of police. Roy had led the investigation, and he oversaw the arrest and prosecution of the accused. The sharpshooter, Satish Kaliya, was arrested. He confessed that he had received Rs 5 lakh for the hit, which he had collected from two unknown people at Chembur and Nallasopara. Kaliya claimed that he had no clue about the identity of the men who had made the last-mile delivery of the supari, and that he only knew that the cash had flowed from Rajan's coffers and found its way to him.

Satish Kaliya was known to be a temperamental and eccentric man. With a gun in his hand, he was all the more dangerous. Even a battle-hardened veteran like Himanshu Roy was stunned by Kaliya's responses during the interrogation.

'Why were none of your associates carrying a weapon?' Roy had asked Kaliya.

Kaliya did not even twitch a muscle. 'They didn't need to because my gun never fails me,' he said.

J Dey was riding his bike when Kaliya shot him. And Kaliya himself was riding pillion on a bike at that time. From a moving position, he was able to fire shots at a moving target with utmost accuracy. The grouping of the bullet wounds was such that all of them were in the range of six inches. Kaliya was indeed a shooter with a cruel, fatal aim.

However, to ease Jigna's worries, I met Himanshu Roy at the 'compound', the name by which the police commissioner's office at Crawford Market was known in reporting circles. Himanshu completely disarmed me with his smile and allayed my fears.

'If Jigna is innocent,' he said, 'no harm will come her way.'

However, Jigna's worst fears came true when she was arrested on 25 November 2011, on the day she was supposed to visit a shrine in Rajasthan for a pilgrimage. Much of Jigna's story has been covered in her book, *Behind Bars in Byculla*. The bestselling book has also been adapted into a web series titled 'Scoop', which has garnered much acclaim.

The media fraternity was quick to throw Jigna to the wolves. She became the subject of a witch-hunt, and the media seemed adamant about burning her image to rags. She was subjected to such intense scrutiny in the case that it appeared as if she was more guilty of the crime than the chief planner (Chhota Rajan) or the chief executioner (Satish Kaliya).

The trial trudged along at a leisurely pace. Himanshu Roy oversaw the collection and analysis of forensic evidence, including DNA samples and mobile phone records, which helped the prosecution to establish the guilt of the accused.

One more arrest in the case was quite interesting: Paulson Joseph. He was one of Rajan's aides and was arrested for being part of the conspiracy to the murder. The cops alleged that three SIM cards with global roaming facilities were distributed between Paulson, Satish Kaliya and Vinod Chembur. All three of them had been in touch with Rajan in the days leading to the murder. However, the cops did not have strong evidence against him, so he was only charged with abetting the crime.

Paulson gained infamy in 2009 when he had organized a party at the Chembur Gymkhana to 'celebrate' the release of D.K. Rao and Farid Tanasha from jail. Both Rao and Tanasha were key members of the Chhota Rajan gang. Havoc broke loose when video footage of the party leaked into the public domain. Several officers of the Mumbai Police, from a DCP to an ACP and a senior police inspector were found dancing at the party, doing the twist alongside the criminal elements from whom they were supposed to protect the public. Soon after the leak, the cops were suspended but Paulson gained notoriety of another level.

Vinod Chembur later obtained bail in the case citing ill health. He was suffering from cirrhosis of the liver. He kept extending his bail by filing applications to travel abroad for treatment. In early 2015, he was granted permission by the court to travel to London for treatment but he did not make the visit. In April 2015, he filed an application to travel to Singapore. The application came up for its final hearing in mid-April. However, Vinod Asrani aka Vinod Chembur expired on the same morning.

Even during court hearings, Satish Kaliya was known to be unrepentant. When the accused were presented before the court, he would ensure that nobody sat near him. He was the sharpshooter in this case, a hero in his own mind, and no one else was allowed to steal the limelight from him. It seemed like there was a social hierarchy among the accused in the case as well.

After Rajan's return to India in 2015, he was also made to stand trial in this case, which he attended via videoconferencing from a high-security cell in Tihar Jail, Delhi. While the prosecution had a strong case against most accused, their evidence against Jigna was pretty weak and could not stand against the cross-examination of the defence counsel. On 2 May 2018, when the judge announced the verdict in the case, Jigna Vora and Paulson Joseph were the only two out of the ten accused who were acquitted in the case. Vinod Asrani was 'appended', considering that he had expired before the final verdict.

Rohit Joseph alias Satish Kaliya was sentenced to life imprisonment. This was the first case in which Chhota Rajan was convicted after his return to India. He casually acknowledged the sentence of the judge by saying '*theek hai*'.

Himanshu Roy, the man who had arrested Kaliya, met with a rather unfortunate end. In the year 2000, Roy had been operated upon as he was suffering from renal cancer. He had to undergo a nephrectomy, i.e. removal of the infected kidney. Even after this, he went on to live an active lifestyle and build a physique like that of a professional bodybuilder. After he was posted to Mumbai, he handled many high-profile cases as well. But in 2016, the disease returned and spread to his bones.

The relapse broke his spirit. The chemotherapy that followed also took a toll on his body. He lost weight and muscle. His physical appearance turned into a pale shadow of his former self.

On 11 May 2018, sometime in the afternoon, he walked into his room, pulled out his service revolver, and fired a shot after placing the barrel in his mouth. Merely four days ago, the doctors had told him that the cancer was under control and that he had a chance of defeating the disease he was fighting. Alas, that was not to be. He was cremated around 10 p.m. on 11 May 2018 at the Chandanwadi crematorium in Marine Lines, Mumbai. Interestingly, around the same time, Jigna Vora was acquitted in the J Dey murder case on 2 May 2018.

The trial court order granting acquittal to Jigna Vora did not sit well with the city police who had arrested her, as well as the CBI. To them, it was a clear case of one-upmanship where one had abetted the murder of another in the quest to gain an upper hand. Her release had perhaps punctured a hole in their ego and the matter was subsequently raised to the high court.

'There is no foundation to the charge that Vora had instigated the murder,' the high court had observed, upholding the trial court's judgment of Vora's acquittal. In a response to the CBI's fixation on Vora's phone conversation with Rajan, the high court simply drew attention to the fact that the transcript of the call produced by the CBI had nothing in it to prove that Vora incited Rajan against J Dey. Adding that Vora was out of station for ten days since the day prior to the murder, the court said that all that the call data record contained was a conversation between Rajan and another accused Manoj Shivdasani.

A real estate agent, Manoj Shivdasani was another accused in the murder case, who had submitted in his initial statement that Rajan had spoken of Vora on a phone call with him. Shivdasani later backtracked from this statement and said the don had called him to simply ask about Asrani's health.

The call in question was said to have been made by Rajan two months after the killing. If anything, the content of the conversation lent some credibility to the theory of Rajan's contempt for J Dey on account of the latter's works that seemingly antagonized Rajan. If at all, the purported phone call made it amply clear that Rajan's perception of J Dey working for Dawood and writing articles disparaging him at the behest of his rival was what led him to order his killing. There was no mention of Vora, and Shivdasani had attested to that much in the later statements he gave in court during the trial.

Jigna Vora bid goodbye to journalism. As of writing this book, she has made her TV debut by appearing on the reality show *Bigg Boss*.

After her acquittal, I gave the following quote in the media: 'At one point, if there were two very good crime journalists in the city, it was Jyoti (J Dey) and Jigna. I would often tell my wife one of them is Amitabh, and the other one is Vinod Khanna; there is very little to choose between them. I was proud to be a mentor to both of them.

Their rivalry was healthy and unmatched, and I enjoyed the kind of sparring between them, which showed in the kind of stories they did. For a crime journalist, the only way to compete is by writing fine stories, not murder.'

30

India's Escobar

Narcos, the series on Netflix, captured the world's attention. Columbian drug lord Pablo Emilio Escobar Gaviria founded the Medellin Cartel and built a narco empire worth $30 billion at the time of his death in 1993. Around the same time, there was a player in India who could arguably be called India's Escobar. This man was none other than Mohammad Iqbal Memon aka Iqbal Mirchi.

'We never stopped chasing him,' Neeraj Kumar told me. 'We went after him in India, and abroad too.'

Kumar was right. He was in the thick of the action when it came to Mirchi. It was a mission that took him to foreign shores. 'It began with that flight to London,' Kumar said.

In 1995, IPS Neeraj Kumar and Hemant Karkare landed in the UK and headed straight for the St James Court Hotel in London. They were among the two most promising police officers of the country. The duo were here for a high-profile mission. They had hardly dropped their luggage and made themselves comfortable when the phone in the room trilled. Kumar was the one who picked up the phone.

'You know we are dangerous,' a hoarse voice said to Kumar. 'And we know that you are here.'

It wasn't the first time that Kumar had been threatened. He took it in his stride. His itinerary had been leaked and relayed to the man they were pursuing—Iqbal Mirchi who was known to be an associate of Dawood Ibrahim and kingpin of a narcotics empire. Mirchi had fled to the UK sometime before the Mumbai bomb blasts of 1993. His name kept cropping up during the subsequent investigation.

Two of the country's best officers were sent to extradite Mirchi back to India. Neeraj Kumar was part of the CBI STF that was probing the blasts and Karkare was involved as he had worked extensively with the Anti-Narcotics Cell.

On Monday, 3 April 1995, Iqbal Mirchi woke up to the sharp raps on the door of his farmhouse located in Essex. Officers of Interpol and Scotland Yard had reached his doorstep with a warrant for his arrest.

An RCN for Mirchi had been issued by Interpol at India's behest in relation to two high-profile narcotics cases. Mandrax tablets and methaqualone powder had been seized by the Anti-Narcotics Cell in India. The estimated worth of the contraband was worth Rs 9 crore.

Mirchi was arrested and was scheduled to be presented at the Bow Street Magistrates' Court the next day. This was the first of the two extradition trials that Mirchi would undergo during his stay in the UK. Neeraj Kumar and Hemant Karkare were in charge of getting Mirchi extradited back to India.

The threatening call that Kumar received upon reaching the hotel left him more surprised than scared. The man they had come after was more of a swindler who ran the biggest narcotics ring in India. But Mirchi's notoriety had grown manifold and he had not shied away from threatening one of the senior police officers of the country.

Mohammad Iqbal Memon aka Iqbal Mirchi was born on 25 April 1950 in Dongri—an area that, until recently, found its mention inseparable from that of the big names of the underworld, such as Haji Mastan and Dawood Ibrahim Kaskar. His family was involved in the business of masala (spices) trading that went back a few generations. Their shop was located in the famous market of Null Bazar. Old-timers recollect that Iqbal would fold the front of his kurta and fill it with chilli powder and then slap his stomach with one hand, exhorting potential customers to buy his wares.

Mirchi took on his family business and continued its march forward. He expanded it from retail to securing orders from big hotels and restaurants that dealt in larger quantities. He started making considerable profits from the sales to these hotels and gained the reputation of a shrewd businessman in his social circles. This provided him with considerable clout, which he used to further his advantage. Even in business, Mirchi followed a take-no-prisoners approach. He wanted to conquer all.

'Stay in your limits,' Mirchi had said to one of his fellow traders in the market. 'Don't even venture near the hotels where I supply. Otherwise, I will wipe your business from the market.'

Mirchi had an insatiable appetite for money. The handsome profits he generated from his masala business were nowhere near the amount of wealth he desired. He craved more and thought of ways to amass more wealth in less time. He zeroed in on smuggling from the docks, the illegal trade which was the reason for the affluence and popularity of men like Haji Mastan.

Full liberalization of the economy was about a decade away. Exploitation of the docks for the smuggling of highly demanded goods was at its peak. Mirchi too, in his quest for making more money in less time, turned his attention to the docks and mobilized a group of men to invade the docks during the night.

Mirchi and his men would steal electronic items, textiles, watches and goods that were high in demand and lucrative in their returns. He came to be called '*godi ka chooha*' (a rat from the docks) by his detractors, who did not want to admit his quick rise to fame and wealth. Mirchi's avarice did not end there. He desired to make more and more. He considered laying his hands on goods that were easy to hide and yet had a bigger market in foreign lands.

'Perhaps we should focus on smuggling gold,' Mirchi's friend suggested.

'One thing is more lucrative than that stupid piece of metal,' Mirchi said.

'What?'

'Drugs.'

He had spoken the word. And then he had gone on to establish a narco empire across the world, which put him on the list of India's most wanted men. Mirchi came up with an ingenious plan. He would break into the docks at night, swipe 2 to 4 kg of cocaine, stow them into a container and note down the container's number before making his way out of there. Then he would convey the container's number to his contacts whom he knew were capable of releasing the pilfered cocaine from the docks by means fair or foul in return for a share in the profit. The cocaine would be released without much difficulty and everybody would make profits from its sale with Mirchi keeping the lion's share. This marked the beginning of Iqbal's journey from being Iqbal Mirchi to ultimately becoming famous by the name Iqbal Powder (powder indicating cocaine).

As the scale of his operations increased, Mirchi started maintaining storehouses wherein he stashed drugs like heroin, hashish and Mandrax. He was arrested in 1982 along with his associate Niaz Khan for smuggling contraband goods, which was a rare blip in his misadventures with drug trafficking that largely went undetected for a while. In 1985, he was detained under National Security Act (NSA) and was described at the time as a 'notorious dock thief'.[1]

Law enforcement agencies began taking notice of Mirchi's antics. They became alert about taking action against him. Their wait ended in 1986 when the Directorate of Revenue Intelligence (DRI) located a farmhouse in Talasari in Thane District, holding 602 kg of heroin, 4564 kg of hashish and 4 kg of Mandrax tablets. The total worth of the seized items was estimated to be around Rs 9 crore; the biggest-ever haul in the history of narcotics in India at that time.

The farmhouse was pinned down to Mirchi and a reward of Rs 5000 was announced for anyone who could provide information on Mirchi or his associate Niaz. But the wily Mirchi had a trick up his sleeve to escape the severe punishment that the seizure of such enormous amounts of drugs called for.

The Mumbai Police, in 1984, had sent summons to Mirchi under the Conservation of Foreign Exchange and Prevention of Smuggling Activities Act (COFEPOSA). But the act, since its passing in 1974 during the Indira Gandhi government, never really took effect and remained restricted to the papers. Mirchi was well aware of the particular law's inefficacy and so didn't bother himself with responding to the summons at that time.

But after the Thane farmhouse seizure, Mirchi saw his illegal trade on the brink of total collapse. As a ploy to escape from the DRI, he turned himself in to the police in reference to the two-year-old summons under COFEPOSA. He was taken into remand, which ensured that he remained out of the reach of the DRI, who wanted to question him on the Thane farmhouse case. He pulled a rabbit out of his hat and managed to escape the clutches of the DRI by a whisker.

Mirchi remained in jail for just over three months. By the month of May, he was out walking free. He appeared before the CBI to mark himself present and was arrested by the DRI the same day. He paid Rs 2 lakh for his bail, which was granted by the order of the additional chief metropolitan magistrate. Thus, by merely serving three months in jail and spending Rs 2 lakh, Mirchi cleared his name from all charges that came under the law of narcotics. Later, he escaped to the UK.

For this reason, Kumar and Karkare had arrived in London to extradite him and they attended the extradition hearing in Westminster. The second day of the hearing fell on 6 April 1995. The prosecution annexed one more case in the list of Mirchi's offences. This one had quite a serious charge.

'The defendant is also accused of carrying out the murder of one Amar Suvarna,' the prosecution said as the hearing began.

Mirchi fumed at the prosecution's move. The defence quickly took recourse to the argument that the prosecution was required to produce the necessary documents to substantiate the accusation of murder. Surprisingly, the prosecution hadn't come equipped with evidence to substantiate the charge. It had to request the magistrate to allow a few days to produce the evidence. The magistrate consented and fixed the date of 9 June as the final date of presentation of the documents. The prosecution was hopeful that the murder of Amar Suvarna, which was committed at the behest of Mirchi in Mumbai, would prove decisive in the successful extradition of Mirchi to India.

Until 1994, Mirchi and Suvarna were good friends. After moving to the UK, Mirchi set out to create the image of a legitimate businessman for himself among the gentry of London. For that, he needed to learn the etiquette and manners befitting a person wanting to become a part of such a community. He asked Suvarna to help with the task.

Suvarna helped Mirchi and also introduced him to the drug syndicates operating in Europe and Canada. Mirchi made Suvarna the manager of his rice mill in the UK. But sharing the spoils of their misdeeds became a bone of contention between the two.

Eventually, Mirchi took Suvarna off the managerial position of the rice mill and sent him to Dubai on the pretext of looking after his businesses there. Later, he packed him off to India and kicked him out of the business completely. Suvarna was enraged and swore revenge.

By then, Neeraj Kumar had joined the CBI. He was sent to Mumbai to investigate the 1993 serial bombings in the city. Kumar's first breakthrough came from none other than Amar Suvarna. The latter passed critical information on Mirchi's transactions to Ranjith Sethi, who was the Indian ambassador to the UAE at the time. Sethi visited Delhi and met CBI Director K. Vijaya Rama Rao and shared the input. Sethi was then referred to Kumar, who began gathering information on Mirchi through Suvarna.

In Mumbai, top police officers would draw a blank whenever Kumar brought up the topic of Iqbal Mirchi. Through his sources, Kumar was successful in tracing down Mirchi's properties around the city. Afraid that his plans would be leaked, Kumar kept Mirchi's investigation under wraps. Still Iqbal Mirchi was made aware of Kumar's interest in smoking him out. During that time, Kumar received a call from Mirchi, who was then based in Dubai where he owned Hotel Imperial Suites along with a shipping company.

'Why are you investigating me?' Mirchi had asked Kumar.

'It's a part of my job,' Kumar had responded.

During this period, the two seizures of Mirchi's drugs occurred; he escaped to the UK and had then been dragged to the London court. Mirchi immediately suspected Suvarna was snitching on him. Days after his telephonic conversation with Kumar, Suvarna was killed near a hotel at Kala Ghoda. The Mumbai Police charged Mirchi in the murder case.

Kumar then got an RCN issued against Mirchi through Interpol, who arrested Mirchi from his farmhouse in Essex. Many properties that Mirchi had purchased became the focus of fresh inquiries by the CBI.

While smuggling and exporting dangerous drugs such as meth and Mandrax gave new wings to Mirchi's business, it also posed a risk due to the sudden influx of large amounts of cash. He ended up making a number of benami investments in real estate to hide his wealth.

Starting with the purchase of Hotel Ashiana, Mirchi went on to buy numerous other properties in the prime locations of the city such as Worli, Crawford Market and Juhu. Though each property stood as a symbol of his financial power, nothing came close to the one that Mirchi held most dear to himself, the notorious Fisherman's Wharf.

Transformed into a disco bar, Fisherman's Wharf was especially chosen by Mirchi to host highly important guests and parties. The bar was specifically targeted by the CBI and the police during their crackdown on Mirchi's properties. It was also seized at least twice. But the battle to bring Mirchi back to India was far from over. He was a seasoned operator who would try every trick in the book to escape from the clutches of the law.

31

Fugitive

The day was 2 September 1993. The Anti-Narcotics Cell (ANC) of the Mumbai Police was on the move. Considering the guile of the man they were up against, the law agency did not have much time to spare. They had to reach the Jewel of India Hotel, located in Worli, before the news of their operation reached Iqbal Mirchi and their quarry slipped out of their hands.

The ANC was acting on a tip-off that promised a big breakthrough in their efforts to stall the rise of the drug empire in the country. According to their information, a jeep containing a big consignment of illegal substances was parked near the Jewel of India Hotel. The officers reached the spot in time. An officer climbed into the jeep from the back while another waited outside with his gun aimed at the rear entrance of the vehicle.

'*Ae*,' the officer inside the jeep called out. 'Look at this. Unbelievable!'

The second officer slipped his gun into the small of his back and scurried towards the jeep. His eyes widened with surprise. He was looking at a pile of nearly 150 kg of Mandrax tablets that were kept hidden under the seat carefully. The officers seized the content as well as the jeep and launched an investigation. Two names, Angelo D'Souza and Dhananjay, emerged as the key players in the handling and delivery of the drugs and the agency quickly made arrests.

The duo spilled a few names involved in the smuggling. In addition, they also revealed one more location where another consignment of an even bigger quantity was waiting for disposal. The officers sprang into action quickly once again and caught hold of the consignment before it was too late. The quantity of the Mandrax tablets seized this time turned out to be higher than the previous one. The total amount of Mandrax climbed to 2000 kg with an estimated worth of over Rs 2 crore. It sent shockwaves through the entire law agency and a case was duly filed in the sessions court.

Around fourteen people were accused of being party to the crime. Six were found absconding, including Iqbal Mirchi. The ANC had also gone to great lengths in gathering witnesses who could testify against the accused and particularly against Mirchi in the court. Statements of close to fifty witnesses were taken. Much to the ANC's surprise, not one of them named Mirchi in their statements. The drug lord had given the law another slip and fled the country.

Years later in the UK, in 1995, Neeraj Kumar and Hemant Karkare were trying to get Mirchi extradited.

The mood in the Bow Street Magistrates' Court was tense. Mirchi's second wife, Heena Kausar, the daughter-actress of the famous director K. Asif, was present at the hearing and was watching the proceedings nervously. Neeraj Kumar and Hemant Karkare were also seated in the courtroom.

'Your Honour,' the prosecution lawyer said, holding a bunch of papers in his hands, 'these papers contain the full statement of Cyrus Cooper, who is the lone witness in the Amar Suvarna murder case.'

The judge was busy perusing the papers. James Lewis, regarded as one of the top solicitors in England, and Clive Nicholls QC, a distinguished and highly acclaimed extradition lawyer, were representing Mirchi. The fugitive's fortune, if anything, had quadrupled from the time he had left Indian borders.

'The date of the said testimony is at least a year after the murder,' the defendant lawyer said. 'This casts a serious doubt on the motivation of the witness and by corollary, on the testimony itself.'

The judge nodded and returned to examining the papers. Kumar and Karkare were visibly anxious.

'I am afraid,' the judge said, 'the documents that I am reading right now do not seem to be attested by the relevant authorities.'

The prosecution lawyer rose from his chair wearily and tried to provide an explanation.

'I am sure you know that's inexcusable,' the judge said. 'According to section 27 of the British Act of Extradition, you need to have the attestation of either a judicial authority or a minister in charge of the prosecuting department in order to have the testimony accepted by the court.'

The prosecution lawyer drooped his shoulders as an indication of being at a loss for a response before sinking down in his chair. Karkare, for some reason, looked unhappy with the judge's remark and whispered something into Kumar's ear, to which Kumar gave a curt nod. They had now become painfully aware that the case was slipping away from their hands. Kumar looked at Mirchi who seemed to be extremely pleased by the remark the judge had just made.

Karkare's resentment with the judge's apparent preference for Mirchi was not without reason. He as well as Kumar had been witness to the police's consistent reluctance in taking appropriate action against Mirchi and dragging him to court for various serious offences that he had committed when he was still in India. According to them, the only reason behind the police's inaction was that Mirchi had been using his enormous wealth to grease the wheels of the system that refused to turn against him until it was too late.

Just a year after the ANC had found and seized Mandrax tablets worth crores of rupees, the police received information of a similar consignment present in Mumbai and Gujarat's Mehsana District. The police reached the locations and conducted a raid. A total of 5000 kg of Mandrax tablets was seized from the two locations—a huge quantity. Despite it being evident that Mirchi was the man behind the gargantuan rise of the illegal drugs business, he was merely mentioned as the 'main supplier of the narcotics drugs' in the remand application filed in relation to the case. Even more surprising was the complete absence of Iqbal Mirchi's name in the first chargesheet drafted by the police in the case!

His name only found a mention in the one-page supplementary chargesheet that was filed later in the same year. Though one good look even at this supplementary chargesheet would tell its reader that Karkare and Kumar's apprehension of the police department's infidelity wasn't entirely unwarranted. The supplementary chargesheet read that an accused named Nitin Bhanushali was told by another accused, Prem Shetty, that he was working for Mirchi. The chargesheet was as vague in terms of accusing Mirchi as it could get.

Going back a year from there, Judge B.M. Gupta of the sessions court found himself being divested of the authority to try any of the narcotics cases in the future. Such an order had come from the then Justice of the Mumbai High Court, Aravind Sawant. Gupta's removal came as a result of a report that found him responsible for granting bail to a person who was a clear offender in a couple of cases filed against him by the Narcotics Control Bureau (NCB). The high court subsequently ordered the cancellation of the said bail and appointed another judge to reopen and re-examine the two cases. The glaring oversight by Gupta that invited the high court's order of barring him from further trying narcotics cases was mentioned by some as a proof of the complicity of the guardians of law in the perpetuation of the illegal narcotics trade in India.

The Bow Street Magistrates' Court judge was still not done studying the documents before him. He flipped through the papers for a while before announcing that the court was adjourned for the day. He fixed the date of the next hearing in the next month. It was going to take a while before Kumar and Karkare could get closure on Mirchi's extradition and fly back to India, hopefully with Mirchi in their custody.

In the days that followed, the prosecution chose to submit additional files and documents in the court that included other instances of Mirchi's stocking and distributing contraband substances from different locations. The activity took extra time, which caused the subsequent hearings to be delayed by at least a month.

Mirchi, meanwhile, remained in the custody of the court. He was infuriated that the agencies have been shadowing him all over the globe even though he kept moving from the UAE to the UK.

The initial pleasure and delight of landing in an opulent Gulf country hadn't lasted long for Mirchi as he got unsettled when he saw that Dubai was overcrowded by the mafia fugitives who were running from Indian law authorities following the 1993 blasts. The one practice that separated Mirchi from fellow criminals of the 1990s and kept him largely out of the law and media's attention was maintaining a distance from glory and glamour.

Unlike his peers in the underworld such as Dawood Ibrahim and Chhota Shakeel, Mirchi displayed no such desire to get close to and rule over the Bollywood industry—despite his wife belonging to a prominent family of that industry.

He preferred carrying out illegitimate activities in the shadows. The idea of sharing the same space with fugitives of the bomb blasts made him feel uneasy. He envisioned himself leaving Dubai soon and now sought a new base. He started expanding and exporting his business to various countries such as South Africa, Germany, Australia, the UK and the US.

From being born and raised in Mumbai to eventually fleeing to Dubai to escape the law, Mirchi had more than one aspect of his life that was common to the head of the gang accused of carrying out the blasts, Dawood Ibrahim Kaskar. But Mirchi's peril did not end there.

The investigation launched into the bomb blasts named Tiger Memon as the prime accused and the mastermind of the serial blasts. And since Iqbal was known to be a D-Company associate in police records and was himself a Memon too, the fingers of his complicity were being pointed at him, though at no point could the CBI or the Mumbai Police ever establish his role or involvement in the serial blasts. This latest development had Mirchi extremely worried. He finally decided that the time had come to leave Dubai and reach the UK.

32

Wily Wolf

On the fifth day of the hearing, Neeraj Kumar and Hemant Karkare got ready to reach the Bow Street Magistrates' Court. The prosecution had a hard time availing itself the additional documents in the court to sufficiently establish the extent of Mirchi's involvement in the crimes he was being accused of. The result was that the evidence submitted in the court appeared ineffective and not efficiently assembled. But it was not just the prosecution that was to be entirely blamed. The weakness of the submitted documents was the result of the cumulative laxity of the police force in general.

Fingers were pointed at an official occupying an important position. Rahul Rai Sur, an IPS officer at the time, was said to have several files in his possession that could have proved Mirchi's involvement in narcotics and drug smuggling. But Sur, reportedly, simply chose to sit on these files and blocked any attempt to have them released.

Not long ago, Mirchi had alleged that a high-ranking official had asked Mirchi for a bribe in exchange for leniency. But later developments in 2021 revealed that Rahul Rai eventually won the case against him in which he was accused of truancy in Mirchi's case. He had also given an interview where he said that he held no such file that documented Mirchi's crimes. None of his seniors, Rahul Rai alleged, who had held the office before him had made any mention of the existence of such a file.

However, during the hearing at the Bow Street Magistrates' Court, Heena Kausar had a gloomy expression on her face and a silent prayer on her lips. Jeremy Connor, the judge, was busy scribbling on a legal pad. Kumar and Karkare sat in their usual places. Their faces showed no sign of delight or despair.

Mirchi sat in the space next to his lawyers. Traces of white had salted his hair. Otherwise, Mirchi was the same innocuous and harmless-looking man, and anyone who passed by him on a street would never suspect that he was one of the biggest drug lords of the era.

While Judge Connor was busy with the papers, the prosecution was preparing to present its arguments in the light of the new documents submitted in the court.

Though the paperwork was lacking in impact, the prosecution was expecting the court to conduct a trial in such a high-profile case. But they were swept off their feet when the judge declared that the case against Mirchi had been quashed as the evidence presented against him was incoherent and failed to justify the grounds for his extradition. Kumar and Karkare seemed surprised but not completely shocked. The only thing that struck them as terribly odd was that the judge seemed to be in a hurry to announce his verdict in just under six hearings and did not allow the case to enter a trial. Two of the country's top cops had to return to India without the man they had come chasing to the UK. Karkare would often cite the court's decision as proof of the 'managed' nature of things.

After fleeing from Dubai and landing in the UK, Mirchi had tried to build a clean image for himself in London. Apart from owning a few properties, a rice mill and restaurants in the city's premiere tourist location, Canary Wharf, Mirchi also started investing in the construction businesses.

Back in India, after failing to get Mirchi extradited, the CBI decided to open an inquiry about the several properties that the drug czar owned in the prime locations of the financial capital of the country. The humiliation in the UK had only spurred the authorities to get more aggressive against Mirchi.

The NCB also proactively examined sources through which Mirchi had acquired multiple properties in Mumbai and around the country. It launched an investigation into this a month before Mirchi's arrest in London. Within two years, eleven properties were seized.

Mirchi leveraged his money power to reclaim the properties that were under the threat of being seized and held by the Indian court. The NCB had ransacked, searched and seized one property after another. Several of Mirchi's properties in Worli were seized along with a Union Bank of India locker in the Juhu branch.

But the most prominent jewel in Mirchi's crown was his hotel-cum-dance bar, Fisherman's Wharf. Mirchi was brazen about the establishment where every vice of the world was available for a price. He claimed that the place had helped him win many contracts. This particular property had been subjected to raids at least a couple times even before Mirchi had moved to the UK.

In one such incident earlier, Mirchi and his clients were sitting at Fisherman's Wharf in Worli. Although the place was run by Mirchi as a dance bar under the guise of a restaurant, striptease would often be held on special occasions. On one such night, a striptease was in overdrive.

Mirchi's clients were enjoying the lusty scenes of beautiful women peeling clothing off their bodies, one piece at a time. But he was also wary of two men sitting at a table away from them. The faces of those men did not seem familiar and that had raised Mirchi's suspicions.

'This is great!' one of the patrons told Mirchi. 'Your club is comparable to those in Vegas.'

Mirchi was gloating from the praise when one of his men walked up to him and whispered something in his ear. A grimace replaced his smile.

'Party's over,' Mirchi told his patrons.

'What happened?' one of the patrons asked.

'My manager said there's something wrong with the electricity system. There is a chance of a short circuit.'

Mirchi was giving his patrons a subtle hint. The two men he had grown suspicious of were police informers. Mirchi ushered his clients out of the building. A few moments later, a posse of policemen raided Fisherman's Wharf. But Mirchi managed to escape by the skin of his teeth. However, he had to face a little difficulty in reinstating the hotel and getting it back into business.

But not all events that Mirchi hosted for his clients ended with the police or other law enforcement agencies invading and carrying out a raid. Most of them went smoothly and met the purpose for which they were organized. Mirchi often boasted to the media about organizing parties for business tycoons. Fisherman's Wharf was raided again by the Vigilance Department of the Mumbai Police in March and a second time in September 1992.

In October 1997, a competent authority under the Narcotic Drugs and Psychotropic Substances (NDPS) Act passed an order demanding the release of six out of the eleven properties that had been seized. 'The six properties in question have been shown to be legally acquired and therefore lie out of the purview of legal confiscation,' the authority had said. It also directed the Juhu locker to be closed and a fresh notice to be issued seeking its seizure.

The Maharashtra government was outraged at the decision and approached the high court to allow the re-seizure of the six properties. The high court too turned down the state's application and held the judgment that those properties be released to Mirchi.

After Mirchi's lawyers had successfully retained the six properties, in January 1999 the chief metropolitan magistrate ordered the attachment of another set of properties. This new round of seizure reportedly included some of Mirchi's prized possessions, such as Hotel Minaz and a couple of flats in Juhu and three sea-facing buildings in Worli.

A later chargesheet filed by the Enforcement Directorate (ED) also mentioned Mirchi's humongous real estate fortune in the UK that amounted to fifteen properties and a hotel in London. The ED, in its investigations, had found out that Mirchi had registered two companies, namely Mihaj Investment Corporation, registered in his first wife Hajra's name in Dubai, and Jamaica Tavern, the directors of which were his second wife Heena and his son from his first wife.

Mihaj Investment Corporation had given loans to Jamaica Tavern in January 2019. The said loans, which were acquired during the period between 2003 and 2010, were used to cover the losses incurred from the restaurant Dockmaster's House. The hotel was owned by Jamaica Tavern. The report made publicly available showed Jamaica Tavern receiving money from Mihaj Investment to the tune of Rs 36 crore.

Years later, Jamaica Tavern went into liquidation. It sold its assets and transferred the proceeds to Mihaj Investment Corporation. Mihaj Investment had invested in a corporation called Country Properties and Mirchi's elder son Junaid was the director of this company.

Country Properties was found to have bought fifteen pieces of property that mostly constituted flats in London. The drug money trail led the agency to emails exchanged between Mirchi, his family members, attorney, fund manager and a contractor. Further investigations revealed that, following its liquidation, Jamaica Tavern had given Rs 45 crore to its creditor Mihaj Investment.

Mirchi was also seeking to clear his name from several legal cases that were booked against him in the Indian courts. But after several failed attempts, he realized that getting away from Indian courts wasn't as easy a job as winning an extradition case from the UK court was. So finally, around the year 1999, Mirchi requested the intervention of the court as he expressed his desire through his lawyer Shyam Keswani that he wanted to return to Mumbai. Mirchi had proved himself to be a wily wolf. The man had thrown another curveball at the authorities. What remained to be seen was how they would react to it.

33

Death of the Kingpin

The year was 2011 and I was the resident editor of the Mumbai edition of *Asian Age*. I had built quite a team of reporters. Each day, we were setting the narrative by breaking big stories way before the TV media could catch a whiff of them. The reporters would usually assemble in my cabin, and we would try to plan the articles for the next few days. Needless to say, the journos I had groomed were relentlessly delivering the goods, one story after another. But sometimes, the story came chasing us. One afternoon, there was a faint knock on the door. I was informed that a lawyer had come to meet me.

'I don't have any legal appointments,' I told my assistant Pramodini, who had brought the message.

'He says it's urgent,' she insisted. 'He says he wants to disclose something about one Iqbal Mirchi to you.'

Wow, I thought and asked for the lawyer to be sent through. He was one of the city's best lawyers with an office at Nariman Point, one of the prime real estate locations in the country. Like a good lawyer, he was sharp and to the point. He didn't waste much time on pleasantries.

'I want you to publish an article conveying my client's wish to return to the country and face the law,' he said.

'And your client happens to be Iqbal Mirchi?'

He nodded and took a sip from his cup of tea before setting it down on the table. I was trying to make sense of the request that had just been made. He was appointed by Iqbal Mirchi to represent him in the Indian courts. While I was aware that Mirchi may be trying to build his case through a PR campaign, I wanted to test the seriousness of the drug baron's intent.

'You are a respected lawyer,' I told the emissary. 'You have complete access to the legal channels and can take this matter up with the court.'

'That's true. But do you know what happened when Ram Jethmalani approached the government of the day carrying a similar proposition made by Dawood Ibrahim?'

I nodded. Public perception was an important factor when it came to making decisions in high places. And whether I liked it or not, Iqbal Mirchi made *news*. In 2004, the US had named him in the list of drug kingpins under the Foreign Narcotics Kingpin Designation Act. The law was designed to prevent narcotics traffickers and their operatives and associates from gaining access to the financial systems of the US. The Bush administration had cited Mirchi's links with Dawood Ibrahim and terrorism as a reason for his appearance on this notorious list.

In 2003, Dawood had been listed as a global terrorist by the US for his role in the 1993 Mumbai bomb blasts. A reward of $25 million was announced for information that could lead to his arrest. Mirchi's appearance on a high-value target list of the US only testified that the notoriety he had gained was second only to Dawood Ibrahim's.

'Okay,' I said. 'My paper can't function as a mouthpiece for your client. But I can publish the facts as they stand.'

He agreed. The government was going all out to capture Mirchi's financial assets. The drug baron appeared desperate to clear his name in the Indian courts. But no legal manoeuvres, similar to the ones he employed during the hearings in London, seemed to work now for Mirchi. Justice Vishnu Sahai of the Bombay High Court said in no uncertain terms that Mirchi was obligated to surrender to the law and submit to the jurisdiction of the court before any petition relating to the discharge of his application could be heard by the court.

Similarly, the petition filed by Mirchi's brother, Aslam Memon, seeking to quash the detention order issued against him by the state government was snubbed by the high court. Justice Aravind Savant and Justice Chandrashekhara Das had observed that such a petition could not be entertained as the petitioner was considered absconding in the eyes of the law. The court upheld the Maharashtra government's objection, which effectively compelled Mirchi to refrain from hoodwinking the Indian courts into granting him a passage of escape.

'He was a soft-spoken person and had a genial personality,' said one of the journalists who had met Mirchi a few times in India and abroad.

In fact, Mirchi had mastered the technique of laying low and kept his professional and particularly private life under cover. Very little is known by way of his behaviour and the treatment he afforded his immediate family and relatives. He was said to have a rocky relationship with his sons who had grown up in boarding schools in Panchgani.

His sons took over and picked up from where their father's deal with Dheeraj Wadhawan, the non-executive head of Dewan Housing Finance Ltd, had reached. Mirchi had sold three of his properties, Rabia Mansion, Sea View and Marium Lodge that were situated in Worli, to Dheeraj Wadhawan for Rs 225 crore. Years later, Mirchi's sons and his first wife, Hajra, got into a dispute with Wadhawan as they claimed that Wadhawan had bought the properties at a much cheaper rate than their actual worth.

Wadhawan found himself in a fix as he had already conceived a residential tower coming up in the place where the three properties had stood. The dispute ultimately gave rise to a legal feud between the two parties, which unearthed ugly truths.

'I have made full payments as per the initial agreement,' Wadhawan would say passionately during the many meetings that took place between the disputing parties in the offices of law firms Hariani and Company and Miskita and Company. The meetings would be mediated by numerous lawyers representing each party and attended by several of Mirchi's relatives.

In reality, the three properties of interest had been entangled in legal controversies long before Mirchi had struck a deal with Wadhawan to sell them during the latter's trip to London in 2010. Mirchi had bought these properties from the Sir Mohammad Yusuf Trust in September 1986 for Rs 6.5 lakh. The ED confiscated these three properties under the Smugglers and Foreign Exchange Manipulators Act (SAFEMA). Investigations by the ED revealed that when the three buildings had come under the authorities' scrutiny and were on the brink of getting freezed, the chairperson of the trust, Haroun Yusuf, came forward with the claim that the buildings still belonged to the trust.

It was a ploy that came out of Mirchi's mischievous mind. He had also planted tenants there to make it appear that the buildings were tenanted properties. But a crafty Mirchi got caught in his own trap when he drew a contract for the redevelopment of the buildings with Joy Home Constructions.

The construction company, however, failed to pay the agreed amount to the trust, resulting in Mirchi entering into a new agreement with Sunblink Real Estate. Yet another farce!

The deal of the sale of the three properties was struck at Rs 225 crore of which Rs 170 crore was said to be received by Mirchi through hawala. The remaining amount was paid through cheques. The investigation led by the ED, however, made yet another damning discovery of Sunblink being linked to Dheeraj Wadhawan, who was found to have given a loan of Rs 2186 crore to the real estate firm. The loan was traced to Mirchi, who simply used the real estate company to route the money to his account in Dubai under the guise of the loan.

The ED filed a chargesheet in 2019 in which it identified Dheeraj Wadhawan as the person behind Mirchi's deal with Sunblink Real Estate. The ED had arrested the Wadhawan brothers Dheeraj and Kapil in 2020 in what came to be known as the biggest bank fraud case. Haroun Yusuf and one Humayun Merchant (responsible for planting the tenants) were also arrested. Two other persons, Ranjeet Bindra, who brokered the deal of Mirchi's property, and Rinku Deshpande, through whom Bindra had allegedly received his commission, were also among those arrested. Haroun Yusuf was granted bail in May 2013.

The special Prevention of Money Laundering Act (PMLA) judge, M.G. Deshpande, while granting bail to Yusuf, had observed that there was nothing by way of evidence to show that Yusuf had knowledge of Mirchi's source of money except bare allegations. Humayun Merchant, however, shared the same fate as that of the Wadhawan brothers. The Special PMLA court refused to grant him bail on the grounds that Merchant was sufficiently shown to be at the forefront of the deals and that meetings between Mirchi and the parties involved led to the deal.

A case was registered in Mumbai on a complaint filed by the Union Bank of India against a certain private borrower whom the bank alleged to have cheated a consortium of seventeen banks. The loss incurred by these banks due to the alleged fraud was calculated to be Rs 34,615 crore. The investigations led the CBI team to the houses of two people, one of which was located in Mumbai and the other in Mahabaleshwar.

The raid carried out by the CBI at both premises unearthed a collection of expensive artworks that were valued at Rs 40 crore as per the initial estimates. By the time the investigation was complete, the Wadhawan brothers were found to have siphoned off loans from the consortium of seventeen banks by creating shell companies, which had come to be known as Bandra Book Entities.

During its probe in a case against Mirchi under the PMLA, the ED was also able to collect enough evidence that established Mirchi as the owner of the three properties that were seized. The fresh evidence led the authorities to declare that Mirchi had shown the property to belong to the Sir Mohammad Yusuf Trust through deceit and therefore the order of 2005 that excluded the three properties from confiscation stood 'non-est'.

The competent authority had also pulled up the Sir Mohammad Yusuf Trust for deception and forgery in concealing vital evidence and facts with respect to the actual ownership of the three properties, thus misleading the additional metropolitan magistrate and chief metropolitan magistrate.

On 13 August 2013, Mirchi stepped out of his London house to take his routine stroll to the city's famous Hyde Park in the evening. He had undergone four bypass surgeries by then. The doctors who operated on him had boasted that they had transformed his heart into that of a thirty-five-year old. Mirchi didn't doubt his doctor's assertion as he strode across the park's enchanting landscape. But a twitch in his heart forced him to stop and plop down on the nearest bench. He was taken to the hospital but did not survive. The doctors said that he died of a heart attack.

The ED attached Mirchi's three properties along with his fifteen Dubai properties under PMLA, making the total worth reach Rs 798 crore. The chargesheet filed by the ED on 9 December 2019 before the special PMLA court prompted the court to open non-bailable warrants (NBWs) against Mirchi's two sons, Asif Memon and Junaid Memon, and his wife Hajra.

The following year, the ED filed a plea in the special PMLA court seeking to declare Mirchi's two sons and his first wife as Fugitive Economic Offenders (FEOs). The court granted the plea and in 2021, declared all three as FEOs, which paved the way for Interpol to issue RCNs against them.

To this day, the ghost of Iqbal Mirchi continues to haunt his survivors and those he had business dealings with. Names of several politicians keep cropping up now and then. In 2016, the US also removed him from the list of drug kingpins.

Mirchi's sons, Asif and Junaid, stated that their father had petitioned authorities in the US to have his name removed from the list. 'At last,' they said, 'the truth has come to light.'

The US Treasury Department noted that following Mirchi's death in 2013, the need for his name to remain on the list as a first-tier drug kingpin was not warranted. It also noted that the removal did not overrule the evidence that had placed him on the list in the first place. But the fact remains that many of Iqbal Mirchi's secrets were buried along with him. Perhaps, they will never come to the fore.

34

Movies and the Mafia

As the country moved towards a more liberalized economy, the mafia also began expanding its footprint. It did not want just a piece in every profitable business, it wanted to dominate those businesses—such as construction, real estate and even the movies. The film industry today might be pan-India but in the 1990s, Bollywood or the Hindi film industry was considered to be mainstream. The biggest stars of the country worked here, right from the great Yusuf Khan aka Dilip Kumar to Dev Anand, Raj Kapoor, Rajesh Khanna and the 'Shahenshah' Amitabh Bachchan. The mega stars of the current day were rising to take the spots that were up for grabs as Bollywood passed through a generational curve. A similar generational shift was evident in the mafia too, with both Dawood Ibrahim and Chhota Rajan investing in movies through their frontmen. Sanjay Dutt's run-in with the law has been well documented in his biopic. But there were more stories to be uncovered here.

Consequently, in the suburbs of Andheri (West), where many film stars live, I caught up with actor Aditya Pancholi at a coffee shop near Versova, not far from his home. His tall frame, fair complexion and booming voice contribute heavily to his strong personality. He is still the good-looking man he was during the times he played the main lead in several films at the same time. 'Thank God I became an actor at nineteen,' he told me. 'Otherwise, I could have been on the other side of the law.'

The admission is not surprising given his acting chops in many movies that were based on the mafia. Aditya Pancholi was, after all, one of the original bad boys of Bollywood. From the mid-1980s to the mid-1990s, he played a string of roles where he was cast as a don or a drug dealer, a top henchman for the mafia boss and or even a cop fighting against the mafia. Aditya had the uncanny ability to make these characters appear real, and he sure did.

One of most memorable performances came as a drug dealer in the 1991 hit movie, *Saathi*, which also starred Pakistani cricketer-turned-actor Mohsin Khan, who was then married to actress Reena Roy. This movie was produced by Mukesh Duggal, with whom Aditya shared a business association that saw several ups and downs.

Another epic performance from Aditya came through his character of Nawab in the 1994 movie *Aatish*, where he was Sanjay Dutt's best friend. He played a character who is ready to sacrifice his life for the sake of friendship. 'Somehow,' he says, 'this has been my philosophy in life too. I value my friends and will go all out for them.'

Aatish was 'inspired' by a 1986 Hong Kong action flick called *A Better Tomorrow*, directed by John Woo. Though the story is heavily borrowed from the 1986 cult classic, the film was one of the slicker mafia-based movies which the industry had seen at that time.

'But in real life,' Aditya says, 'it was the mafia that came after the movies. It was not the other way around.'

'How did all of it happen?' I ask.

In this trademark style, Aditya Pancholi takes each question on the front foot.

In February 1993, after the release of his movie *Game* (1993), Aditya was partying in a room of a five-star hotel in Dubai. His Bollywood career was at its peak. He had visited the UAE for a special cricket match organized for celebrities such as Bollywood stars, cricketers and even businessmen. Many prominent personalities from India and other countries were attending this event.

After a tiring day, Aditya was enjoying a round of drinks with his gang of buddies whom he had taken along on the tour. Some of them were staying in his suite. Those days, Aditya was fascinated by a dialogue he had heard from one of the greatest actors in the industry, Sanjeev Kumar. The dialogue went like this: 'I the lalu, five the fifty five.' It became Aditya's pet phrase which he used to spray around with a combination of humour and some expletives.

The party in Aditya's hotel room was going on in full swing until the doorbell rang. Aditya cast a glance at the ornate clock hanging on the wall. It was 1.30 a.m. He was surprised to have a visitor this late. Must be some crazy fan, he thought. Aditya asked one of his friends to check. Opening the door, his friend found a portly man with unremarkable features standing at the door.

'Is Aditya Pancholi inside?' the man said gravely.

'Who are you?' the friend asked.

'Tell him that Vijay bhai has come to meet him.'

The friend informed Aditya about the visitor. Aditya was too drunk to process the information and too unwilling to rise from his place and go to meet the man at the door whom he didn't recognize anyway. 'I the lalu, five the fifty five,' Aditya said. 'Who the heck is this Vijay bhai? Tell him to get-t-tt-ttt out!'

When the same message was conveyed to Vijay bhai, his expression turned grim and he revealed his real identity. 'Tell Aditya that Chhota Rajan has come to meet him,' the man said.

Aditya was shell-shocked. A shiver went down his spine as soon as he heard the moniker of the man visiting him. The dreaded gangster of the mafia and Dawood's right-hand man, Chhota Rajan had come looking for him. Dawood and Rajan were still working together as the Mumbai bomb blasts had not been executed at that time. Aditya's elated state of inebriation and mirth quickly vanished, and he sobered himself to meet the man waiting for him at the door. The don walked in and introduced himself again.

'I'm not fond of film stars,' Rajan told Aditya. 'But you've played the role of my ex-boss in your latest movie. I loved your performance. That's why I came to meet you.'

Chhota Rajan was referring to Aditya's role in the movie *Game*, where Aditya had played the role of a man who sells movie tickets in black and becomes a don, only to get killed in a courtroom when attending a hearing in a murder case. The character was heavily inspired by Bada Rajan aka Rajan Mahadevan Nair, the former boss of

Chhota Rajan, who was eventually killed while attending a court hearing. Incidentally, Aditya's character in the movie was also called Raja. But Aditya had no plans to become an actor. It was only a matter of chance, and when the opportunity came his way, he grabbed it with both hands.

Aditya's blonde hair, blue eyes and good looks had earned him his debut in the cinema in the movie *Sasti Dulhan Mahenga Dulha* (1986). He belonged to a middle-class family. He was born and raised in the low-income areas of Juhu. The fair complexion earned him the nickname 'Gorya' (foreigner) among his circle of friends. But his hero-like features had little influence on the inclinations he grew up with in areas where local thugs and small-time criminals thrived to the fullest.

Robert, Bastya and Gabi were a gang of three in Pancholi's neighbourhood. They were famous for committing petty crimes such as chain-snatching and pickpocketing around the area. They were also involved in smuggling gold, silver and electronic items, an unlawful but lucrative business during the 1980s and 1990s in Mumbai. The gang of three would unload the smuggled items at the Ruia park (near Juhu) before infiltrating the market with the contraband and making a quick buck. Mora Gaon in Juhu, which wasn't all plush buildings back then and was made up of narrow and puzzling lanes formed by haphazardly placed small huts, was the trio's favourite place to hide whenever the cops put some heat on them.

Aditya and his friends looked up to the three hoodlums as their role models and desired to follow in their footsteps and make quick money. He was merely fourteen when he had formed a group of boys whose age and aspirations conformed to his. He would roam the streets of his area while being surrounded by his boys in a display of the power he sought to attain in the locality.

All went well for him except for the person named Alus, who claimed the entire strip of hutments for himself, posing as its sole don. In his early twenties, the man was also a bully who would go about harassing the local boys just so he could assert his dominance in the area. Aditya was aware of the man's chicanery but only decided to take action against it when one of the boys from his gang became the subject of the thug's bullying.

Aditya and his friend Hari grabbed a few sugarcane sticks from a nearby juice shop and landed outside the thug's house. When the thug stepped outside, Pancholi and Hari rained blows upon him with the sugarcane sticks. Soon, the locals gathered to watch Alus being beaten up and were overjoyed that someone had meted out justice to him. Aditya did not stop until the thug started begging to let him go and promised that he would not come near him or his gang ever again.

Over a period of time, Aditya's involvement in the gang culture deepened. His friends learnt the art of pickpocketing. They would particularly look out for film shootings because crowds would gather in large numbers to watch and it gave them enough targets to zero in on. Aditya would stand in the crowd, blocking the target so that one of his friends could swoop down on their wallet. But he had never thought that one day he would be on the other side of the camera, and that too as a mainstream hero.

While he was studying at Mithibai College in Mumbai, Aditya used to travel in the first-class compartments of local trains without buying a ticket. Once, he was leaning outside a moving train, hanging on to the rod in the middle of the door. Pancholi's antics caught the attention of a man sitting nearby, who was amazed by the young boy's extraordinary features. The man's name was Bali and he used to work for Bhappi Soni, a film producer. Bali ji walked up to Aditya and, drawing him inside, asked if he would like to work in films.

'Why not?' Aditya said promptly. 'If I get paid well, I will do whatever is asked of me.'

This event landed Aditya a meeting with director Bhappi Soni, who took five seconds to offer him one of the lead roles in his upcoming movie *Sasti Dulhan Mahenga Dulha*. The signing amount was a cheque of Rs 5000, which Aditya happily took home. Then he realized that he did not have a bank account to deposit the cheque into! Finally, his maternal aunt helped him open a bank account. The amount was such a huge one for Aditya that he felt like a king that day.

Media magnate and producer Nari Hira, who would produce movies and publish magazines like *Stardust*, also signed Aditya to act in his movies for a salary of Rs 5000 a month. Aditya had not seen such kind of money before. Working with Nari Hira resulted in Aditya getting constant work even though some of his initial movies didn't exactly set the cash registers ringing at the box office.

His acting skills, however, reached its zenith when he acted in the 1993 movie *Game* and essayed the role inspired by Bada Rajan. His acting was admired by many from within the film fraternity. And outside of the industry, Chhota Rajan liked his performance so much that he had turned up at Aditya's hotel room in Dubai. Aditya and his friends kept staring at the don with no one daring to speak a word.

'What's wrong?' Rajan asked. 'Why are you guys acting like you've come to a funeral?'

'Actually bhai,' Aditya said, 'one of my friend's bags got misplaced while exiting Dubai Airport today. It contained important items.'

'That's it?' Rajan said, as if it was a non-issue.

Rajan made a call to Dubai Airport and gave the details of the mislaid bag to the person on the line. Within the next half an hour, the lost bag magically turned up at the hotel room while Rajan was still present. Aditya was amazed at the influence that Dawood and Rajan exercised in Dubai during those days. After talking for a few more minutes, Rajan bid goodbye to Aditya with the promise that he would accompany Aditya to Dubai Airport to see him off on the return flight. Aditya certainly wasn't looking forward to another meeting with the don and sought to steer clear of him.

'Why do you bother, bhai?' Aditya said. 'I will manage it.'

'*Arey raja-a-a,*' Rajan said. '*Tu ne mere boss ka role kiya hai. Tujhe itna respect toh dena padega.*'

Rajan often used the word 'raja' as a term of endearment. Even today, that term is popular among locals who hail from Chembur and the areas of central Mumbai where Rajan once held sway. Aditya thought it was better not to get into a disagreement with the don.

'Okay bhai,' he said, 'as you wish.'

Aditya was hoping that Rajan would forget about the arrangement. But true to his word, Rajan landed at the hotel to drop Aditya at the airport for his return to Mumbai. During their journey to the airport, Rajan regaled Aditya with stories spanning his childhood to teenage years. Aditya found the stories amusing even though he did not believe all of it.

They reached the airport. Aditya wanted to get on the flight as soon as he could. But Rajan's eyes fell on an actor who was queued up at the checkpoint that allows passengers inside the airport. The man was a budding star who had only recently made his appearance on the big screen. Rajan was fond of the star and wanted to meet him.

'Do you know that guy?' Rajan said, pointing to the star.

'Yes,' Aditya said.

'I want to meet him.'

Aditya tried to avoid putting the new star in a sticky position, but Rajan wasn't letting go. Time was running out. The man was about to enter the airport when Aditya marched in the man's direction and tapped him on his shoulder. The actor turned around.

'Someone wants to meet you,' Aditya said, pointing towards Rajan.

'Who's he?' the actor asked.

Aditya leaned into the star's shoulder. 'Chhota Rajan,' he whispered.

The actor stopped what he was doing and almost ran to meet Rajan to exchange some pleasantries. Such was the fear the mafia had instilled in the industry during those days. Even if people did not recognize their faces, the mere mention of the names of Dawood or Chhota Rajan was enough to induce fear among the rich and the wealthy. The star spoke with Rajan for a few minutes before quickly making his way into the airport.

Aditya was finally relieved to be back on the flight to Mumbai. But this was certainly not the last he would hear from Rajan. His first meeting with Chhota Rajan happened due to his role in *Game*. When he had signed the movie, he had no idea that the man behind the movie was also connected to Rajan. This man was a much-feared name within the industry and even among the mafia circles. And he had a very peculiar nickname. *Goonga bhai*.

35

Life Is a Game

Defying conventional practices, Aditya Pancholi was hardly twenty-two years old when he got married to the prolific and popular movie actress, Zarina Wahab. The couple met on the sets of their 1986 film *Kalank Ka Tika*. By the time the shooting came to an end, the two were dating each other. They tied the knot the same year.

Aditya's marriage to a woman who was older than him kicked off gossip within the film fraternity that he had married Zarina because of her fame and money. Generally, heroes were not supposed to marry at such a young age as it alienates their female following. On top of it, Zarina was already a big name in the industry, with hits such as *Chitchor* (1976) and *Gharonda* (1977) under her belt. They also came from different religious backgrounds, which added more complexity to the situation.

'I married Zarina because she is a wonderful human being,' Aditya says. Despite being a top actress, she was abstemious of a lavish lifestyle. She would take an autorickshaw for her daily travels and would book a train ticket whenever she had to visit her hometown, Hyderabad.

Nari Hira was among the first to whom Aditya spoke about his marriage. Aditya was expecting Hira to lambast him for marrying so early but Hira treated Aditya like a son, and wished him well.

'But sir,' Aditya said, 'I have a request. The five thousand rupees you pay me each month will not be sufficient to sustain a family.'

'No problem,' Nari Hira said. 'I'll pay you ten thousand then!'

Aditya was thankful for Nari Hira's magnanimity. Aditya and his wife moved to the latter's house in Bandra. Three years later, they were blessed with their first child, a baby girl whom they named Sana. The introduction of one more member into the household was an added responsibility and Aditya felt the need to do more films to provide a good life for his family.

It was a peculiar period in the industry. Several actors would simply accept every single offer sent their way without asking about the story or their role in the film. Aditya too joined the race by signing over sixty films within the span of five months. 'Perhaps only Mithun da and Govinda had signed more movies than me,' Aditya says.

He would work five shifts in a day and had appointed Ajit Dewani as his manager. Ajit belonged to the Sindhi community and would often visit Tilak Nagar near Chembur. He was also the manager of the sensational actress Mandakini and would later go on to be Manisha

Koirala's manager. During the last-mentioned stint, he was shot dead by Abu Salem's men.

Aditya believes that Ajit was a pretty straight man with no active dealings with the underworld. 'In fact,' Aditya says, 'he would start shivering even if I raised my voice to ask why the heck he had scheduled so many shifts in a day for me.'

However, Dewani was quite familiar with the happenings in Chembur, which was Chhota Rajan's stronghold. At most, he liked talking about the mafia—about how dons like Rajan and Dawood functioned. He was simply fascinated by the amount of knowledge that he would be privy to due to his mingling with the underworld people who wanted to make movies. He would divulge the most discreet knowledge of the gangs to flaunt his reach among his circle of his friends and acquaintances.

'You should know where to speak and where to keep your mouth shut,' Aditya used to tell him.

Aditya's cautionary words to Ajit turned prophetic years later when Ajit was working as the manager of actress Manisha Koirala. He was shot dead by two of Salem's men, Upendra Singh and Deepak Singh. Though Salem's confession says that he ordered the killing due to Ajit's refusal to pay the demanded extortion money, Aditya believes that it was Ajit's irresponsible handling of the intimate knowledge of gangs and ganglords that cost him his life. Mingling with even theoretical knowledge of the mafia was a dangerous *game* in those days.

In the early 1990s, Aditya was contacted by producer Pammi Sandhu over an offer for a role in an upcoming movie. This movie was titled, ironically, *Game*.

'It's a mind-blowing mafia story,' Pammi ji said. 'You'll be playing the role of Bada Rajan.'

The mafia was reaching its zenith in the late 1980s and early 1990s. Pammi ji announced that he had signed megastars such as Naseeruddin Shah and Rahul Roy (a sensation at the time after his 1990 blockbuster *Aashiqui*) for the film. Former Miss India Sangeeta Bijlani was going to play the female lead opposite Aditya.

But none of this mattered to Aditya. Very rare are those actors who can work in the industry for decades. Most actors, even fairly successful ones, vanish within five to seven years. Some others turn out to be one-race horses, disappearing into obscurity right after their first hit. Aditya wanted to make sure that he made enough money while he could.

'All of that is fine, Pammi ji,' he said. 'How much will I be paid?'

Aditya wanted to buy a house and a car of his own. Pammi offered a decent remuneration and Aditya accepted the signing amount without inquiring about the script or the financiers. At that time, he was only concerned about the remuneration. He was comfortable with the idea that he would come to know everything about the film and the role as the shooting progressed. The movie was greenlighted. On the day of the *mahurat* shot (first shot of a film marking the commencement of the principal photography), Aditya got ready and headed for Bhaidas Hall near the renowned Mithibai College in Mumbai, not knowing that he was in for a surprise.

Reaching the venue, Aditya encountered a jam-packed crowd in the hall. Everyone was waiting for Naseeruddin

Shah to arrive as he was reportedly stuck in a traffic jam. While waiting, Aditya couldn't help but notice a man who seemed to be given to incessant jabbering. But more than his rambling, it was the man's peculiar voice that had caught Aditya's attention. Though he clearly commanded a kind of fearful respect from those who flocked near him, his voice gave him the image of a small boy stuck in an adult male's body. His vocal chords didn't function effectively and muffled his words. Aditya thought it to be an irony of ironies that the man was nicknamed 'Goonga bhai'.

The word *goonga* meant someone who could not speak, but Goonga bhai was abusing everyone's mother and sister, not even sparing the producers and actors. '*Oye chutiye*,' he said to no one in particular. 'Why hasn't the mahurat happened yet?'

Someone from the production team gave him a reason but Goonga was in no mood to listen. He was getting angrier by the minute. No one had the gall to even go near him at this time as they feared becoming the subject of his ire.

Aditya asked Pammi ji about the identity of this man. 'Who is he?'

'He is none other than Goonga bhai,' Pammi ji whispered.

Aditya later learnt that Goonga bhai was the best friend of Chhota Rajan, who was working for Dawood Ibrahim at that time. The actor now became suspicious of the kind of movie and the role he had signed up for.

But it was when he met Goonga that he was in for a real shocker. Goonga was once involved in selling tickets in black at Sahakar Cinema, Chembur by partnering with

Chhota Rajan. This fact swept Aditya off his feet. He cursed himself for not reading the script or doing any due diligence.

Now that Aditya had taken the signing amount and even spent it, he had no option but to keep his commitment. He would participate in the activities around the movie that Goonga used to plan and invite each member of the crew to join him in. During those days, there were no TV shows where actors could promote their movies. Outside of the screen, their interactions with fans were limited to public appearances. Actors would often visit Ganpati pandals or *dahi handi* gatherings to let fans have a glimpse of them.

During the shooting of *Game*, the Ganesh Chaturthi festival came around. The festival is marked by the erection of makeshift temples called pandals at various spots. Organizers of these pandals are usually a group of local boys who raise funds from the neighbourhood and other sponsors. Sometimes, these pandals also become a mark of the power and influence of those who organize them. Chembur was famous for its pandals that were controlled and managed by Goonga's dearest friend, Chhota Rajan.

Goonga resided in the same area. He used to ask his film's cast and crew members to visit these pandals. This was often followed by a drink at his place. Nobody would dare to say no and would bend backwards to oblige Goonga bhai.

Goonga, like any other underworld member, was ostentatious in the display of his power and influence. Along with glasses of alcohol, he would also place his two revolvers out on the table for everyone to see and marvel at.

Once an actor, very famous for his comic timing and villainous roles, got a little too drunk and began nagging Goonga to lend him one of his revolvers. Goonga ignored him and carried on his conversation with other guests. The actor began throwing tantrums and demanded that he be given one of those revolvers. The don's denials seemed to have no effect on him. Finally, Goonga ran out of patience. He looked at the actor furiously and slid one of the guns across the table towards the actor. 'Take it,' he said.

The guests looked at Goonga in disbelief. The actor was extremely high and wasn't even remotely conscious of his actions. He picked up the gun and guffawed in the same manner he would do when playing a comedian in a movie.

That night, the actor took the gun home with him, placed it under his pillow and went off to sleep. He woke up sober in the morning and was startled to find a revolver under his pillow. 'Where the heck did this come from?' he mumbled.

After thinking hard, he recollected his antics of the previous night and called Goonga's house to return the revolver. But Goonga wasn't ready to forgive him easily.

'That revolver had been used for a couple of killings,' Goonga said, merely to instil fear in the actor. 'The gun is yours now. You asked for it. So you better keep it.'

The trick worked. The actor melted in fear as soon as he heard the gun's past record and beseeched Goonga all the more earnestly to take it back.

'Please, take it back, bhai,' the actor said. 'I beg you.'

Goonga refused and insulted the actor before telling him to disappear. The actor had to plead with Goonga and be humiliated for the next six days before the don agreed to take the gun back.

'*Chutiye,*' Goonga said as he took the gun back, 'will you dare to ask me for a gun again?'

'No bhai,' the actor pleaded. 'Never!'

That taught the actor a lesson about dealing with dons. Although being a member of the underworld, Goonga possessed a decent understanding of commercial cinema. One day, Aditya was scheduled for a shoot and rushed to the sets. He didn't want to provide Goonga bhai a reason to be upset with him. He landed on the set and was making his way towards the make-up man when Goonga bhai pulled him aside.

'*Ae* Aditya,' Goonga said in his gruff voice, 'why didn't you show up at the recording of the title song?'

'Bhai,' Aditya said, 'I had another shooting to attend. Please understand.'

'Boss,' Goonga said. 'What a track we have recorded!'

'Amazing bhai,' Aditya said perfunctorily. 'Should I go for my shot?'

'Not until you hear the song!' Goonga said.

He asked the production crew to hand him the recording of the song. The whole production team began running helter-skelter in search of the recording. Goonga heaped abuses on them for not keeping up with his demands.

'No stress,' Aditya said. 'I'll hear the song some other day, bhai.'

'No!' Goonga said. 'You *have to* hear it today.'

'How bhai? The recording isn't available.'

'So what?! I will sing it for you.'

Aditya rolled his eyes and braced himself for the most bizarre vocal rendition on the foot-tapping music that famous music directors Anand-Milind had composed. Pin-drop silence descended upon the set. Goonga cleared his throat.

'*Na chahat. Na daulat.*

'*Na izzat. Na fame.*

'*Zindagi ha-iii game*!' Goonga crooned while raising his eyebrows in sync with the beats.

The lyrics meant that life is not about love, money, respect or fame. *Life is a game.*

Fuck my life, Aditya thought. *I can't even laugh!* The gun tucked under Goonga's shirt didn't allow him to even break into a smile. Instead, Aditya had to praise his producer.

'*Saaton sur barabar lage hain, bhai* (You hit all the notes perfectly),' Aditya said.

Goonga's chest swelled with pride. Later, when Aditya heard the full version sung by the ever-fantastic Suneeta Rao, he realized that the song was actually mind-blowing. He congratulated Goonga bhai for the awesome work.

'There you go, my brother,' Goonga said. 'I am not a chutiya when it comes to films. Nana and I would sell tickets in black together at Sahakar Cinema. We know the pulse of the public.'

Chhota Rajan was addressed as Nana bhai because it was disrespectful to call a don by his first name. Aditya could not help but notice the seriousness on Goonga's face. He gave him a wholesome nod indicating his agreement.

The shooting of the film was complete and its premiere was held two days prior to its official release date at a prominent theatre—Metro Cinema—in Mumbai. The entire crew along with a few guests were attending the event.

Aditya took his seat in the front row alongside other cast members. Each attendee settled in their place and the hall was enveloped in pin-drop silence. The lights in the hall went off and the large screen lit up with the censor board certificate filling it up first, followed by a 'Triple AAR Films Presents' written in large, bold letters. The audience was bracing themselves to spend their next three hours in quality entertainment when they heard frantic screams for help.

Each neck turned around to look curiously at the cries for help coming from the back. It was only when the lights were turned back on that people saw Goonga shouting for help. A sizable contingent of the Mumbai Police was literally carrying him away from the hall. Aditya took out a handkerchief and wiped the sweat off his face. What on earth had he got into?

36

Arrest at the Premiere

Some patrons in the cinema hall stood up from their seats and craned their necks to watch Goonga being carried away by the cops. He was thrashing and smashing his legs on the seats to resist the attempt by the policemen, who were holding him from both sides and forcibly carrying him out of the hall. The resulting commotion caused the screen to go off and the lights to be turned on again.

'Mandira,' Goonga screamed, 'save me, help me!'

Mandira, Goonga's wife, ran after the policemen but they were in no mood to listen. The attendees in the hall stared at each other in complete bewilderment. Nobody knew that they were witness to the advent of a watershed moment in the city's history. The ever-growing mafia menace had the city in its grip for too long. It had permeated the city's significant industries such as Bollywood and business, and was now threatening to turn into an epidemic.

The Mumbai Police finally decided that enough was enough. It was time to steady their ranks and initiate a major crackdown against the mafia world. Dawood and Chhota Rajan had shifted their base to the Gulf, but their frontmen were still here, operating their businesses and running their operations. The cops had decided to go for these men to instil the fear of god in the dons. Goonga, being Chhota Rajan's close friend, became one of their first targets.

Goonga was taken to the Crime Branch at Crawford Market where he was given a taste of the Mumbai Police's famous thrashing. The city's police wanted to send a message to the mafia that their gory business wasn't going to be tolerated any more, and they were trying to make an example out of goons like Goonga.

Aditya might have imagined that the premiere of the film marked the end of his interactions with the mafia and its members. He imagined that he would never have to see or come in contact with people such as Goonga and Chhota Rajan. But he couldn't have been more wrong. As soon as Chhota Rajan heard the news of Goonga's arrest, the don contacted Aditya on the phone.

'Raja-a-a,' Chhota Rajan said, 'arrange bail for Goonga.'

Wow, Aditya thought. Now he had to arrange bail for a *bhai*. Rajan made it clear to Aditya that getting Goonga released from prison was his responsibility. The don had great affection for Goonga as the man was his long-standing friend, and put subtle pressure on Aditya in the form of appeals for help. Aditya knew better than to argue with the don. Although reluctantly, he decided to pitch in.

Mandira, Goonga's wife, was very cordial with Aditya during the shooting of the movie and considered him to be her *rakhi* brother. She visited Aditya's house and asked for help to hire a good lawyer and get her husband out of jail.

'The lawyers are asking for a lot of money for a case like this,' she told Aditya.

Aditya didn't have much money in cash. But he went to the vault in his house and picked up a few gold biscuits that he had acquired as an investment. He handed over the biscuits to Mandira. 'Get the best possible lawyers for your husband,' Aditya said.

Mandira raised the remaining amount by contacting a few of her relatives and friends and hired a top lawyer. Goonga's case ran for several months. During the time he was inside, the harrowing March 1993 serial blasts incident took place. It sent the entire industry scampering, after the names of Hanif Kadawala and Samir Hingorani of Magnum Video cropped up during the investigation. The duo, seeing their necks on the line, brought forth the subject of Sanjay Dutt acquiring weapons during this period. Again, much of these developments have been covered in Sanjay Dutt's biopic.

Goonga eventually got released and his family heaved a mighty sigh of relief. Aditya also went to see him out of courtesy. But the actor was amused to find Goonga extremely happy despite the police giving him an extremely tough time during his incarceration.

'What's the matter, bhai?' Aditya asked. 'You look more happy than when you were taken to jail.'

'I am glad that they arrested me,' Goonga said.

Aditya gave him a puzzled look. 'Why?'

'These cops would have framed me in the bomb blasts and got me killed in an encounter,' Goonga said and laughed. 'The arrest saved my life!'

Aditya laughed too. But Goonga was right in his assessment. The war on the mafia that the Mumbai Police had declared ramped up multifold in the aftermath of the blasts. Soon, central agencies like the CBI got involved. The police and the CBI showed no mercy in nabbing and bringing the culprits to book. The serial bombing was also responsible for the widely famous Dawood Ibrahim–Chhota Rajan split.

Chhota Rajan continued to keep in touch with Aditya even in the midst of the raging gang war between him and Dawood. Aditya knew that being in contact with him in such a volatile situation was extremely dangerous but there wasn't much he could do about it. Some of his well-wishers suggested he change his phone number. 'How long will it take for him to get my new number?' Aditya would say tersely in response.

Though well aware of the extremely risky situation, Aditya did not resort to unlawful means to get out of it, nor did he ask anyone else to help him out. 'Rajan would call me but I have never called him,' Aditya said. 'Not even once.'

In 1999, the Dawood and Chhota Rajan gang war was at its peak. Both of them were looking to gun down each other's friends, associates and financiers. During this time, Goonga decided to produce another movie starring Sanjay Dutt, Aditya Pancholi and Inder Kumar. Two brother musicians who were also on their way to fame and success, Sajid-Wajid, were signed as music composers. Aditya gave a nod to doing the film and got on with the shooting.

It had been days since Chhota Rajan had last contacted Aditya, which proved to be a breather for him. But the pleasure was short-lived. During the shooting of the film, Aditya got an unusual call. Only zeros were displayed on the caller identification screen. Aditya was baffled and picked up the call. It turned out to be none other than Chhota Shakeel.

'Are you doing Goonga's movie?' Shakeel asked.

Aditya was aghast. Now not only Chhota Rajan but Chhota Shakeel was also calling him.

'Yes bhai, I am doing the movie,' Aditya said. 'But if you want me to drop it, I can do that in a jiffy. I have a family to take care of. I don't want to be involved in these games.'

'*Ek minute seth se baat kar*,' Chhota Shakeel said.

Shakeel passed the phone to *seth* (boss) who turned out to be none other than Dawood Ibrahim. Dawood asked Aditya the same question, if he was doing Goonga's movie and Aditya repeated what he had told Shakeel seconds ago. The movie was not more important than his life or his family's future.

'You are an actor,' Dawood said, with a smirk in his voice. 'You continue doing your job. I have no problems with you. But how will the movie get released if it never gets made?'

Dawood cut the call tersely before Aditya could react. The actor immediately gauged that something nasty was afoot. He wasted no time before visiting Goonga's house. Goonga's mother, whom Aditya admired and respected a lot due to her religiosity, informed him that Goonga wasn't home. 'Ask him to call me immediately,' Aditya told Goonga's family.

That same night, Goonga got in touch with Aditya. The actor told him about the phone call and the veiled threat from Dawood Ibrahim. Goonga became alert and petitioned the court to provide him security. The court directed the state government to grant him security. On 2 September 1998, the state government passed an order directing the police commissioner, Mumbai to provide armed security to Goonga. However, the order was later cancelled.

Goonga smartened up and arranged for his own men as personal bodyguards to accompany him at all times. All of them had weapons. Goonga was now of the opinion that the cops couldn't be trusted more than his boys. If the time came, his boys would take a bullet for him. But the same could not be said about the cops.

The shooting of the film went on for a while with no sign of a threat to its continuity. Encouraged, Goonga went on a tour to Himachal on some personal business. Goonga had to discard the weapons he usually carried as he was travelling by plane. He stayed there for a few days. Over the phone, he also coordinated the logistics for a huge set that was being constructed for the film in Mumbai. When he landed back in the city on 19 March 1999, Goonga promptly headed for the film's set, which was located near Hotel Rangsharda in Bandra.

The holiday had caused Goonga to lower his guard. The air travelling also meant that he did not have any of his boys for security nor was his gun with him. In these circumstances, he made the mistake of visiting the set directly from the airport.

Unbeknownst to him, a group of gun-wielding men from the D-Company were waiting for him at the spot where the set was built. He was met with a barrage of gunshots as soon as his car reached the place, around 6 p.m., causing the common public to panic and run helter-skelter. The flurry of bullets reduced the car into a battered piece of scrap. A few bullets hit Goonga and he got injured. Seeing the attackers zero in, Goonga stepped out of the car and made a run for his life. But Dawood's boys caught hold of him.

One of them held his pistol near Goonga's head and shot him. Point blank. Goonga dropped to the ground and a stream of blood issued from the side of his head. The shooter skipped to his bike and triumphantly motioned the rider to start moving. The bike blew smoke, burning rubber on the tar and vanished in no time.

The entire stretch appeared deserted except for the bleeding Goonga, who lay sprawled on the ground. He raised his head furtively to make sure that his attackers had completely gone before he pulled himself up to his feet. The bullet had only grazed the side of his temple! Multiple bullets had punctured his body. But like Rasputin, he was alive; even if barely. He was rushed to Lilavati Hospital.

Meanwhile Aditya was buying a DVD from a famous video library where most of Bollywood purchased Hollywood flicks to base their films upon. The actor's phone rang. It was Chhota Rajan.

'Raja-a-a,' Chhota Rajan said, '*Goonga marna nahi chahiye.*'

Fuck my life, Aditya thought. Now he had to save a dying man. Rajan had one and only one concern. His friend shouldn't die. Aditya rushed to the hospital and took charge. Goonga was indeed in a bad shape. But importantly, he was alive and would eventually live to tell the tale.

By the time the film's shooting was completed, Goonga had borrowed around Rs 5 lakh from Aditya. The film was released in the year 2000, in the month of April. It performed relatively well at the box office and Goonga made a profit of a few crores from the movie. But apart from not returning Aditya's Rs 5 lakh, Goonga had also not paid his acting fee for the movie. Months passed while Aditya followed up respectfully. Goonga showed no signs of paying his dues. Aditya was enraged and decided to confront him by visiting him at his place.

'When are you going to pay me?' Aditya asked Goonga.

Goonga tried to postpone the payment once again. Aditya lashed out at him in his booming voice. The entire neighbourhood gathered. Aditya raised his voice purposefully to humiliate Goonga before his people for whom he was a *bhai*. Losing his patience, Aditya grabbed the don by his collar.

'One backhanded slap is all it will take to send your *bhaigiri* crashing down!' Aditya thundered.

Goonga was taken aback. He had never seen such rage in Aditya's eyes before. The actor let go of the don's collar in a way that shook Goonga from head to toe. Then he strutted out of that place. Any residual hope of recovering his money from Goonga had evaporated on account of his aggressive behaviour. But Aditya was glad that he had unloaded his frustrations on the man. To his surprise, a few days later, Aditya was meeting a producer in Juhu when he got a call from Goonga.

'How are you, my friend?' Goonga said. 'Come and collect your money.'

'Wow. Really?' Aditya said, pleasantly surprised. 'My manager will come over to collect it.'

'No, no. You raised such a hullabaloo the other day,' Goonga said, 'I will only get peace after I hand over the money to you personally.'

Aditya agreed and drove to Goonga's office in Juhu. Surprisingly, there was no crowd of favour-seekers at his office that evening. The bhai was sprawled in his chair. Relaxed.

'I have another meeting to attend,' Aditya told him as he sat down. 'Please be quick with the money.'

'What's the rush, my friend?' Goonga said. 'I have a surprise for you.'

Something in Goonga's tone unsettled Aditya. The office door flung open, and a couple of men stormed in with pistols in their hands. Aditya tried to get up from his chair but the men thrust their pistols at either side of his temple. He sunk back into his chair with his eyes darting from side to side. He looked at Goonga who now had a smug smile on his face.

'What's all this *chutiyagiri, haan*?' Aditya said.

'You humiliated me in my locality,' Goonga said. 'For this, you will pay with your life.'

Aditya was flustered and expected a bullet to rip through his head at any second. In the melee, one of Goonga's boys fumbled with the gun and its magazine fell upon Aditya's ear, cutting it sharply. He started bleeding profusely and had to stem the flow of blood by holding a handkerchief to his ear. Surprisingly, both Goonga and his boys were flustered at the sight of his blood; as if something had gone wrong.

Aditya looked around and got back his bearings. He realized that if Goonga wanted to kill him, he wouldn't have called him to his office. That type of deed demanded that the perpetrator conduct the *business* at a place far away from his personal or professional premises. Aditya smartened up that Goonga's intention was only to scare him. And now Aditya was anything but scared! He went on the offensive.

'You forgot the times when I stood by you?' Aditya bellowed. 'Call Nana right now.'

'*Ae*!' Goonga shouted. 'Not Nana, address him as Nana bhai.'

'Oh yes, why not!' Aditya shouted back. 'Call Nana bhai!'

At that moment, Goonga's phone rang. Chhota Rajan was calling. Goonga quickly picked up the call, and Rajan gave him quite a earful before asking him to put the phone on speaker.

'Nana bhai,' Aditya said, 'he has forgotten the gold that I gave away to get him out of jail. And when he was shot, who was the first one to reach the hospital? Who made sure he received timely medical attention? Who handled the cops? And now he wants to put a gun to my head?!'

Rajan placated Aditya by saying that he knew Goonga was wrong. He asked Aditya to pass the phone to Goonga. He excoriated Goonga for his impertinence and instructed him to order his men out of there immediately and deflate the situation at once. No sooner had the word been given than Goonga's men left the room with their tails between their legs.

As soon as Rajan hung up, Goonga also got a call from his wife, Mandira. She too came down heavily on her husband in condemnation of his ill behaviour with Aditya before exhorting him to apologize and come to a compromise. Goonga shook hands with Aditya and later gave him a cheque for his payment for the film. They eventually managed to bury the hatchet. Today, when they bump into each other, the two talk cordially, even if a lot of water has flowed under the bridge.

37

Five-Crore Bet

In the mid-1990s, Aditya was in touch with a businessman named Suresh Devadiga. They had been friends for a while. Among many businesses, Devadiga owned a bar in an upmarket area of Mumbai. The bar was one of the topmost in the city, a money-minting machine for its promoters and dancers. Among other shady businesses, Devadiga was also into cricket betting to make more money. He acted like a middleman who'd accept bets from punters and pass them to the top bookie of the day. The book through which he conducted betting was named Samrat. Devadiga used to visit Aditya often to spend some leisure time.

Aditya used to find Devadiga's way of pronouncing certain words very funny. When Devadiga had purchased a new car, he called Aditya to pass on the good news that he had purchased a 'Lolls-Loyce'. Another time, he purchased a plot at a prime location in Bandra, which was as expensive as buying a plot on the moon. He wanted Aditya to meet the 'arch-e-tekt'. Aditya laughed and reminded Devadiga of the correct pronunciation, making sure to add a friendly expletive or two with his counsel.

On 13 July 2002, India was playing England in the final of Natwest Series. A powerful politician from the north, Choudhary, was visiting Mumbai and called Aditya over to the hotel where he was staying. Aditya had known the politician for years, and considered him to be an elder brother and even addressed him as such.

Since Aditya was hanging around with Devadiga, he took his friend along to meet the leader. The trio talked in the hotel's restaurant. The TV perched on the wooden stand showed the Indian team reeling under the pressure to chase down a massive score of 325 put up by the English team in the first innings.

After a brilliant innings of 60 off just 43 balls, Indian captain Sourav Ganguly was clean bowled by fast-paced bowler Alex Tudor. In just under an over, Virender Sehwag followed the captain into the stands as he fell victim to a mind-boggling spin delivery by Ashley Giles. The prospects of the Indian team winning the match had started to appear grim.

Aditya introduced the politician, who was based in another state, to Devadiga. The latter was delighted to meet such a powerful man and had high hopes of striking some kind of business deal with him.

'What do you do for a living?' Choudhary asked Devadiga.

Aditya said that his friend owned a very famous bar in the city. Seeing that it didn't evoke much excitement on the part of the politician, Devadiga rushed to add that he was also into cricket betting. Aditya cast an angry glance at Devadiga. He wasn't pleased with Devadiga's impatience.

Devadiga paid little attention to Aditya's silent remonstrance and went ahead with rattling out the list of rich people who placed their bets through him. He tried to make it sound very exciting, dropping names and huge figures left, right and centre.

By then, the match on TV had already seemed to slip out of Team India's hands. The middle order quickly collapsed and India were at a miserable 146 for 5. England were the favourites from this point.

'Good sir,' Devadiga said, 'would you want to place a bet?'

'Yes,' Choudhary said. 'Five crores on England's victory.'

Devadiga's jaw hit the floor. He had not anticipated such a big amount to be thrown in so casually. At that moment, Aditya knew this discussion had taken a wrong turn but he chose to maintain silence rather than ruffle any feathers. Devadiga hastened to make a call to the betting house and asked to enter the amount against the favourites in his book. The man seemed pleased with the bet, whereas it seemed like no big deal for the politician.

The trio called an end to their meeting just as the new batsman, Mohammad Kaif, made his way to the middle to join Yuvraj Singh on the crease. Aditya, who had also downed a few rounds of drinks, went home and slept as soon as his head hit the pillow. The next morning, the actor got a call from a harried Devadiga. Still in his sleep, Aditya struggled to determine what the fuss was all about.

'What's wrong, Devadiga?' Aditya asked. 'You sound as if you've seen a ghost.'

'The match!' Devadiga mewled. 'The match!!'

'What about it?'

'India won,' Devadiga said. 'Didn't you see it? India won. Oh, what am I going to do now?!'

Aditya looked up the newspaper to confirm the news. It was true after all. India had beaten England to lift the NatWest series trophy. Sourav Ganguly had celebrated by taking off his T-shirt and waving it in the air to get back at England's Andrew Flintoff, who had celebrated his team's victory against India previously in the same manner.

But all of that didn't matter to the bookies. All they knew was that India had won and Devadiga was due to turn in the Rs 5 crore he had betted on England, on behalf of *someone*. Devadiga had lost the count of the number of times he had called Choudhary as soon as he received the bad news. 'But bhaiya is not answering my call!'

'Listen, my friend,' Aditya raged. 'You are a chutiya. Who asked you to flaunt your betting business in front of him?'

Devadiga apologized and implored Aditya to get him out of this mess worth Rs 5 crore. Aditya agreed to take Devadiga to the politician's hometown. There was a long list of visitors waiting for an audience with Choudhary. But Aditya's good rapport with the politician enabled them to get into his office without much hassle. Choudhary laughed his heart out after listening to Devadiga's ordeal.

'Aditya,' he said, 'who on earth pays money they've lost on a bet?!'

Devadiga felt like he was slipping into a coma. The bet was nothing but a joke for the politician. But for Devadiga, it was a matter of life and death. He'd have to pay, even if he had to sell his house and live on the road.

Aditya held a brief conversation with Choudhary in private while Devadiga waited outside. He explained to the politician that Devadiga was a good friend and had a family to look after. If the amount was not paid to the syndicate, they would find ways to hound Devadiga and extract the money from him. Aditya was concerned about the safety of his friend and his family.

'How do you want to handle this?' Choudhary asked.

Aditya suggested that the amount could be paid to Devadiga in parts instead of leaving the fellow in the lurch. Choudhary agreed to pay Devadiga on Aditya's request. Importantly, the politician kept the promise he made to Aditya and paid the entire Rs 5 crore to Devadiga in a few months. The timely intervention by Aditya was greatly appreciated by Devadiga and his already strong friendship with Aditya grew to a completely different level from that point.

Devadiga had by then become the owner of several properties located in the posh areas of the city. His dance bar business had reached astronomical proportions, thanks to a fruit-seller turned businessman, Abdul Karim Telgi, who made frequent visits to Devadiga's bar.

Scamster in reality, Abdul Karim Telgi hailed from the state of Karnataka and used to deal in stamp papers. However, the real nature of his business was to mix the fake stamp papers that he had learnt to produce along with the genuine ones and sell them to major institutions such as banks, insurance companies and brokerage firms in return for massive profits. He had even set up his own printing press on Mint Road where he appointed nearly 300 agents to conduct business meetings and bring in bulk orders from major firms and institutions. He soon became the man with a net worth that figured in billions.

He was a big Bollywood enthusiast and nursed dreams of meeting some of its famous superstars. He found his dream semi-fulfilled when he set eyes on a dancer in Devadiga's bar whose name was Tarannum Khan. She was said to possess features that closely resembled Madhuri Dixit and Telgi was starstruck.

Telgi would show up at the bar regularly for Tarannum and shower note after note of the highest denominations on her dance performance. On one such night, he went berserk and bathed Tarannum in a sea of notes that was supposed to have amounted to around Rs 90 lakh. It is said that Telgi's racket was going on discreetly until his daily splurging in the bar was noticed by several others who wondered where this guy was minting the kind of money he was spending each night.

Devadiga became the owner of several properties due to Telgi. Also, Tarannum bought quite a few properties in the city where only days before she was barely able to make ends meet. She had reportedly even financed some construction projects.

But Devadiga's growing wealth was soon going to cause him much trouble. Aditya and Devadiga grew so close that one was rarely seen hanging out without the other. One day, Aditya got a call on his cell phone. Chhota Rajan was calling after a long time. He wanted to put a garland of flowers around Aditya's photograph, a warning sign that he wanted the man dead, even if he mentioned it as half a joke.

'Raja-a-a,' Rajan said in his signature style, '*teri photo pe maala chadhani padhegi.*'

'What's wrong, bhai?' Aditya asked.

'Three times. Three times! Three times my men attempted to counter Devadiga near Juhu and Andheri. Each time, you were hanging around him. My boys had to return empty-handed. I won't be able to stop them the fourth time.'

'But why are you going after him, bhai?'

'The man owes us some protection money.'

After a moment of pondering, Aditya mustered a reply. 'In that case,' he said, 'you can arrange for a garland to be put over my photograph.'

'Are you out of your mind?' Rajan said.

'He is my friend. I can't abandon him.'

Rajan was perhaps amazed as a moment of silence lingered before Aditya spoke again and repeated his resolve to stand by his friend. Rajan was impressed by Aditya's words and show of loyalty and decided to go slow on Devadiga.

Back in Mumbai, Aditya never left Devadiga to venture out alone until the matter cooled down completely. This incident had alarmed Devadiga to the dangers of being rich and famous in a city where the mafia still wielded control. He decided to acquire a licensed weapon which he could keep with him at all times. He urged Aditya to arrange a meeting with Choudhary to get the requisite permissions.

Being a high-profile politician of his state, Choudhary went one step ahead in granting Devadiga's wish. Instead of just assisting him with a licence for a normal pistol, Choudhary arranged for a mammoth .45 for which the formalities were completed in no time.

Since the weapon was acquired for personal security purposes, Devadiga was left wondering about the ways he could carry and conceal the weapon during the course of his normal day. Aditya once again stepped up to rescue his friend and took him to a tailor of his acquaintance.

The tailor was well known among the film fraternity for his excellent craftsmanship and long years of stitching clothes for all occasions. The tailor obliged by agreeing to stitch clothes for Devadiga with a large-sized pocket that would hold and conceal the weapon as he went around. Devadiga was happy with all this until Aditya observed him walking in an awkward gait that bordered on severe limping.

'What happened to your legs?' Aditya asked.

Without saying anything, Devadiga peeled off his pants to reveal an ugly wound that covered more than half of his thigh. The gun had caused quite a wound by rubbing against his thigh all the time. Aditya had a good laugh about it. Devadiga realized that acquiring the weapon was a bad idea. He eventually surrendered the licence and returned the weapon to the government. Again, the formalities were completed in no time due to Aditya's contacts with Choudhary.

In 2005, the Sri Lankan cricket team was on a tour of India for a series of matches. The team was in Mumbai when a common friend introduced Aditya to spin bowler

Muttiah Muralitharan through a common friend. The foxy spinner with an unorthodox bowling action had heard a lot about the city's booming dance bar business and expressed his desire to Aditya to witness the spectacle first-hand. It was plain curiosity on the cricketer's part. Mumbai's bars were famous in the entire country at that time. Even people from neighbouring states would visit Mumbai to experience this type of nightlife. So, within a microsecond of hearing Murali's request, Aditya called up Devadiga to arrange a visit to his bar.

'But we'll use the back entrance to avoid any *hungama* (ruckus),' Aditya said.

'Sure,' Devadiga said. He was excited to meet Murali too. 'Come over.'

Aditya and Murali hardly remained in the bar for thirty minutes to an hour, and exited without touching the drinks or spending any money on the female dancers. But their brief presence in the bar was enough for a certain journalist, who spotted the cricketer and the actor and reported that the duo was trying to fix a match in connivance with Tarannum.

The news was quickly picked up by other editorials and news channels. The police took cognizance and arrested Tarannum Khan in the case. She was brutally thrashed while in police custody and was asked to confess to the match-fixing taking place between Murali and Aditya in her presence. After getting a coerced confession out of Tarannum, the cops started pressuring Aditya.

The police made Aditya go through a round of interrogation where they employed every tactic to intimidate him. Unlike Tarannum, Aditya was a star and a public figure which made him immune from the police's high-handedness. Aditya was stubborn in his denial of the betting accusations and maintained that he and Muralitharan were there only on account of the latter's curiosity to witness Mumbai's dance bar scene.

The cop interrogating him gestured to the *havaldar* (constable) by bobbing his head. The havaldar quickly disappeared and returned with a couple of lady constables who hauled Tarannum into the room. Aditya was shocked to see that Tarannum's face was swollen and bruised. She wobbled and the lady constables kept pulling her up to prevent her from falling.

'Did you fix the match with Aditya Pancholi and Muralitharan?' the cop asked Tarannum.

She barely nodded. The cop bobbed his head once again and the havaldar motioned towards the lady constables to lead Tarannum out of the interrogation room. The cop turned to Aditya with a triumphant look on his face.

'See?' he said. 'She has already confessed to the crime.'

'Really, Inspector?' Aditya said. 'You believe this custodial confession will stand in a court of law?'

The triumphant look on the cop's face vanished and was replaced by a scowl.

The police had no option but to release Aditya on account of zero evidence. Aditya, as soon as he came out, called the press and gave a series of interviews declaring his innocence and challenging the accusations levelled against him.

After trying hard to gather evidence in establishing the match-fixing allegations and finding none, the police closed the case and released Tarannum. No charges were pressed against Aditya and the Sri Lankan team's star spin bowler, Muttiah Muralitharan.

Aditya's non-negotiable loyalty towards his friends, which included Devadiga, never found the recognition and appreciation that it deserved. In any kind of trouble, his friends invariably found Aditya on their side, bestowing whatever help was needed to get them out of their woes. But when his son, Sooraj, was accused in actress Jiah Khan's suicide case, Aditya found himself on the other side and in a most vulnerable state of mind.

Not that he asked, but Devadiga offered to help him through legal means to get Sooraj acquitted in the case. Devadiga, however, did not keep his promise, which ultimately resulted in the end of their long friendship. 'I have paid my dues for my friends in ways they can't even imagine,' Aditya says. 'And if any of them, including Devadiga, need me by their side, I will continue to stand by them.'

38

Snippets from Three Decades

Aditya formed quite a few professional associations during his film career, which has spanned more than three decades. He was right in the thick of the action when the mafia began making inroads into the industry. But it was never easy to figure out who was linked where. It wasn't as if Chhota Rajan or Dawood Ibrahim or Chhota Shakeel would come down personally to make offers to actors. Everything happened through a screen of smoke and mirrors. Just like Goonga bhai was a front man for Chhota Rajan, there were other producers who had links to the D-Company.

Having started their office in a garage at Bandra, Magnum Films International was founded by Hanif Kadawala and Sameer Hingora. In Aditya's words, Haneef and Sameer had a lot of clout in Bollywood during the early 1990s. They could make or break things by fair means or foul. Aditya was approached for one movie by the duo which was titled *Baap Numbri Beta Dus Numbri*.

Co-starring Jackie Shroff, Shakti Kapoor and Kader Khan, the film went on to become the eighth highest-grossing film of 1990.

On account of working with Magnum Films, Aditya became a regular visitor to their office. Apart from lengthy conversations, he used to spend time in the office playing carrom.

One fine day, a jovial man came to their office to see the producer duo. Aditya later learnt that the man was none other than Tiger Memon. This was a year before the Mumbai bomb blasts occurred; and Aditya had no idea that Tiger would go on to engineer such a huge act of terror. In fact, Aditya never felt uneasy around Hanif, Sameer or even Tiger during their early days.

Aditya continued his occasional visits to the Magnum office and maintained his relationship with Hanif and Sameer. But with the passing of time, Aditya noticed a subtle but definite transformation in Tiger's nature and attitude. Tiger's visits to the office became less frequent to the point where he completely vanished from the scene.

But just three or four months before the blasts, Tiger reappeared at the Magnum office.

Aditya was shocked to see the remarkable transformation the man had undergone. He had grown a long beard that came down to his chest and carried himself in the manner of a cleric. His conduct was in stark contrast to the jovial man who used to visit the office earlier. Aditya was puzzled. What on earth was going on? He got his answer a few months later, on 12 March 1993, when Mumbai once again fell victim to yet another gruesome terrorist attack.

Investigations revealed Tiger Memon to be its key perpetrator. Aditya came to fully realize the basis of the radical transformation he had seen Tiger undergo. Hanif and Sameer also turned persona non grata in the industry and Aditya never did another movie for them. They were also shunned by others who had worked with them regularly. It was during Hanif and Sameer's interrogation conducted by Rakesh Maria that Sanjay Dutt's name cropped up. The superstar had to spend numerous years fighting a lengthy trial and did considerable jail time for possession of weapons that he self-admittedly acquired for his own safety and that of his family during the Mumbai riots.

Aditya had also come in contact with another film producer by the name of Mukesh Duggal. He had started his career as producer with a movie titled *Fateh* (1991) starring Sanjay Dutt.

In the same year, he also produced *Saathi* with Aditya Pancholi and Pakistani cricketer turned actor Mohsin Khan in the lead roles. The film portrayed the story of two friends, Suraj and Amar, who take to a life of crime and become drug peddlers. The movie was high on raw violence. The famous (or infamous) chainsaw hacking scene from the Al Pacino classic *Scarface* (1983) was lifted in the movie. Aditya's performance stands out and garnered much applause. In 1994, Duggal would also go on to become a director with *Gopi Kishan*, starring Suniel Shetty in a double lead role.

The success of *Saathi* prompted Duggal to venture into another project with Aditya. This movie was titled *Khilona* (1996). Aditya was cast in a lead negative role where he sets out to put the whole world to flames in the course of his criminalistic and romantic pursuits. Besides Aditya, the film's cast included Ayyub Khan and Monica Bedi. Aditya met Monica for the first time on the set of this movie. He found her to be very kind and humble.

'She was a very well-behaved girl,' Aditya says. 'Stories about her *connections* were flourishing by then but she never threw her weight around.'

The rumours connecting her to gangster Abu Salem were doing the rounds and were ultimately found to be true many years later when she was arrested along with Salem in Portugal in 2005.

Though his professional relationship with Monica during the making of *Khilona* was amicable, creative differences created a rift between Aditya and the director of the movie. The story had been narrated to Aditya in a certain manner but improvisations in the script were making his on-screen character lose its weight. Like any other actor, Aditya felt the need to stand his ground and protect his on-screen space. Last-minute modifications resulted in frequent quarrels with the director. Things finally came to such a boiling point that Aditya put his foot down and stopped shooting on the set.

The news of Aditya throwing a fit on the set didn't go well with Duggal. He called Aditya and asked to meet him. Aditya agreed and showed up at the producer's office.

'*Khilona* is my film,' Duggal said.

'I never claimed it to be mine,' Aditya retorted sharply.

'Then how dare you stop the shooting?'

'You should focus on resolving the creative issues, which are the root of the problem,' Aditya said.

The next moment, Duggal pulled out a pistol from underneath his shirt and placed it neatly on the table. An expression of disbelief spread across Aditya's face. Duggal, with whom he had worked so closely, was issuing a death threat to him. The message from Duggal was clear in typical *filmi* style. Complete the film, or else . . .

'Okay,' Aditya said, glaring into Duggal's eyes. 'I'll complete the film. But never will I work with you again.'

Duggal picked up the pistol and stuffed it back inside his shirt.

Aditya added that he wanted the full payment right away. 'You can hold back a certain portion until I complete the dubbing. The rest of the payment must be delivered before my next shot.'

Duggal acquiesced. Aditya went back to the film knowing that the plot was going haywire. But he wanted to keep his professional commitments and the shooting was finally completed. The movie was released in December 1996 and tanked at the box office. It was a commercial failure. Aditya kept his word and never associated with Duggal again.

On 7 March 1998, Duggal was stepping out of his office at Seven Bungalows and had almost got into his car when a couple of bike-borne boys stopped him and asked him for his autograph. He was about to oblige them when one of the boys pulled out a pistol from underneath his shirt and shot Duggal at point-blank range. Duggal collapsed and the boys fled. He was gunned down right outside his office.

Multiple theories behind the producer's killing were propounded in the days following his death. Aditya remains of the opinion that Duggal was talking to both warring parties (Dawood and Chhota Rajan) and paid the cost for such misadventures with his life. There was also an indication of a property dispute being a factor in the murder. Abu Salem and Chhota Shakeel's name also cropped up during the investigation.

After his extradition from Portugal, Abu Salem was subjected to a narco test in which he named a popular actress of the time as the person who had ordered the killing. It is important to note that statements obtained by the police under a narco test are not admissible in a court of law.

Aditya was also good friends with a person named Dheeraj Emerald. Dheeraj ran a high-profile betting ring in the Emerald Club. Hence, the name of the club became inseparable from his name. Once Aditya was sitting with Dheeraj in the club when his phone rang. He glanced at the screen which displayed the same ominous number that featured only zeros from start to end. *D was calling*. Aditya picked up the call.

'Are you sitting with Dheeraj at the Emerald?' Chhota Shakeel asked.

'Yes,' Aditya said.

'*Yeh le, seth se baat kar*,' Shakeel said and passed the phone to Dawood.

'Your friend is going to get a bullet in his ass,' Dawood said.

'Why? What did he do?' Aditya asked.

'He is giving *hafta* (extortion money) to the enemy,' Dawood said, without taking Rajan's name. '*Hum kya chutiye baithe hain*? Tell him to pay us too.'

Aditya just looked at Dheeraj in bewilderment. 'I am sure there is some misunderstanding,' he said over the phone.

He asked Dawood and Shakeel to call back later so he could get more information from Dheeraj. Aditya was assured by Dheeraj that he hadn't given a single penny to anyone as hafta till date. When Shakeel called again, Aditya clarified that Dheeraj wasn't involved in any hafta transactions and that he hadn't given a single penny to the other gang.

'And if my words turn out to be wrong,' Aditya said confidently, 'then you can shoot me before you kill him.'

Dawood was amazed. '*Tu jaanta hai tu kya maang raha hai?!*'

Aditya said that he was fully aware and that he was ready to put his neck under the guillotine by becoming a guarantor for his friend. Without speaking any further, Dawood disconnected the call. This was one of the many instances that served as a reminder that the general perception about him using *connections* for his gain was in stark opposition to what actually was the case.

Aditya, in his entire life, met only one person in the film industry whom he never saw caving in to the incessant demands and pressures of the mafia. He remembers the moment to this day when he was with the said actor at Mehboob Studios. The actor, who was the reigning superstar of Bollywood, got the dreaded call from a prominent member of the underworld. The caller was pressuring the actor to work in a film for one of his acquaintances. The response that came from the actor blew Aditya away. 'I don't tell you whom to shoot,' the actor said. 'So you don't tell me which film to choose.'

Aditya felt immensely proud of him. The respect and admiration that he already had for the actor grew even higher. This actor was none other than the *badshah* of Bollywood: Shah Rukh Khan.

Aditya also had the chance to interact with the controversial and self-styled godman, Chandraswami. Nemi Chand Jain was said to have been attracted to the study of Tantra from an early age. He left home while still young to come under the tutelage of Upadhyay Amar Muni and the renowned tantric scholar, Mahamohopadhyay Gopinath Kaviraj. After spending several years as their student, he ventured into the jungles of Bihar where he remained for four years. He claimed to have acquired extraordinary tantric skills—*siddhi*—during those four years. He then christened himself Chandraswami.

Chandraswami remained an unknown figure until he met P.V. Narasimha Rao. His fortunes soared when Rao became the prime minister and he became the founder of Vishwa Dharmayatan Sanathan, which was built in Qutab Institutional Area in Delhi. The land for the erection of the building was said to have been allotted by the government.

Aditya remembers how the man had the ability to influence anybody with his magnetic personality. He would sit cross-legged, and fold his fist in such a manner that a loud clap would resound in the room due to the clashing of many big rings and gemstones that adorned his fingers. 'If there ever existed a man who could clap with one hand,' Aditya says, 'it is none other than Chandraswami.'

Within a short period, Chandraswami became a famous figure who was sought by rich and influential personalities from all over the world. From politicians to celebrities to big businessmen, the list of Chandraswami's visitors went across the board. He would make his seekers wait for a long time before granting them an audience.

'Why do you make them wait, Swami ji?' Aditya had asked him.

'An exercise in sifting,' Chandraswami said. 'Those who need me will wait as long as I want them to.'

Once when Aditya was visiting Chandraswami, the godman asked him to make a phone call to a number that he dictated. The call connected and the man on the other end asked in broken English who was calling. The grim tone and strange accent of the man made Aditya wonder about his identity. Aditya said that he was calling on behalf of Chandraswami. 'Swami ji wishes to speak to you,' Aditya said.

Swami's name effected a change of tone and the man immediately broke into a soft voice. 'Please put him on the line.'

Aditya gave the phone to the self-styled swami, who spoke to the man for a long time. The conversation veered around several different topics and Aditya overheard some interesting parts. Once the call ended, Aditya asked Chandraswami about the identity of the person on the other end of the line.

'The Sultan of Brunei,' Chandraswami said.

Aditya couldn't believe his ears. The sultan was one of the few remaining absolute monarchs in the world and was also among the world's richest men. But with Chandraswami, nothing seemed too far-fetched.

Aditya got busy with work and a long period passed before he met Chandraswami again in London.

Chandraswami was craving vegetarian food. Aditya was staying with a friend who had employed a *maharaj* (cook) who could make delicious vegetarian food.

'Please come over, Swami ji,' Aditya said.

Chandraswami came to meet Aditya in the company of a man who was swanky in his appearance and polite in his mannerisms. They chatted, ate and spent some time together before calling it a day and going their separate ways. It was later that Aditya came to know that the man accompanying Chandraswami that day was none other than Adnan Khashoggi, a businessman and arms dealer from Saudi Arabia, known for his lavish lifestyle.

There was no dearth of high political and business connections that Aditya made during his career, which spanned more than three decades. But instead of exploiting these connections for his personal gain, he would always be the first line of defence when his friends would fall into any kind of trouble. However, when his son Sooraj was accused in the suicide case of an actress, Aditya was left to fend for himself. After many years, during which he attended all the hearings, Sooraj was finally acquitted by the court.

Reclining in a chair in his house at Versova, Aditya assumes the grim air of some of the intense characters he had portrayed on the screen. 'I like to fight my own battles,' he says.

There are other cases involving him that have been dissected widely in the media.

'But those stories are for another day,' Aditya Pancholi says, as he signs off in style.

39

A Tale of Two Brothers

The taxi crossed Chhatrapati Shivaji Maharaj Terminus Railway Station. I was in the back seat, as the vehicle submerged into the rush hour traffic of Mumbai. The majestic railway station building was built by the Britishers and thus has a Gothic architectural style. Construction of the building began in 1878 and was completed by 1887. It was earlier named Victoria Terminus. In 1996, the station was named after Chhatrapati Shivaji Maharaj, the great Maratha warrior king. This detail gains importance because it was a part of the city's transformation from Bombay to Mumbai. The mention of the bomb blasts found its way into this change too. Very famously, a politician had justified the name change by asking, 'Why do we want to attach a bomb to our bay?'

The taxi driver navigated through the overcrowded roads. Traffic crawled. The footpaths were full of hawkers. The cab stopped outside a shopping complex near Dhobi

Talao. No, this was different from Dhobi Ghat (most people who don't know the city well enough think both are the same). Dhobi Ghat is the world's largest open air laundromat. Reportedly, half a million pieces of cloth are painstakingly handwashed by laundry men and women each day here. But it is located near Mahalakshmi, and I was a fair distance away from that place.

At the shopping complex, I took the stairs to the dimly lit basement and found the office I came looking for. I had an appointment with its proprietor. There were no signboards outside. A lanky man was seated at the door. He didn't look dangerous but I wondered if he was armed.

'Is Tarique Parveen inside?' I asked.

The lanky man measured me with his gaze and checked with his boss. Soon, I was inside a small cabin filled with the strong fragrance of musk. Tarique Parveen owned a perfumery business. Vials of attar and perfume were stacked inside the cabinet on the wall. But there was a time when he used to work closely with Chhota Shakeel. The shadows of his past have not been dispelled completely. There was a CCTV monitor to his right and he kept throwing regular, purposeful glances at it.

Just like Sabir had introduced Dawood to a life of crime, Tarique was introduced to the underworld on account of his elder brother whose name was Zubair Parveen. But the brothers had to pay a heavy price for playing this game.

'Zubair was an outspoken man,' Tarique said. 'Being outspoken in this business has its own consequences.'

I leaned back into the chair and listened.

Zubair Parveen entered a godown in Crawford Market where Mustafa Dossa aka Mustafa Majnu was planning another killing based on his whims and fancies. The godown was filled with Dossa's cronies; yes-men all of them. Zubair sat across the table, and heard that Mustafa wanted to give out a supari for a certain Farooq, who belonged to a family of hoteliers in Mumbai. Zubair knew Farooq pretty well and they were good friends. There was no way he would allow Farooq to be thrown under the bus.

'Why are you after his life?' Zubair asked.

'See what he has done!' Dossa said.

He pulled out a newspaper clipping and thumped it on the wooden table. On the page, dated sometime in 1987, there was news about a smuggling consignment being caught by the customs department off the Gujarat coast. This consignment belonged to the D-Company for whom the Dossa brothers worked. According to Mustafa, Farooq was responsible for leaking the details and the route of the vessel carrying the goods to the authorities. Thus, he was *wajib-ul-qatl* (mandated to be killed) like other informers.

But Zubair was not convinced by any margin. Dossa was known for his troublemaking tendencies. Also, during that time, incidents of double-crossing in the smuggling game were happening with alarming regularity. These seemed to have sanction from the top.

As unbelievable as it may sound, the D-Company was looting businessmen who wanted to work with them. There was always a long queue of people who wanted to do business with Dawood. These included businessmen from all religions and communities. The D-Company would keep them waiting and then dangle the carrot of a 'jacket' being smuggled into India for them, through which they could make a lot of money. In the smuggling parlance of those years, one jacket of goods was worth Rs 5 lakh.

So, the D-Company would ask the businessman to invest Rs 5 lakh and the mark would agree immediately. Similarly, they would take money from nine others on the pretext of smuggling a jacket for them. Each of these ten businessmen would be ordered to maintain strict confidentiality about the deal. Such was the fear of the D-Company that even the businessman's left hand was unaware what the right was doing.

In this manner, ten boats with a jacket each, with Rs 50 lakh worth of goods in total, would sail from Dubai. With the blessings from the top leadership of the D-Company, details about one boat would be leaked to the customs who would intercept the boat at sea and seize the goods. The next day, the news of the capture would be plastered all over the newspapers.

The D-Company would then summon each of the ten businessmen separately. Each one would be told that *their* jacket, in which they had invested, was seized by the customs! The newspaper clipping would serve as proof of their alleged misfortune.

Now even if the businessman's innards were boiling, he would have to grin and bear the situation because he was powerless in front of Dawood's or Shakeel's men. And he couldn't even complain to the cops because it was a smuggling operation in the first place! In such a manner, the D-Company would sacrifice one jacket of goods worth Rs 5 lakh but pocket the nine other jackets worth Rs 45 lakh. In short, they were duping their own investors.

So, Zubair Parveen was thinking that this confiscated consignment—which Mustafa Dossa was furious about—was also sleight of hand played by the Dossa brothers on the D-Company. Dossa was looking to pin the blame on someone to evade suspicion from Dawood. Thus, he had zeroed on Farooq. But Zubair could vouch for Farooq's innocence. The man was anything but a rat. Zubair tried to convince Dossa about it but Dossa (being Dossa) was in no mood to listen.

'Fine,' Zubair told Dossa. 'Give me three days. I will find out who the mole was. If Farooq squealed on us, go ahead and shoot him in the head. If not, you have to stay clear of him.'

Zubair would throw cuss words with abandon and generally had a rough manner of speaking. He had got involved with the underworld because he had grown up around the same areas where it had bloomed and then mushroomed into a Frankenstein-esque monster, which threatened to destroy everything in its path. On Zubair's insistence, Dossa agreed to the three-day time limit and not go after Farooq until then.

Knowing that he was racing against time, Zubair rushed to Tiger Memon's office at Mahim. The two were good friends and discussed the situation at hand. Tiger and the Dossas always had a cold war going between them. Hence, Tiger took an unusual interest in wanting to prove that Mustafa Dossa aka Mustafa Majnu was good for nothing except lusting after beautiful women.

Zubair and Tiger came up with a trick that had earlier been used by none other than Dawood Ibrahim. A few years ago, another of the don's consignments had been caught by the customs. He was livid at that time. But he was also sure that one of his own men had stabbed him in the back by leaking the information to the authorities. During those days, if any consignment was caught on the basis of information provided by a *khabri* (informant), the general practice in the customs department was to pay a certain percentage value of the confiscated goods to the khabri.

Since this was government money, the transaction needed to be confidential, but it also needed to be on record. To find the mole, Dawood had bribed a top customs official and gained documentary evidence about the identity of the mole. Needless to say, the mole soon met a ghastly end.

Tiger was aware of this incident. He called people who knew people. Soon, Zubair and Tiger were able to find a contact in the customs who would part with the information for the right price. Zubair put in nearly Rs 30,000 of his personal money to bribe this contact.

When Zubair finally got documentary evidence about the identity of the mole, he was unable to believe his eyes. The man who had leaked the information to the customs and even got paid for it was none other than Siddik, a relative of Mustafa Dossa!

Zubair stormed into Dossa's office and confronted him with his evidence. Even Dossa did not believe the news until Zubair showed him the documents. Then, to save Siddik, Dossa tried to pin the blame on Zubair himself.

'Only an informant can get such documents from the customs,' Dossa told Zubair. 'Maybe you are the informant.'

'Let's assume I am.' Zubair laughed. 'But Dawood bhai also has a history of procuring such documents from the customs. Is he also a police informer then?'

Dossa was aghast. 'None can speak Dawood bhai's name with such insolence,' he said, even though he knew that Zubair's impudence was directed towards him and not Dawood.

'You were about to kill an innocent man,' Zubair thundered. 'Why don't you show the same urgency to kill Siddik that you were showing to kill Farooq?'

'No,' Dossa said. 'Siddik is my flesh and blood.'

'*Madarchod*,' Zubair said. 'What happened to your loyalty to Dawood bhai now? *Haan*?'

At that time, Dossa took that insult on his chin and appeared to calm down. He told Zubair that he had casually spoken about the route of the consignment to Siddik a few weeks ago. He had no idea that Siddik would leak the information to the customs to make a quick buck. He also pleaded with Zubair to finish the matter at this point.

'I will personally slap Siddik with my Bata chappal,' he said.

Zubair knew that Dossa was on good terms with Dawood at that time. Since Dawood had set up a new base in Dubai with Chhota Shakeel and Anees, Mohammed Dossa and Mustafa Dossa were handling most of Mumbai under the don's command. Even if Dawood came to know of Siddik's misdeeds, he would probably finish off Siddik, who was anyway a small player in the game. Dossa would probably escape with a slap on the wrist on account of his proximity to Dawood. Zubair had managed to save

Farooq, which was his primary objective. So he shook hands with Dossa and laid the matter to rest.

But he had no idea he was shaking hands with a snake who would never change its stripes. Dossa would never forget the humiliation Zubair had heaped on him in front of the boys. He swore to avenge this insult. He knew that as long as Tiger was allying with Zubair, he would not be able to harm him without the fear of retribution from Tiger. He would have to wait for the right moment, even if it took years.

40

If You Can't Beat Them . . .

On 24 September 1994, Tarique Parveen was busy making arrangements to repay the loan of Rs 2 lakh which he had taken from his brother Zubair. The two brothers shared a very close bond. Zubair was protective of Tarique and wanted to keep him away from the life of crime. Tarique planned to use the funds given by his brother to start a new business and earn a legitimate living. But fate had other plans for him and his brother.

While Tarique was mobilizing resources to repay the money, Zubair was sitting inside his office when he heard a knock on the door. An acquaintance, a young man named Faheem, had shown up unexpectedly. Zubair greeted Faheem heartily at the door. The two knew each other.

'Won't you invite me inside?' Faheem asked.

'Of course, brother,' Zubair said without realizing that he had opened the door for the messenger of death. 'Come in.'

'Where is Tarique?' Faheem asked. 'Is he coming here any time soon?'

Zubair told Faheem that Tarique wasn't expected to return until the evening prayers. He thought that Faheem had asked a casual question. But the man was shrewd and he was trying to gauge if Zubair would have his brother by his side any time soon. Faheem breathed easy knowing that there was quite some time for Tarique to return, and for him to be able to put a sinister plan into action.

Zubair ordered lunch from a nearby Irani hotel.

'Break bread with me, brother,' Zubair said.

'Yes, yes,' Faheem replied. 'Why not!'

Faheem obliged even though he was here to perform a ghastly ritual of the underworld called *'chehra-patti'*. This was a process through which a target was positively identified as the one who was to be killed. Chehra-patti was a must before a contract killing was executed. This was done to ensure that the person who was killed was indeed the one for whom the supari had been floated. While the identification was done by Faheem, the supari had been assigned to one of the most lethal contract killers of the underworld.

The supari for Zubair's murder had been assigned to none other than Feroz Konkani, a lanky young man, a college dropout from Nagpada. By the time Feroz Konkani was twenty-four years old, he was already the most feared sharpshooter in the history of the Mumbai mafia. Terror of him reigned not only among his victims but also among his colleagues, who were too afraid to take any chances with his mercurial temper. Later, he also gained the infamous distinction of being the first gangster to use an AK-47 in a contract killing. Zubair was to be among the initial victims of his killing reign.

Not long after he had broken bread with Zubair, Faheem stepped outside and signalled to Feroz Konkani (who was waiting nearby) that his target was alone inside the office. But who had assigned the supari to Feroz Konkani?

It was none other than Mustafa Dossa aka Mustafa Majnu. As the Dossa brothers began to grow closer to Dawood, their notoriety within the gang had increased manifold. After the episode with Siddik, Mustafa was trying to build a case against Zubair on each visit to Dubai. His general refrain was that Zubair had a sharp tongue. Initially, his plans didn't cut much ice with either Chhota Shakeel or Anees. As long as Tiger was with Zubair, he was well protected.

Soon after 6 December 1992, riots broke out in Mumbai following the demolition of the Babri Masjid in Ayodhya. Until that moment, the Mumbai mafia was not divided on communal lines. It is said that Dawood did not want to get involved in the retaliation of the riots in which his community had suffered much loss of life and property. But community pressure was mounting upon him steeply. Residents of Dongri shouted slogans around Musafirkhana to the tone of 'Dawood Ibrahim Kaskar, *tu hamara bhai nahi hai*'. They publicly shamed Dawood for his failure to stand up for them. Another reported incident is that Dawood received a parcel at his residence in Dubai, which was sent from Dongri. When he opened the box, he was aghast to find that it was filled with bangles and a note which lamented that these bangles were the perfect gift for a brother who wasn't man enough to protect his sisters.

The ISI was keen on creating a disturbance in India and exploiting the religious fault lines. Pakistan's secret service agency had spent much of the 1980s providing support to the Taliban after the USSR invaded Afghanistan. The Soviets withdrew in 1989 and this established the ISI as an agency that had defeated a professional, trained and highly powerful army by using a ragtag assembly of Afghan mujahideen.

Buoyed by their success, the ISI wanted to use Dawood's network to execute the March 1993 blasts in India. They sent him feelers but Dawood wasn't ready to play ball. Then the ISI played their stronger cards. Through Aslam Bhatti and Dawood Jatt, both of whom were Pakistani smugglers, the ISI began intercepting and confiscating Dawood's smuggling consignments in the Arabian Sea. The message was clear. Dawood had to cooperate or they wouldn't let him operate. With such factors at play, both in Mumbai and in Islamabad, Dawood embarked on the mission of avenging the riots.

Tiger Memon emerged as the mascot of the mission but Mohammad Dossa was also a key player. The key difference was that Tiger was the more flamboyant of the two, whereas Dossa managed to keep a relatively low profile. Tiger and his entire family moved out of India before the blasts were triggered on 12 March 1993.

As soon as the news of Tiger's involvement in the blasts started doing the rounds, Siddik (Dossa's relative) sensed an opportunity to create trouble for Zubair, with whom he had unfinished business. He went to the cops and told them about Zubair's proximity to Tiger. The cops picked up Zubair for questioning and detained him in the lock-up. No arrest was shown. Tarique began mobilizing all resources to secure his brother's release. As Zubair had no role to play in the blasts, the cops released him after twenty days. This again caused much pain to Siddik and Dossa.

But Dossa was not one to let go of a relatively petty rift. As soon as the heat of the bomb blasts began to die down, he floated a supari for Zubair Parveen's murder, which was picked up by the hot-headed Feroz Konkani. And that is how Konkani had landed outside Zubair's office.

After the chehra-patti was done by Faheem, Konkani saw Zubair heading out for prayers at the local mosque. He followed Zubair to the mosque like a shadow but maintained a distance.

Konkani was known for his violent ways. Reportedly, he had committed his first murder when he was barely sixteen or seventeen years old. Such was his infamy that even Dawood would address Konkani as 'darling'. Now the hitman was about to add another strike to his list of kills.

Inside the mosque, Zubair performed the ablutions and prayed. As soon as he stepped outside the mosque, he found himself staring at the barrel of Konkani's gun. The sharpshooter pulled the trigger. Taking advantage of the ensuing chaos, the killer vanished into the crowd. Zubair's lifeless body lay on the crowded road, but no one took him to the hospital. Konkani had shot his victim several times and left him no chance of survival.

News of the incident soon reached Tarique. He was broken to the core. He rushed to the hospital where his brother's body had been taken. Devastated. A respected police officer of the area placed a hand on Tarique's shoulder. 'Mustafa Dossa and Ejaz Pathan are behind your brother's killing,' the cop told Tahir. 'And now they are also planning to take your wicket.'

In a state of helplessness, Tarique put in a call to Chhota Shakeel, who was in Dubai. Until that time, Chhota Shakeel did not seem to know what had transpired on the streets of Mumbai. Tarique had his doubts that something like this would have happened without Shakeel's approval.

'Bhai,' Tarique said, 'if my brother caused you any trouble, I could have fallen at your feet and begged for your pardon.' He sobbed, 'Why did you allow him to be punished like this?'

'What happened?' Shakeel asked.

'They killed my brother, bhai!'

Shakeel told Tarique to wait for a few minutes and disconnected the call. He made a few inquiries and called Tarique again. He reconfirmed that Mustafa Dossa was behind the killing. 'But I have issued orders that whoever lays a finger on you will be my personal enemy,' Shakeel said. 'No one can touch you now.'

After the blasts were executed, Dossa had climbed higher in the pecking order of the D-Company. At most, Dossa's indiscretion with Zubair would lead to a verbal lashing from Dawood but nothing beyond that. Tarique had no option but to thank Shakeel for his supposed magnanimity.

But his brother's death had broken him. Tarique was inconsolable for days. One of his business associates came to meet him a few days later. He saw Tarique's miserable condition and asked him a simple question.

'Can you beat them, Tarique?'

'No,' Tarique said.

'Then join them.'

Tarique realized that power was the key to his family's survival. He had to keep himself and his family safe from the likes of Dossa. He immediately called Shakeel and told him that he wanted to work for the D-Company. Chhota Shakeel agreed and found an excellent manager in Tarique who would answer phone calls even in the middle of the night and show the required results.

Tarique started off by doing small jobs like getting files cleared from various departments. He later became Shakeel's man Friday in Mumbai. Shakeel was so pleased with his new lieutenant that in the year 2000, Tarique was called to Dubai.

As the flight took off from Mumbai Airport, Tarique thought about his decision. Once he would get into the don's inner coterie, there would be no coming back. He would get access to a lot of power and money, but there would be a price to pay—he would be tied to Shakeel for life. If some day, Tarique would ever want to give up the life of crime and return to Mumbai, Shakeel would probably kill him rather than let him go. Of this, Tarique was already aware. The biggest proof was in his hands; a one-way ticket to Dubai sent by none other than Chhota Shakeel.

41

Come to Dubai

After landing in Dubai, Tarique began managing Chhota Shakeel's work across the UAE. He would coordinate payments from various parties. Shakeel began trusting and relying on Tarique's sound judgement. One of the earliest matters that Tarique 'managed' was that of a businessman in Dubai who was supposed to repay Rs 50 lakh that he had borrowed from the D-Company. The businessman, however, had fallen upon bad times and was unable to repay the loan. Tarique called the businessman to Shakeel's office where Chhota Shakeel gave the man quite a earful.

Shakeel's condition was simple. 'Repay the money,' he said, 'or eat a bullet.'

However, Tarique had sensed that the businessman wasn't short-changing the D-Company but was genuinely short of funds. He proposed to Shakeel that the businessman be allowed to repay in instalments. Shakeel was reluctant initially but agreed when he saw rationale in Tarique's thought. Tarique proposed that the yearly instalment be Rs 20 lakh. And that the businessman would pay four annual instalments.

'Bhai,' the businessman pleaded. 'Why four?'

'EMI payments attract interest,' Tarique said. 'Bank *se kabhi* loan *nahi liya kya*? (Haven't you ever taken a loan from a bank?)'

Ultimately, even the businessman found it wiser to pay a lesser amount across a longer period of time. In this manner, Tarique was able to recover Rs 80 lakh for Shakeel without firing even a single bullet.

Soon, Tarique began mingling with other key members of the D-Company. He met another D-Company man named Salim Chiplun. Chiplun is a small town in Maharashtra. Since there was a surfeit of Salims in the underworld, they were identified by their origin. Salim had a few extortion cases registered against him in Mumbai and was very close to Anees Ibrahim. Many years later (around 2010), the marriage ceremony of Salim Chiplun's son took place with Anees Ibrahim's daughter at the Star Gymkhana in Karachi. In the early 2000s, the bond of friendship between Chiplun and Anees was only growing by leaps and bounds.

During those days, a Kashmiri named Jaan was Anees's new bodyguard. Everybody in the D-Company was in awe of Jaan because he had an imposing personality. He also had huge hands, with which he threatened to strangle his enemies. Salim Chiplun and Tarique were partying at a club in Dubai when Chiplun introduced him to the bodyguard. As soon as Jaan stepped away, Tarique told Salim Chiplun that though everybody seemed to have a very high opinion of Jaan, it was in Anees Ibrahim's best interest to find a new bodyguard.

'Why?' Salim asked.

'I have measured this man,' Tarique said. 'He is a big *gaand-fattu (coward)*!'

Salim laughed it off. The party at the club continued for a while. But Tarique's judgement about Jaan was soon going to come true. Tarique had just left the club when Salim frantically began calling him on his cell phone. Apparently, a fight had broken out at the club and more men were needed to control the situation.

'Come back,' Salim said. 'We need backup!'

'All right,' Tarique said as he prepared to take a U-turn. 'But what happened to the Kashmiri bodyguard? Didn't he fight?'

Salim grunted with anger. 'The motherfucker ran away at the first sign of trouble!'

At that time, Tarique could not stop laughing. But a friendship formed between Tarique and Jaan despite this incident. The duo would often hang out together. Once, Tarique was sitting in his office in Dubai when he received a call from Jaan, who was waiting at the salon on the opposite side of the road. Jaan apparently wanted to discuss a pressing matter. All this time, Tarique had noticed that while Shakeel was very close to him, he (Tarique) was not allowed anywhere near Dawood Ibrahim.

'How come they've never sent you to Karachi?' Jaan asked Tarique.

'Dubai is good enough for me,' Tarique said. 'I don't want to go elsewhere.'

Jaan then told Tarique that he had overheard a conversation between Anees, Shakeel and Dawood Ibrahim. The chief of the D-Company had given strict orders to Shakeel that Tarique was not supposed to be called to Karachi. Shakeel assured his boss that such a situation would never arise.

'If he ever lands in Karachi,' Dawood had said, 'just finish him.'

Tarique now understood that while Shakeel trusted him, Dawood still had some vestiges of doubt in his mind that Tarique would seek revenge for the killing of his brother, Zubair. Still, Tarique continued to work for the D-Company.

In 2003, Tarique had a surprise visitor at his Dubai office in the form of Khalid Pehelwan. Khalid was an old-timer in the D-Company, who had once saved Shakeel from certain death when the latter was caught by Mehmood Kalia and his men during a gunfight at the AC Market in Tardeo. Secondly, Khalid had also saved Dawood Ibrahim after the Pathans had attacked Musafirkhana following Sabir's gruesome killing. In many ways, Khalid was considered Dawood's mentor and thus his words carried a lot of weight in the D-Company.

Khalid Pehelwan was a wrestler from Bhopal in Madhya Pradesh. He arrived in Bombay to work with Bashu Dada, who ran an *akhara* (traditional wrestling centre) at Teli Mohalla. In the ensuing turf wars, Bashu's gang was pitted against the Dawood Ibrahim-led D-Company.

The D-Company boys picked up Bashu and brought him to Dawood Ibrahim's office. People thought that Bashu would meet his end. But Dawood sprung a surprise by allowing Bashu to sit on his own chair and treated him like an equal. Bashu was confused at this show of respect. Dawood stared back at him with a cold gaze.

'*Tu Bambai ka purana shaana hai,*' Dawood said. '*Teri izzat toh karunga.*' (You are an old-timer from the Bombay mafia, and thus you deserve respect).

Such an incident also made Khalid switch sides to Dawood's gang. For a man who could move mountains, Khalid Pehelwan had a very low-pitched voice.

He brought up the matter that had brought him to Tarique's office. A property had come under dispute between two business partners. Shakeel had been approached by one of the parties to resolve the matter. Now, the other party also needed someone of the stature of Chhota Shakeel to negotiate on their behalf and had brought the issue to Khalid Pehelwan. The erstwhile wrestler asked Tarique to call Shakeel immediately.

Tarique called Chhota Shakeel and informed him that Khalid Pehelwan wanted to talk to him. Then Tarique offered the phone to Khalid but the mighty Pehelwan simply ordered him to put the phone on speaker. 'Your party can keep the land for himself,' Khalid told Shakeel. 'But he has to pay for it.'

'How much?' Shakeel said.

'One crore rupees.'

'Company *mein jitni izzat Dawood bhai ki hai, utni aap ki bhi hai*,' Shakeel said, implying that he was as respected as Dawood in the gang. 'Whatever you say is the final verdict.'

Khalid appeared pleased with Shakeel's response. The deal was agreed to in principle. Shakeel hung up the phone.

Since Tarique and Khalid knew each other, Tarique ordered some tea for both of them. The duo joked and laughed about a few incidents of the past. Seeing that Khalid was in a jovial mood, Tarique began negotiating on behalf of Chhota Shakeel.

'One crore is a lot for that piece of land,' Tarique said. 'Give some discount for Shakeel bhai at least.'

Khalid smiled. 'Twenty lakhs less for his sake.'

Tarique grinned. 'And how about some discount for me?'

'Ten lakhs less for you,' Khalid said. 'But not a penny less than seventy lakhs.'

'*Shukriya*, Khalid bhai. Give me some time to arrange for the money.'

'Arrange? *Kya* arrange?!' Khalid shouted. 'I want the cash now!'

Tarique's jaw almost hit the floor. Khalid was insistent that he needed the money now or he would take the entire Rs 1 crore instead of Rs 70 lakh. Tarique scoured through all the drawers in his office. All his cash amounted to a mere Rs 20 lakh. He called Chhota Shakeel again. '*Yeh pehelwan ko paisa abhi chahiye* (this wrestler wants the money now),' he whispered. 'I have only twenty lakhs with me.'

Even Shakeel was surprised. But he could not say no to Khalid Pehelwan. He asked Tarique to wait for ten minutes. Before the stipulated time, a car stopped outside Tarique's office and two boys delivered two bags filled with cash to Tarique. Several minutes later, Tarique had painfully counted each note, locked it all up in several briefcases and bid the Pehelwan a cheerful goodbye. An hour later, Khalid called Tarique's phone.

'The cash is less than what you promised me!' Khalid said.

'What are you saying, bhai?' Tarique pleaded. 'I counted each note myself.'

'The five hundred wads are less than they should be!'

Tarique cussed under his breath. 'Bhai, there are bundles of thousands in the bag too. Check *toh karo*!'

Khalid asked Tarique to stay on the line as he rustled through the money again. Indeed, Tarique was speaking the truth. Then Khalid Pehelwan laughed heartily and hung up. In this manner, Tarique was able to save Rs 30 lakh for Shakeel in a matter of minutes.

Things were going well for Tarique in Dubai. One day, he was summoned by Chhota Shakeel to the latter's office. Shakeel seemed to be in a very serious mood. As soon as Tarique stepped inside, Shakeel asked the other boys to vacate the room as he wanted to talk to Tarique in private. Shakeel leaned back on the sofa. 'I have some news for you,' he said.

Tarique wondered what the news was because he had never seen Shakeel so serious before. He did not ask any questions but waited for his boss to reveal the situation. Shakeel took a long pause and then he said, 'Feroz Konkani is dead.' Another pause. 'I got him bumped off in Karachi.'

Tarique remembered the dreadful day he had seen his brother's bullet-ridden body. Konkani had killed his brother Zubair in the most brutal manner. Tarique covered his eyes to hide his tears, but he was unable to stop the tears from overflowing. He stood up to leave the room.

'Stay seated,' Shakeel shouted. 'I have not asked you to move yet. This news should stay between you and me.'

Tarique sat back in the chair, and covered his face with his palm. He had heard on the rumour mill that Feroz Konkani was getting too big for his boots. Konkani was in the custody of the Mumbai Police in 1998 but had escaped while being taken for a medical check-up at the JJ Hospital. It was one of the most dramatic escapes in the history of the Mumbai underworld. He escaped on a bike ridden by Zahoor Makanda, who was later shot dead by Vijay Salaskar, the encounter specialist of the Mumbai Police.

Konkani moved to Nepal, and then to Bangkok before making his way to Karachi. But over a period of time, he had started becoming too big for his boots. One of his conversations in which he abused Anees and Shakeel and threatened to bump them off came under the scanner of Dawood Ibrahim. The don immediately asked Shakeel to take countermeasures. Chhota Shakeel's men captured Konkani in Karachi and gave him a painful death. The renegade threat was eliminated forever.

Tarique's trail of thought was broken when one of the boys asked for Shakeel's permission to enter the room as an important matter needed his attention. Shakeel asked the boy what was so urgent that he deemed fit to disturb him.

'Bhai,' the young man said. 'Do you know? Feroz Konkani is dead. Someone bumped him off in Karachi.'

Shakeel shook his head and dismissed the boy after throwing a few cuss words. But now Shakeel was surprised that the news had reached Dubai even though he hadn't told anyone about it. Tarique was thankful that Shakeel had stopped him from leaving the room.

'Bhai,' Tarique said. 'Had I left the room, wouldn't you have blamed me for leaking the news of Feroz's death?'

'Guess I would,' Shakeel said.

'Misunderstandings like these caused my brother's death,' Tarique said.

Life had turned full circle for Tarique. Feroz Konkani was dead. Dossa was also arrested in 2003. In many ways, those who had wronged Tarique's brother had paid for their misdeeds. The feeling of helplessness that Tarique had experienced when his brother had died had now been eliminated to a great degree. In 2004, Tarique decided to return to India. But he feared for his life and opened back-channel negotiations with Indian agencies to return to the country. Although Tarique wanted to return, he was not sure if Shakeel would allow him to return alive.

42

Dubai to Jail

Chhota Shakeel was furious. He was trying to change Tarique's decision of returning to India but the latter had already made up his mind. After his brother's killers had been murdered or arrested, he found no point in continuing to work in the underworld. In 2003, Iqbal Kaskar (Dawood's brother) and Tarique were detained in Dubai following the murder of Sharad Shetty. Shetty was an aide of Dawood Ibrahim who owned several hotels in the UAE. It is suspected that Chhota Rajan bumped him off for his apparent involvement in the Bangkok attack in which Rajan was nearly killed.

In the year 2000, a hit squad sent by Chhota Shakeel and led by sharpshooter Munna Jhingada managed to corner Chhota Rajan in the plush neighbourhood of 26th Street, Sukhumvit Soi in Bangkok. Rajan was grievously hurt in the attack but he managed to escape. He took out Sharad Shetty by having him killed outside the plush India Club in Dubai.

The UAE authorities, who hadn't taken much action against Dawood while he was living there, suddenly found that the level of violence on their land was growing to a whole new level. They also upped the ante against the underworld.

After Iqbal's release, Dawood insisted that Iqbal should shift to Karachi but the latter wanted to return to Mumbai. The Indian authorities also began negotiations to bring Iqbal back to the country. The top bosses in the Mumbai Crime Branch assigned police inspector Aslam Momin to convince Iqbal to return to Mumbai and he would be kept safe. Inspector Momin was an honest officer and never faced the slightest doubt or question regarding his integrity. Iqbal, after having received enough assurances from Inspector Momin and the Crime Branch, decided to return to Mumbai. He was extradited and charged in the cases he was involved in and had apparently received assurance of a fair trial by the authorities.

But the powers-that-be made a U-turn and immediately arrested Iqbal on his return to India. When he mentioned his conversations with Inspector Momin, the government initiated action against the honest cop and suspended him, and instituted an inquiry against Momin.

Incidentally, when Tarique also announced his intention to return to India in 2004, he came under relentless pressure from Chhota Shakeel.

'The cops will bump you off in an encounter,' Shakeel said.

'Death will come to me only once, bhai,' Tarique said. 'If you have no objection to my return, then I have nothing to fear.'

Shakeel understood that Tarique could no longer be convinced to stay back. Like Iqbal, Tarique was also being persuaded by the agencies to return and face the law. The agencies felt that he could provide crucial information about Dawood's operations in the Middle East. Shakeel was also aware of this fact. He was trying to decide if he should let Tarique go back or bump him off.

'Call me before you board flight AI-717 tomorrow,' Shakeel told Tarique.

Tarique was not surprised that Shakeel knew of his travel itinerary. Shakeel had informers who worked for the national carrier, and he was able to obtain the details of Tarique's travel plans. However, Tarique did not make the final call to Shakeel, who had decided to let the man go. Shakeel was of the opinion that even if Tarique revealed any information to the cops, Indian agencies would not be able to harm the men and assets of D-Company on foreign soil without causing diplomatic turbulence. Tarique returned to India, safe and sound, where he was taken into police custody.

This was not the first time that Tarique had been arrested. Earlier, an influential businessman who was close to Chhota Rajan came under Shakeel's scanner. Shakeel called up Tarique's office in Mumbai to get an update. Apparently, Shakeel had decided to bump off the businessman. Tarique warned him against such misadventures.

'He is a big fish, bhai.'

'So what?' Shakeel said. 'Even big fish can be fried!'

That call was traced by the law enforcement agencies and Tarique was called for questioning. Tarique explained to the authorities that he was too small to influence Shakeel one way or the other. The police slapped a case under the Maharashtra Prevention of Dangerous Activities (MPDA) Act and arrested him.

The next day, he was packed off to Akola Jail. The entire jail was abuzz with activity even at 11.30 p.m. All lights were switched on the orders of Swati Sathe, who was in charge of the jail. She was known for her integrity and was unlikely to give in to pressure from Tarique's clout.

'Do not create any trouble here,' Swati warned.

'Madam,' Tarique said, 'as long as I am treated fairly, you will have no complaints.'

Tarique was placed alone in a huge cell. He spent most of his time reading the newspaper and gardening. Swati Sathe kept a strict vigil on his movements. Once when he was meeting his lawyer, Swati insisted that the meeting should take place in her presence. She was not ready to yield to his objections. Tarique finally agreed to talk to the lawyer in her presence. When they went to the mulaqat room, Tarique asked his lawyer directly, 'So whom does Shakeel plan to bump off next?'

Swati was taken aback. She chided him for starting such a conversation in her presence. Tarique responded by saying that he would continue to have such frivolous dialogue if she insisted on staying in the room. Ultimately, Tarique was allowed a few minutes with his lawyer. But even after that incident, Swati did not let her guard down.

Once, Tarique wanted to come out of jail to get a breath of fresh air. He clutched his chest and feigned a heart attack. Swati saw through his game and insisted that an entire fleet of doctors would show up inside Akola Jail, but there was no way Tarique was going out even for a moment. Finally, Tarique pleaded with her. 'Madam, why are you putting so much pressure on me?'

Swati conceded that she was getting daily calls from R&AW and IB to track Tarique's activities. On a review petition filed in the high court, Tarique was released after eight months in Akola Jail.

When he was deported from Dubai, he was again placed in the jail where Swati Sathe was in charge. Iqbal Kaskar was also in the same jail. It was a reunion of sorts. Tarique suggested to Iqbal that he should contest the upcoming municipal election. Iqbal was averse to the idea but Tarique reasoned that it was a good time to test the waters.

Tarique managed to get an order from the high court, which allowed Iqbal the permission to contest the election. The news reached Swati Sathe and she came under severe pressure from her superiors to ensure that a fugitive don's brother would not contest an election in India while still being lodged in jail. She called Iqbal to her cabin.

'Madam,' Tarique said. 'I will accompany Iqbal to your office.'

'*Ae*, what business is it of yours?' Swati said.

'He is the brother of my boss. I cannot leave him alone.'

Grudgingly, Swati allowed Tarique to tag along. She asked the two men about their recent antics. Tarique replied that it was no crime to fight an election. When Swati insisted that they disclose their true intentions, Tarique told her that they would withdraw at the last moment.

Eventually, the form was filled. Many local politicians turned up to ask Iqbal to back out as they feared he would eat into their votes. One politician offered a sum of Rs 50 lakh for the withdrawal. As the election came closer, a horde of people turned up to meet Iqbal including his sister—Haseena Parkar. Some acquaintances suggested that Iqbal would win the election because a seer whom Haseena Parkar held in high regard had predicted the result in Iqbal's favour. Dawood's sisters revered seers as much as her other family members, including Dawood Ibrahim. But after Haseena Parkar got involved, Tarique realized that an election contest that had begun as a joke had gone too far. Iqbal began to believe his own hype and thought he had a good chance of winning the post.

'Bhai, this baba is making a chutiya out of us,' Tarique told Iqbal. 'Please withdraw your nomination.'

But now, Iqbal did not want to take back his candidature. With great effort, Tarique convinced Iqbal to sign a blank paper and used it to withdraw Iqbal's name from the election. A few days later, Chhota Shakeel sent a message through an emissary to Tarique. Dawood Ibrahim was very angry that Tarique had taken Iqbal's signature on a blank paper. Tarique sent back an apology with a footnote: if Iqbal had contested the election, he would not have got even 500 votes, which would have been a huge loss of face.

During Tarique's stint at Akola Jail, Abu Salem was also lodged in solitary confinement in the opposite barracks. Salem lived under constant fear of his life from other inmates, who included his rivals like D.K. Rao. Other D-Company members tried to boost his morale but Salem was apparently very scared about the threat from Rajan's men. Before Salem carried out Gulshan Kumar's murder in 1997, there was a famous saying in the underworld that *'Salem phone pe goli chalata hai'*, which meant that he was only giving extortion threats over the phone but lacked the spunk to follow them up. The killing of Gulshan Kumar made him an overnight terror.

As per Tarique, when the D-Company was trying to extort money from producer Mukesh Duggal, the filmmaker had apparently agreed to pay the requisite amount. But Salem did not relay this to Chhota Shakeel, either purposely or not. Duggal was killed in the Seven Bungalows area of Mumbai on 7 March 1998.

Back in Akola Jail, Swati Sathe had put Salem under a strict vigil. To tighten the screws further, a mobile phone was placed inside the jail by the police authorities themselves and was shown to be recovered from Salem's barracks. As Salem was being dragged to face the wrath of Swati Sathe, Tarique insisted he would accompany the don. Swati was taken aback to see Tarique tagging along with Salem.

'Why are you here?' Swati asked Tarique.

'What has he done, Madam?' Tarique asked, pointing a finger at Salem.

'He smuggled a mobile inside the jail,' Swati said.

'Impossible,' Tarique said. 'He is a big *fattu*, Madam. *Yeh* barracks *se bahar nikalne darta hai. Mobile kaise andar layega?!* (He is such a coward that he can never smuggle a phone inside the jail).'

Legal processes continued in the cases in which Tarique was named as an accused. The major one was the Sara Sahara case. A slum-dweller had told the police that they were being forcibly evicted from the land that belonged to the Central Public Works Department. The D-Company had plans to build two shopping malls on that land by the name of Sara Sahara Complex. Tarique was convicted in that case, but he filed an appeal in the high court against the verdict. In 2007, he was released on bail.

In April 2018, a local informer in Mumbai advised Tarique Parveen that Pradeep Sharma, an encounter specialist cop, was planning to arrest him. Nearly two decades ago, Tarique's name had figured in the murder of a cable operator in Mumbra. The informer told Tarique that he should clear the air with Sharma immediately, and that he (the informer) was happy to mediate. Tarique replied that, if summoned, he would go to Pradeep Sharma and that he did not need petty intermediaries.

On 26 April 2018, Sharma's men picked up Tarique from the gates of Ashoka Shopping Centre, near GT Hospital in south Mumbai. Tarique was put into the lock-up. At 3 a.m., he ate a light meal and went to sleep. The next day, Pradeep Sharma arrived at the police station at around 11 a.m. Tarique thought Pradeep Sharma would humiliate and torture him, but his fears proved unfounded when Sharma asked him to sit on a chair.

'Sir,' Tarique said, 'do you want money for releasing me?'

'No.'

'Have you arrested me on a personal grudge?'

'No.'

'Then why am I here?'

'I had a misunderstanding about you,' Sharma said. 'It has been cleared.'

Sharma called Tarique's relatives inside his cabin and ordered tea for them. He told them that they would be able to secure his bail from the Mumbra Court. Tarique could never figure out why Sharma had arrested him. His hunch was that the department wanted some dirt against an officer who was tipped to be the next commissioner of police of Mumbai. Some officers also raised questions over the manner of Tarique's arrest as he was not an accused who was on the run. Rather, he had been deported in 2004 from Dubai and all law enforcement agencies, including the Mumbai Police, were aware of this fact. They also knew his location and he wasn't hiding anywhere. Satisfied that his suspect was up to no mischief, Pradeep Sharma let Tarique go.

But controversy continued to follow Tarique. In February 2020, he was arrested by the Anti-Extortion Cell of the Mumbai Police after they had detained gangster Ejaz Ladkawala, who claimed that Tarique was helping him extort money from his targets. It only goes to show that once a man enters the underworld, it becomes extremely difficult for him to move away from such a life. Tarique had been thrown in at the deep end due to his brother's killing, and continues to swim in these troubled waters.

43

Legal Eagle

Back in Delhi, I was waiting at a junction near Lajpat Nagar. Located in the south-east of the capital, the neighbourhood was named after freedom fighter Lala Lajpat Rai. Today, the area is a vibrant neighbourhood with shopping malls, boutiques and hotels. I was waiting for my friend Neeraj Kumar to arrive.

A car stopped at the junction and the window rolled down. Neeraj Kumar waved me over from the back seat. I squeezed through the accumulating traffic and slipped inside the car. The air conditioning inside was a respite from the Delhi heat. Our driver steered the vehicle towards the CGO complex where the CBI headquarters are located. Kumar was due to meet a former colleague from his agency. I asked him about Manish Lala, the man who was known to be the 'law minister' of Dawood Ibrahim. Kumar remembered the man distinctly for a specific reason.

'Not many come to the law and ask to be put into CBI's custody,' Neeraj Kumar elaborated. 'Our *khatirdari* (treatment of guests) is quite unconventional.'

Kumar was right. After being accused in the infamous shoot-out at JJ Hospital in Mumbai in 1992, Manish Lala surrendered before the court. Then he sought to be put into CBI custody, during which Neeraj Kumar had interrogated him. Lala was a street-smart man. But once he got sucked into the vortex of the underworld, there was no turning back.

'His descent into crime started on an ordinary afternoon in 1981,' Neeraj Kumar said.

A few gruff-looking men entered an office located at 75, Poddar Chambers. The building was located in Fort, Mumbai and Manish Lala was the proprietor of the legal 'consultancy' business he was running from that premises. Lala was successful even though he was not a qualified lawyer. He had, however, cut his teeth with some of the most brilliant lawyers in the country. He had also worked with exporters and architects, and had provided them legal opinions.

But the men who had entered the office were not looking for any legal advice. In fact, these men had scant respect for the law. Their leader stepped forward, thumped his hand on the table and stared into Lala's eyes. Instantly, Lala recognized that the man was from the underworld.

'Where is that chutiya?' the leader said.

'Who?' Lala asked. 'Who are you talking about?'

'Sageer Ahmed.'

In 1981, Manish Lala had given a part of his office to a subtenant named Sageer Ahmed. Sageer ran a travel agency from the same space but was not in the office at that time. Lala conveyed this to the men who were now running out of patience.

'Leave your number,' Lala said. 'I will ask him to call you.'

The leader pulled out a country-made revolver from the small of his back. He asked Lala about his relationship with Sageer and Lala duly explained that Sageer was his subtenant. But the men were not convinced and asked Lala to come along with them. Lala was flustered on seeing the weapon.

'Where are you taking me?' he asked.

'Shut up,' the leader said, 'and start moving your legs.'

Lala tried to keep his calm and not piss off the men any more than they already were. He followed them to their car, which then started moving towards Musafirkhana, Pakmodia Street. Lala knew that Sageer was in deep trouble because Musafirkhana was the headquarters of Dawood Ibrahim and the D-Company.

The area had seen the rise of the don from being just another teenage boy roaming aimlessly on its streets to becoming the head of a gang that wiped out the presence of the dreaded Pathan gang from the area.

As late as 2017, three properties that stood on Pakmodia street, which were included among the host of properties that Dawood owned in the city, were declared illegal and put out for auction. Damarwala building was located at the corner of Pakmodia and Yakub streets. The two-storey building that Dawood was said to have bought in his wife's name was called Shabnam Guest House. The property that the don had bought in his early years, which was also perhaps the most famous among the three auctioned buildings, was Hotel Ronak Afroz, now famously known as Delhi Zaika.

After the former journalist S. Balakrishnan bid for but failed to raise Rs 4.28 crore to buy the hotel, it was auctioned a second time after lowering both the earnest price (Rs 6.28 lakh) and reserve price (Rs 1.18 crore) of the property. The low reserve price in each instance of the auction of the three properties was attributed to the prevailing fear that the mafia boss kept a vigilant eye on all his properties even while sitting in Dubai and there was a threat to the life of the person who bought them in auction. According to his own admission, journalist Balakrishnan had come forward to place a bid on the hotel to prove a point that there was no need to fear a criminal and a fugitive, and that the buying of the property would not bring anyone harm.

But Manish Lala lived during the time when Dawood's power was about to reach its zenith, through the early 1980s to the mid-1990s. The dread that Lala felt after finding himself being brought to the notorious Pakmodia Street was real and unnerving. Earlier, he had been scared for Sageer but now he even began fearing for his own life. The men took him inside the building and dragged him to a cabin. Inside, Anees Ibrahim was rocking back and forth on a chair behind a wooden table. Manish Lala almost froze to death at the sight.

Anees glanced at Manish Lala and then turned to his men. '*Kisko uthane bola tha? Aur yeh kisko utha ke laaya?* (Whom did I order you guys to bring here? And whom have you brought?)'

The three men tried to explain to Anees that since Sageer was not there at the office, they did the next logical thing by picking up the man in whose office their quarry was operating. Anees was not too happy about the fact that his boys had missed their target. They should have made sure Sageer was in the office before storming inside. He began abusing them for not being able to do a simple job without screwing up. Manish Lala sensed an opportunity and gathered all his confidence.

'Bhai,' Lala said, 'what is the matter about? Perhaps I can help.'

Anees looked at Manish Lala more closely now. He weighed him in his mind. Then he proceeded to tell Lala that Sageer Ahmed had made some dubious transactions with a certain client. The client knew Anees and had approached the D-Company to 'settle' the matter. Anees being Anees Ibrahim Kaskar jumped at the opportunity to make a quick buck.

Lala heard the details. He had the gift of the gab and managed to convince Anees that he would ensure that the matter would be resolved to the don's satisfaction. Anees was assured by Lala's persuasive manner of speaking. He let go of Lala but not before sending a chilling warning down his spine. 'If you don't keep your word,' Anees told Lala, 'you will be as guilty as Sageer and meet the same fate as him.'

But Manish Lala was a sharp man. He convinced Sageer to talk with Anees over the phone and resolved the matter in a way that Anees had no reason to be angry with Sageer any more. In fact, Anees was so impressed with Lala that he began keeping in touch with him regularly. Lala would attend parties and weddings whenever Anees would invite him. Soon he became a trusted man of not just Anees, but also Dawood.

Born on 23 May 1952, Manish Lala studied in some of the best schools in the city, including a very esteemed public school located in Andheri (West). His father, Ganga Ram Lala, worked for the Maharaja of Narsinghgarh and Santrampur. When he was four years old, Lala was adopted by the childless family of one of his father's friends. The man who adopted Manish Lala was also a senior advocate. Thus, Manish developed an early affinity for the law. From his natural family, Manish had one brother and sister but he had been separated from them due to the adoption.

Between 1973 and 1978, Manish Lala worked with Barrister Manchent and B.K. Gupta. This led him to develop a deep interest in the law, which rendered him indispensable for the D-Company. Not only Anees but even Dawood took a liking to Lala, who could talk his way out of most situations. Lala would often provide the D-Company with legal advice and settle their matters with cops. Law was his subject of expertise, but he was not even a qualified lawyer. Yet, his knowledge of the various sections of the Indian Penal Code and his ability to make a point was second to none.

A formidable challenge awaited Lala. In the same year (1981) during which Lala met the Kaskar brothers, another event changed the course of the city. An erstwhile rich but quiet town turned into a battlefield between Dawood Ibrahim's D-Company and the Pathan gang, which was run by Karim Lala and his family. This event was the brazen murder of Sabir Kaskar, the eldest child of the Kaskar clan, who was not only Dawood's closest sibling but also his confidant. The result was a massive earthquake, and Manish Lala had no idea that its tremors were going to shake the foundations of his life.

44

Law Minister

In 1983, Manish Lala walked into Anees Ibrahim's office at Musafirkhana. It was the same office he had been brought to after being forcibly picked up by Anees's men in 1981. But now, times had changed, and Lala had been accorded due respect and protocol. His association with the D-Company had gone from strength to strength in the past two years.

That evening, Anees was in a very pensive mood. Dawood was on the run from the Mumbai Police after being named as a conspirator in one of the most audacious shoot-outs in the criminal history of the city. Anees was fighting tooth and nail to secure anticipatory bail for his brother. But he seemed to have hit a roadblock and had thus called Lala to figure out a solution. Anees had approached many police officers, lawyers, politicians and resourceful people. But none of them wanted to touch this case. Anees was tired of hearing non-committal responses from his contacts. Still, he explained the situation to Lala.

Lala listened to the entire case patiently. Then he nodded. '*Ho jayega*, bhai.'

Anees knew that the job was easier said than done. Still, he had a glimmer of hope in despondent times. But what was the case in which Dawood was seeking bail? The path to that answer passed through a rather fateful night that had threatened the existence of the entire Kaskar clan.

On 12 February 1981, Sabir Ibrahim Kaskar, the eldest of the Kaskar brothers, was driving around the city in his white Fiat. According to some sources, the last four digits of his number plate were 3266. Seated beside him was Chitra, his lady-love, who was a dancer at a brothel named Congress House. Though Sabir was married for about two years and his wife was pregnant at that time, it did not stop him from courting other women. His wife's name was Shahnaaz and she was quite a good-looking woman. Yet, Sabir's lust for adventure had driven him into the arms of Chitra.

Noticing that the car was running low on fuel, Sabir turned into the Servo Care petrol pump near Prabhadevi. He had barely stepped out of the car when an Ambassador pulled up behind him.

The Ambassador was covered in flowers, making it appear that it had been decked up to ferry a bride or groom for their marriage. Sabir then realized that the car had been tailing him for a while. But his defences had been lowered on account of the woman who was seated beside him. Sabir and Chitra were having a passionate affair at that time, and Sabir could think of little else when Chitra was close to his arm.

Seven men stepped out of the Ambassador. Prominent among them were Alamzeb and Amirzada from the Pathan gang, of which Karim Lala was the patriarch. They were accompanied by the hot-headed Manya Surve. The Pathans had been at constant loggerheads with the D-Company for control of the city. Things had come to a point where Jenabai Daruwali and Haji Mastan had negotiated a truce between the two gangs in July 1980.

Known to run rationing and bootlegging operations, Jenabai had good relationships with cops and gangsters. In many ways, she would act as a bridge between them. When the war between the Kaskars and the Pathans was peaking, Jenabai heralded a meeting between various factions. Haji Mastan used to address Jenabai as Jena Bahen (sister), whereas Dawood used to call her *maasi* (maternal aunt).

The truce conducted by Jenabai was held at Haji Mastan's bungalow. Alamzeb and Amirzada were present as representatives of the Pathan gang, whereas Sabir, Dawood and Anees had attended from the D-Company's side. At that time, Sabir was the leader of the D-Company and Dawood was under the heavy influence of his brother, whom he idolized.

Alamzeb and Amirzada had no intention of keeping the peace. They wanted to destroy the D-Company; and believed that finishing Sabir would be the final nail in its coffin.

Manya Surve, who was looking to make his mark in the underworld, came up with a rather ingenious plan to trap Sabir. He was an independent operator who had studied at Kirti College in Dadar (West) before he adopted a life of crime. Manya was fond of reading novels written by British author James Hadley Chase and often planned robberies and murders based on the plots of such crime novels. He offered his services to the Pathan gang who were looking to take Sabir down.

It was common knowledge that Sabir was deeply involved with Chitra. She was also close friends with another dancer named Nanda. Based on Manya's plan, Amirzada befriended Nanda and started keeping tabs on Sabir through her association with Chitra. This is how the Pathans had managed to trap Sabir on that fateful night in Prabhadevi. They were well prepared and well armed.

At the petrol pump, Sabir was hopelessly outnumbered. The Pathans made Chitra step out of the car and move away. There was a telephone booth near the petrol pump in which Chitra sought refuge. And then she shrieked in horror when the Pathans and Manya emptied their guns on Sabir. They also slit his wrists, which was the signature of the Mumbai mafia at that time. A lifeless Sabir collapsed while his brothers and associates—including Dawood—were waiting for him to return to Musafirkhana.

The killers then raced towards Pakmodia Street with the intention of finishing off the remaining Kaskar brothers. But as soon as the car made its way towards Musafirkhana, they ran into a roadblock in the form of Khalid Pehelwan.

Khalid, an erstwhile wrestler from Madhya Pradesh, was one of Dawood's closest associates and also his mentor. The burly pehelwan ordered the wrought iron gate of Musafirkhana to be shut and took an offensive position on the first floor of the building. He opened fire on the approaching enemy. The hail of bullets shocked the Pathans and Manya Surve. They beat a hasty retreat.

When Dawood learnt of Sabir's death, he was inconsolable and furious. But if the Pathans thought that Sabir's killing would finish the D-Company, they were badly mistaken. This killing made Dawood go on such a revenge-seeking spree that it changed the entire character of the city for nearly two and a half decades. Dawood swore to take no prisoners. The D-Company was not finished. It was only getting started.

The first to pay the price for Sabir's murder was Manya Surve. His dossier of crime was gaining weight by the day. To instil a sense of fear among criminals, the then commissioner of police, Julio Ribeiro, decided to make an example out of Manya late in 1981. It was ironic that a woman had played a part in Sabir's downfall and another woman played a role in Manya's downfall. Sub-inspector Isaque Bagwan and Raja Tambat were assigned the task of eliminating Manya. The cops are said to have pressured a woman whom Manya was dating at that time to call him to Ambedkar College in Wadala. On 11 January 1982, Manya arrived at around 10.45 a.m. to meet the woman at the specified location.

Bagwan and Tambat had already set a trap around the premises. They confronted Manya with their guns drawn. Manya pulled out his Mauser pistol and fired at the cops. In return, both Bagwan and Tambat pumped three bullets each into Manya's muscular body. The official version is that the cops tried taking him to Sion Hospital but he was declared dead before admission.

Amirzada was next on the D-Company's hitlist. By then, he had also executed the daylight kidnapping of film producer Mushir Ahmed from a busy junction near Worli

Sea Face for ransom and extortion. This was a shocking event and none other than superstar Dilip Kumar walked into the office of Ribeiro to seek justice for Ahmed. Ribeiro assigned the case to Inspector Zende and Isaque Bagwan. The cops finally traced Amirzada to Gujarat and arrested him.

If Amirzada thought he was safe in police custody, he was badly mistaken. Dawood assigned the task of eliminating Amirzada to Rajan Nair aka Bada Rajan. Nair had his base in central Mumbai and used to steal branded typewriters and sell them in the black market during his early days. In fact, Chhota Rajan, who went on to become Dawood's most trusted man first and his arch-enemy later, used to work for Bada Rajan.

Bada Rajan was looking to get into the good books of Dawood and hired a shooter named David Pardesi, who shot Amirzada dead on 6 September 1983 at the City Civil and Sessions Court. This courtroom shoot-out remains a testimony to the ferocity of the Mumbai mafia and their utter disregard for the law.

But Pardesi could not escape from the court as he was arrested by Isaque Bagwan. Goaded by Bagwan, Pardesi decided to turn approver in the case and named Bada Rajan and Dawood Ibrahim as the key conspirators. Seven months after Sabir was killed, Dawood had exacted his revenge.

Dawood absconded to evade police action. So Anees approached Manish Lala to help secure anticipatory bail for Dawood. The legal frontman immediately began tapping into his network. Lala engaged a senior counsel named Samant from Mumbai who filed an application of anticipatory bail for Dawood in this case.

Not just the Mumbai Police, but even the Mumbai mafia was shocked when the anticipatory bail was granted by the court! Anees was surprised that Lala was able to execute a task that no one else wanted to take ownership of. In fact, Dawood was so pleased with Lala that he called a special meeting of the D-Company and crowned Manish Lala as his law minister. From that day onwards, Lala began handling all legal matters of the D-Company.

45

Calling D

June 1994: DIG Neeraj Kumar and Manish Lala were seated inside the former's cabin at the CBI headquarters in Delhi. On Kumar's approval, Manish Lala picked up the telephone on the desk, which was connected by a secure and encrypted line. Lala dialled a number after turning on the speaker.

The phone was answered by Sunil Sawant aka Sautya, who had played a key role in the shoot-out at JJ Hospital. After speaking with Lala, Sautya passed the line to Iqbal Kaskar, who then brought another person on the conference call. This man, with a cold and confident voice, was none other than the man whom the Indian authorities had been chasing at all costs. This man was Dawood Ibrahim Kaskar.

Neeraj Kumar held three parleys with Dawood on 10 June, 20 June and 22 June 1994. Manish Lala was the go-between. On the first call, Lala explained to Dawood about the circumstances under which he found himself in CBI's custody. He assured Dawood Ibrahim of fair treatment from the CBI if he returned to the country. The conversations between Neeraj Kumar and Dawood Ibrahim played out like a game of chess. Kumar's opening move was in line with his departmental approach.

'Manish said you wanted to tell me something,' he said. 'Go ahead.'

'Do you feel I had a role to play in the bomb blasts?'

Dawood had countered Kumar's opening salvo with a question of his own. On 12 March 1993, a series of twelve bomb blasts shook Mumbai—then known as Bombay—killing 257 people and injuring over 1400 civilians. Initial investigations by the Mumbai Police revealed that the bombings were repercussions of the riots that shook the city in December 1992 and January 1993 following the demolition of the Babri Masjid in Ayodhya.

Fugitive gangster Dawood Ibrahim was named as the mastermind behind the attack. He had been on the run from law enforcement agencies since 1986 after facing a battery of charges for assault, extortion and murder.

Six months after the bomb blasts, the Mumbai Police claimed to have cracked the case. But reports of excesses continued to mar the investigation. The state police were accused of targeting and harassing many individuals, mostly from the minority community, who were not even remotely connected to the blasts. Under such circumstances, the probe was handed over to the CBI on the directives of the Central government. A Special Task Force (STF) was formed by the CBI for the probe. The STF, led by DIG-ranked Neeraj Kumar, formally took charge of the case in late November, 1993.

'I have been falsely implicated in the bomb blasts,' Dawood told Kumar on the phone. 'But I am not a fool who can be used as a pawn by others.'

The don claimed that he had been approached by various people to intervene in the aftermath of the riots in which the minority community had suffered the loss of life and business. If reports were to be believed, a parcel had been sent to him containing a set of bangles. It was meant to be a taunt for his inaction against the communal violence in which a particular community had faced heavy losses in economic sense and even loss of lives.

'Did you meet Tiger Memon and Dawood Phanse for planning the blasts?' asked Kumar.

'I met the two around the end of 1992,' Dawood said. 'Or early 1993.'

A namesake of the don, Dawood Phanse aka Taklya was a landing agent who would bribe customs, revenue and police officials to ensure goods smuggled by sea could be landed and transported to their destination. As a part of the larger conspiracy of the blasts, Tiger wanted Phanse to 'manage' a landing at the Shekhadi coast. But Phanse had recently begun working for another smuggling syndicate consisting of Haji Ahmed, Salim Sarang and Aslam Patni, which had caused disputes between Phanse and Tiger.

According to Dawood, Tiger brought Phanse to the White House (as the don's bungalow in Dubai was named) for a meeting. But the matter for discussion was Phanse's switching of allegiance rather than landing the RDX needed for the bombings.

'I decreed that Phanse should work for Tiger Memon and not for Haji Ahmed,' Dawood said. The reasoning behind this decision was that Phanse had worked for Tiger way before he met Haji Ahmed. Hence, Phanse's loyalties should remain with Tiger. The decision made in the don's court was deemed to be final and binding on all parties. Phanse had no option but to agree even though Haji Ahmed was paying him better than Tiger.

Phanse had also brought up the topic of a well that was to be constructed in his village during the meeting. Dawood had contributed funds in the memory of his late father as charity for this task. The work of constructing the well had been assigned to one Sayed Munim.

'But Munim has misappropriated those funds,' said Phanse.

Dawood Ibrahim reassured Phanse that he would look into the matter. Phanse was so awestruck by the presence of Dawood Ibrahim and the glitter of the White House that he agreed to do whatever the don wanted him to do. At that time, Tiger proclaimed that Phanse was very *mazhabi* (religious). 'He can do anything for the sake of religion,' Tiger had said.

The don patted Phanse on the back and encouraged him to work with zeal. But according to Dawood, Tiger had succeeded in creating an impression on Phanse that the plan to land RDX and weapons at Shekhadi had the blessings of the head honcho of the D-Company. In this manner, Tiger was able to elicit the services of Dawood Phanse for landing the RDX which was eventually used in the blasts. When the investigations began, Phanse's name cropped up immediately. The cops picked him up in no time.

After being arrested, Phanse claimed that he had to pay higher bribes to various government agencies because their officers seemed to know that the *maal* (stuff) being delivered was coming from the ISI. Yet, they allowed all this to happen.

Neeraj Kumar then probed a topic that had sent shockwaves around the Hindi film industry during those years. 'What about the weapons that were recovered from Sanjay Dutt?'

Dutt was one of the top bracket movie stars of those years. His stardom would have reached another level had he not got embroiled in this mess. It is said that Abu Salem and his men delivered an AK-56 rifle to Dutt, who claimed that he had procured the weapon to protect his family as riots were raging throughout the city.

'Anees ordered those weapons to be delivered without consulting me,' Dawood Ibrahim told Neeraj Kumar. 'I beat him up for this mistake.'

Dawood also said he was aware that his statement was implicating his own brother in the crime but that is what had happened and he was obliged to say it likewise. Perhaps it was his way of trying to convince Neeraj Kumar that there was truth in his other statements as well.

'What about the boats that carried the explosives from Dubai to India?' Kumar asked.

'Check the movements of the boats belonging to Mustafa Dossa and Mohammad Dossa,' Dawood said. His statement acknowledged the involvement of the Dossa brothers in the blasts. The don also said that if he were to plan an attack like the bomb blasts, he would plan it in a more sophisticated manner and would not leave any evidence behind. 'Also, if I was involved in the blasts,' the don proceeded to raise a counter question, 'would I have not moved my entire family out of India just like Tiger had done?' He paused. 'My mother, sister and other family members, many of them, are still in *Bambai*.'

Tiger Memon had moved his entire family to Dubai only days before the blasts. When the cops began investigating the bombings, they found an abandoned Maruti van that was used to transport explosives around the city. Javed Chikna—a close associate of Tiger—and a few other men had used this van. On the day of the blasts, they were on their way to attack the Municipal Corporation building when a small explosion occurred in the van. In utter panic, Chikna and his men abandoned the vehicle near Worli.

Later, the cops found seven AK-56 rifles and four hand grenades in the Maruti. The Regional Transport Office confirmed that the vehicle was registered in the name of Rubina Memon, who was Tiger's sister-in-law and the wife of his brother Suleman. It was the first breakthrough in the investigation, which led the cops to the Al-Hussaini building at Dargah Road, Mahim, where the Memons lived. But by the time the cops barged through the door of the house, the entire Memon family had moved to Dubai.

Several members of the Memon family would return to the country to face the law. Rubina Memon is still serving a life sentence in this case. Tiger's brother, Yakub Memon, was sentenced to death. The death warrant was executed on 30 July 2015.

Dawood's family, on the other hand, had stayed put in the city. He used this fact as a supposed pointer to his innocence. When Manish Lala later mediated on the call, he urged Dawood to surrender by attributing Kumar as an even-handed and unbiased cop. He likened Kumar's impartiality and sense of fairness to Dawood himself.

During the conversation, Dawood said he would consider surrendering to Kumar. Then he elaborated on the terms and conditions of the surrender. Firstly, he wanted to be tried only in the Bombay bomb blasts case and asked for other cases against him to be dropped. He also listed that he should not be bundled with other prisoners in a cell and no physical torture in custody should be inflicted upon him. He said that he had tried contacting the police commissioner of Bombay after the blasts to explain his position. 'But the commissioner did not answer my calls,' he said.

Kumar told Dawood that he would convey the don's demands to his bosses in the department. Kumar's superiors clearly stated that Dawood should surrender unconditionally. There was no other way.

Additionally, one of Kumar's bosses felt that he should discontinue these conversations as Kumar was stepping into the turf of other agencies. Accordingly, Kumar had to stop his telephonic meetings with Dawood, which were mediated by none other than Manish Lala. And with that, any chances of the fugitive gangster returning to the country faded away forever. However, Manish Lala was soon going to pay an expensive price for his association with Dawood Ibrahim.

The vehicle in which I was seated was about to reach its intended destination. But after hearing Neeraj Kumar's tale, I was intrigued by the life and times of Manish Lala. Here was a boy who had studied at a prestigious public school, worked for the underworld and met a violent end. I wanted to know more about him.

'You should talk to his wife,' Neeraj Kumar said. 'She still lives in Mumbai.'

That sounded like an interesting proposition. After noting down Shaheda's address, I bid goodbye to Neeraj Kumar, until we would meet again and unearth more stories together.

46

Casualties of War

I faced trouble finding the building in Powai. I typed out the name of the tower that Neeraj Kumar had given to me into Google Maps and followed the trail. This complex, where Manish Lala's wife lived, was built along with many others during the construction boom of the late 1980s and early 1990s. The development eventually transformed the landscape of Powai and pushed the value of its real estate through the roof.

The house I was looking for, once owned by Manish Lala, was located on the first floor. I took the stairs instead of the elevator. The woman who answered the doorbell was in her sixties. Her name was Shaheda.

'Please come in,' she said.

Inside, the house was well maintained. At the time of Manish Lala's death, Shaheda was his life partner. Shaheda pulled out some photographs and documents for this conversation. I understand that it takes a lot of strength to talk about the past, especially if it is riddled with bullets. Shaheda is a casualty of a war she never wanted. But knowingly or unknowingly, she ended up getting caught in the frenzy. Widowed at forty in 1998, she remembers Manish as a man who was always smiling. 'He even used to exchange cooking recipes with me,' she said.

I could not imagine Dawood's law minister as a man who'd have an interest in cooking. But I made no mention of this to her. Instead, I asked her how she met Manish Lala, and she just smiled.

Outside the streamlined offices at Flora Fountain, Manish Lala was waiting near an advertising agency. Along with his 'legal' consultancy business, Manish also used to run a pest control company called Pest Proof from a nearby building. It was evening and people were stepping out of their workplaces after a tiring day. Manish glanced at his wristwatch. He was waiting for Shaheda, a family friend, who used to work at the advertising agency. Soon, he spotted her in the crowd and casually walked up to her.

'Going home?' he asked.

Shaheda laughed. 'Where else will I go at this hour, Manish?'

Manish had been pursuing Shaheda for a while now. Each day, he would come to the advertising agency where she worked as a telephone operator and wait for her outside. He would then make it appear as if he'd bumped into her coincidentally. Manish was good friends with Shaheda's sister. So Shaheda was already aware that he was living separately from his wife and two children. Shaheda was also married but her personal life was in great turmoil as she was also separated from her husband.

'I have some work at Vakola,' Manish said. 'Can I drop you there?'

Shaheda was staying with her sister at Vakola. She knew that Manish had no work over there, that his words were only a ruse to spend time with her. For the same reason, she had been avoiding him for weeks. But his perseverance, without any kind of aggression, had finally paid off and made an impression on her. That day, she finally agreed and got into his car.

On the drive back home, Manish Lala turned on the stereo and began playing romantic songs. Shaheda was surprised to find that their taste in music was similar. When they reached Vakola, Manish asked for her phone number. Shaheda thought about it for a while. Her marriage was on the rocks. She was feeling the need for companionship more than anything else. So she dictated her office number, which he wrote on a piece of paper and carefully placed it in his shirt pocket. For Shaheda, it was the beginning of something special.

Manish later began visiting Shaheda's sister more often on one pretext or another. His real motive, however, was to get closer to Shaheda. He would call Shaheda on her office number and play romantic songs in the background. He also purchased a new Kenwood stereo system for his car just because Shaheda liked listening to music. Shaheda also began enjoying this attention.

Notwithstanding Shaheda's tragic personal life, her family was very fun-loving. They loved partying and eating out. But due to her prevailing personal circumstances, Shaheda had retreated into a shell. The separation with her husband was taking a toll on her. She would get attention from many other men but never reciprocated. She wasn't interested in beginning a new relationship until Manish entered her life. When he saw that she was still undecided about him, Manish began taking her entire family out to the best eateries in town, including the famous Delhi Darbar at Colaba, Mumbai. Still, Shaheda refused to reciprocate his feelings.

Once, Manish had taken Shaheda's family for dinner to a famous hotel at Kemps Corner. As they stepped outside, Manish asked Shaheda if she had made up her mind about him.

'We can *only* be friends,' Shaheda made her position clear. 'Nothing more.'

Manish laughed it off. 'Everybody will grow fat from all this eating out,' he said. 'But you will never get convinced about me.'

Shaheda was a good dancer. Whenever they had a party at home, she would jive and Manish was fascinated with her moves, the chasse to the left and the chasse to the right. He would watch like a man totally fascinated by her. Even after Shaheda's initial refusal to reciprocate his feelings, Manish treated her with the same care and respect that he accorded to her always.

At an appropriate time, Manish proposed to Shaheda again. She gave it some serious thought. She had no idea about how deeply Manish was involved with the underworld. To her, he was an affable and charming man. Finally, she relented and became his partner for life. But Shaheda had no idea that the worst was yet to come.

When Manish got associated with Shaheda, his relationship with his children from his previous marriage also improved. Manish and Shaheda used to visit Chowpatty in their car and buy eatables like jalebi, fafda and dhokla from a famous eatery. Then they would visit Manish's children and spend some time with them. So far, so good.

Shaheda's alarm bells began ringing when she noticed that Manish would never introduce her to his work associates. He would take her along to his meetings at plush hotels but Shaheda would be seated at a separate table while Manish conducted his *business* talks at a different table. Shaheda didn't like it one bit. She felt that Manish was not giving her the respect she deserved and that he did not see her as a woman who was worthy enough to be introduced to her life partner's friends. But at that time, she did not know that Manish was trying to protect her.

In July 1992, Ismail Parkar—who was married to Dawood's sister Haseena Parkar—was murdered in their stronghold of Nagpada. Shailesh Haldankar, a shooter of the Arun Gawli gang, was identified as the key person in this attack. This attack was a retaliation by the Gawli gang as Dawood's men had killed Kishore Gawli aka Papa Gawli, brother of Arun, on 22 July 1990 near the Sitladevi temple at Mahim.

Only a month after Ismail's killing, Haldankar shot dead another businessman at Nagpada. But he was caught in the melee and thrashed black and blue by the locals. Haldankar was moved to JJ Hospital in Mumbai for treatment.

For Dawood, the death of his brother-in-law brought back memories of the time when his brother (Sabir) was killed. Revenge had to be extracted at all costs. Dawood knew that it would be nearly impossible to kill Haldankar if he was moved to jail. He decided to turn the hospital into Haldankar's graveyard. A team of nearly two dozen shooters, some of them armed with AK-47s, descended on JJ Hospital on 12 September 1992. It was an audacious attack launched at 3.40 a.m. Nearly 500 rounds were fired. The whiplash of the machine guns shook the entire city. Key shooters who led this assault for the D-Company were Sunil Sawant aka Sautya, Subash Singh Thakur and Shyam Garikapatti.

Haldankar was killed but the volley of bullets also took the lives of two constables from the Mumbai Police who were deployed as security cover at the hospital. The government had to act strongly.

Manish Lala, on account of his association with the D-Company, was also made an accused in the JJ shoot-out case. The charge against him was that he had provided shelter to Sunil Sawant aka Sautya and Subash Singh Thakur while they were on the run from the police. His dealings with the D-Company came under the scanner. He was now a wanted man.

Soon after, the Mumbai riots started in December 1992 and the bomb blasts took place in March 1993. The government went hard after Dawood Ibrahim's associates. Manish Lala was now on the run and looking for a way out of this situation.

In August 1993, Manish was in Delhi and Shaheda was alone at home. Two cops—she remembers their names distinctly—from the Mumbai Police knocked on the door. Shaheda told them that Manish was out of town. Still, they barged into the house and ransacked everything. They checked the whole house. His cupboard. His room. His camera. Everything. Then they took Shaheda to Ghatkopar Police Station where they interrogated her for nearly twelve days. But Shaheda did not have much clue about Manish's dealings. It was then she realized why Manish would not introduce her to his associates.

Shaheda was tortured while she was in custody. Due to Manish's influence in legal circles, one of the city's top criminal lawyers visited her and started legal proceedings to secure her release. Shaheda was finally able to return home on 14 August 1993.

Manish Lala surrendered before the Mumbai court on 7 January 1994. As the CBI had also got involved with investigation of the bomb blasts, Neeraj Kumar arrived in Mumbai and interrogated Manish Lala at Arthur Road Jail. There, Manish asked Neeraj Kumar to move him into CBI's remand. Kumar was surprised at this move by Lala. But Kumar was looking for more information on Dawood and agreed to the proposal. When the CBI applied for Manish's custody, there was no opposition from Manish's side.

Manish was then moved to Delhi and he put Neeraj Kumar in contact with Dawood Ibrahim, who was trying to negotiate a conditional surrender with the Government of India. The surrender never happened. While Manish was in jail, he would still write letters to Shaheda and become angry if she didn't respond to them.

'But his anger would vanish as instantly as it would appear,' Shaheda said.

Manish was able to secure bail and come out of prison. He suffered a personal tragedy when his son met with a fatal accident in 1995. There was further trouble when underworld don Chhota Rajan, who had parted ways with Dawood Ibrahim over the bomb blasts, began targeting Dawood's associates—especially those who were named in the bomb blasts case.

On 4 June 1998, Manish was cornered by three shooters of the Chhota Rajan gang and shot dead at his second-floor office at the Old Oriental building. One of the men whose name cropped up during the investigation of the murder was none other than Lakhan bhaiya, a Rajan loyalist who was known to be a mentor to gangsters like D.K. Rao.

The news of Manish's death shattered Shaheda to pieces and she cried for days on end. He had willed his home and car to her. His remaining assets were to be given to his children.

In a strange twist of fate, in November 2006, the Mumbai Police shot dead Lakhan bhaiya near the Nana Nani Park in Versova. The encounter of Lakhan bhaiya also caused quite a scandal. Cops were accused of staging the encounter and killing Lakhan in cold blood. The matter got so heated that even encounter specialist Pradeep Sharma had to spend considerable time behind bars before he would finally be acquitted in the case.

As for Shaheda, Manish's death broke the strands that had tied her to his children. They are no longer in touch. In the wars of the underworld, Shaheda has managed to preserve her life and sanity. She is soon moving to a new place where perhaps the past can be buried for good, if not erased forever.

47

Dangerous Debts

Firoz, one of my go-to persons for information on the underworld, was waiting for me at Pydhonie in Mumbai. He grew up in the same area as Dawood Ibrahim and has seen the don at close quarters when Dawood was just a new jack on the block, trying to make his mark in the world of crime. Firoz has narrated many stories about Dawood Ibrahim and even those who preceded him. It was in the context of gaining more such information that I met him near Pydhonie.

The name of the place, etymologically, means 'foot wash' and derives from a small creek where the locals would once wash their feet before the land was reclaimed from the sea. Once upon a time, Pydhonie also housed the office of Yusuf Patel, who was one of the earliest kingpins of the smuggling business in Mumbai. Abdul Majid Abdul Patel aka Yusuf Patel was a shrewd smuggler who was involved with Haji Mastan, the most famous gold smuggler in the history of the city.

'During Dawood's early days in the badlands of crime,' Firoz said, 'his gang would do many small-time jobs for Yusuf Patel.'

These jobs were as simple as evicting tenants from a plot of land, or giving someone a thrashing to make sure they complied with whatever Patel wanted them to do. But Patel failed to measure Dawood Ibrahim's ambition.

Dawood was not going to wait and watch and slowly climb up the ladder of the mafia. He was hell-bent on taking the escalator to the top. 'Many years later,' Firoz said, 'Dawood would teach Yusuf Patel a lesson he would never forget.'

'How did that happen?' I asked.

Firoz explained that Dawood had once proclaimed that *'tera sabse bada dushman woh, jis pe tera paisa banta hai'*. The inference was that the one who had loaned money to another, and the one who had borrowed from him, could go on to become sworn enemies of each other. Yusuf Patel had a long list of repayments that he should have cleared. Alas, that was not to be. And it led to a dramatic consequence.

In the early 1980s, Yusuf Patel was sitting inside his office at Pydhonie. One of Patel's boys came inside and told him that a businessman to whom Patel owed money was waiting outside to meet him.

Patel waved his hand dismissively. 'Tell him to come next week.'

But the lender would have none of it. He had made several trips to Patel's office earlier and was tired of lame excuses. He wanted his money, promptly. This got Patel thinking, and he decided to play another of his tricks.

'Ok,' he said to the assistant. 'Send him in.'

On the wall behind Patel's chair, there were photographs of him with several political leaders of the day, including an ex-chief minister of Maharashtra. In the late 1970s, Patel was trying to move away from the smuggling business. He then began moving towards the construction business, which was then booming in the city. After the national Emergency declared by Indira Gandhi in 1975 was revoked in 1977, the Janata government came to power after gaining a majority in the general elections. J.P. Narayan was the soul-keeper of the new government headed by Morarji Desai, who had become the first prime minister of the country who did not belong to the Indian National Congress party.

J.P. Narayan offered an amnesty scheme to the smugglers of the country if they 'pledged' to reform their ways. Unbelievable as it may sound now, a total of eighty smugglers, including Haji Mastan and Yusuf Patel, took such a pledge at the Jaslok Hospital auditorium in the presence of J.P. Narayan on 30 April 1977. Sukur Narain Bakhia, another big smuggler, had consulted his lawyers who advised him against the pledge.

Many smugglers faced tough times during the Emergency. Their properties were attached to the Foreign Exchange Manipulators Act, known as FEMA. Various sections of COFEPOSA, i.e. Conservation of Foreign Exchange and Prevention of Smuggling Act, were applied upon their activities. Mastan was even jailed for approximately eighteen months under the draconian Maintenance of Internal Security Act (MISA). Yusuf Patel also came under the scanner of the Income Tax department and the ED.

Patel had famously stated that the pledge he had taken before Narayan did not imply that he was a smuggler. He generalized the event and said that all citizens of the country should take this pledge to not indulge in smuggling.

He was looking for other avenues and took to construction by starting the Patel Brothers Construction Company. To construct, one needed land. And if such land was occupied by slum dwellers or owners who did not want to sell, they needed to be evicted or their hand needed to be forced into selling their properties. Patel had often employed Dawood Ibrahim and his gang to perform such activities.

Construction was also a capital-intensive business. At that time, the financial sector was also not very formal and borrowing from the market was a common practice. Not that it would have made a difference to Patel anyway because the crux of their business was unaccounted black money. The lender who had shown up at Patel's office had loaned him a huge amount for building a residential complex. But the project, and Yusuf Patel in general, had begun falling into financial doldrums. He was stalling the repayment, citing losses and various other pretexts.

'Yusuf bhai,' the lender said. 'My patience is drying up. You promised to return the money three months ago.'

Patel tried to pacify the lender with his smooth talk. But when he saw that the lender was not ready to yield, Patel played an old trick from his book. He signalled to his aide, who promptly rushed out of the office and went to a nearby phone booth. From there, the aide dialled the office number. Patel picked up the receiver and put on an act while speaking in his Gujarati accent.

'*Haa Indira ben*,' he said aloud. 'How are things in Delhi?' Then he put his hand on the mouthpiece and whispered to the lender, '*Indira bai nu phone che.*'

Yusuf Patel was making it appear that he was a close associate of the then prime minister, Indira Gandhi, who had come back to power at the start of 1980. It was true that Patel had a lot of political influence, but he definitely did not have a direct line to the prime minister. But such was his confidence and his manner of speaking, that even a sceptical man would think there was truth in Patel's talks.

So now, the lender began to believe that rubbing Patel too strongly would only lead to more trouble as Patel had big political contacts. He left without collecting his money and with the promise of another date that Patel gave him. It was a promise that Patel had no intention of keeping.

This was not the first time Patel had failed to keep his word. Around 1968, Haji Mastan and Yusuf Patel had conducted a lot of business with each other. Haji Mastan was known as the Gold King, who had established a hegemony in the smuggling business. While gold remained the item of choice for his smuggling operations, he did not shy away from smuggling silver as well.

In a deal set with some associates from Dubai, Mastan had to send a consignment of silver to Dubai from where it was supposed to be sent to another country. Mastan asked Yusuf Patel to send this consignment on his behalf. Mastan did not consider smuggling a crime but as *tijarat*, which meant 'business' in Arabic. And trust was a basic pillar of this tijarat.

Mastan attached great value to keeping one's word. '*Hamara dhanda zabaan pe chalta hai*,' he'd often say. It meant that there was a code of honour even among thieves. Keeping one's word was an infallible dictum. But Patel did not share the same sentiment. He considered all this talk of honesty nothing but hogwash.

Apparently, he packed the consignment to be sent to Dubai with chunks of iron instead of silver. The party in Dubai was aghast at this insanity and connected with Mastan. Haji Mastan was furious. He tried to get in touch with Patel but the latter had gone underground, hoping that the matter would die its own death.

Mastan's anger was growing by the minute. He wanted to pronounce the death sentence on Patel. Mastan generally did not subscribe to violence as he was happy making money through smuggling and generally did not have an affinity towards gunshots and bloodshed.

But Patel's treachery had hurt him a great deal. His boys began tracking Patel's movements and a few shooters were sent to make an example of Patel. The shooters intercepted Patel's car on the streets of Mumbai and opened fire. A pathan bodyguard who was accompanying Patel managed to save him. But the bodyguard lost his life in the process. This event is generally viewed as the first instance when a gunshot from the gangs of Bombay had spilled on to the streets. It created quite a furore even in the mafia circles.

The Mumbai mafia then decided to resolve the matter as bloodshed was generally considered bad for business in those days. A meeting was arranged between Mastan and Patel in which peace and amity were restored. The duo began working together again.

However, Patel did not mend his ways when it came to keeping his accounts clean. It was a mistake that would eventually cost him dearly—the man who would make him pay was none other than Dawood Ibrahim Kaskar.

48

Bankrupted

In the late 1980s, Firoz explained to me, Dawood Ibrahim found a surprise visitor knocking at the door of one of his many bungalows in Dubai. It was located in Naif Road and had a swimming pool and a meeting room on the floors above. The middle-aged visitor was a godman from Mumbai, who had a huge following among the local populace. The don's family often relied heavily on seers while making decisions.

Interactions between dons and godmen, however, often produce volatile results. Dawood Ibrahim was buried neck-deep in the sands of crime. But that never stopped him from invoking religious references when speaking to his boys. When one of Dawood's long-time associates had indicated that he wanted to give up crime and turn towards the path of religion and righteousness, the don had merely laughed and retorted that 'the mercy of our creator is far greater than our sins'. For him, there was no need to give up crime. It was a classic case of a religious doctrine being deliberately misinterpreted to suit an ulterior motive.

Many of Dawood's siblings had high regard for babas or peer sahabs. Haseena Parkar was known to revere the same seer whom even Haji Mastan had held in high regard. This seer had now come to Dubai. When Dawood saw the peer, he stood up from his chair as a mark of his veneration.

'What was the need to come here, peer sahab?' Dawood said. 'I am always a phone call away for you.'

'If this were a matter of lakhs, I would have called,' the seer said. 'But this is way beyond.'

Dawood raised his brow high above his black sunglasses. Now he was interested in knowing more. The seer explained that he had visited the don on behalf of his brother-in-law, Zahir (name changed), who also ran an airline office at the World Trade Centre in the plush Cuffe Parade area of Mumbai. The core of Zahir's problem was that he had invested a huge sum in a real-estate project. The man was now in a fix because his *partner* was neither able to complete the project nor repay his money.

'So,' Dawood said as he leaned back into his chair, 'the money must be recovered from the partner.' He paused. 'And the partner's name is Yusuf Patel.'

In a role reversal of sorts, the don's clairvoyance managed to shock the seer. But there were no magical forces working for Dawood Ibrahim. He just had a very strong network on the ground. Nothing that happened on the streets of Dongri and its surrounding areas escaped the don's attention. Every day, his lieutenants would brief him about the developments taking place in the city.

Dawood had been hearing stories of how construction projects in which Yusuf Patel was involved were going bust or landing in trouble. He was also aware that Yusuf Patel had started a joint venture called Patel and Soni Arcade. Hence, Dawood was already aware of the matter.

'Indeed,' the seer said. 'The recovery needs to be made from Yusuf Patel.'

Dawood now thought about this matter. At that moment, he did not agree, nor did he refuse. He just nodded. The peer returned to Mumbai and prayed that the seed he had planted in Dubai would bear fruit.

But the seer was not the only one who had a score to settle with Yusuf Patel. Around 1987–88, Mustafa Dossa had also opened his office in Nakhuda Mohalla. Soon, there would be fights between him and Yusuf Patel on the issue of parking scooters. Dossa's shop was near one of Yusuf Patel's offices. And Dossa's boys would park their scooters outside Patel's office as the neighbourhood was very congested.

The scooters used to be loaded with smuggled silver. In those days, *chaar aana* (four quarters of a rupee) was the codename for twenty-five bricks of silver. Fifty bricks were called *aanth-aana* (half a rupee) and 100 bricks were called *ek rupya* (one rupee). Smuggled gold biscuits in the slab form were called Parle-G, while smuggled gold coins were called Marie. This is because the disc form of the coins resembled the shape of the Marie brand of biscuits, which were popular cookie snacks in those days.

Patel was scared that he would get into unnecessary problems due to Dossa's scooters being parked in front of his office. He had not forgotten the troubles he had faced during the Emergency. After all, in the post-Emergency era, had he also not pledged in front of J.P. Narayan, the patron saint of the country, that he would not indulge in smuggling again?

Patel was also trying to turn into a legit businessman through his construction business. But there was always a question mark over his dealings. He had gained expertise in acquiring illegal floor space index (FSI) by manipulating records and bribing his way through. By 1984, five cases of FSI violations were filed against him after much pressure from Arun Bhatia, who was the collector of Bombay at the time. Surprisingly (or not), Bhatia was summarily transferred from the job. Patel's political clout largely protected him.

Soon, Patel was pumping crores of rupees into redevelopment projects and making many more by exploiting the loopholes in the system. The real estate sector was not very tightly regulated at that time. It was commonplace for builders to not deliver the homes after taking money from buyers. Builders would also construct illegal buildings and sell the flats while the authorities looked the other way. All of this would cause heavy losses to buyers and genuine businessmen who became partners in the project after falling prey to false promises of these dons-turned-builders.

One of the living examples of illegal construction where Yusuf Patel was involved is the Campa Cola Complex in Worli. Located in the heart of the city, amidst prime real estate, this complex stands on land owned by the Brihanmumbai Municipal Corporation (BMC). In the 1980s, this land was leased to a company named

Pure Drinks Private Limited, which manufactured Campa Cola—a popular soft drink of the day. This company in turn sold redevelopment rights of the land to a group of three builders, one of whom was Yusuf Patel and the other was B.K. Gupta of B.Y. Builders.

In those years, it was common practice for builders to build beyond the approved height of the apartment in the hope that the construction would get 'regularized' by paying a penalty (or more) to the concerned authorities. In flagrant violation of FSI norms, between 1984 to 1989, the builders constructed thirty-five more floors in the Campa Cola complex than what was approved by the BMC. Buyers also purchased flats in this property on the promises of the promoters that the occupation certificate (OC) for the apartments would be made available by the authorities.

But to the shock of the residents, the absence of the OC and the irregularities in construction were brought to light in 1999. Civic authorities turned up to cut off the water and electricity supply while the residents protested and put up a brave face. The matter is still sub judice but it is a living testimony to the nexus between builders, politicians and the authorities.

The project of Patel and Soni Arcade, in which the seer had sought Dawood's intervention, was also mired by similar issues. Around the same time, Mustafa Dossa also landed in Dubai to build a case against Yusuf Patel.

'The *zulm* (injustice) of Yusuf Patel has breached all boundaries,' Dossa told the don.

Dawood tried conservative methods to recover the funds from Yusuf Patel at first. But whenever his boys would reach out to Patel, he would simply tell them that he had gone bankrupt. In the lingo of the underworld, declaring such bankruptcy was called '*deewaliya ka billa bandh lena*' (to wear a certificate of one's bankruptcy around one's neck).

Dawood realized that he would have to force Patel's hand. Summarily, he ordered Chhota Shakeel to prepare a list of Yusuf Patel's immovable properties and assets. Then Dawood asked Dossa if he was willing to buy Yusuf Patel's properties at a bargain. It only took a heartbeat for Dossa to agree to the proposition. Where else would he get such a deal? Finally, the don put in a call to Yusuf Patel himself.

'Yusuf bhai,' said Dawood. 'My men will deliver a ticket to Dubai to you tonight. Board the flight tomorrow. Understood?'

Yusuf Patel was hurt at Dawood's orders but his best years were past him. Much water had passed under the bridge since Dawood was a young lad who had worked odd jobs for Patel. Now Dawood was bigger than all the dons of Mumbai put together. Haji Mastan had faded away. The Pathans had been nearly finished off. There was no one in the city, or in the country, who could stand up to Dawood Ibrahim. Patel had no option but to obey the don's decree.

When Patel landed up at the Naif Road bungalow, Dawood asked him to repay the money he owed to Zahir, the brother-in-law of the seer. Patel had only begun to proclaim his bankruptcy again when Dawood pulled out his revolver and pointed it at his former boss. Then Shakeel placed the list of Patel's properties on the table.

'Sell all these properties,' Dawood said, 'and pay your dues.'

Yusuf Patel protested that he needed some time to find a buyer. Dawood turned his head sideways where Mustafa Dossa was sitting with a bearish grin on his face. 'The buyer is also ready, Yusuf bhai,' proclaimed Dawood. 'Dossa will buy your properties. He will even pay you a *fair* price.'

Dossa quoted an amount he was willing to pay for Patel's assets. It was a pittance. Patel had no option but to put pen to paper and sign the deal. Zahir got his money back, but the incident put an already struggling Yusuf Patel into more trouble. Things reached a point where he had to sell many of the cars he owned, including a famous garage business. He was left with only non-performing assets. Patel could never recover from this humiliation. Quietly, he faded into the sunset. A few years later, he died of a brain tumour.

49

The Don's Garage

Firoz and I were passing by the Chowpatty beach in a taxi. It was one of those things I wanted to do, out of pure nostalgia—ride in the legacy black and yellow top cabs (called *kaali-peeli* in local slang) before they went off the roads. Chowpatty, arguably, remains the most iconic beach in the country. It has been featured in many movies and remains a favourite spot among tourists. The surrounding area is also one of the plushest in the country.

When the taxi stopped at a signal, we were surrounded by a Jaguar on one side and a Bentley on the other. Firoz seemed to admire these beauties. Growing up, there weren't many fancy cars in the city but many of them could be found in a garage that used to be located in the vicinity.

'The famous Bombay Garage was located in a nearby building,' I said. 'They literally introduced imported cars to the gentry of the city.'

'Oh yes,' Firoz said. 'Haji Mastan also used to operate from the same building.' He paused. 'But Mastan was convinced that it was a *panauti* (jinxed) place.'

'What do you mean?' I asked, knowing fully well that panauti meant—that the place would bring bad luck to those who were associated with it. But I was interested in knowing the circumstances under which the term got associated with the property.

Firoz smiled. He knew the answer to my question in detail.

One thing that was certain about Haji Mastan was that he operated with a certain flair. He loved luxury watches and luxury cars. Mastan's love affair with cars gained steam when he moved into the Meher building near Chowpatty. The building was famous for the prestigious Bombay Garage, which was a showroom and service centre for imported cars.

The garage was started by the illustrious Chinoy family. In 1916, Meherally Chinoy had moved to Bombay from Bhuj and acquired an agency for Chevrolet and General Motors and petrol pumps. But Bombay Garage was the jewel in the crown of the family. It also housed a private petrol pump. Truly, the stuff of royalty. The showroom, sprawled across 45,000 square feet, was a distribution centre for sleek Pontiacs, Lanchesters, Vauxhalls and Armstrong Siddeleys.

Around the 1970s, Haji Mastan reportedly purchased this property for lakhs of rupees. Haji Mastan dismantled the garage and began operating from the premises. Mastan's fleet of cars included Mustangs and Mercedes. He would often use these cars to move his smuggled gold.

Mastan also had a mechanic called Ashok who worked for him in the early 1970s. It is said that Ashok was such a good mechanic that he could recognize faults in imported cars by merely listening to the sound of the engine.

One of the offices in Meher building was empty. A car dealer approached Mastan to check if the don was willing to rent out that particular office. Surprisingly, Mastan was more than open to the idea. Radhe Kishan, who was Mastan's manager at that time, called the dealer to Mastan's office to negotiate the terms of the lease.

'Mastan bhai,' said the dealer, 'will you rent the office on a *pagdi* system?'

Mastan smiled and shook his head. 'No.'

The pagdi system worked on the premise that the tenant would pay a nominal rent and become part owner of the property (not the land). The tenant had the right to even sell the property if he paid a certain percentage to the land owner. This ensured that the landowner gained on every sale while retaining the rights to the land. But Mastan had no intention of leasing the property on a pagdi agreement.

The dealer thought that maybe Mastan wanted a heavy deposit for the place. Under the heavy deposit system, the property was rented out on payment of a huge sum, which would be returned to the tenant at the end of the agreed term.

'Then should I pay a heavy deposit?' the dealer said.

Mastan shook his head again. 'No.'

'Then how much will the rent be?'

In his trademark style, Mastan raised one finger to denote the amount. The dealer wasn't accustomed to Mastan's methods so Radhe Kishan explained that the rent would be Rs 1000 a month. The dealer felt that was a really sweet deal for a property at such a prime location.

'But,' said Mastan, 'there is one condition.' He paused. 'Whenever I ask you to vacate the premises, you must vacate without making me ask twice.'

Mastan further explained that, whenever the time came, he would provide the dealer with fair notice before asking him to vacate. The dealer wondered why Mastan was insisting on such a condition. Mastan replied that he was planning to build a movie theatre at that spot in partnership with a big movie star of that era (the late 1960s and early 1970s). A famous producer and director was also involved in the project. The dealer had no qualms about this.

'Mastan bhai,' said the dealer, 'I will need rent receipts for my payments.'

To say that Mastan was shocked at this would be an understatement. He stayed silent for a long minute while the dealer wondered if he had asked for the don's kidneys. The meeting suddenly turned awkward. Even Radhe Kishan, Mastan's manager, was shocked at this suggestion.

'Listen son,' said Mastan. 'There's no *likha-padhi* (paperwork) in our business. My word is not just our agreement; it is also your rent receipt.'

Mastan's affinity towards operating on the spoken word was well known. He showed a lot of documentation to the dealer, which included the map of the Bombay Garage as of 1939, the agreement that was submitted to the municipal corporation of Bombay and the property tax receipts. But the don was firm that no rent receipts could exist in his scheme of things.

The dealer did not want to lose out on the opportunity as the office was in one of the best locations in the city. He finally moved into the shop and started paying Rs 1000 as rent.

But soon, a notion took seed in Mastan's head that the place was a panauti. Firstly, his plan for the movie theatre did not materialize. The authorities did not give the requisite permissions for the cinema. The superstar and the director who were involved in the project also backed out.

Mastan then tried to develop a mall at the site but even that plan was thwarted by the authorities. In 1975, Mastan was arrested during the Emergency under the Maintenance of Internal Security Act. Many of his properties were sealed. He was in jail for eighteen months before being released. Mastan was reported to have lamented that those politicians who abused him by day would come seeking favours from him at night.

Now, the car dealer who had rented the property also began experiencing uncanny incidents. When he would lock the office at 9 p.m., he would often hear unusual noises from different corners. Sometimes, he would feel that shadows on the wall behind him were moving in different directions. He spoke about these incidents to Mastan, who called a baba to cleanse the place. Just like Dawood's family, even Mastan had a certain veneration for seers. The incidents stopped for a while.

Later, Mastan asked the car dealer to vacate the property. He explained to the dealer that the office was now in the hands of Yusuf Patel, who had also become Mastan's business partner. The new tenant (Patel) did not make much use of the space and it remained unoccupied for a while. But soon, bad times struck Yusuf Patel. His real estate business went bust and his debts mounted astronomically. Patel's debtors soon approached Dawood to settle their dues. That was the beginning of the end for the once-powerful smuggler.

Dawood Ibrahim called Yusuf Patel to Dubai and annexed all his properties, including his office in Pydhonie. This incident broke Yusuf Patel to such an extent that his finances and his clout were completely destroyed. Patel then contacted the same car dealer to whom Mastan had leased the property earlier.

Reluctantly, Patel asked if the dealer would help him sell his cars so that he could generate liquid cash. The dealer, who was now operating in the Gamdevi area, told Yusuf Patel that he would be happy to assist. 'But I can't get clients all the way to Pydhonie for a test drive,' the dealer said. 'That will be a great headache.'

He asked Patel to let him keep the cars at his place in Gamdevi. Patel was so bereft at that time that he agreed to the dealer's conditions. It was a complete reversal of fortunes for the strongman that he now had to agree to a car dealer's demands. Soon after, Yusuf Patel died, reportedly from a brain tumour.

In the 1990s, the name of a popular film financier was also reportedly associated with this property. This producer was also arrested on charges that the mafia was involved in financing a mainstream Bollywood movie. The financier had pumped Rs 1.2 billion ($26.4 million) into the movie's budget. As evidence, the police had submitted tapes of the financier's conversations with Chhota Shakeel where the two were discussing an extortion case involving another businessman. The financier has since maintained a low profile.

'Whether the place was jinxed or not,' Firoz said, 'it had surely seen a motley crowd of characters from the underworld who met with unfortunate incidents.'

50

The Gold King

I stand outside the door of Bismillah Shah Baba's dargah while Firoz pays his respects at Baba's mausoleum. The dargah is located inside the Chhatrapati Shivaji Terminus near platform number seventeen and is over two centuries old. An apocryphal story goes that when the Britishers were building the grand station, they found that railway tracks being laid over a particular patch of land would vanish mysteriously. Later, the architects learnt that the land was the final resting place of a revered Sufi saint who went by the name of Bismillah Shah Baba. So, the Britishers constructed a mausoleum, following which the unusual occurrences stopped and the construction was completed.

When Firoz returned, he began narrating another interesting anecdote about the dargah. 'In the 1930s,' he said, 'an eight-year-old boy visited this dargah with his father.'

I listened to the tale with rapt attention. The father of this boy used to work as a daily wage labourer in Cuddalore (Tamil Nadu) and had migrated to Bombay in search of a better life with his family. Still, the family lived in great poverty. But the father had faith in God and those who were deemed close to the creator. This is why he would often visit the dargah with his son.

A *faquir* baba, who was sitting at the dargah, with many colourful rings on his fingers, noticed the boy and called him over. The baba measured the boy with his gaze and closed his eyes. Perhaps, the baba was witnessing the boy's destiny. The faquir opened his eyes and said: '*Beta, tere naseeb mein hikmat hai. Aur hukumat bhi.*' He paused. '*Is shahar mein tera naam hoga. Tu waqt ka Suleman hoga.*'

The faquir was predicting that the young boy would earn great riches. Suleman was a rich, pious and wise king who has been referred to as King Solomon in the Old Testament and revered as Hazrat Sulaiman in the Holy Quran and Muslim Hadith. Back then, the boy stifled a sneer purely out of respect for the aged clairvoyant. How would he rule a city like Bombay when the sword of starvation was always dangling above his head? But the faquir's prophecy would eventually come true.

'This eight-year-old boy went on to become the Gold King of the city,' Firoz said. 'And came to be known as Haji Mastan Mirza.'

The young Mastan's fortunes changed when he landed a job as a porter at the Bombay Docks. A chance encounter with an Arab smuggler named Ghalib introduced him to the world of smuggling. Gold, silver, imported watches and electronic equipment were often smuggled from other countries. It was a lucrative business at that time since the government used to levy high duties on these items. If these goods could make it past the maritime borders by escaping the scrutiny of the customs department, there was a lot of money to be made. Mastan took to smuggling like a fish to water.

There came a time when Mastan completely dominated the smuggling routes in the city. He was a suave operator, fond of cars and good quality clothes. It is said that Amitabh Bachchan's character in *Deewar* (1975) was inspired by Haji Mastan.

Though Mastan did not have an affinity towards violence, he was not averse to courting muscle power. To this extent, Mastan quickly formed an alliance with Varadarajan Mudaliar, who was a strongman controlling the central Mumbai region. The slums of Dharavi were Varada's territory and he operated illegal businesses of bootlegging, extortion and contract killing with impunity.

To establish his hold in south Mumbai, Haji Mastan allied with Karim Lala, who was the patriarch of the Pathan gang that operated in the areas of Dongri, Nagpada, Bhendi Bazaar and Mohammad Ali Road. These were the same areas from which Sabir and Dawood's gang emerged. Pitched battles involving soda bottles, blades and swords would take place between the two gangs. Another popular weapon used on the streets was the Rampuri knife, a sharp switchblade originating from Rampur, Uttar Pradesh.

Things finally exploded when Amirzada and Alamzeb of the Pathan gang murdered Sabir. But even then, Mastan was clear that he was not going to take sides in the war between the Pathans and Dawood. In fact, along with others, Mastan tried to negotiate a truce between the rivals.

But Dawood wanted more than an eye for an eye; he insisted on dissecting each appendage from the body of each Pathan who had played a role in his brother's killing. On the other hand, it is said about Mastan that he did not fire even a single bullet in his life. Mastan had other ways by which he could force someone's hand. His spoken word and one tight slap was sufficient to make people do his bidding. An advocate learnt this lesson the hard way in the early 1980s.

At that time, Mastan was approached by an advocate and a cop from Pune. As much as one could have expected from people connected to the legal system, the duo had not turned up to issue any legal notice from the courts to the don. Rather, they needed his assistance. Mastan amicably received the visitors at his palatial bungalow at Peddar Road, named Bait-ul-Suroor (abode of happiness). He knew the cop personally, and asked what had brought the policeman to his doorstep. The cop then introduced the advocate to Mastan and asked him to state the problem.

'Mastan bhai,' said the advocate. 'I own a plot of land in Pune. I leased the property to a party who operates a guest house at that site.'

'Now that you want the plot back,' Mastan said.

'Yes, but the party is refusing to vacate it.'

The advocate folded his hands in front of Mastan and nodded. The don had caught on to the rest of the story quickly. There were umpteen cases during those days where tenants refused to vacate properties they had rented. Tenancy laws were not highly regulated at that time. Legal cases would drag on for years. The early norm for renting out properties was in the form of rent agreements and not leave and licence agreements that stand cancelled after eleven months. Under the rent agreement, the tenant could occupy the property as long as he was paying the rent. And even if he were not, the existing laws prevented owners from evicting tenants.

Hence, tenants would stay put on the property forever, paying the same amount of meagre rent for decades while the property owner could only tear his hair in frustration. So when legal systems failed, property owners would seek help from the dons of the day—and Haji Mastan Mirza was the king of the smugglers during that time.

In fact, Mastan would often use the services of a young Dawood Ibrahim and his gang to evict people from properties regularly. During those days, the *baithak* of Dawood and his boys used to be outside a shop located at Maulana Shaukat Ali Road near JJ Hospital. Ironically, this shop was known as the '*kafan waali dukaan*' because it would sell shrouds, garlands and *itr*, pronounced as *attar* (perfumes), which are generally used in the funeral rituals of the Muslim community. It was a prophecy of sorts, that a man who made death and destruction his business used to assemble his gang outside a shop that sold materials for funeral proceedings.

As soon as the shopkeeper would lower his shutter after sunset, the D-Company boys would start assembling to plan their devious schemes. Dawood bhai would order cups of '*paani-kam chai*' (tea with more milk and less water) from the nearby Nilgiri Hotel for them. He would also order jalebis from a famous sweetmeats shop that was located at the right end of the street. If word was sent to Dawood that Haji Mastan had called, the young don would show up and get the job done for the right price. Today, the whole topography and important landmarks have been altered or revamped. However, these now are part of the Mumbai mafia folklore or history of the underworld.

But since the matter in which the advocate was seeking Mastan's help was in the Pune jurisdiction, Mastan decided to use some of his contacts who were based in Pune. He had a number of boys working for him in Pune too.

'*Ho jayega*,' Mastan said, providing his word that the tenant would be evicted.

'How much time will it take, bhai?' the advocate asked.

Mastan had a habit of denoting numbers with his fingers. He raised all five fingers of his right hand. The advocate did not seem to understand but the cop had frequent dealings with Mastan and understood the sign. He told the advocate that Mastan was promising to get the property evacuated in five days.

'And what will be the honorarium for this service?' the advocate asked.

Mastan raised three fingers.

'Three lakh rupees,' the cop explained.

The advocate agreed in a heartbeat. Rs 3 lakh was a fair price for such a job, given the value of the property. The men shook hands over the deal. Mastan then set about the job. He always believed in keeping his word and expected others to do the same. His boys from Pune got the property evicted by the fourth day itself. On Mastan's command, they also handed over the property to the advocate and then asked for the payment. The advocate assured them that he'd send over the payment to Mastan's office in two days.

However, Mastan was shocked to know that the advocate had only sent Rs 2 lakh instead of Rs 3 lakh upon which the deal had been made. The advocate started giving lame excuses, like he was short of money. It was only a matter of time before Mastan lost his patience. He ordered his boys to bundle the advocate into a van and drag him to Bombay. Accordingly, the advocate was produced in front of the don.

Again, Mastan raised his three fingers. 'Where are the three lakh rupees we agreed upon, *vakeel* sahab?'

The advocate opened his mouth to provide another lame excuse. But Mastan stood up, swung his arm and slapped the advocate so hard across the face that his cheek turned red with the imprint of Mastan's fingers!

Mastan then warned the advocate that if the pending payment was not delivered before sunset, his boys would occupy the property in Pune and no power in the world would be able to evict them. The worried advocate apologized profusely and promised to deliver Rs 1 lakh before the evening.

But this time, Mastan raised two fingers. 'One lakh rupees is the pending payment,' he said. 'And the extra one lakh is the penalty you must pay for not keeping your word.'

The advocate had no option but to pay up. When the money came to Mastan, he kept a portion of it and distributed the rest among the boys who had done the job.

Haji Mastan believed that the entire *dhanda* (business) worked on one factor, and one factor alone: trust. He believed in not breaking the trust of those he conducted business with and expected the same from them. Dawood, on the other hand, never shied away from underhanded moves and backstabbing his enemies if the situation warranted.

A differentiating factor between Mastan and Dawood is that the two had completely opposite views on violence and bloodshed. Mastan believed that killing and bloodshed would attract severe action from the authorities. Dawood would settle for nothing less than absolute domination. He was ready to crush whoever stood in his way. In those ways, Dawood Ibrahim was a ruthless man who could go to any extent to achieve his objective. It is not surprising that when Mastan's era was coming to an end, there would be only one solid contender for the throne—and his name was Dawood Ibrahim Kaskar.

51

The Adopted Son

My conversations about Mastan with Firoz made me think. What happened to Mastan's legacy? Where were his heirs? It was common knowledge that Mastan's children ran into a lot of disputes regarding the inheritance of his property. Three of Mastan's daughters were locked in a bitter legal battle with the children of Mastan's one-time aide, Karim. The fiasco even resulted in the arrest of Karim's children. Around 2016, the property at Mumbai's famous Peddar Road was estimated to be worth at least Rs 100 crore. After years of legal tussle, the two warring parties decided to settle the matter out of court.

There was a well-kept secret of Haji Mastan Mirza that not many people were aware of. A lot has been written about Mastan. Major superstars have played his characters in the movies but some aspects of his life have escaped the public eye till date. Not many who have not experienced the reign of Mastan know that he had an adopted son who went by the name of Sundar Shekhar aka Suleiman Mirza. I had known him since my early days as a crime reporter. I tracked down Shekhar at his residence in Colaba and we settled down for a chat.

Shekhar is a religious man. Photographs of the Hindu deities he worships adorn the walls of his home in Colaba. A photograph of Mastan is also present in the same room. Shekhar reveres his father though there is a difference in the religions they follow.

In the 1980s, Mastan felt the need to organize minorities politically and started a party called Dalit Muslim Suraksha Mahasangh. None of his friends or biological children supported him but Sundar Shekhar became the successor of his father and managed the party. The name of the party has now been changed to Bharatiya Minorities Suraksha Mahasangh. Their office is located at Nagpada, which is also near the areas where Dawood Ibrahim grew up.

'How old were you when Mastan adopted you?' I asked Shekhar.

Shekhar didn't remember exactly his age at that time. 'I have known him since I was a child,' he said.

Like his foster father, Shekhar was also born in poverty. His family used to live in Madras. To earn two square meals a day, he had to move across several states. From Madras, he went to Karnataka, to Andhra Pradesh and then he came to Maharashtra. Survival was always difficult for him until Mastan adopted him.

It is said that Mastan had great reverence for Mumbai and the Arabian Sea as he was making a living in the city and through its waters. Shekhar also imbibed this trait and considers Maharashtra as his symbolic mother. 'Maharashtra is my *maa*,' he said.

When Shekhar arrived at Mumbai Central, he was terribly hungry and was looking for food to eat. He went to a canteen without too much money in his pocket. The sight of cooked rice made him even more hungry. In Tamil, rice is called *chor* so he started shouting '*chor chor*' to ask for food. As *chor* means thief in Hindi, a man started beating Shekhar thinking that the boy was a thief. Getting angrier by the second, Shekhar picked up a stone and hit the man who was attacking him.

Cops arrived soon after and took Shekhar to the police station where he was fed three times a day. This was a eureka moment for him. He realized that throwing stones at people and injuring them would ensure that he wouldn't have to sleep on an empty stomach! So he started doing this frequently to keep himself in jail. The lock-up became like a hotel for him.

He was sent to the lock-up at least fifty times, for anywhere between five days to a month at a given time. Since Mastan was into the smuggling business, he was also a regular at police stations during that era.

Mastan was said to have a Robin Hood kind of image as he used to say that he was stealing from the government and helping the poor. Shekhar also considers his foster father a messiah (though my personal view is slightly different). I feel that Mastan was a stingy man and never believed in charity. In fact, the Haj that he performed was on the government dole through the Haj House scheme and not from his hard-earned money.

Once when Shekhar was in the lock-up, Mastan happened to visit the police station. He immediately bonded with Shekhar since they both spoke the Tamil language. Mastan slapped Shekhar twice for getting involved in many police cases. But then, he also arranged for his release from the lock-up and took him to his bungalow. From that day, Shekhar began staying with Haji Mastan and began unloading Mastan's shipments at Cuffe Parade and other places.

Shekhar has retained many of Mastan's personal belongings as souvenirs. The don's skull cap. Lighter. Handkerchief. A packet of 555 cigarettes. When Mastan passed away, he had Rs 5700 in cash in his pocket. Shekhar has those notes saved to this day.

Shekhar also believes that Mastan was adept at forming alliances. A famous strongman from Daman—Lallu Jogi—was one of Mastan's close associates. Jogi was also fond of the lavish life, just like Mastan. He owned farmhouses spread over as wide as 200 acres. Stables for horses were also built around the farmhouse. Like a king, Jogi would often survey the property on horseback. His bungalows had lifts to move between the floors. Such was his domination in Daman that people even feared overtaking his car.

Jogi was known to have good contacts in the customs department. Once an officer dared to stop one of the don's consignments. When Jogi came to know of this, he was furious. He rushed to the spot and asked the officer why the consignment had been stopped when he had already made arrangements for its smooth passage with the higher-ups. But the officer refused to relent. This angered Jogi so much that he reportedly pulled out his weapon and aimed it at the officer. The sight was enough for the officer to let the consignment pass.

When Dawood Ibrahim was working for Mastan, he had also attended a function in Daman that was organized by Lallu Jogi as Mastan's representative. Jogi was one of those who could stand at the gates of Musafirkhana (Dawood's headquarters while he was in Mumbai) and order Dawood's acolytes to let their boss know that 'Lallu bhai' was here to meet him. Dawood would immediately meet Lallu Jogi without making him wait for a second.

During those days, the religious divide in the underworld was almost non-existent. Shekhar also seconded this fact.

'My *baap* wore silk clothes at my wedding,' he says. Baap is the Hindi term for father, with which Shekhar addresses Mastan. Muslims are known to avoid silk clothes due to religious considerations, but Mastan wore a silk kurta and dhoti at his foster child's wedding. Mastan would also visit temples, mosques and churches. Shekhar has a particular memory of visiting Babulnath temple with Mastan. The don also built a dormitory at Haji Ali for the followers of the seer.

During the time he was trying to turn legit, Shekhar reveals, Mastan also made a film called *Mere Garib Nawaz* (1973). This again goes to prove the reverence that the dons of the Mumbai mafia had for seers. The star cast included Agha, Anwar Ali (ace comedian Mehmood's brother), Veena and Nazneen.

It is through his love for films that Mastan found a life partner in the later stages of his life. Mastan, when he was younger, was enamoured of Madhubala. But the actress unfortunately died at a young age. Health complications caused the death of the extremely beautiful actress in 1969, only a few days after she had turned thirty-six years of age.

As fate would have it, during the production of one of his films, Mastan met Shahjahan Begum. She was an actress in small-budget films but she bore a striking resemblance to Madhubala. Thinking that fate had fulfilled his wishes, Mastan married Shahjahan Begum in 1984. This was Mastan's second marriage. He had three children from his first marriage, all daughters.

During the later years of his life, Mastan's influence faded with the rise of Dawood Ibrahim. The D-Company had gone international by moving its base to Dubai and there was no holding them back as they steamrolled their opponents in the arena of crime.

'My father's death was very sudden,' Shekhar says, with a forlorn look on his face. On 25 June 1994, Mastan had spoken to his foster son around 3 p.m. in the afternoon. But then the don suffered a heart attack and was taken to Breach Candy Hospital. A famous doctor from Bombay Hospital, who was close to Mastan, also arrived to treat him. However, Haji Mastan Mirza was declared dead around 5 p.m. He was sixty-eight years old. And thus, ended the story of the man who was known as the Gold King.

52

Return of the Badshah

One of my favourite protégés, who also wanted to become a writer, had reached out to me after reading my first book—*Black Friday: The True Story of the Bombay Bomb Blasts*. He had been deeply influenced by the book and the movie, directed by Anurag Kashyap. The boy had good writing chops but I gave him a fair warning about working with me. It was not for the faint-hearted. One had to interact with all kinds of people, each with different motives and agendas. Some of my subjects and contacts were truly dangerous men, or women. But my warnings failed to dissuade the young lad. He was ready to walk the talk.

Over our association of many years, my protégé maintained that the character of Badshah Khan (portrayed by Aditya Srivastava in the film) had been an enigma for him. He was right to a great extent. Here was a man—codenamed Badshah Khan to protect his identity—who had played a part in the deadliest terror attack of the time, the one who'd been on a desperate run from the cops for days after being betrayed by those who had pushed him into this grave conspiracy. Disillusioned, Badshah Khan finally switched sides and turned into a prosecution witness for the government, which led to the arrest and conviction of many others. For this, he became a marked man for the mafia, who felt that he had betrayed them.

I could understand my protégé's fascination with the character from a storytelling perspective. The character of Badshah Khan is truly complex. To test my protégé's mettle, I called him to an address in suburban Mumbai. We landed at an apartment and were seated in the hall. I hadn't told him whom we were about to meet until a man with a white beard, smiling politely, entered the room.

Respecting the bearded man's age, my young protégé stood up to shake hands with him and exchange salutations. The boy was truly well mannered. As soon as the two settled on the sofa next to each other, I asked my protégé if he knew who the bearded man was.

'No, sir,' the boy said.

I pointed towards the bearded man. 'He is the *real* Badshah Khan from *Black Friday*.'

The whites of my protégé's eyes expanded like an ocean. He froze. He kept his head low, trying to catch a glimpse of the bearded man again, who was smiling. The boy's face paled, as if he had sighted Count Dracula on a moonless night. After a few moments, he regained his composure and we finally delved into how life had turned out for Badshah Khan since he was released from jail.

Until the proceedings of the 1993 bomb blasts were in progress, he was referred to as Badshah Khan (police witness number 2) to protect his identity. But now that much water has flowed under the bridge, he has no qualms about revealing his true identity. His name is Usman Jan Khan.

Once a TADA convict, Badshah Khan lived under protection provided by the government to ensure his safety. Khan was part of the core group that attended the first conspiracy meeting convened by Tiger Memon at Hotel Big Splash in Alibaug in December 1992. He was recruited by Javed Chikna, who was close to Tiger Memon. Khan was one of the members of the team that conducted a recce of the spots that were chosen as bomb sites. He also took part in assembling the bombs, which took place at Tiger's residence in Al-Hussaini building in Mahim.

After the blasts, when the Mumbai Police turned up the heat against the conspirators, Khan travelled to Uttar Pradesh from where he made his way to Rajasthan and later to Delhi. He was finally arrested by the Crime Branch of the Mumbai Police.

Khan was an educated man, a fact attested to by the then Anti-Terrorism Squad (ATS) chief, Rakesh Maria. Like any other educated person, he harboured aspirations of making something good out of his life. But it was his habit of getting into bad company that resulted in his fall and he ended up participating in the gruesome crime. After his conviction under TADA, Khan decided to atone for his sins by becoming an approver for the government. His testimony was a game changer for the prosecution, who were finding it difficult to produce concrete evidence of meetings conducted in Dubai for the conspiracy or the arms training in Pakistan.

He testified to the meetings held in Dubai to discuss the blasts and gave the names of thirty-three accused who had participated in the crime. The TADA court let Khan and one other approver walk free in lieu of becoming approvers for the court.

To this day, an armed police escort has been provided to Khan by the government. The policeman was stationed in the watchman's cabin of the building where Khan currently lives.

'We last met during the days you were writing *Black Friday*,' he tells me. 'My bad times also ended around that time. And now when we meet after so many years, good news is around the corner again.'

'May I ask about the good news?' I said.

'I am expecting the news of the birth of my first grandchild any minute now.'

When I first met Badshah, he was in his early thirties, a young man whose rage against the riots had been exploited to the hilt. He had played a part in a deadly terror conspiracy and paid the price for it. Now in his fifties, he was talking about taking his soon-to-be-born grandchild to the various gardens around the city, like an affable grandfather.

After he was released from jail, his family arranged his marriage. The marriage has withstood the test of time and the couple has three children. Two boys and a girl. The girl studied law and was married into a good family. The elder of the two boys works in a visual effects company while the youngest is also studying law.

'My children have seen the mistakes I made and the legal turmoil I faced,' he says. 'They chose law so that they could contribute to the betterment of society and the country.'

How had he managed to afford such excellent education and the upbringing of his kids? The question took us back to the days when Khan had just been acquitted by the court and was struggling to get his wrecked life back on its feet. Khan used to work as a real estate agent when he got sucked into the vortex of the 1992–93 riots and the bomb blasts.

After his release, Khan resumed his real estate dealings as that was the only trade he was adept at. Some of the properties that he hadn't been able to dispose of due to his arrest were lying unattended after he came out. He sold those properties to breathe life back into his business and sustain his married life from the proceeds.

But as Khan and his wife braced themselves for their first child, he realized that the real estate business wouldn't be enough to sustain them. He started thinking of new ways of making money. He got in contact with a person with whom he started the import–export business. They established contact with some businesses based in Dubai and started exporting fruits and vegetables, which they sourced from the Agricultural Produce Market Committee (APMC) market. Khan wistfully recalled the nights he would spend sleeping on the gunny bags in trucks while he transported the produce from one point to another.

'I had a police escort for my protection at that time too,' Khan says. 'People would wonder why a man with an armed guard was sleeping in trucks. The answer was simple. I wanted to make an honest living.'

Somewhat irritated, Khan revealed that his security was reduced from two guards to one following Rakesh Maria's departure from the corridors of the Mumbai Police. Rakesh Maria was DCP (Traffic) when the blasts occurred, but his investigation had led to the arrest of several accused and put Maria on a pedestal for future postings and promotions.

'Have you been in touch with Rakesh Maria?' I asked.

'He is like a godfather to me,' Khan said, with a hint of gratitude in his voice.

After Badshah Khan forayed into the construction business, he met a few sketchy personalities once again. During those days, he also ventured into the media business by starting a weekly newspaper with a partner. The business did not fetch good returns. 'I had purchased a white elephant,' Khan said.

The financial losses notwithstanding, it turned out that his partner had some links with men of the D-Company. Maria, during the entire stint of the newspaper business, warned Khan to stay away from people of dubious reputation. 'If he saw I was going wrong, he would scold me just like a father scolds a petulant child.'

Maria's cop instincts turned out to be true when Khan's newspaper buddy left the business and enrolled himself back into the D-Company.

'He just couldn't get over his obsession with the D-Company,' Khan said.

'Rakesh Maria's association turned out to be a blessing for you,' I said.

'And so did yours.'

'Mine?' I laughed. 'How?'

'After being released by the authorities, I was facing a lot of difficulty in obtaining a passport. It was also hampering my export business, which required me to travel to Dubai.'

Not only did the police refuse to process the passport applications for Khan but they also rejected clearances for his wife, who had applied for a passport too. Each time, the police would reject the application citing the charges relating to the blasts that Khan had faced in the TADA court. If reminded that the court had cleared Khan of all charges and allowed him to start his life anew, the police would ask his wife to produce the court's judgment citing the same. Khan had all the clearances from the CBI and the government for his passport to be processed. But the cops were still giving him a tough time. He was distressed when journalist Anand Holla called him up on his landline number.

Anand Holla was one of the many journalists who worked with me. I introduced Khan to Holla when I was writing *Black Friday*. Holla asked Khan to narrate his ordeal in full detail so that he could write an article about it and help him out of his misery.

'The government has banned me from giving any interviews,' Khan said.

'But they haven't banned your wife,' Holla said.

Holla was a smart man. He asked Khan to bring his wife on the phone so that she could tell him all. Khan quickly passed the receiver to his wife, who was sitting beside him. His wife narrated the inconvenience she had to face on a daily basis to get the passport approved by the police department.

Holla noted everything down and came up with an article dated 11 January 2008 in *Mumbai Mirror*. The article was scathing and uncompromising in its criticism of the police department to deny Khan and his wife their passports and lent a voice to the aggrieved couple who expressed that they had decided to move to the high court if they faced more delays.

The article pushed the police station to call up Khan and assure him that he would get an approval for his passport at the earliest. Khan thanked Holla profusely for his assistance.[1]

'And now I can thank you for putting me in touch with Holla,' Khan told me.

'So when you finally got your passport,' I said, 'where did you first travel?'

'I first went on to the holy pilgrimage to Makkah with my wife and son,' Khan said. 'Then I took my family on a tour.'

'You must have skipped Dubai,' I quipped.

Khan laughed. 'The D-Company and the fear it commanded in Dubai is a thing of the past now. They have been virtually wiped out there. Any businesses they may have there are operated remotely.'

Khan said that his export business had crashed badly by then. He then started a restaurant in the area where he lived and had to put in a lot of hard work in the initial phase. On some occasions, he would find himself multitasking, where he would serve a customer and come running to the billing counter when it was time for the same customer to pay. 'One fine day,' he said, 'Anurag Kashyap came to the restaurant for a meal. I walked up to him and introduced myself.'

I smiled at the coincidence. 'Do you still get threats?'

Khan nodded. The last threat he had received was from a prolific member of the D-Company who went by the name of Fahim Machmach.

A trusted aide and lieutenant to Dawood Ibrahim and Chhota Shakeel, Fahim Shaikh aka Fahim Machmach was wanted in several cases that ranged from murder, attempted murder and extortion. He was seen as the right man by his bosses and given the responsibility of handling the affairs of the D-Company in Mumbai. Fahim had the habit of nagging his victims on the call until they paid him the extortion money, which earned him the sobriquet 'Machmach'. He later fled to Pakistan where he reportedly died of Covid in 2021.

'But no one could touch me as I had protection from the state. Rakesh Maria sir took a personal interest in ensuring my safety.' Khan pauses. 'Even big cops, the famous encounter specialists from the Mumbai Police, wouldn't trouble me as Maria sir's hand was on my head.'

'What would Fahim tell you on those calls?'

'He told me I was a traitor.'

'Was he wrong in saying that you betrayed your one-time associates?' I asked curtly.

A tense expression spread across Khan's face. 'They brainwashed and used me for their own purposes. I made the mistake of falling into their trap.' He paused. 'I spent most of my time in jail praying. I also read many religious texts during this time and learnt that a righteous Muslim abides by the law of the land that he lives in.'

Khan also cited various sayings of the Prophet that proved that the spilling of innocent blood was frowned upon. He condemned the violence unleashed by those involved in the deadly riots and the blasts, irrespective of religion.

Khan recalled an incident during his trial when advocate Waris Pathan (who went on to become the MLA from the Byculla constituency in Maharashtra from 2014–19) was about to cross-examine him. Khan and Pathan kept looking at each other, as if they were exchanging some words in silence, prompting the judge to ask what was going on.

'Waris and I were classmates in school,' Khan told the judge. 'It is a travesty that he is now a respected lawyer, and I am on the stand with other criminals and terrorists.'

'Is that true, Waris?' the honourable judge asked Waris Pathan.

Waris Pathan nodded. He looked at Khan again and paused. Then he turned towards the judge. There was pity in the lawyer's voice. 'I do not wish to cross-examine him, sir,' Pathan said.

That moment was also a turning point for Badshah Khan. He realized that he should have been leading a respectable life like some of his classmates. Instead, he got embroiled in a massive terror conspiracy and had to spend the best years of his youth in jail and go through a great turmoil.

'How do you feel when you hear any news about your ex-colleagues?' I asked.

Often there have been news reports about the deaths of the blast accused like Yeda Yakub, who reportedly died in Pakistan in 2015. Yakub Memon was hanged in Nagpur Central Jail in the same year.

'Nothing,' Badshah Khan says. 'I just whisper a prayer, which is mandated by my faith. I have had no contact with them or their families. Now, I just want to atone for my past and lead a good life.'

He has started a charity organization that gives free food and medicines to those in need. It also provides assistance to jobless youth. The organization's affiliate runs a 'Roti Bank' in Malegaon to provide food to the poor and orphans. Besides this, Badshah Khan also owns a shop where food for dogs is sold. He has political ambitions and with that intent, he joined the Bharatiya Janata Party (BJP) as a part of their minority cell.

He is also contemplating filing a couple of petitions with the aim of bringing relief to the police department.

'What are these petitions?' I asked.

Khan was happy to elaborate. A police person has to face a great ordeal in making residential, educational and other arrangements for their family after being transferred to a new place. The exercise, Khan said, takes at least fifteen days every time they get transferred to another city or state. He wants to make this process easier by ensuring there are adequate arrangements made for those who are being transferred.

The second petition, Khan said, concerns the poor conditions of the quarters that the jailers are allotted to live in with their family. As jails are mostly situated on the outskirts of a city where there is a scarcity of resources, jailers often find themselves helpless to provide even a basic standard of lavatory facilities for their family. Members of the jailers' family, including women, have to walk long distances to use the washroom facilities. The cramped alleys that lead to these washrooms have a solitary dim bulb as the only source of light to navigate their way.

'It is my responsibility to do whatever I can to ease such ordeals that police personnel face,' Khan says.

What a twist of fate! A man whom the cops went chasing across the country wanted to bring some relief to their lives. By the time we ended our meeting, my protégé had gotten a first-hand taste of writing about crime and criminals. But not all stories need to have a gory ending. Sometimes, life throws up a second chance. It is up to the person to take the chance, which Badshah Khan did. He wants to spend the rest of his life ensuring that his children and grandchildren lead respectful, law-abiding lives.

Badshah Khan now turned the tables and asked a question about my protégé, who'd been making notes and asking the right questions. 'Who is this boy?'

'His name is Kashif,' I said. 'Kashif Mashaikh. And I brought him here because he was riveted by your character in *Black Friday*.'

Badshah Khan smiled at Kashif, who had edited several books for me. Two very special people in my life, my friend and mentor Vikram Chandra, and my wife Velly Thevar, also held the boy in high regard. I told Badshah Khan that Kashif was on his way to becoming an accomplished writer. He had already authored one published book, and had two more in the pipeline. Hearing this, Badshah Khan promised my protégé that he would share more stories when we met next. I look forward to that day too.

53

New Lamps for Old

The areas of Bhendi Bazar and Dongri are among the oldest native markets of Mumbai. This iconic part of south Mumbai occupied a significant position in the making of the city since British rule.

Predominantly a Muslim locality, it boasts of several freedom fighters, litterateurs, eminent journalists and social activists, and is a hub of several historical structures occupying pride of place in the city. Unfortunately, it is also in the news for the wrong reasons.

Dongri, Bhendi Bazar and Pydhonie are also referred to as the epicentre of the Mumbai underworld. Haji Mastan, Karim Lala and Dawood Ibrahim and his cronies came from this geographical region. Bringing so much infamy and embarrassment to the residents of the area.

Bhendi Bazar, Null Bazar, Nakhuda Mohalla and such other markets in south Mumbai are some of the most prominent addresses in the country and not just the city.

The market is a one-stop solution for all shoppers. But apart from its vibrant shops that sell everything from clothes to fishing equipment, the place is also notorious for being home to some of the most dreadful gangsters that the country has witnessed.

Demolishing old structures and constructing new ones can signify a change in more ways than one. Perhaps this is why the Saifee Burhani Upliftment Project (SBUP), established by a trust of the same name, circa 2009, is of much importance.

While Dawood Ibrahim moved from one country to another, some of his family members remained in Mumbai, the most prominent of them being his sister Haseena Parkar, who stayed right in the middle of the city, at Gordon Hall apartments in Nagpada until she passed away in 2014.

The infrastructural growth of Bhendi Bazar and its surrounding areas was haphazard and chaotic. Buildings almost tilted upon each other. There was no space for footpaths. The roads were congested by traffic jams. Conditions were unhygienic due to open gutters and a lack of sanitation. Things came to a point where any redevelopment was possible only by pulling down the dilapidated structures and constructing a new, integrated township. This was the basis of the SBUP, which had its own execution problems, some of which were spurred by the vestigial elements of the D-Company who had stayed behind in the area.

To trace some of these stories, I met Taizun Hassonjee, who manages an engineering company that was involved in the SBUP. Their office in Nariman Point, Mumbai, provides a breathtaking view of the Arabian Sea. Hassonjee showed me a blueprint of the project and got straight to the point.

SBUT stands for Saifee Burhani Upliftment Trust (SBUT), which is managing the SBUP. The ambitious plan is aimed at uplifting the Bhendi Bazaar area by launching a redevelopment drive over 16.5 acres of land comprising 250 buildings that are inhabited by 3200 families and has 1250 shops.

Taizun Hassonjee was born and raised in Nagpur. He studied law and later migrated to the US. His brother was an expert architect and town planner, and they were selected by the SBUT committee to take on the redevelopment project in the beginning.

'What kinds of challenges did you face as you took on the project?' I asked.

'The challenges were too many and too ridiculous,' he said.

In the year when this project was launched, the city streets had long been sanitized of the mafia rule. But that is not to say that the city, particularly the area at the centre of the project, had completely got rid of its traces. Musafirkhana was the place where Dawood started his career as a small-time smuggler and eventually turned into his hub from where he conducted his illegal activities.

'Many people would call up and seek acts of omission or commission after dropping the names of Dawood Ibrahim's siblings,' Hassonjee said.

His reference is to Iqbal Kaskar, who was deported from the UAE in 2003. After the encounter specialist Pradeep Sharma was reinstated in the force following his suspension in the Lakhan bhaiya encounter, the cop arrested

Iqbal in 2017. Iqbal is still in jail as of writing this book. But controversy refused to leave Pradeep Sharma alone. He also landed behind bars after being arrested by the National Investigation Agency (NIA) for his involvement in the murder of Mansukh Hiren, whose vehicle, filled with explosives, was found near the residence of India's biggest industrialist in what is now known as the 'Antilia Bomb Scare' case.

'But we never entertained these callers who dropped the names of Dawood's siblings,' Hassonjee said. 'We had a job to do, and we were focused on that.'

The project was spread over seven clusters. When the top priests of the Bohra community announced the project, Tricone Engineering was one of the firms that put in the quotation to secure it. After their credentials were deemed appropriate for a task of such magnitude, they started with the process to get buy-ins from the residents of the area to have the redevelopment of their properties and land conducted.

'No one believed that this project could be done,' Hassonjee said. 'Everyone thought we'd burn our hands.'

There was sufficient reasoning for such fears. Previous negotiations had seen resistance from the residents that was deemed impossible to overcome. Most of the buildings were as old as a hundred years and had been long due for reconstruction. The decrepit conditions of these buildings lay especially bare in each monsoon season where a few of them would collapse due to heavy rain. It was a nightmare for the authorities too.

Construction and maintenance of the buildings was MHADA's responsibility. Keeping in mind the precarious situation of the buildings, MHADA had issued notices to the inhabitants to evacuate the premises for the maintenance work several times in the past. But the plan of the corporation was never realized owing to some of the unreasonable occupants of these buildings who simply refused to move out. The public sphere was replete with tales of residents beating up the men who had been sent by MHADA to instruct the residents to comply with the evacuation notice.

Hassonjee and his younger brother had studied building planning in the US. Inspired by the architectural genius of the country, they were filled with a fervent desire to replicate the same in their home country. The operations they carried out initially in trying to get the occupants to agree to the redevelopment of the premises met a similar fate as that experienced by the MHADA. As soon as any team connected to the project reached the spot, they would face a huge crowd that would gather to stop them. How were they getting news of the team's arrival?

After a few days of careful observation, Hassonjee had his first breakthrough. 'It was the hawkers on the street who'd alert everyone,' he said.

The street was filled with such hawkers. A close observation of their activities through cameras installed at different spots across the street revealed that there was something far more sinister taking place under the cover of selling their wares. Apart from obstructing the vehicles from passing the stretch of the road, these small shops played an important role in concealing the weapons that their owners possessed for the purpose of threatening and dissuading anyone who tried to carry out any operation.

'You came here walking,' the hawkers would say to the ones who had come to them with evacuation orders, 'but you will return on a stretcher.'

They would also act as informants to the local hoodlums. Hassonjee had figured that this menace should be tackled first to kick-start the project.

However, the foundation for such a massive project cannot be established on violence but on smart manoeuvres that would ensure everlasting peace and harmony in the region, so Hassonjee decided to adopt non-forceful means to carry out the evacuations. He approached these hawkers and offered them sufficient remuneration in lieu of moving out from the place. He was delighted to find out that some of them responded to his offer positively and moved out.

But his joy was short-lived when he saw that the same shops that had moved returned after a few days, albeit with a new face that claimed to be its owner. One such shopkeeper was the owner of a famous mutton paaya shop.

Hassonjee first offered him the rent for three months to ask him to vacate the place. He agreed, took the money and promised to move out. But, within a week he was seen back at the hotel accepting customers. Hassonjee was surprised and reminded him of his promise to leave the premises.

'It would take more money to shift the entire set-up to a different place,' the owner said.

'How much?' Hassonjee asked.

He quoted an amount, and Hassonjee agreed again.

'What about my inventory that will be rendered useless?' he said.

Hassonjee understood that all he needed was more money. But he wasn't going to be penny-wise and pound-foolish. He paid the man and helped him set up his shop elsewhere. He raised the amount of his offer and dealt with each according to his need. After moving out the hawkers, Hassonjee launched the project in the cluster 2 area. Demolition of structures was underway when Hassonjee was approached by Salim Fruit.

'You'll need my help with demolition in this area,' Salim said. 'All demolition contracts here are assigned to me.'

Chhota Shakeel's brother-in-law and a key member of the D-Company, Salim Qureshi was making news for all the wrong reasons. His association with Shakeel and Dawood had made him a feared name in the neighbourhood. His family business of selling fruit got attached to his name and he became famous with the name Salim Fruit. He was arrested by the NIA in 2022 for his alleged involvement in aiding the D-Company's activities.

Hassonjee was aware of big names such as Dawood and Chhota Shakeel, but his knowledge of the underworld didn't go much beyond that. Besides, the project had the full backing of successive state governments in Maharashtra. Combining that with his own belief and staunch resolve, Hassonjee wasn't afraid of such developments. He did not entertain Salim Fruit any further.

Salim was visibly incensed. To decline his offer was one thing, but the fact that someone was claiming to have heard of him for the first time in his life was something that he found difficult to digest.

Salim used to leverage his kinship with Chhota Shakeel to intimidate his competitors into silence and win the demolition contract of the area for himself. It was apparent that his dominance in the area was met with zero resistance and Hassonjee had all the intentions of bringing an end to that tradition.

'Our company is the sole contractor of this project,' Hassonjee said, 'and I possess enough means to complete the demolition without needing any help.'

Salim was fuming. He got into an altercation with one of Hassonjee's employees during one of the demolitions. The employee also stood his ground. The incident was video-recorded by one of the onlookers; it garnered several views and remained viral for a brief period of time. However, when Salim Fruit was arrested by the NIA, the employee in question was also asked to record a statement. 'But there was little connection in our run-in with Salim Fruit and his other activities,' Hassonjee said.

Facing the mafia menace wasn't the only thing that was a new experience for Hassonjee while he worked incessantly to evacuate the properties in the area. He also came across realities that were novel in his long career in the construction domain.

Hassonjee was trying everything in his power to try and convince people of the significance of the project and the benefit it was going to bring them. He was not oblivious to the fact that the residents suspected the kind of projects he was overseeing. There have been instances where they had evacuated the premises on account of similar promises made to them in the past that never came to fruition. They had to face the brunt of the whole phony process. Many times, spurious builders would get a building vacated but failed to deliver on their promises of completing the redevelopment in time.

So Hassonjee would meet prominent figures in the locality personally and sometimes even the locals to build the required trust and confidence. He used to show them the videos and photos of the conceived plans in addition to explaining to them the worth it was going to add to society. The meetings would prove successful in convincing the part of the group who came from an educated background. But to the ones who fell on the opposite side of the spectrum the whole plan appeared suspicious, leaving no option for Hassonjee but to deal with them on an individual basis.

And it was during one such dealing that he got to witness a totally peculiar and ridiculous situation. It was the curious case of a property owned by six people and which measured a mere 1.5 sq. ft.

The paan shops in the city are makeshift shops that are built out of a single slab of tile. The tile is sheared from the middle to make a slot of the size sufficient for the shopkeeper to stand in. The items are vertically arranged on the remaining portion of tile and small packets of tobacco and gutkha are hung from the makeshift ceiling. Though the legally owned space of the shop was 1.5 sq. ft, the owners had made minor illegal expansions.

The owner of the paan shop said that he had five other partners who were residing in their native village in UP. The paan shop did its business on a rotational basis where each partner ran the shop for a year and kept whatever profit the shop made during those twelve months. Hassonjee had to move heaven and earth to gather all the six partners and convince them to evacuate the place. He explained to them that the management had decided to allot the standard size of 30 sq. ft of plot to those who currently owned an area less than 25 sq. ft. The owners agreed and Hassonjee was able to evacuate the last stretch of land that cleared the way for the redevelopment work for cluster 2.

But that's not to say that Hassonjee was left alone and did not have to deal with the bhais of the town till the time he successfully completed the work of the cluster 2. Apart from gangsters such as Salim Fruit, the area was also riddled with small-time bhais who conceived themselves to be the don of the locality. One such person was Sikander, who claimed to be Khalid Pehelwan's brother-in-law.

Though Khalid Pehelwan is a well-known name in the underworld, Hassonjee's lack of mafia knowledge made him look up the Internet. He saw that most search results for Khalid Pehelwan were references from my book *Dawood's Mentor*, which I had written in 2019. Khalid Pehelwan was the man who mentored Dawood Ibrahim while he was fighting his wars with rival gangs. On the night Sabir Kaskar was murdered, Manya Surve and the Pathan gang had tried to attack Dawood Ibrahim as well, but it was Khalid Pathan who had opened fire and rebuffed the attack. In another instance, he is also known to have saved Chhota Shakeel after Mehmood Kalia had trapped him in the AC market at Tardeo.

But much water had flowed under the bridge since then. The D-Company was no longer the violent force it had once been. Khalid Pehelwan himself was living in another country.

So Hassonjee showed the orders under which the BMC had granted permission to evacuate 1200 houses for the purpose of the redevelopment project. Sikander read the letter and tossed it at Hassonjee in irritation.

'I don't care what the BMC has to say,' Sikander said. 'This is my area and I disapprove of the operations that you are performing here.'

'If you have any objections,' Hassonjee said, 'please raise them with the corporation.'

After this interaction, Sikander did not come in contact with Hassonjee nor was he seen around the site of operation. But the encounter with Sikander was a portent of a much larger nuisance that Hassonjee was going to face in the coming days. The project was going to the next stage, which included the neighbourhood that became immortal in the pages of the country's underworld history, namely Pakmodia Street. This was where Dawood Ibrahim once used to live, on the second floor of what came to be known as Musafirkhana.

And the architect of the new menace was going to be none other than Imran Kalia, the son of the driver and long-standing aide of Dawood, Haneef Kutta.

54

Where There's a Will

The word *Bohra* draws its meaning from the Gujarati root word *vohrvu* or *vyavahar*, which means trading or business. So Bohra basically translates as 'to trade'. The Bohra community is a brand of Shia Islam that is mainly involved in trading and business. Natives of Gujarat, the Bohra population is concentrated in India with a sizeable number also found in Southeast Asia, Europe, the US and the Middle East. One of the central beliefs of the Shia faith is that there will always be an Imam on earth to show them the right path. But a proviso to this belief says that there will be times when this Imam will choose to remain out of the public view. This is where the various sects among Shia Muslims have serious differences of opinions.

The Da'i al-Mutlaq, as the head of the Bohra community, presides in a mosque that acts as the headquarters. Since a large chunk of the Indian Bohra population reside in Bhendi Bazaar, the role of the congregational centre is played by the Saifee Masjid, which at the time of the redevelopment project had become a century old.

The biggest advantage for Taizun Hassonjee was that he was an outsider. He did not belong to the area to get intimidated by the local bhais. Despite being a Bohra from Nagpur, Hassonjee was a US citizen. The colour of his passport brought him much needed clout and resources for the task.

Hassonjee started operations from a trailer that was parked near Saifee Masjid at the periphery of the whole cluster block. Soon he got entrenched into the project and decided to move out of the trailer and get a proper war room or operational office.

When Hassonjee started the evacuation process, he had managed to get the owner of Noor Hotel, located next to Saifee Masjid, to evacuate the hotel and set up a temporary office there. He operated from this office till the time he was done with all the reconstruction work of all the clusters he had signed up for. One day, when Hassonjee was sitting in the office discussing the plans related to the current cluster, there was a knock on the door. He had got used to the constant visits paid to him by the locals by this time. But this time it was not a regular local who had come to see him. The person to walk in was Imran Kalia.

Apart from being Dawood's driver, Imran Kalia's father, Hanif Shaikh was a notable member of the D-Company. He was among the first buddies of Dawood to join the don in his smuggling and extortion shenanigans. He was believed to have been handling Dawood's illegal businesses in Mumbai. Imran Kalia leveraged his father's reputation and posed as the don of the area. The redevelopment work of the cluster included one of Dawood's infamous properties.

It was a crudely built shed that was covered with metal sheets for walls. The shed was once used by Dawood and Chhota Shakeel as the torture room where they would bring their victims, bind them and serve them incessant thrashings. Kalia enjoyed considerable clout in the area and led expansive extortion operations with the help of his lackeys. He had lodged three tenants in the property with strict instructions that they were not to move out of the property no matter what. The tenants stuck to the role they were given by Kalia and clung to the property, shunting every effort made by Hassonjee to come to common terms.

'We have many ways to stop you,' Kalia said to Hassonjee.

Hassonjee had understood Kalia enough to know that he was self-delusional and that he wouldn't hesitate to go out of his way to save the property. Hassonjee wanted to try his best to not allow things to turn violent. But at the same time, he was also getting to hear that Kalia was up to something mischievous. Though he continued paying visits to the tenants to try and persuade them to empty the plot, he also got engaged in coming up with a countermeasure for whatever Kalia was planning. The air was thick with premonitions of sectarian conflict. Whipped up by Kalia, the bad elements from both the communities were quick to take the cue and brew communal tensions in the locality. There were also rumours insinuating that the redevelopment was a way of emptying the area of the residents belonging to the Sunni community and converting it into a Bohra-only locality. Hassonjee did not waste a single second in scotching such a rumour.

'I will be needing the services of four more bouncers,' Hassonjee spoke on the phone from his temporary office.

Over the past few days, Hassonjee had assembled an army of bouncers, whom he had hired from various agencies. He had no plans of getting embroiled in a physical conflict. He had only gathered the party of bouncers so that on the day when Kalia decided to execute his mischievous plan, he would be meeting him on an equal footing.

And the day had arrived. With the addition of four more bouncers, Hassonjee had a face-off with Kalia, with almost double the number of men on Hassonjee's side. The face-offs went on for a while. Every time Kalia added more numbers to his force, Hassonjee would procure the services of additional bouncers, ending up meeting Kalia with double the strength and warding off the violence and disruption. Kalia gave up at last when Hassonjee was successful in getting the tenants to leave the property in exchange for a better and more hygienic place. The tenants also thanked Hassonjee that the alternative accommodation provided to them was of a good standard.

Having dealt with the Kalia issue, the person Hassonjee was lined up to lock horns with next was none other than the don's own brother, Iqbal Kaskar.

Younger brother of Dawood, Iqbal Kaskar oversaw the functioning of Dawood's famous property on Pakmodia Street, Shabnam Guest House. As soon as Iqbal heard about the project, he had planted tenants there and placed his man named Goga to ensure the house remained with them. Goga tried playing smart and brought religious scriptures into the house so that Hassonjee and his team would hold back from demolishing it.

He also started tuitions on the first floor for kindergarten children, who used to come at nine in the morning. The guest house leaned on the building next to it which, like most buildings in the locality, was in a dilapidated condition. During the period when Hassonjee was engaged in talks with the owners of the property to hand it over for redevelopment work, the building next to it collapsed under a night of pounding rain.

Hassonjee did not wait for the authorities to react before instructing his assistants to reach the spot with their personal force and get out the people who must have got stuck under the debris. Unfortunately, they couldn't pull out a single person alive except for a man who had gone to the basement of the sweet shop next door to spend the night. The accident killed forty people. The children who used to come for tuitions at Shabnam Guest house were lucky as the incident took place thirty minutes before their tuition time.

The incident paved the way for the equally dilapidated Shabnam Guest House getting auctioned to the SBUT and becoming a part of the demolition and redevelopment process. Hassonjee made sure that he took a *maulana* (Muslim priest) along into the house and removed the religious scriptures kept in there on purpose before ordering the demolition of the building.

Residents kept coming to Hassonjee with ridiculous claims. Some asserted that the SBUT had undertaken a similar project in the past and its members owed them a certain amount of money. Without paying any attention to their bickering, Hassonjee simply directed them to contact those members and ask them for their outstanding money. He was also summoned to the local police station once. The police had got information that he had a beef with Kalia and wanted him to lodge a complaint against the latter on the grounds that he was trying to dominate and threaten the continuation of the project.

'Have you watched the videos captured by the locals of my confrontation with Kalia?' Hassonjee told the police. 'From no angle does it appear that he was dominating me.'

He reminded the police that Kalia had been found engaging in crimes much more serious than this and that there were enough cases against him to put him behind bars. There was also resistance from some of the residents who simply wanted to create issues and delay the project. Hassonjee held a few meetings with the local BJP minister, who assured him of taking appropriate action against the notorious elements. He also got good support from Devendra Fadnavis, the chief minister of Maharashtra, during his tenure from 2014 to 2019.

'The chief minister was of the opinion that there was a general perception that his government did not want minorities to develop,' Hassonjee said. 'But the CM wanted to prove this notion wrong and showcase that all communities and neighbourhoods should reap the benefits of development.'

The chief minister provided them with the full backing of the law and wanted all legal processes to be followed. He also directed the police officers to act without fear or favour.

Soon the 95A notice was issued in the area, which gave the authorities the power to evict a resident from the premises after three notices warning them to move out had been served.

The visits paid to Hassonjee by the petty bhais of the area never stopped. But over the years, he gained expertise in how to deal with each situation without resorting to violent means.

The result amazed the locals and the SBUT management alike. Not only were the newly constructed buildings beautiful, sturdy and hygiene-friendly, there was also enough space between the two buildings in compliance with the local laws. The plan had allowed for the otherwise congested streets to widen and make sufficient space for parking and pedestrians to easily pass by.

Hassonjee was overjoyed at the positive response and was looking ahead to finish the rest of the clusters he was allotted without much hassle. He was speaking to his assistant in the office regarding the project when there was another knock on his door.

'Can't you see I am busy?'

'It is Aapa (elder sister) on the call,' the person at the door said. 'She wants to talk to you.'

Hassonjee had no idea at the time who Aapa was in the underworld.

The assistant was a little well versed in the crime world to know who aapa was. His expression turned sombre as he leaned forward to whisper to Hassonjee.

'It's Haseena Parkar,' the assistant said. 'Dawood's sister. Aapa.'

Hassonjee got alert and asked the person at the door to step inside. Though he took the phone from the person with a determined hand, he did not know what to expect.

He had no idea that the person he was about to speak with was someone who always had the last say in almost every issue concerned with the illegal world of the place she lived in, Nagpada. The murder of her husband, Ismail Parkar, by the Gawli gang in 1991 was the event that marked the entry of Haseena Parkar into the underworld. Her prominence in the world of crime grew rapidly until she attained the image of Aapa among the locals.

According to the Crime Branch, Haseena was appointed by Dawood as the caretaker of the fifty-four benami properties he left behind when he fled the country. She also owned a famous hotel on Peer Khan Road in Nagpada that served as a rent accumulation unit for her. It was said that she owned six more hotels in Nagpada. From settling family disputes to arbitrating in a business matter, Aapa was the go-to person for the locals in their everyday affairs.

Imran Kalia was also one of the lackeys who worked for Haseena Parkar. It was at her behest that he was later sent off to Dubai on account of a fall-out. But putting all of that aside, the major area that Parkar had her keen eyes on was the projects launched by the Slum Rehabilitation Authority (SRA) in carrying out the redevelopment plans in Nagpada. She would procure most of these redevelopment projects for herself and it was in this context that she was booked in the extortion case. Hassonjee greeted the lady with due respect.

'What can I do for you?'

'I've heard that SBUT is conducting redevelopment operations in Bhendi Bazar,' she said, 'and they have put you in charge.'

Hassonjee confirmed that what she heard was right and expected a threatening warning to back off from the project. But to his utter surprise, none of that happened. All that Parkar asked of him was to be fair in allocating the properties before praising the work and ending the call. Hassonjee was relieved to find out that he was spared another episode of a daunting task in getting someone like Haseena Parkar to give in and not become an obstacle in continuing the project.

After long years of haggling, buttering-up, reasoning and sometimes vehement arguing, Hassonjee had finished the redevelopment work of the area that had been assigned to him. 'It is well known that the crime rate in the area has gone down after the redevelopment began,' Hassonjee said.

He had successfully managed to overcome the situation each time he was challenged by the dons who still ruled the vibrant and bustling area of Bhendi Bazaar and brought the drive to its completion. With the emergence of new buildings and expansive infrastructure, Bhendi Bazaar is stepping into a new era that will be free of the influence of the mafia and anti-law elements.

55

Ghosts of the Past

Nawab Malik, a seasoned politician and a prominent leader of the Nationalist Congress Party (NCP), remained a significant figure in Maharashtra's political landscape. Known for his sharp rhetoric and strong grassroots connections, Malik had held various ministerial portfolios. His influence extends beyond the confines of his party, making him a well-recognized name in both political and public spheres. However, his career took a tumultuous turn when he found himself at the centre of a high-profile legal battle, challenging the very foundations of his political legacy.

The ED sought the custody of Nawab Malik in connection with allegations of money laundering linked to a property deal involving underworld figures.[1] The ED was investigating a property transaction in Kurla involving Nawab Malik, where they initially claimed that a payment of Rs 55 lakh had been made to Haseena Parkar, the sister of Dawood Ibrahim, for a 3-acre plot of land. According to the ED, this payment included Rs 5 lakh via cheque and Rs 50 lakh in cash. The agency also stated that the Kurla land had originally belonged to Munira Plumber before it was taken over by Haseena Parkar. Later, the ED changed its stance and said that the amount paid to Haseena Parkar was not Rs 55 lakh but Rs 5 lakh and their initial submission of the higher number was a typo.[2]

On 23 February 2022, Malik was first called to the ED office at Ballard Estate and subjected to questioning for several hours, at the end of which he was placed under arrest.[3]

The next morning, he was produced in a special PMLA court and the ED filed its remand application, which ran into several pages. Next came the fact that the NIA had recently registered a case against Dawood, his right-hand man Chhota Shakeel and his gang for their anti-India activities, and that several 'elements' in India were funding the said activities through their crimes.

Every reporter who read the remand application that day—it was doing the rounds on WhatsApp hours after being filed in court—waited patiently for the ED to cut to the chase.[4] What did all of this have to do with Nawab Malik and how did it fit into the PMLA, they wondered.

The next person to be introduced was Haseena Parkar, Dawood's sister who stayed in Mumbai till she died in 2014. Unlike her brothers, she never quit the *mohalla* (locality) she grew up in, and breathed her last at the Habib Hospital in Dongri on 6 July 2014.

After Parkar came the next character in the story—Sardar Shahwali Khan.[5] His background was pretty uninteresting; he was a real estate agent and stayed in Kurla. The only interesting part was that he was a convict in the 1993 blasts case. And there, finally, the remand application came to the point.

The ED claimed in its remand application, and later in its 5000-page chargesheet, that Malik bought a plot of land in Goawala Compound, Kurla from Parkar, with her driver-cum-bodyguard Salim Patil acting as an intermediary.[6] The land was allegedly usurped by Parkar from a woman at a much lower price than the market rate at the time, after which it was sold to Malik. Thus, the ED charged Malik for 'funding' Dawood's terrorist activities by buying land from his sister. Malik filed a habeas corpus petition in the Bombay High Court stating that the arrest was illegal.

The entire allegation of the ED hinged on a statement recorded by Sardar Shahwali Khan, who was at the time lodged in the Aurangabad Central Jail after being convicted for the 1993 blasts. Khan had allegedly witnessed this entire deal and sworn to it in writing.

He worked as a real estate agent, attended one of the many meetings held by Tiger Memon in Mumbai to radicalize the youth for his nefarious mission and was picked up after the blasts for withholding information about an impending terrorist attack. He subsequently gave the investigating team a list of names and all these people were arrested and later convicted.

Malik's fate, however, was sealed for the moment. While the hearings went on and Malik stayed behind bars, the sequence of events started becoming clear to those who could look beyond the immediate; beyond the loud headlines of how 'Nawab Malik funded Dawood's terrorist activities'.

In January 2021, Malik's son-in-law Sameer Khan was arrested by the NCB for alleged procurement, sale, purchase and transport of illegal narcotics.[7] Khan and five others were charged under the Narcotic Drugs and Psychotropic Substances Act and it was eight whole months till Sameer got bail in September.

Since Sameer's arrest, however, Malik was on the warpath against the NCB and its then zonal director, Sameer Wankhede. The IRS officer himself was something of a media darling. He was married to an actress, frequently seen wearing expensive shirts, and had lately taken to parading film stars to and from the NCB office. It began with a viral video, supposedly of a group of film stars being 'high' during a party at a filmmaker's home. For several days, the filmmaker and the stars seen in the video were summoned to the NCB office, a few blocks away from the ED while the news media gleefully clicked pictures and ran prime-time debates about the 'drug menace in Bollywood'.

Then came actor Sushant Singh Rajput's untimely demise and the alleged drug angle, in which his girlfriend Rhea Chakraborty became the target of a nationwide witch hunt. Again, Wankhede was hailed as the hero for 'cleaning up' Mumbai's film industry of the bane of drugs.

Shortly after Sameer's arrest came Wankhede's pièce de résistance—the arrest of Shah Rukh Khan's son Aryan in a drugs case.[8] For the first twenty-four hours, it was never specified if Aryan was arrested for consumption, possession or peddling.

Aryan Khan's arrest, however, was confirmed by Wankhede on a WhatsApp group composed of officers and journalists, hours after Aryan was picked up. The news went viral and later the same night, a picture surfaced—a bald man in a selfie with Aryan inside the NCB headquarters. The picture made its way to the WhatsApp group and, of course, without verifying it, someone had added a caption—'NCB Officer with Aryan inside NCB Office'. The response came from Wankhede himself, 'Do not spread rumours. That is not an NCB officer.' 'Well,' the reporters asked, 'who is he?' There was no answer.

The answer, of all places, came from Nawab Malik. In a press conference that Malik took a day after Aryan's arrest, he revealed that the man was K.P. Gosavi, a history-sheeter with several cases registered against him in Mumbai and Thane.[9] Gosavi was also seen escorting Aryan from the cruise ship dock after he was detained, along with Manish Bhanushali, a BJP member.[10]

That, however, was just the beginning. Over the next couple of weeks, Malik went on to address several press conferences, making serious allegations of misconduct against the NCB and Wankhede.

Malik wasn't the only one asking questions. In an online news debate shortly after the arrest, journalist Gautam S. Mengle asked, 'If no drugs were found on Aryan Khan's person, and his blood and urine samples were never taken to be tested for consumption—a fact admitted by the NCB in court—what exactly is the charge against him?'

The anchor threw the question across to retired IPS officer Meeran Borwankar Chadha, who was also in the same debate. She replied saying, 'I wouldn't want to comment on the NCB's way of working, but I will say that if I were the investigating officer, I would have definitely taken blood and urine samples.'

The backlash against Malik was severe. Online trolls attacked him constantly. Threat calls were received on his office landline. BJP leaders then 'revealed' his 'Dawood connection' in the form of the alleged land deal.

And then, finally, in February 2022, Malik was arrested by the ED, based on a statement from persona non grata Shahwali Khan, who said that Malik bought land from Parkar, which is how he funded anti-India activities of Dawood, who was also involved in the 1993 serial blasts along with Tiger Memon and Javed Chikna.[11]

The ever-useful Dawood and the 1993 blasts, which had till then been a useful card to play during election time, had now come in handy to put a stop to Malik's press conferences.

Malik spent over a year in jail before being granted medical bail in August 2023.[12] His tweet before he was arrested had been, *'idhar aa sitamgar, hunar azmaye; tu teer aazma, hum jigar aazmayein.'* Immediately after his release, he changed it to, *'Mai jhukega nahi.'*[13]

But perhaps Malik's biggest vindication came in May 2022, when the NCB filed a chargesheet in the Aryan Khan case, but did not include Aryan Khan's name in it. The investigating team stated that it had not found enough material to prosecute him, and gave him and five others a clean chit.[14]

Epilogue

PAKmodia Street to PAKistan State

'Who is more powerful than the king?' asked Kamaal Hasan.

I had requested for one last meeting with Kamaal Hasan—my latest periscope in Dawood Ibrahim's current life, power play and his unchallenged reign in the Islamic Republic of Pakistan.

Kamaal was laughing so loudly that many snobbish business class travellers sitting in the premium lounge of Dubai Airport raised their brows in disapproval. But his expensive suit and his heavily accented Americanese forced them to back off. My experience has been that US-returned Pakistanis and Indian Gujaratis love to speak with an American accent. Kamaal started getting into his cynical philosophical mode.

'You Indians are quite naïve,' he said. 'There is nothing Islamic or *paak* (as in sacred) about my country. It has been a disastrous failure since the beginning, and I guess our friend Dawood Ibrahim has contributed to its massive decline.'

I had to agree with Kamaal on his statement. Also, the same could be said about the Islamic Republic of Iran. There is nothing Islamic and nothing is remotely republic in the country. For the last year and a half, Kamaal was mercilessly hauling me from one foreign city to another, subjecting me to a lot of travel and travails, not to mention causing a hole in my small pocket. This time, on my request, he deigned to meet me only at the Emirates terminal at Dubai Airport and not to step into the city.

I thought I had finished this book and sent my manuscript to the ever-charming Milee Ashwarya from Penguin India. But then suddenly, Pakistani politics went into extreme turbulence and Asif Ali Zardari managed to bag the Pakistani presidency again. Strange, how the capital of the country is named after a religion—which I haven't found in any of the Arab countries. Hejaz, which was the birthplace of Islam, was renamed Saudi Arabia after the Saud dynasty took over. But after these developments, I had been expecting a call from Kamaal.

I got a familiar Dark Knight Icon on my Facetime. I steeled myself again to speak to that Batman voice, which I knew would ask me to travel again. And here I was, seated in front of him trying to take notes and keep up with his fast-paced conversation.

'Among the thirteen presidents of Pakistan so far, Zardari is the only exception who has replicated this feat twice since the formation of the country,' Kamaal said.

I was listening with rapt attention. In 2008, Zardari became the Pakistan President within months of his wife Benazir Bhutto's assassination in December 2007. The then President Parvez Musharraf had blatantly accused Zardari of killing his wife. The same year, in 2008, he was acquitted of the murder charges of his brother-in-law Murtaza Bhutto, who was killed in 1996.

The year also changed the fortunes of Malik Riaz Husain, who started the construction of Bahria Icon Tower (Pakistan's first skyscraper), the same year Bahria Town Karachi was launched. One of Pakistan's largest malls, Dolmen, was constructed by Malik Riaz's son in 2008.

Another interesting thing is that Mohsin Naqvi started his news channel in C42 soon after Zardari took over as President. Both of them have had deep connections since then. Naqvi was always surrounded by controversies right from the bribe imbroglio of his news channel to his being caretaker chief minister of Punjab to his taking over the chairmanship of the Pakistan Cricket Board (PCB) in 2023 without any prior or negligible experience in cricket.

Ironically, he was elevated to the post of chairman only a few days ahead of the Pakistan general elections and commencement of the Pakistan Super League.

Naqvi's ambitious journey included his rise to the senate of Pakistan. While he contested it on an independent ticket, he got the support of all four parties of Pakistan. He was widely seen as Rawalpindi man, which means he had the army's support. Imran Khan also made a cryptic statement that 'The king is sitting behind.'[1]

Javed Miandad, Imran Khan's former teammate, had clearly said in his television interview that Imran rose and fell because of a few powerful people in Pakistan, which is clearly interpreted as Dawood Ibrahim. Javed Miandad had no qualms in acknowledging his relations with Dawood as well. Javed's son Junaid is married to Dawood's daughter Mahrukh.

Shehbaz Sharif was never seen as a man who had public support and popularity to become the Pakistani prime minister nor does his political background indicate any clout and resourcefulness. In the elections of February 2024, Shehbaz Sharif's Pakistan Muslim League-Nawaz (PML-N) didn't have enough seats to form a government; they needed alliances and Zardari's PPP as an ally.

Perhaps Kamaal would have continued incessantly but I interjected and said this was too much to process. I also suddenly felt hungry.

Kamaal went to the food corner and got a tray overflowing with all kinds of exotic food. I envied his metabolism. How could he wolf down such a rich serving of food and still remain slim and trim while I put on weight just by looking at food? I got my home-made barley roti, methi and cheese. We both finished it with a soothing chamomile tea that had a dash of honey and cinnamon in it, and then resumed our conversation with unabated gusto.

I asked him to take me through this intricate puzzle of Pakistan, which seemed to be too spread out and complex.

'Instability has seeped deep into Pakistan, turning it into Fasad-istaan ruled by Corruption-abad. *Fasad* in Urdu means riots and *Fasad* in Arabic means corruption and both are applicable to my country,' Kamaal said.

I refused to laugh but asked Kamaal to summarize it for me. He began his own intellectual spiel. The whole chessboard of Pakistani politics and power when laid out looks like a weak prime minister, dependent on his coalition partner PPP, whose chief Zardari is the President. Perhaps the most controversial president of not just Pakistan but of any democracy in the world. The interior minister, media mogul and chairman of the Pakistan Cricket Board, Naqvi, and Zardari are inseparable friends.

The third angle to the troika is 'money bag' Malik Riaz, a man with unlimited support of the Pakistani judiciary, who went on their knees to recover his dues from the government. Riaz was a civil contractor who rose to affluence in 2008.

So, the king, bishop and knight are already aligned as per the much touted and infamous London Plan. The London Plan is a concept in Pakistan much written about in Pakistani newspapers like *Dawn* and recently alluded to by Imran Khan while pointing an accusatory finger towards the current government.

In short, the way the Indian diaspora, including commercial centres and crime czars, finds Dubai a convenient location for expanding businesses and making crafty plans, Pakistanis seek solace in London. In fact, parts of London are now resembling Karachi and Dongri a lot, and it is bustling with Muslim immigrants.

Malik Riaz made an office in London and funnelled all his illicit money to London headquarters, though he landed in trouble with the Metropolitan Police. The British National Crime Agency has already named Russia and Pakistan as two main countries stashing their money from corruption in London.[2]

Pakistani film production houses have established overseas offices in London, including that of Mehwish

Hayat, rumoured friend of Dawood Ibrahim. Pakistanis are now convinced that the privacy of London provides them with the vantage to plan, plot and upstage their enemies. In simple terms, it is referred to as the London Plan.

Nevertheless, all the important pieces of the jigsaw are under the influence of Dawood Ibrahim—the PM, the President, a businessman who can influence top judges, the interior minister who is also chairman of the cricket board facilitating betting for the gamblers in the game.

Last but not least, Dawood may have lost his hold over the Indian film industry but found an all-pervasive sway in the Pakistani film industry. Kamaal leaves me curious and anxious every time we meet. For me, Dawood was a small-time gangster from a lane in Dongri called Pakmodia Street who has now gone on to dominate Pakistan. Some obsession with Pak, I surmised.

It was now time for Kamaal's sting in the tale observation. 'Who is bigger than the king?'

I replied, 'God the Almighty.'

He chided me again. *Grow up old boy, can't think beyond God.*

'The kingmaker is more powerful than the king. Didn't Chanakya install Chandragupta Maurya as a king after he was insulted by Nanda?'

I wasn't so impressed though.

Regarded as kingmaker, Dawood prefers to play demigod. Pakistan has realized the usefulness of Dawood, which is why they continue to protect him. They do not want the incident of Abbottabad repeated, where US special officers found Osama bin Laden and shot him dead, taking Pakistan totally by surprise.

With Dawood's food poisoning incident going viral in December 2023 following his treatment at Aga Khan University Hospital in Karachi, Pakistan did not want to face the same embarrassment, and they decided to take extreme caution with Dawood. They shifted him to a location called Dhabeji near the Karachi Naval Base. This is one of the most secure locations in Pakistan with state-of-the-art security, fitted with Japanese radar that can detect any low-flying aircraft or drone.

The base has direct access to Karachi and also the sea. The area has several farmhouses, including those of the PPP's leaders. However, Dawood's farmhouses are not just the most secure ones but also convenient places for calling the shots in Pakistan.

After the Indian government's surgical strikes at Balakot, Pakistan was quite wary of US-style Indian special ops of elimination of their arch-enemy. However, Pakistan is now aware that the Indian government has no plans to kill or bring back Dawood; they are happy where he is. The question is: For how long?

Acknowledgements

This book marks a sort of challenging feat for me, being my fourteenth. It is an ambitious project as it attempts something no other writer I know of has tried before. I have made my best efforts to conclude two books through a single work of research—the book in your hands. It is the sequel to two of my bestsellers—a conclusion to *Black Friday* and a culmination of *Dongri to Dubai*. With this, we are moving towards a final, definitive end in the saga. Whether I have succeeded, only time will tell.

The journey to create this work was gruelling, filled with uncertainties, challenges and moments of self-doubt. There were days when I feared I would not have the content, the stamina or even the focus to see it through. But, as with every book I have written, I did not expect this to be a simple task. Every story I undertake is a trial, a challenge, and this one felt the most serious, most daunting. I believe it is a good sign, yet I did sweat through the ordeal.

I've done my best throughout to blend research, storytelling, analysis and reportage in a way that is honest and without judgement. I wanted this to be a raw, undiluted account, without an endeavour to sensationalize or embellish or garnish it with fiction and imagination, no matter how tempting it was at times.

A particular example that comes to mind is how Dawood Ibrahim, despite amassing wealth through various illegitimate means, tried to exploit religious tourism for his own gain. I heard apocryphal stories of Dawood Ibrahim having shares in the fancy towers that surround the sacred mosque of Masjidul Haram of Holy Kaaba. In fact, I was sent subtle invitations to be a guest in those Haram view suites. Of course, I straightaway declined those invitations, but I also refused to build a chapter around Dawood's presence in Mecca.

Nevertheless, I also felt rumours walking over me about Dawood's alleged involvement in a luxury hotel in Karbala. The compelling nature of the stories; Pakistani management and high-end clientele pointed towards the unmistakable backing of a powerful, unseen force. Everything pointed to Dawood Ibrahim. The hotel, located at a distance of few kilometres from the Holy Shrine in Karbala, was repeatedly claimed to be part of Dawood's legit assets. However, I chose to exclude these details, as they could not be verified through reliable sources. My aim, always, has been to present only what can be corroborated through government documents, court records or credible media reports.

I would like to acknowledge that, without a few key pillars of support, this book would not have turned out the way it has. This is one of my most detailed works, double the length of some of my earlier works. At one point, I thought I needed to stop before my readers refused to take in any more chapters of this research-heavy tome. I want to express my profound gratitude to those who selflessly devoted their time, expertise and skills to this project. Their contributions made the journey worthwhile, and I hope readers will find it equally worth their time, effort and attention.

First and foremost, my friend Neeraj Kumar, former commissioner of police, Delhi. We started this book together, and I had originally wanted him to co-author it with me. It felt only right, given his immense contribution—his knowledge, experience and the stories he shared from his extraordinary career. However, in an act of generosity and magnanimity, Neeraj sahab decided to step back. He felt that sharing the laurels with me wouldn't do justice to the book, and insisted I be the sole author, though he continued to offer his support in every way possible. Much of the intricate details, complex information and valuable insights you will find in these pages are thanks to him. His years of policing, research and investigation, and experiences from various other roles in the Indian government, are deeply embedded in this work.

Film actor Aditya Pancholi was graceful and generous with his time and narrated interesting anecdotes, some of which have become part of a few chapters in this book.

Adrian Levy, bestselling author and journalist from London, encouraged and inspired me to complete the tome of research on Dawood without giving up.

I would like to thank my friends and fellow journalists, Gautam Mengle, who has worked for the top newspapers in Mumbai, and Danish Khan, who has been covering the UK and Europe for Times Now. I also received significant assistance from Pakistani journalists and writers, though I cannot name them for obvious reasons. Some were open and willing to share valuable information with anonymity, while others, unfortunately, were biased in favour of Dawood and their own government, which made their contributions less reliable and disappointing.

Needless to say, the man who made this book possible and constantly boosted my morale and confidence is my protégé, Kashif Mashaikh. He is decades younger than me but has the maturity of an established thinker, writer and editor. He is my go-to person for almost everything. I sincerely hope my competition never discovers Kashif, so he stays with me as the bulwark I know him to be.

I would also like to express my heartfelt thanks to Velly Thevar, who has stood by me through thick and thin, and through the places the book took me: whether here, in Dubai or in Pakistan. The best part about Velly is that she doesn't always conform with me. In our disagreements, she never lets me forget that I am, first and foremost, a journalist, and I must remain objective. I publicly acknowledge that she keeps me grounded, not letting my arrogance and overconfidence as a writer and reporter creep into my work. Thank you, Velly.

Finally, I want to thank the team at Penguin for their unwavering support, patience and understanding, especially for forgiving my delays and constant revisions. Special mention must be made of Hitha Haridas, my editor, and the fabulous and beautiful Milee Ashwarya, who remained rock-solid throughout this journey. For a year and a half, they waited steadfastly for everything to come together and encouraged me every step of the way. Thank you, everyone, especially Milee.

Finally, thank you, my readers. I hope you all enjoy reading this book and continue to support me in my future endeavours.

The factual accuracies are due to all those who helped me in compiling this book, though mistakes or errors in this work are solely mine.

Notes

Prologue: Kamaal to Kamal

1   Neha Khan, 'Ex-Pak Cricketer Javed Miandad Acknowledges Family Ties with Dawood Ibrahim', *Siasat Daily*, 19 March 2024, available at https://www.siasat.com/ex-pak-cricketer-javed-miandad-acknowledges-family-ties-with-dawood-ibrahim-2994850/.

Chapter 1: The Blue Fox

1   [Interview with source] The 1992 Karachi Incident - Unveiling the Blue Fox Operation document.
2   [Interview with source] The 1992 Karachi Incident - Unveiling the Blue Fox Operation document.
3   'Remembering History: What Happened on 19th June 1992 in Karachi?', MM News, 19 June 2022, available at https://mmnews.tv/remembering-history-what-happened-on-19th-june-199-in-karachi/.
4   [Interview with source] The 1992 Karachi Incident - Unveiling the Blue Fox Operation document.

5 'Zardari Who Sold Tickets in Black Became Billionaire: Imran', *News International*, 20 September 2017, available at https://www.thenews.com.pk/print/231170-Zardari-who-sold-tickets-in-black-became-billionaire-Imran.
6 [Interview with source] The 1992 Karachi Incident - Unveiling the Blue Fox Operation document.

Chapter 2: Pakistan's First Ten-Per Cent President

1 'Musharraf: Pakistan's "Rogue" State May Have Helped Kill Benazir Bhutto', Daily Beast, 27 December 2017, available at https://www.thedailybeast.com/musharraf-pakistans-rogue-state-may-have-helped-kill-benazir-bhutto.
2 '2 Blasts Strike Crowd Celebrating Bhutto's Return', NBC News, 17 October 2007, available at https://www.nbcnews.com/id/wbna21344367.
3 Neena Gopal, 'The Guard Who Did Benazir Bhutto In!', *Deccan Chronicle*, 22 September 2017, available at https://www.deccanchronicle.com/nation/current-affairs/220917/the-guard-who-did-benazir-bhutto-in.html.
4 Owen Bennett Jones, 'Benazir Bhutto Assassination: How Pakistan Covered Up Killing', BBC, 27 December 2017, available at https://www.bbc.com/news/world-asia-42409374.
5 Tariq Ali, 'Asif Ali Zardari: the godfather as president', *Guardian*, 7 September 2008, available at https://www.theguardian.com/commentisfree/2008/sep/07/pakistan.usa.
6 'Singapore Airlines Flight 117', Wikipedia, available at https://en.wikipedia.org/wiki/Singapore_Airlines_Flight_117.

Chapter 3: A Tale of Two Arrests

1 Interview with Neeraj Kumar; Aviral Virk, 'Yakub Memon's Surrender and Arrest: What Really Happened', Quint, 25 July 2015, available at https://www.thequint.com/

videos/the-gripping-and-uncertain-tale-of-yakub-memons-surrender#read-more#read-more.
2. B. Raman, 'Why Yakub Memon Must Not Be Hanged', Rediff, 24 July 2015, available at https://m.rediff.com/news/column/exclusive-b-ramans-unpublished-2007-article-why-yakub-memon-must-not-be-hanged/20150723.htm?sc_cid=fbshare.
3. Shekhar Gupta et al., '1993 Bombay Serial Blasts: Search on for Bombay's 12-Member Memon Family', *India Today*, 30 July 2015, available at https://www.indiatoday.in/magazine/india-today-archives/story/19930415-bombay-serial-blasts-search-on-for-bombay-12-member-memon-family-810940-1993-04-15.
4. 'Bombay Riots', Wikipedia, available at https://en.wikipedia.org/wiki/Bombay_riots.

Chapter 4: Grand Guest House

1. Interview with Neeraj Kumar.
2. Interview with Neeraj Kumar and confidential documents.
3. B. Raman, 'Why Yakub Memon Must Not Be Hanged', Rediff, 24 July 2015, available at https://m.rediff.com/news/column/exclusive-b-ramans-unpublished-2007-article-why-yakub-memon-must-not-be-hanged/20150723.htm?sc_cid=fbshare.

Chapter 5: The Interrogation

1. This chapter is based on personal interviews with Neeraj Kumar.
2. Sheela Bhatt, 'Dawood Ibrahim: "I Had Nothing to Do with Yakub Memon, Never Seen His Face"', *India Today*, 12 September 2022, available at https://www.indiatoday.in/india-today-insight/story/from-the-india-today-archives-1994-dawood-ibrahim-i-had-nothing-to-do-with-yakub-memon-never-seen-his-face-1999385-2022-09-12.

Chapter 6: Taufique Jaliawala

1. M. Rahman and Lekha Rattanani, 'Bombay Blasts Case: With the Memons' Dramatic Return, CBI Tantalizingly Close to Solving the Puzzle', *India Today*, 30 July 2015, available at https://www.indiatoday.in/magazine/india-today-archives/story/19940915-in-major-coup-with-memons-dramatic-return-cbi-tantalisingly-close-to-solving-the-puzzle-809634-1999-11-29.

Chapter 8: The Aftermath

1. 'Yakub's Final Journey in Mumbai Draws Crowd of 15,000', *Times of India*, 31 July 2015, available at https://timesofindia.indiatimes.com/india/yakubs-final-journey-in-mumbai-draws-crowd-of-15000/articleshow/48289743.cms.
2. Aakar Patel, 'The Reality of Being Muslim in India', Rediff, 3 August 2015, available at https://www.rediff.com/news/column/aakar-patel-the-reality-of-being-muslim-in-india/20150803.htm.
3. 'Any Memon Would Do', *Telegraph*, 26 July 2015, available at https://www.telegraphindia.com/7-days/any-memon-would-do/cid/1313993.
4. 'If Yakub Never Came Back from Pakistan', *Mumbai Mirror*, 31 July 2015, available at https://mumbaimirror.indiatimes.com/mumbai/cover-story/if-yakub-never-came-back-from-pakistan/articleshow/48288742.cms.
5. 'Chhota Shakeel Speaks on Yakub Memon's Hanging, Says Yakub Punished for Tiger's Deeds', *India Today*, 31 July 2015, available at https://www.indiatoday.in/india/story/yakub-memon-hanging-chhota-shakeel-dawood-ibrahim-1993-mumbai-terror-attack-285611-2015-07-30.

Chapter 9: Stockholm Syndrome

1. 'Pakistan Court Issues Notice to Ex-Prez Zardari for Hiding Assets Worth over USD 1 Mn', *Indian Express*, 4 April

2019, available at https://indianexpress.com/article/pakistan/pakistan-court-issues-notice-to-ex-prez-zardari-for-hiding-assets-worth-over-usd-1-mn-5658652/.

Sagnik Chowdhury, 'Dawood Ibrahim's New Residence in Karachi near Bilawal's residence', *Indian Express,* 23 August 2015, available at https://indianexpress.com/article/india/india-others/india-has-evidence-of-dawood-ibrahim-living-in-pakistan-report/.

2. Abid Hussain, 'Former Pakistani PM Imran Khan Arrested at Islamabad Court', *Al Jazeera,* 9 May 2023, available at https://www.aljazeera.com/news/2023/5/9/former-pakistan-pm-imran-khan-arrested-outside-islamabad-court; 'Imran Khan to join NAB Investigation in Al-Qadir Trust Case today', *Nation,* 23 May 2023, available at https://www.nation.com.pk/23-May-2023/imran-khan-to-join-nab-investigation-in-al-qadir-trust-case-today.; Hawwa Fazal, 'Imran Arrest: What Is the Al Qadir Trust Case?', *Dawn,* 9 May 2023, available at https://www.dawn.com/news/1751790#:~:text=Subsequently%2C%20Islamabad%20Police%20released%20a,a%20real%20estate%20firm%20for.

Chapter 10: Mehwish Hayat

1. 'This Dev Anand heroine was rumoured to be Dawood's girlfriend, left India after allegations of spying for Pakistan', DNA, 26 September 2023, available at https://www.dnaindia.com/bollywood/report-bollywood-actress-anita-ayoob-dawood-ibrahim-girlfriend-called-pakistani-spy-dev-anand-gangster-javed-siddique-3061368.

Chapter 12: Mexican Stand-Off in Bombay

1. Amaresh Misra, 'Pune Blasts: The Story behind the Story', *Times of India,* 5 August 2012, available at https://timesofindia.indiatimes.com/blogs/the-mainstream-maverick/pune-blasts-the-story-behind-the-story/.

Chapter 14: Do I Look like a Dog?

1. Amaresh Misra, 'Pune Blasts: The Story Behind the Story', *Times of India*, 5 August 2012, available at https://timesofindia.indiatimes.com/blogs/the-mainstream-maverick/pune-blasts-the-story-behind-the-story/.

Chapter 17: Volcano of Weapons

1. Interview with source and 'State of Maharashtra v. Abdul Hamid Haji Mohammed', Case Mine, 21 February 1994, available at https://www.casemine.com/judgement/in/5609acb2e4b014971140f766.

Chapter 18: Suburban Drug Lord

1. Mowgli Productions, 'Chhota Shakeel Interview 1st Time Talk About His Personal Life Lalit Modi 93 Blast Chota Rajan', YouTube, 18 September 2016, 32:00-35:00, https://www.youtube.com/watch?v=boK7fdtl4GU.
2. 'Why Chhota Rajan and Dawood Ibrahim Parted Ways', *Deccan Chronicle*, 26 October 2015, available at https://www.deccanchronicle.com/151026/nation-current-affairs/article/why-chhota-rajan-and-dawood-ibrahim-parted-ways.
3. Interview with the source.

Chapter 19: Trapped in Thailand

1. 'Dawood Ibrahim's aide, on the run for 20 years, arrested', *DNA*, 14 March 2016, available at https://www.dnaindia.com/india/report-dawood-ibrahim-s-aide-on-the-run-for-20-years-arrested-2188918.

Chapter 20: Shoot-Out at Bandra

1. Asif Rizvi, 'Chhota Rajan to Be Tried for 2001 Murder of 1993 Mumbai Blasts Accused', *Mid-Day,* 25 September 2017, available at https://www.mid-day.com/mumbai/mumbai-news/article/chhota-rajan-underworld-gangster-2001-murder-hotelier-1993-blasts-case-hanif-kadawala-18605151.

Chapter 21: A Long Trial

1. Jake Khan, 'Chhota Rajan Picks off Blasts Accused like Flies', Rediff, 6 April 2001, available at https://www.rediff.com/news/2001/apr/06jake.htm.
2. The dialogue is dramatized from the judgment papers of the case. PDF available on request.

Chapter 23: *Yeda* on the Run

1. Shubhangi Khapre, 'Sharad Pawar: Jethmalani's Proposal on Dawood Ibrahim Was Conditional', *Indian Express*, 5 July 2015, available at https://indianexpress.com/article/india/india-others/ram-jethmalanis-proposal-on-dawood-was-conditional-sharad-pawar/.
2. '1993 Blasts Accused Yeda Yakub Dies in Karachi of Heart Attack', *Economic Times,* 7 August 2015, available at https://economictimes.indiatimes.com/news/politics-and-nation/1993-blasts-accused-yeda-yakub-dies-in-karachi-of-heart-attack/articleshow/48386680.cms.

Chapter 25: With Friends Like These . . .

1. Praveen Swami, 'FBI Fallen Agent Is Returning Home. Kamran Faridi's Story Shows How Drug Cartels Have Rotted Pakistan', ThePrint, 14 May 2024, available at https://theprint.in/theprint-explorer/fbi-fallen-agent-is-returning-home-

kamran-faridis-story-shows-how-drug-cartels-have-rotted-pakistan/2078958/?amp.
2. Based on interview with source.

Chapter 26: Kamran Faridi and The Beatles

1. 'Machine Gun Kelly (gangster)', Wikipedia, available at https://en.wikipedia.org/wiki/Machine_Gun_Kelly_(gangster).

Chapter 27: Jostling for Jabir

1. M. Khan, 'FBI Violated Pakistan Laws by Secretly Filming Karachi Businessman, UK Court Told', *Daily Jasarat,* 3 July 2019, available at https://www.jasarat.com/en/fbi-violated-pakistan-laws-by-secretly-filming-karachi-businessman-uk-court-told/.
2. 'Guantanamo Bay detention camp', Wikipedia, available at https://en.wikipedia.org/wiki/Guantanamo_Bay_detention_camp.
3. 'Shaker Aamer', Wikipedia, available at https://en.wikipedia.org/wiki/Shaker_Aamer.

    Aamer says that the 'MI5' interrogators told him he had two choices: (1) agree to spy on suspected jihadists in the United Kingdom; or (2) remain in US custody.
4. Murtaza Ali Shah, 'Kamran Faridi—Karachi Criminal Who Turned FBI Spy before Losing It All', *Geo News,* 22 November 2021, available at https://www.geo.tv/latest/383615-kamran-faridi-karachi-criminal-who-turned-fbi-spy-before-losing-it-all.

Chapter 28: Fallen Comrade

1. 'Why Chhota Rajan got J Dey—the fearless crime journalist—murdered', DailyO, 3 May 2018, available at https://www.dailyo.in/variety/j-dey-murder-chhota-rajan-convicted-mumbai-underworld-dawood-ibrahim-jigna-vora-23853.

Chapter 30: India's Escobar

1. 'Iqbal Mirchi', Wikipedia, available at https://en.wikipedia.org/wiki/Iqbal_Mirchi; Rajesh Ahuja, 'Mirchi's journey: From petty thief to drug lord', *Hindustan Times,* 12 October 2011, available at https://www.hindustantimes.com/delhi/mirchi-s-journey-from-petty-thief-to-drug-lord/story-KctwcQ9cppPpAMzQKBOuwN.html.

Chapter 52: Return of the Badshah

1. Anand Holla, '93 Blasts Approver Accuses Police of Refusing to Clear Family's Passports', *Mumbai Mirror,* 11 January 2008, available at https://mumbaimirror.indiatimes.com/mumbai/other/93-blasts-approver-accuses-police-of-refusing-to-clear-familys-passports/articleshow/15775380.cms.

Chapter 55: Ghosts of the Past

1. Vijay V. Singh and Swati Deshpande, 'Mumbai: Special court send Nawab Malik to ED custody till March 3', *Times of India,* 24 February 2022, available at https://timesofindia.indiatimes.com/city/mumbai/mumbai-special-court-sends-nawab-malik-to-ed-custody-till-march-3/articleshow/89782743.cms.
2. Rebecca Samervel and Vijay V. Singh, 'ED accepts typo, says Nawab Malik paid Rs 5 lakh, not Rs 55 lakh', *Times of India,* 4 March 2022, available at https://timesofindia.indiatimes.com/india/ed-accepts-typo-says-nawab-malik-paid-rs-5-lakh-not-rs-55-lakh/articleshow/89980466.cms.
3. 'Maharashtra minister Nawab Malik sent to ED custody till March 3 by Mumbai court', *Business Today,* 23 February 2022, available at https://www.businesstoday.in/latest/politics/story/maharashtra-minister-nawab-malik-sent-to-ed-custody-till-march-3-by-mumbai-court-323701-2022-02-23.
4. Interview with crime journalist Gautam Mengle.

5 Shoumojit Banerjee, 'Fadnavis objects to Ajit Pawar-NCP faction hobnobbing with NCP's Nawab Malik', *The Hindu*, 7 December 2013, available at https://www.thehindu.com/news/national/other-states/ncp-leader-nawab-malik-out-on-bail-hobnobs-with-ajit-pawar-faction-at-maharashtra-assembly/article67614141.ece.

6 Munish Chandra Pandey, 'Nawab Malik bought Rs 300 crore plot for few lakhs with help from D-gang, says ED', *India Today*, 24 February 2022, available at https://www.indiatoday.in/india/story/nawab-malik-arrest-ed-d-gang-dawood-munira-plumber-property-1917062-2022-02-24.

7 'Drugs case: Special court grants bail to Sameer Khan, son-in-law of Maharashtra Nawab Malik', *Times of India*, 27 September 2021, available at https://timesofindia.indiatimes.com/city/mumbai/drugs-case-special-court-grants-bail-to-sameer-khan-son-in-law-of-maharashtra-minister-nawab-malik/articleshow/86559123.cms.

8 Aloke Deshpande, 'Shah Rukh Khan's son Aryan Khan among three arrested after drug bust on cruise ship off Mumbai', *The Hindu*, 3 October 2021, available at https://www.thehindu.com/news/cities/mumbai/shah-rukh-khans-son-aryan-khan-arrested-after-ncb-busts-drugs-party-off-mumbai/article36806752.ece.

9 Faizan Khan, 'Man who "accompanied" NCB on cruise raid has 4 cheating cases against him', *Mid-Day*, 8 October 2021, available at https://www.mid-day.com/mumbai/mumbai-news/article/live-updates-no-drugs-seized-at-cruise-aryan-khans-panchnama-manipulated-claims-nawab-malik-23195659

10 Shweta Sengar, 'Who Is Manish Bhanushali, the Alleged BJP Leader Involved in Aryan Khan's Arrest Case', Indiatimes.com, 7 October 2021, available at https://www.indiatimes.com/news/india/aryan-khan-drugs-case-manish-bhanushali-551104.html.

11 Faizan Khan, 'Man who "accompanied" NCB on cruise raid has 4 cheating cases against him', *Mid-Day*, 8 October 2021, https://www.mid-day.com/mumbai/mumbai-news/article/live-

updates-no-drugs-seized-at-cruise-aryan-khans-panchnama-manipulated-claims-nawab-malik-23195659.

12. Rebecca Samervel and Vijay V. Singh, 'NCP leader Nawab Malik goes home from Mumbai hospital after bail', *Times of India*, 15 August 2023, available at https://timesofindia.indiatimes.com/city/mumbai/nawab-malik-goes-home-from-hospital-after-bail/articleshow/102735758.cms
13. https://x.com/OfficeofNM/status/1496427148105875456.
14. Aryan Prakash, 'Aryan Khan gets clean chit in drugs case. Who were chargesheeted?' *Hindustan Times*, 27 May 2022, available at https://www.hindustantimes.com/india-news/aryan-khan-gets-clean-chit-in-drugs-case-who-were-chargesheeted-full-list-101653640464495.html.

Epilogue: PAKmodia Street to PAKistan State

1. Rameez Khan, 'PML-N, PPP both deny Naqvi is "their man"', *Tribune*, 11 March 2024, available at https://tribune.com.pk/story/2459004/pml-n-ppp-both-deny-naqvi-is-their-man.
2. Prasun Sonwalkar, 'Lens on corrupt Pakistani politicians investing in UK', *Hindustan Times*, 15 May 2018, available at https://www.hindustantimes.com/world-news/lens-on-corrupt-pakistani-politicians-investing-in-uk/story-RapRNHG6B3OEPixc57gmdP.html.

Scan QR code to access the
Penguin Random House India website